CLARENDON LAW SERIES

Edited by

H. L. A. HART

CLARENDON LAW SERIES

The Concept of Law
By H. L. A. HART

Introduction to the Law of Property
By F. H. LAWSON

Introduction to the Law of Contract (2nd edition)
By P. S. ATIYAH

Precedent in English Law (3rd edition)
By RUPERT CROSS

Criminal Law and Punishment
By P. J. FITZGERALD

Introduction to Roman Law
By BARRY NICHOLAS

An Introduction to the Law of Torts
By JOHN G. FLEMING

Constitutional Theory
By GEOFFREY MARSHALL

Legal Reasoning and Legal Theory
By NEIL MACCORMICK

K 460 .F57
Finnis, John.
Natural law and natural
 rights /

NATURAL LAW
AND
NATURAL
RIGHTS

BY

JOHN FINNIS

Fellow of University College, Oxford

RITTER LIBRARY
BALDWIN-WALLACE COLLEGE

WITHDRAWN

CLARENDON PRESS · OXFORD

1980

Oxford University Press, Walton Street, Oxford OX2 6DP

OXFORD LONDON GLASGOW
NEW YORK TORONTO MELBOURNE WELLINGTON
KUALA LUMPUR SINGAPORE JAKARTA HONG KONG TOKYO
DELHI BOMBAY CALCUTTA MADRAS KARACHI
NAIROBI DAR ES SALAAM CAPE TOWN

© *John Finnis 1980*

Published in the United States
by Oxford University Press
New York

*All rights reserved. No part of this publication may be reproduced,
stored in a retrieval system, or transmitted, in any form or by any means,
electronic, mechanical, photocopying, recording, or otherwise, without
the prior permission of Oxford University Press*

British Library Cataloguing in Publication Data

Finnis, John Mitchell
    Natural law and natural rights. –
    (Clarendon law series).
    1. Law
    I. Title
    340   K230   79–41092

ISBN 0–19–876110–4

*Filmset in Great Britain by
Northumberland Press Ltd, Gateshead Tyne and Wear
Printed by
Richard Clay (The Chaucer Press) Ltd, Bungay, Suffolk*

PREFACE

THE core of this book is its second Part. In one long movement of thought, these chapters (III–XII) sketch what the textbook taxonomists would label an 'ethics', a 'political philosophy', and a 'philosophy of law' or 'jurisprudence'. We may accept the labels, as a scholarly convenience, but not the implication that the 'disciplines' they identify are really distinct and can safely be pursued apart. Parts One and Three are, in a sense, out-riders. Anyone interested in natural law simply as an ethics may omit Chapter I; anyone whose concerns are limited to juris-prudence may omit Chapter XIII. And those who want to see, in advance, how the whole study yields an understanding very different from the accounts of 'natural law' in their textbooks of jurisprudence and philosophy might turn first to Chapter XII, and then perhaps to Chapter II.

The book is no more than introductory. Countless relevant matters are merely touched upon or are passed over altogether. Innumerable objections receive no more than the silent tribute of an effort to draft statements that would prove defensible if a defence against objections were explicitly undertaken. No effort is made to give an ordered account of the long history of theorizing about natural law and natural rights. For experience suggests that such accounts lull rather than stimulate an interest in their subject-matter. And indeed, the history of these theories can only be properly understood by one who appreciates the in-trinsic problems of human good and practical reasonableness with which the theorists were grappling. So my prior concern is to give my own response to those problems, mentioning other theories only where I think they can both illuminate and be illuminated by the theory presented in this book. My hope is that a re-presentation and development of main elements of the 'classical' or 'main stream' theories of natural law, by way of an argument on the merits (as lawyers say), will be found useful by those who want to understand the history of ideas as well

as by those interested in forming or reforming their own view
of the merits.

Every author has his milieu; this book has roots in a modern
tradition that can be labelled 'analytical jurisprudence', and my
own interest in that tradition antedates the time when I first
began to suspect that there might be more to theories of natural
law than superstition and darkness. Someone who shared my
theory of natural law, but whose focus of interest and
competence was, say, sociological jurisprudence or political
theory or moral theology, would have written a different book.

In 1953 Leo Strauss prefaced his study of natural law with
the warning that 'the issue of natural right presents itself
today as a matter of party allegiance. Looking around us, we see
two hostile camps, heavily fortified and guarded. One is
occupied by the liberals of various descriptions, the other by the
Catholic and non-Catholic disciples of Thomas Aquinas.'[1]
Things have changed during the last twenty-five years, and the
debate need no longer be regarded as so polarized. Still, the
issues tackled in this book go to the root of every human
effort, commitment, and allegiance, and at the same time are
overlaid with a long and continuing history of fierce partisan-
ship. So it may be as well to point out that in this book
nothing is asserted or defended by appeal to the authority of any
person or body. I do quite frequently refer to Thomas Aquinas,
because on any view he occupies a uniquely strategic place in
the history of natural law theorizing. Likewise, I refer occasionally to the Roman Catholic Church's pronouncements on
natural law, because that body is perhaps unique in the
modern world in claiming to be an authoritative exponent of
natural law. But, while there is place for appeal to, and
deference to, authority, that place is not in philosophical argument about the merits of theories or the right response to practical problems, and so is not in this book.

My arguments, then, stand or fall by their own reasonableness or otherwise. But that is not to say there is much that is
original in them. My debts to Plato, Aristotle, Aquinas, and
other authors in that 'classical' tradition are recorded in the

[1] Strauss, *Natural Right and History* (Chicago: 1953), p. 7.

footnotes and in the more discursive notes following each chapter. My debt to Germain Grisez is similarly acknowledged, but calls for explicit mention here. The ethical theory advanced in Chapters III–V and the theoretical arguments in sections VI.2 and XIII.2 are squarely based on my understanding of his vigorous re-presentation and very substantial development of the classical arguments on these matters.

I have, of course, many other debts, particularly to David Alston, David Braine, Michael Detmold, Germain Grisez, H. L. A. Hart, Neil MacCormick, J. L. Mackie, Carlos Nino. and Joseph Raz, who from their diverse standpoints offered comments on the whole or substantial parts of a draft.

The book was conceived, begun, and finished in the University of Oxford, whose motto could be placed at the end of Part III. But the book was mainly written in Africa, in Chancellor College at the University of Malawi, in an environment at once congenial and conducive to contemplation of the problems of justice, law, authority, and rights.

March 1979

CONTENTS

ABBREVIATIONS

Adel. L. R.	*Adelaide Law Review.*
Am. J. Int. L.	*American Journal of International Law.*
Am. J. Juris.	*American Journal of Jurisprudence* (formerly *Nat.L.F.*).
Arch.Phil.Dr.	*Archives de Philosophie du Droit.*
Arch.R.S.P.	*Archiv für Rechts- und Sozialphilosophie.*
British Moralists	D. D. Raphael (ed.), *British Moralists 1650–1800* (Oxford: 1969).
Camb. L.J.	*Cambridge Law Journal.*
Comm.	William Blackstone, *Commentaries on the Laws of England* ((Oxford: 1765–9) cited to 9th ed., 1783, the last revised by Blackstone).
Concept of Law	H. L. A. Hart, *The Concept of Law* (Oxford: 1961).
De Legibus	Francisco Suarez, SJ, *De Legibus ac Deo Legislatore* (Coimbra: 1612).
Doctor and Student	Christopher St. German, *Doctor and Student* [1523 (First Dialogue, Latin), 1530 (Second Dialogue, English), 1531 (First Dialogue, English)], ed. Plucknett and Barton (London: 1975).
Essays	P. M. S. Hacker and J. Raz, *Law, Morality and Society: Essays in honour of H. L. A. Hart* (Oxford: 1977).
Eud. Eth.	Aristotle, *Eudemian Ethics.*
Gauthier–Jolif	R. A. Gauthier and J. Y. Jolif, *L'Ethique à Nicomaque* (revised ed., Paris: 1970).
General Theory	Hans Kelsen, *General Theory of Law and State* (Cambridge, Mass.: 1945; reprint, New York: 1961).
Harv. L. Rev.	*Harvard Law Review.*
I. C. J. Rep.	*Reports of the International Court of Justice.*

in Eth.	Thomas Aquinas, *In Decem Libros Ethicorum Aristotelis ad Nicomachum Expositio*, ed. R. M. Spiazzi (Turin and Rome: 1949).
in Pol.	Thomas Aquinas, *In Octo Libros Politicorum Aristotelis Expositio*, ed. R. M. Spiazzi (Turin and Rome: 1951).
in Primam Secundae	Gabriel Vazquez, SJ, *Commentariorum ac Disputationum in Primam Secundae Sancti Thomae* ... (1605).
Int. J. Ethics	*International Journal of Ethics*
Legal System	J. Raz, *The Concept of a Legal System* (Oxford: 1970).
L.Q.R.	*Law Quarterly Review*
Meta.	Aristotle, *Metaphysics*.
Methodology	E. A. Shils and H. A. Finch (eds.), *Max Weber on the Methodology of the Social Sciences* (Glencoe, Ill.: 1949).
Morality of Law	Lon L. Fuller, *The Morality of Law* (revised ed., 1969, New Haven and London).
Nat. L.F.	*Natural Law Forum* (now *Am.J.Juris.*).
Nic. Eth.	Aristotle, *Nicomachean Ethics*.
Of Laws	Jeremy Bentham, *Of Laws in General* (ed. H. L. A. Hart, London: 1970).
On Law	Max Rheinstein (ed.), *Max Weber on Law in Economy and Society* (Cambridge, Mass.: 1954).
Oxford Essays II	A. W. B. Simpson (ed.), *Oxford Essays in Jurisprudence: Second Series* (Oxford: 1971).
Phil. Pub. Aff.	*Philosophy and Public Affairs*.
Pol.	Aristotle, *Politics*.
Post. Anal.	Aristotle, *Posterior Analytics*.
Practical Reason	J. Raz, *Practical Reason and Norms* (London: 1975).
Proc. Aris. Soc.	*Proceedings of the Aristotelian Society*.
Province	John Austin, *The Province of Jurisprudence Determined* (1832; ed. H. L. A. Hart, London: 1954).
Rev. Thom.	*Revue Thomiste*.
S.T.	Thomas Aquinas, *Summa Theologiae*, cited

by Part (I, I–II, II–II, III), Question
(q. 94), and Article (a. 2); (a. 2c = body
of the reply, in a. 2; ad 4 = reply to
fourth objection in relevant Article).

Theory of Justice   John Rawls, *A Theory of Justice* (Cambridge, Mass.: 1971, Oxford:1972).

U. Pa. L. Rev.   *University of Pennsylvania Law Review.*

Part One

I

EVALUATION AND THE DESCRIPTION OF LAW

I.1 THE FORMATION OF CONCEPTS FOR DESCRIPTIVE SOCIAL SCIENCE

THERE are human goods that can be secured only through the institutions of human law, and requirements of practical reasonableness that only those institutions can satisfy. It is the object of this book to identify those goods, and those requirements of practical reasonableness, and thus to show how and on what conditions such institutions are justified and the ways in which they can be (and often are) defective.

It is often supposed that an evaluation of law as a type of social institution, if it is to be undertaken at all, must be preceded by a value-free description and analysis of that institution as it exists in fact. But the development of modern jurisprudence suggests, and reflection on the methodology of any social science confirms, that a theorist cannot give a theoretical description and analysis of social facts, unless he also participates in the work of evaluation, of understanding what is really good for human persons, and what is really required by practical reasonableness.

A social science, such as analytical or sociological jurisprudence, seeks to describe, analyse, and explain some object or subject-matter. This object is constituted by human actions, practices, habits, dispositions and by human discourse. The actions, practices, etc., are certainly influenced by the 'natural' causes properly investigated by the methods of the natural sciences, including a part of the science of psychology. But the actions, practices, etc., can be fully understood only by understanding their point, that is to say their objective, their value, their significance or importance, as conceived by the people who performed them, engaged in them, etc. And these conceptions of point, value, significance, and importance will be reflected in the discourse of those same people, in the conceptual distinctions they draw and fail or refuse to draw. More-over, these actions, practices, etc., and correspondingly these concepts, vary greatly from person to person, from one society to another, from one time and place to other times and places. *How, then, is there to be a general descriptive theory of these varying particulars?*

A theorist wishes to describe, say, law as a social institution. But the conceptions of law (and of *jus, lex, droit, nomos, ...*) which people have entertained, and have used to shape their own conduct, are quite varied. The subject-matter of the theorist's description does not come neatly demarcated from other features of social life and practice. Moreover, this social life and practice bears labels in many languages. The languages can be learned by speakers of other languages, but the principles on which labels are adopted and applied—i.e. the practical concerns and the self-interpretations of the people whose conduct and dispositions go to make up the theorist's subject-matter—are not uniform. Can the theorist do more, then, than list these varying conceptions and practices and their correspon-ding labels? Even a list requires some principle of selection of items for inclusion in the list. And jurisprudence, like other social sciences, aspires to be more than a conjunction of lexi-cography with local history, or even than a juxtaposition of all lexicographies conjoined with all local histories.

How does the theorist decide what is to count as law for the purposes of his description? The early analytical jurists do not show much awareness of the problem. Neither Bentham nor Austin advances any reason or justification for the definitions of law and jurisprudence which he favours. Each tries to show how the data of legal experience can be explained in terms of those definitions. But the definitions are simply posited at the outset and thereafter taken for granted. Bentham's notion of the 'real elements' of ideas encourages us to speculate that he was attracted to his definition of a law ('an assemblage of signs de-clarative of a volition conceived or adopted by the sovereign in a state . . .'[1]) by the fact that assemblages of signs (and the commands and prohibitions of a definite individual or set of individuals) are 'real entities' that make an empirical impres-

---

[1] Bentham, *Of Laws*, p. 1; on 'real elements' and 'real entities', see ibid., pp. 2–3, 251–2, 278, 294, and *A Fragment on Government* (1776), ch. V, para. vi, note 1(6).

sion on the mind. Austin's *obiter dicta* on methodology suggest that for him the attraction of the notions of command, political superior, and habit of obedience was precisely their simplicity and definiteness. He seems to have wanted the 'leading terms' of his explanatory system to have the 'simplicity and definiteness' found in the 'method so successfully pursued by geometers'.[2] So he did not mind either the complexity of some of the conclusions (e.g. as to sovereignty in federations) necessitated by his definitional premises, or the novelty and artificiality of others among those conclusions (e.g. as to the extralegal character of constitutional law, or the non-existence of legal rights of the sovereign). He prized the 'fewness' of his leading terms;[3] every reader of Austin becomes aware of the consequent flattening or thinning out of the account of legal experience.

In Kelsen's 'general theory of law' we find no critical attention to the methodological problem of selecting concepts for the purposes of a value-free or descriptive general theory. We do find an awareness, not apparent in Bentham and Austin, that point or function is intrinsic to the constitution, and hence to the descriptive understanding, of the subject-matter. So Kelsen defines law as a specific social technique: 'the social technique which consists in bringing about the desired social conduct of men through the threat of a measure of coercion which is to be applied in case of contrary conduct'.[4] From this he derives his characterization of the individual legal norm as a norm for the application of a sanction, and from this in turn follow the other features of his 'nomostatics' and several features of his 'nomodynamics'. But how does Kelsen propose to justify the definition itself? Simply as follows:

What could the social order of a negro tribe under the leadership of a despotic chieftain—an order likewise called 'law'—have in common with the constitution of the Swiss republic?

---

[2] Austin, *Province*, pp. 77–8.

[3] Ibid., p. 78.

[4] Kelsen, *General Theory*, p. 19. So law is a specific means to a specific end: 'The law is ... an ordering for the promotion of peace' (ibid., p. 21); hence 'Law is an order according to which the use of force is generally forbidden but exceptionally, under certain circumstances and for certain individuals, permitted as a sanction' (p. 22); see also ibid., pp. 392, 399.

[Let us interject to ask: Who is doing this calling, this naming? Whose willingness so to refer to the tribe's social order (in language expressing distinctions which the despotic chieftain and his subjects do not care to make) is thus being made decisive?]

Yet there is a common element that fully justifies this terminology ... for the word refers to that specific social technique which, despite the vast differences ... is yet essentially the same for all these peoples differing so much in time, in place, and in culture ...

What could be simpler? One takes the word 'law'. Ignoring a wide range of meanings and reference (as in 'law of nature', 'moral law', 'sociological law', 'international law', 'ecclesiastical law', 'law of grammar'), and further ignoring alternative ways of referring to, e.g., the 'negro tribe's' social order, one looks at the range of subject-matter signified by the word in the usage which one has (without explanation) selected. One looks for 'a common element'. This *one thing common* is the criterion of the 'essence' of law, and thus *the one feature* used to characterize and to explain descriptively the whole subject-matter. There is thus one concept, which can be predicated equally and *in the same sense* (i.e. univocally) of everything which, in a pre-theoretical usage (which the theorist allows to determine his theoretical usage), somebody was willing to call 'law'.

The noticeably greater explanatory power of later descriptive analyses of law, such as those of H. L. A. Hart and Joseph Raz, is to be attributed to their fairly decisive break with the rather naïve methodologies of Bentham, Austin, and Kelsen. This sophistication of method has three principal features, discussed in the following three sections.

I.2   ATTENTION TO PRACTICAL POINT

Hart's critique of Austin and Kelsen retains their fundamentally descriptive theoretical purpose: for his objection is that their theory 'failed to fit the facts'.[5] But the facts which their theory failed to fit, according to Hart, were facts about function. If Kelsen identifies law as a 'specific social technique', Hart replies that Kelsen's description in fact obscures 'the specific character of law as a means of social control' by 'distorting the different social functions which different types of legal rule

---

[5] Hart, *Concept of Law*, p. 78.

perform'.[6] Hart's description ('concept') of law is built up by appealing, again and again, to the practical point of the components of the concept. Law is to be described in terms of rules *for* the guidance of officials and citizens alike, not merely as a set of predictions of what officials will do. A legal system is a system in which 'secondary' rules have emerged *in order to* remedy the *defects* of a pre-legal regime comprising only 'primary rules'. Law must[7] have a minimum content of primary rules and sanctions *in order to* ensure the survival of the society or its members and to give them *practical reason for* compliance with it.

Raz refines these elements by a description of law which moves still further away from the 'despotic chieftain's' monopolization of force by threats of force. For Raz, as for Hart, the law is not any set of norms; it is a system of norms which provides a method (i.e. technique) of settling disputes authoritatively, by means of norms which both (*a*) provide binding guidance for 'primary institutions' (which settle the disputes by 'binding applicative determinations') and (*b*) also ('the very same norms') guide the individuals whose behaviour may fall to be evaluated and judged by those institutions.[8] Because of this dual function of its norms, a legal system differs fundamentally from any social order in which an authority may determine matters by deciding each problem as it thinks best, in its unfettered discretion.[9] Moreover, law does not seek merely to monopolize the use of force and thus to secure peace; it characteristically claims authority to regulate any form of behaviour, and to regulate all normative institutions to which the members of its subject-community belong;[10] finally, it contains norms 'the purpose of which is to give binding force within the system to norms which do not belong to it'.[11] 'By making these claims the law claims to provide the general framework for the

---

[6] Ibid., pp. 38, 39. For a brief account of these differing 'social functions', see ibid., pp. 27–8.

[7] See ibid., pp. 189–90, 193, 194–5; also Hart, 'Positivism and the Separation of Law and Morals' (1958) 71 *Harvard L. Rev.* 593, in Dworkin (ed.), *The Philosophy of Law*. (Oxford: 1977), 17 at p. 35.

[8] Raz, *Practical Reason*, pp. 136, 137, 139.

[9] Ibid., pp. 138, 141.

[10] Ibid., p. 151.

[11] Ibid., p. 153.

conduct of all aspects of social life and sets itself as the supreme guardian of society.'[12] It follows, of course, that sanctions and their enforcement by force, so far from being the specific identifying criterion of law as a social order, are 'not a feature which forms part of our concept of law'.[13] Human nature being what it is, resort to sanctions is universal and the operation of law without such resort, though 'logically possible', is 'humanly impossible'.[14] But the co-ordinating, dispute-resolving, and damage-remedying functions of law would require a *fully* legal social order even in 'a society of angels' which would have no use for sanctions.[15]

Raz builds up his account of law with a full awareness (not apparent in the earlier theorists of law) that there are social scientists who find no use for the concept of law or legal system in their description of human social, even political order.[16] He is aware that their theoretical decision to replace it with other concepts can be contested (as he wishes to contest it) only by showing that they have overlooked (i) important functions (or objectives and techniques) of social order, and (ii) the way in which those functions can be interrelated in a multi-faceted institution worth maintaining as a distinct unit of or component in social order.

By emphasizing (in his recent work) the distinction between law and social systems of absolute discretion, inasmuch as legal norms for guiding the citizen are also *binding* upon the courts (the legal 'primary organs'), Raz goes far towards Lon Fuller's analysis of the social function of law. Where Hart had retained Kelsen's notion that law is a method of social control but rejected as insufficiently differentiated Kelsen's account of the method, Fuller rejects, as an insufficiently differentiated and inappropriate general category, the notion of a 'means of social control'. For Fuller, law is indeed a social order in which there are rulers and subjects, but it is to be distinguished from any social order in which the rulers are exercising a 'managerial

---

[12] Ibid., p. 154.
[13] Ibid., p. 159.
[14] Ibid., p. 158.
[15] Ibid., p. 159.
[16] See his 'On the Functions of the Law', in *Oxford Essays II*, pp. 278–304, at pp. 300–3, analysing G. A. Almond and G. B. Powell's *Comparative Politics* (Boston: 1966).

direction' over their subjects. Law is distinguished from such managerial direction partly by the generality of its major rules, and above all by the fact that its officials are bound to apply the rules which they have previously announced to their subjects. There is thus an essential component of collaboration and reciprocity in the enterprise of subjecting human conduct to the governance of legal as distinct from merely managerial norms.[17]

All these accounts of law, even that part of Fuller's which I have just mentioned, are intended as descriptive. They seek to 'identify law on the basis of non-evaluative characteristics only'.[18] As Raz says, such 'non-evaluative identifying criteria ... should single out those phenomena which form a special sort of social institution, an institution to be found as an important component of many social systems and which differs significantly from other social institutions'.[19] It is obvious, then, that the differences in description derive from differences of opinion, amongst the descriptive theorists, about what is *important* and *significant* in the field of data and experience with which they are all equally and thoroughly familiar.

I.3 SELECTION OF CENTRAL CASE AND FOCAL MEANING

The obvious question provoked by the course of theorizing sketched in the preceding section is: From what viewpoint, and relative to what concerns, are *importance* and *significance* to be assessed? Before we consider that question, however, it will be as well to identify the philosophical device which enables an increasingly *differentiated* description of law to be offered as still a *general* theory of law.

Aristotle introduced, discussed, and regularly employed the device, not least in his philosophy of human affairs. He called it the identification of *focal meaning* (*pros hen* or *aph henos homonymy*). The device is or corresponds to a main component in Max Weber's not too clearly explained methodological device, the *ideal-type*. It involves a conscious departure from the assumption upon which, as we saw, Kelsen proceeded: that

---

[17] *Morality of Law*, pp. 210, 214, 216; 39–40, 61, 155; 20.
[18] Raz, *Practical Reason*, p. 165.
[19] Ibid., p. 165.

descriptive or explanatory terms must be employed by the theorist in such a way that they extend, straightforwardly and in the same sense, to *all* the states of affairs which could reasonably, in non-theoretical discourse, be 'called "law"', however undeveloped those states of affairs may be, and however little those states of affairs may manifest any concern of their authors (e.g. the 'despotic chieftains') to differentiate between law and force, law and morality, law and custom, law and politics, law and absolute discretion, or law and anything else. Such insistence on a flatly univocal meaning of theoretical terms, leading to the search for a lowest common denominator or highest *common* factor or for the 'one thing common', was directly attacked by Aristotle,[20] and is consciously abandoned by Hart and Raz. Thus Hart rejects the view that 'the several instances of a general term must have the same characteristics'. Instead, he proceeds on the assumption that 'the extension of the general terms of any serious discipline is never without its principle or rationale'.[21] What Aristotle says in relation to 'friend[ship]', 'constitution[ality]', and 'citizen-[ship]'[22] is well said by Raz in relation to 'legal system':

The general traits which mark a system as a legal one are several and each of them admits, in principle, of various degrees. In typical instances of legal systems all these traits are manifested to a very high degree. But it is possible to find systems in which all or some are present only to a lesser degree or in which one or two are absent altogether ... When faced with borderline cases it is best to admit their problematic credentials, to enumerate their similarities and dissimilarities to the typical cases, and leave it at that.[23]

Because the word 'typical' may suggest that the relevant criterion is statistical frequency (whether in human history, or today), I prefer to call the states of affairs referred to by a theoretical concept in its focal meaning the *central case(s)*.

By exploiting the systematic multi-significance of one's theoretical terms (without losing sight of the 'principle or rationale' of this multi-significance), one can differentiate the mature from the undeveloped in human affairs, the sophis-

[20] *Eud. Eth.* VII, 2: 1236a16–30.
[21] *Concept of Law*, pp. 15, 210; see also p. 234.
[22] *Nic. Eth.* VIII, 4: 1157a30–3; *Pol.* III, 1:1275a33–1276b4.
[23] *Practical Reason*, p. 150.

ticated from the primitive, the flourishing from the corrupt, the fine specimen from the deviant case, the 'straightforwardly', 'simply speaking' (*simpliciter*), and 'without qualification' from the 'in a sense', 'in a manner of speaking', and 'in a way' (*secundum quid*)—but all without ignoring or banishing to another discipline the undeveloped, primitive, corrupt, deviant or other 'qualified sense' or 'extended sense' instances of the subject-matter: see XII.4, below.

So there are central cases, as Aristotle insisted, of friendship, and there are more or less peripheral cases (business friendship, friendship of convenience, cupboard love, casual and play relations, and so on: see VI.4, below). There are central cases of constitutional government, and there are peripheral cases (such as Hitler's Germany, Stalin's Russia, or even Amin's Uganda). On the one hand, there is no point in denying that the peripheral cases *are* instances (of friendship, constitutionality ...). Indeed, the study of them is illuminated by thinking of them as watered-down versions of the central cases, or sometimes as exploitations of human attitudes shaped by reference to the central case. And, on the other hand, there is no point in restricting one's explanation of the central cases to those features which are present not only in the central but also in each of the peripheral cases. Rather, one's descriptive explanation of the central cases should be as conceptually rich and complex as is required to answer all appropriate questions about those central cases. And then one's account of the other instances can trace the network of similarities and differences, the analogies and disanalogies, for example, of form, function, or content, between them and the central cases. In this way, one uncovers the 'principle or rationale' on which the general term ('constitution', 'friend', 'law' ...) is extended from the central to the more or less borderline cases, from its focal to its secondary meanings.

I.4 SELECTION OF VIEWPOINT

But by what criteria is one meaning to be accounted focal and another secondary, one state of affairs central and another borderline? This is simply a reformulation of the question left over from I.2: From what viewpoint, and relative to what concerns, are *importance* and *significance* to be assessed?

Hart and Raz are clear that a descriptive theorist, in 'deciding to attribute a central role'[24] to some particular feature or features in his description of a field of human affairs, must 'be concerned with',[25] 'refer to',[26] or 'reproduce'[27] one particular *practical* point of view (or set of similar viewpoints). By 'practical', here as throughout this book, I do not mean 'workable' as opposed to unworkable, efficient as opposed to inefficient; I mean 'with a view to decision and action'. Practical thought is thinking about what (one ought) to do. Practical reasonableness is reasonableness in deciding, in adopting commitments, in choosing and executing projects, and in general in acting. Practical philosophy is a disciplined and critical reflection on the goods that can be realized in human action and the requirements of practical reasonableness. So when we say that the descriptive theorist (whose purposes are not practical) must proceed, in his indispensable selection and formation of concepts, by adopting a practical point of view, we mean that he must assess importance or significance in similarities and differences within his subject-matter by asking what would be considered important or significant in that field by those whose concerns, decisions, and activities create or constitute the subject-matter.

Thus Hart gives descriptive explanatory priority to the concerns and evaluations (and consequently to the language) of people with an 'internal point of view', viz. those who do not 'merely record and predict behaviour conforming to rules', or attend to rules 'only from the external point of view as a sign of possible punishment', but rather '*use* the rules as standards for the appraisal of their own and others' behaviour'.[28] Raz, in his earlier work, adopts 'the ordinary man's point of view',[29] but in his more recent work shifts to 'the legal point of view', which is the point of view of people who 'believe in the

---

[24] See Raz, *Legal System*, p. 201.
[25] Ibid., p. 200 n. 2.
[26] Hart, *Concept of Law*, p. 96.
[27] Ibid., p. 88.
[28] Ibid., pp. 95–6; also 86–8, 59–60, 113, 197, 226.
[29] *Legal System*, p. 200 n. 2.

validity of the norms and follow them' (paradigmatically, the viewpoint of the judge *qua* judge).[30]

Rather obviously, this position of Hart and Raz is unstable and unsatisfactory. As against Austin and Kelsen they have sharply differentiated the 'internal' or 'legal' point of view from the point of view of the man who merely acquiesces in the law and who does so only because, when, and to the extent that he fears the punishments that will follow non-acquiescence. But they firmly refuse to differentiate further. They recognize that the 'internal' or 'legal' viewpoint, as they describe it, is an amalgam of very different viewpoints. '[A]llegiance to the system may be based on many different considerations: calculations of long-term interest, disinterested interest in others; an unreflecting or traditional attitude; or the mere wish to do as others do.'[31] Raz is willing to extend his conception of 'the legal point of view' to encompass the viewpoint of 'an anarchist' who becomes a judge 'on the ground that if he follows the law most of the time he will be able to disobey it on the few but important occasions when to do so will most undermine it'.[32] But all this is unstable and unsatisfactory because it involves a refusal to attribute significance to differences that any actor in the field (whether the subversive anarchist or his opponent the 'ideal law-abiding citizen'[33]) would count as practically significant. And, given the technique of analysis by central case and focal meaning, which elsewhere Hart and Raz use with such fruitful resolution, there seems to be no good reason for this refusal to differentiate the central from the peripheral cases *of the internal or legal point of view itself.*

For it is not difficult to discern that the viewpoint of Raz's anarchistic judge, who covertly picks and chooses amongst the laws he will enforce, with the intention of overthrowing the whole system, is not a paradigm of either the judicial or the legal point of view. Neither the anarchist nor his fellows would consider it as such. Why then should the descriptive theorist? Similarly with Hart's 'unreflecting inherited

---

[30] *Practical Reason*, pp. 177, 171.
[31] Hart, *Concept of Law*, p. 198; also pp. 111, 226.
[32] *Practical Reason*, p. 148.
[33] Ibid., p. 171.

or traditional attitude ... or mere wish to do as others do'. These are attitudes which will, up to a point, tend to maintain in existence a legal system (as distinct from, say, a system of despotic discretion) if one already exists. But they will not bring about the transition from the pre-legal (or post-legal!) social order of custom or discretion to a legal order, for they do not share the concern, which Hart himself recognizes as the explanatory source of legal order, to remedy the defects of pre-legal social orders. Similarly, Hart's man who is moved by 'calculations of long-term interest' (sc. self-interest) waters down any concern he may have for the function of law as an answer to real social problems; like Raz's anarchistic judge, he dilutes his allegiance to law and his pursuit of legal methods of thought with doses of that very self-interest which it is an elementary function of law (on everybody's view) to subordinate to social needs. All these considerations and attitudes, then, are manifestly deviant, diluted or watered-down instances of the practical viewpoint that brings law into being as a significantly differentiated type of social order and maintains it as such. Indeed, they are parasitic upon that viewpoint.

From the list of types of internal or legal viewpoint offered by Hart and Raz, we are now left only with 'disinterested interest in others', and the view of those who consider the rules, or at least the rules of recognition, to be 'morally justified'.[34] If disinterested concern for others is detached from moral concern, as it is by Hart,[35] then what it involves is quite unclear, and, in the absence of clarification, it must be considered to have a relationship to law and legal concerns as uncertain and floating as its relationship (on this view) to moral concern.

The conclusion we should draw is clear. If there is a point of view in which legal obligation is treated as at least presumptively a moral obligation (and thus as of 'great importance', to be maintained 'against the drive of strong passions' and 'at the cost of sacrificing considerable personal interest'),[36] a viewpoint in which the establishment and maintenance of legal as distinct from discretionary or statically customary order is regarded as a moral ideal if not a compelling demand of justice, then such a

[34] See Raz, *Practical Reason*, pp. 147–8.
[35] *Concept of Law*, p. 226.
[36] Ibid., p. 169.

viewpoint will constitute the central case of the legal viewpoint. For only in such a viewpoint is it a matter of overriding importance that law as distinct from other forms of social order should come into being, and thus become an object of the theorist's description. But the term 'moral' is of somewhat uncertain connotation. So it is preferable to frame our conclusion in terms of practical reasonableness (see V.1, V.10, VI.1, XI.1, XI.4). If there is a viewpoint in which the institution of the Rule of Law (X.5), and compliance with rules and principles of law according to their tenor, are regarded as at least presumptive requirements of practical reasonableness itself, such a viewpoint is the viewpoint which should be used as the standard of reference by the theorist describing the features of legal order.

One further differentiation remains possible. Among those who, from a practical viewpoint, treat law as an aspect of practical reasonableness, there will be some whose views about what practical reasonableness actually requires in this domain are, in detail, more reasonable than others. Thus the central case viewpoint itself is the viewpoint of those who not only appeal to practical reasonableness but also *are* practically reasonable, that is to say: consistent; attentive to all aspects of human opportunity and flourishing, and aware of their limited commensurability; concerned to remedy deficiencies and breakdowns, and aware of their roots in the various aspects of human personality and in the economic and other material conditions of social interaction.[37] What reason could the descriptive theorist have for rejecting the conceptual choices and discriminations of these persons, when he is selecting the concepts with which he will construct his description of the central case and then of all the other instances of law as a specific social institution?

The descriptive theorist is indeed not bound to adopt into his theory all the concepts which the societies he is studying have

---

[37] Behind Aristotle's cardinal principle of method in the study of human affairs—viz. that concepts are to be selected and employed substantially as they are used in practice by the *spoudaios* (the mature man of practical reasonableness): see XII.4, below— lies Plato's argument (*Rep.* IX: 582a–e) that the lover of wisdom can understand the concerns of men of other character, while the converse does not hold; in other words, the concerns and understanding of the mature and reasonable man provide a better *empirical* basis for the reflective account of human affairs: see also *Rep.* III: 408d–409e.

used in their own self-interpretation of their own practices. Many such concepts betray a weak sensitivity to certain aspects of human well-being; others betray the influence of ideological myth, for example, that 'the people' rules 'itself' (cf. IX.4), or that 'the revolution' is replacing the rule of law with 'the administration of things'. But it is precisely a disciplined and informed *practical* thought (whether 'theoretical', i.e. reflective, in intent, or more immediately directed to action) that can provide a critique of these concepts, in order to overcome the obstacles they place in the way of clear thinking about what ought to be done. Descriptive social theory does not share this concern about what ought to be done. But it cannot in its descriptions do without the concepts found appropriate by men of *practical* reasonableness to *describe to themselves* what they think worth doing and achieving in the face of all the contingencies, misunderstandings, and myths confronting them in their practice.

Thus by a long march through the working or implicit methodology of contemporary analytical jurisprudence, we arrive at the conclusion reached more rapidly (though on the basis of a much wider social science) by Max Weber: namely, that the evaluations of the theorist himself are an indispensable and decisive component in the selection or formation of any concepts for use in description of such aspects of human affairs as law or legal order. For the theorist cannot identify the central case of that practical viewpoint which he uses to identify the central case of his subject-matter, unless he decides what the requirements of practical reasonableness really are, in relation to this whole aspect of human affairs and concerns. In relation to law, the most important things for the theorist to know and describe are the things which, in the judgment of the theorist, make it important from a *practical* viewpoint to have law—the things which it is, therefore, important in practice to 'see to' when ordering human affairs. And when these 'important things' are (in some or even in many societies) in fact missing, or debased, or exploited or otherwise deficient, then the most important things for the theorist to describe are those aspects of the situation that manifest this absence, debasement, exploitation, or deficiency.

Does this mean that descriptive jurisprudence (and social

science as a whole) is inevitably subject to every theorist's conceptions and prejudices about what is good and practically reasonable? Yes and no. 'Yes', in so far as there is no escaping the theoretical requirement that a judgment of *significance* and *importance* must be made if theory is to be more than a vast rubbish heap of miscellaneous facts described in a multitude of incommensurable terminologies. 'No', in so far as the disciplined acquisition of accurate knowledge about human affairs—and thus about what other men have considered practically important, and about the actual results of their concern—is an important help to the reflective and critical theorist in his effort to convert his own (and his culture's) practical 'prejudices' into truly reasonable judgments about what is good and practically reasonable. Descriptive knowledge thus can occasion a modification of the judgments of importance and significance with which the theorist first approached his data, and can suggest a reconceptualization. But the knowledge will not have been attained without a preliminary conceptualization and thus a preliminary set of principles of selection and relevance drawn from some practical viewpoint.

There is thus a movement to and fro between, on the one hand, assessments of human good and of its practical requirements, and on the other hand, explanatory descriptions (using all appropriate historical, experimental, and statistical techniques to trace all relevant causal interrelationships) of the human context in which human well-being is variously realized and variously ruined. Just as (as we shall see: II.4) there is no question of deriving one's basic judgments about human values and the requirements of practical reasonableness by some inference from the facts of the human situation, so there is no question of reducing descriptive social science to an apologia for one's ethical or political judgments, or to a project for apportioning praise or blame among the actors on the human scene: in this sense, descriptive social science is 'value-free'. But when all due emphasis has been given to the differences of objective and method between practical philosophy and descriptive social science, the methodological problems of concept-formation as we have traced it in this chapter compel us to recognize that the point of reflective equilibrium in descriptive social science is attainable only by one in whom wide knowledge of the data, and penetrating understanding of other men's practical viewpoints and concerns, are allied to a sound judgment about all aspects of genuine human flourishing and authentic practical reasonableness.

I.5   THE THEORY OF NATURAL LAW

Bentham, Austin, Kelsen, Weber, Hart, and Raz all published stern repudiations of what they understood to be the theory of natural law; and Fuller carefully dissociated himself from that theory in its classical forms. But the theoretical work of each of these writers was controlled by the adoption, on grounds left inexplicit and inadequately justified, of some practical viewpoint as the standard of relevance and significance in the construction of his descriptive analysis. A sound theory of natural law is one that explicitly, with full awareness of the methodological situation just described, undertakes a critique of practical viewpoints, in order to distinguish the practically unreasonable from the practically reasonable, and thus to differentiate the really important from that which is unimportant or is important only by its opposition to or unreasonable exploitation of the really important. A theory of natural law claims to be able to identify conditions and principles of practical right-mindedness, of good and proper order among men and in individual conduct. Unless some such claim is justified, analytical jurisprudence in particular and (at least the major part of) all the social sciences in general can have no critically justified criteria for the formation of general concepts, and must be content to be no more than manifestations of the various concepts peculiar to particular peoples and/or to the particular theorists who concern themselves with those people.

A theory of natural law need not be undertaken primarily for the purpose of thus providing a justified conceptual framework for descriptive social science. It may be undertaken, as this book is, primarily to assist the practical reflections of those concerned to act, whether as judges or as statesmen or as citizens. But in either case, the undertaking cannot proceed securely without a knowledge of the whole range of human possibilities and opportunities, inclinations and capacities, a knowledge that requires the assistance of descriptive and analytical social science. There is thus a mutual though not quite symmetrical interdependence between the project of describing human affairs by way of theory and the project of evaluating human options with a view, at least remotely, to acting reasonably and well. The evaluations are in no way deduced from the descriptions (see II.4); but one whose knowledge of the facts of the human situation is very limited is unlikely to judge well in discerning the practical implications of the basic values. Equally, the descriptions are not deduced from the evaluations; but without the evaluations one cannot determine what descriptions are really illuminating and significant.

NOTES

I.1

Description of human institutions and practices requires identification of their point ... See Max Weber, *Theory of Social and Economic Organization* (ed. T. Parsons, New York and London: 1947), pp. 88–126; *On Law*, pp. 1–10; Alfred Schütz, 'Concept and Theory Formation in the Social Sciences' (1954) 5 *J. of Philosophy* reprinted in his *Collected Papers*, vol. I (ed. M. Natanson, The Hague: 1967), 48 at pp. 58–9; Eric Voegelin, *The New Science of Politics* (Chicago and London: 1952), pp. 27–9.

Bentham on definition of law ... See also Bentham, *Collected Works* (ed. J. Bowring, Edinburgh: 1863), vol. IV, p. 483; and excursus to XI.8 (notes), below.

Kelsen's technique of definition ... See also Hans Kelsen, *Pure Theory of Law* (Berkeley and Los Angeles: 1967), pp. 30–1.

Description of social institutions, such as law, requires identification of their point or function(s) ... See also J. Raz, 'On the Functions of the Law', in *Oxford Essays II*, pp. 278–304, at 278; *Legal System*, p. 145.

Raz on the criterion of law ... Raz is clear that any theorist seeking to describe law must decide between different theoretical concepts, and that 'the explicit formulation of meta-theoretical criteria is a condition for a rational and reasoned comparison of theories': Raz, *Legal System*, p. 146. Central to his own account of meta-theoretical criteria is his decision that legal theory should explicate 'common sense and professional opinion': p. 201. In *Legal System*, he offers a 'jurisprudential criterion' (p. 200): viz. that 'a momentary legal system contains all, and only all, the laws recognized by a primary law-applying organ which it institutes' (p. 192). He underlines that this criterion 'is concerned with the actual behaviour of primary organs, not with what they ought to do ...' (p. 198). But in *Practical Reason* he criticizes those legal theorists 'who concluded that the law consists of all the standards which the courts do apply. This ... confuses institutionalized systems with systems of absolute discretion' (p. 142). So his new criterion is: a legal system contains 'only those norms which its primary organs are bound to obey' (p. 142; also p. 148). This shift in Raz's jurisprudential criterion for membership of a legal system is to be traced to his shift from a concern to reproduce the rather undifferentiated 'ordinary man's' point of view to a concern to reproduce the 'legal point of view', the view of one (paradigmatically a judge, or an 'ideal law-abiding citizen') who believes that people are in some way *justified* in following the rules of the system: pp. 139, 143, 171.

I.3

Aristotle on focal meaning and analysis of central cases ... See W. F. R. Hardie, *Aristotle's Ethical Theory* (Oxford: 1968), pp. 59–60, 63–5; *Gauthier–Jolif*, II, 1, pp. 45–6; II, 2, pp. 686ff.; cf. W. W. Fortenbaugh, 'Aristotle's Analysis of Friendship: Function and Analogy, Resemblance and Focal Meaning' (1975) 20 *Phronesis* 51–62; and XII.4, below. Hart's discussion, *Concept of Law*, pp. 15–16, 234, does not clearly distinguish what Aristotle called analogy (and the medievals called 'analogy of proportionality') from what he called *pros hen* homonymy or focal meaning (called by the medievals 'analogy of attribution or proportion'). Hart's account on pp. 15–16 seems to concentrate on the former, but the latter is the more important device in the theory of human affairs. Having noted this distinction, however, I find it convenient to use the broad concept of 'analogy' and 'analogical', introduced by the medievals and more or less retained in philosophical usage thereafter. In this broad sense, a term is analogical when its meaning shifts systematically (i.e. according to some principle or rationale) as one shifts from one context or use to another. On the search for the principle or rationale in such cases, see also Hart, 'Definition and Theory in Jurisprudence' (1954) 70 *L.Q.R.* 37 at pp. 38, 44n., 56–9.

Max Weber on the construction of ideal-type concepts for general sociology ... See *Methodology*, pp. 89–93. See also Alfred Schütz, 'The Problem of Rationality in the Social World', in his *Collected Papers*, vol. II (The Hague: 1964), 64 at pp. 81–8.

Differentiation of 'mature' from 'impoverished' specimens of law and legal system ... Austin recognized that jurisprudence should study primarily the 'ampler and maturer' legal systems: see *Province*, p. 367. See also Raz, *Legal System*, p. 140; *Practical Reason*, p. 150.

Frequency of occurrence or instantiation is not a decisive criterion of relevance or centrality ... See Weber, *Methodology* at pp. 72–80; Eric Voegelin, 'The Theory of Legal Science: a Review' (1942) 4 *Louisiana Law Rev.* 554 at pp. 558–64.

I.4

Practical thought, reasonableness, philosophy, etc. ... For my use of 'practical', throughout the book, see Aristotle, *Nic. Eth.* VI, 2: 1139a26–31; *De Anima* III, 9: 432b27; Aquinas, *S.T.* I, q. 79, a. 11; Raz, *Practical Reason*, pp. 10–13. In Aristotle, 'practical' is distinguished from *theoretike*, translated by the medievals as *speculativa*: see Aristotle, locc. citt. and *Meta* VI, 1: 1025b19–29. Neither 'theoretical' nor 'speculative' is very suitable for drawing the necessary distinctions in English; in this chapter 'descriptive' and 'descriptive explanation' have been used for the purpose. The Aristotelian/Thomist distinction has intrinsic difficulties, since practical philosophy is 'directed to action' only somewhat remotely, i.e. in a 'theoretical way'. Despite the difficulties, the distinction should be retained; it witnesses to the ancient awareness of the basic distinction between 'is' and 'ought' (a distinction which itself is not altogether simple in its applications).

Weber on the necessity of the theorist using his own evaluations in order to assess significance for descriptive theory ... See, above all, *Methodology*, pp. 58, 76–82, 24; also Julien Freund, *The Sociology of Max Weber* (London: 1968), pp. 51–61. Of course, Weber regarded these evaluations by the theorist as non-scientific, i.e. as lacking the dignity of objectivity: see II.3 (notes). Hence he would not accept that the theorist's task, in this part of his work, is to decide what the basic forms of human good and the requirements of practical reasonableness 'really are'. I may add that in referring to Weber's contention that evaluation is necessary for any social science, I am not subscribing to every aspect of his argument for this contention, an argument not free from the neo-Kantian notion that all concepts have to be imposed by the human mind on the flux of phenomena, a flux that has no intelligible structure of its own to be discovered.

Descriptive social theory is not about what ought to be done ... Thus the objective and methods of a general descriptive and analytical jurisprudence such as Hart's or Raz's are to be clearly distinguished from the objective and methods of a 'legal theory' as conceived by R. M. Dworkin. For Dworkin, a main function of a 'theory of law' is 'to provide a basis for judicial duty'; 'the principles it sets out must try to *justify* the settled rules [of a given community] by identifying the political or moral concerns and traditions which, in the opinion of the lawyer whose theory it is, do in fact support the rules': Dworkin, *Taking Rights Seriously* (London; 1977), p. 67. (The phrase 'in fact' here means 'really' (as assessed normatively), not 'as a matter of cause-and-effect'; see also p. 51, lines 6, 11.) See also, p. 117; Dworkin, 'No Right Answer?', in *Essays* at p. 82. Of course, a theory so relative to the moral opinions and practices of a given community is not a general theory such as theories of natural law aspire to be. But Dworkin contemplates a 'general theory of law' which in its (quite ambitious) 'normative part' would set out, *inter alia*, 'standards that judges should use to decide hard cases at law' and would explain 'why and when judges, rather than other groups or institutions, should make the decisions required by the theory ...' (*Taking Rights Seriously*, pp. vii–viii). For reasons that are unclear, he contemplates a distinct though related 'conceptual part' that would determine (how is not explained) such questions as 'Can the most fundamental principles of the constitution ... themselves be considered as part of the law?'. In any event, his debate with 'positivists' such as Hart and Raz miscarries, because he fails to acknowledge that their theoretical interest is not, like his, to identify a fundamental 'test for law' in order to identify (even in the most disputed 'hard' cases) where a judge's legal (moral and political) duty really lies, in a given community at a given time. Rather, their interest is in describing what is treated (i.e. accepted and effective) as law in a given community at a given time, and in generating concepts that will allow such descriptions to be clear and explanatory, but without intent to offer solutions (whether 'right answers' or standards that would if properly applied yield right answers) to questions disputed among competent lawyers. The 'embarrassing questions' listed by Dworkin, op. cit., pp. 14, 15, 44, are not questions that either Hart or Raz offers to answer. So Dworkin's is, fundamentally (though with many illuminating moments of description), a normative theory of law, offering guidance to the judge as to his judicial duty; theirs is a descriptive theory, offered to historians to enable a discriminating history of legal systems to be written. The fact that, as I have argued in this chapter, the descriptive theorist needs the assistance of a general normative theory in developing sufficiently differentiated concepts and reasonable standards of relevance does not eliminate the different uses to which the more or less common stock of theoretical concepts will be put by the normative and the descriptive (historical) theorists, respectively.

Reflective equilibrium in descriptive social science ... The theorist who could attain this point would be one whose viewpoint systematically approximated the 'universal viewpoint' postulated by B. J. F. Lonergan, *Insight: A Study of Human Understanding* (London: 1957), pp. 554–68. As Lonergan remarks (p. 566), such a viewpoint 'is universal not by abstractness but by potential completeness. It attains its inclusiveness, not by stripping objects of their peculiarities' (cf. Kelsen, Austin ...) 'but by envisaging subjects' (i.e. persons) 'in their necessities'.

II

IMAGES AND OBJECTIONS

II.1 NATURAL LAW AND THEORIES OF NATURAL LAW

WHAT are *principles of natural law?* The sense that the phrase 'natural law' has in this book can be indicated in the following rather bald assertions, formulations which will seem perhaps empty or question-begging until explicated in Part Two: There is (i) a set of basic practical principles which indicate the basic forms of human flourishing as goods to be pursued and realized, and which are in one way or another used by everyone who considers what to do, however unsound his conclusions; and (ii) a set of basic methodological requirements of practical reasonableness (itself one of the basic forms of human flourishing) which distinguish sound from unsound practical thinking and which, when all brought to bear, provide the criteria for distinguishing between acts that (always or in particular circumstances) are reasonable-all-things-considered (and not merely relative-to-a-particular purpose) and acts that are unreasonable-all-things-considered, i.e. between ways of acting that are morally right or morally wrong—thus enabling one to formulate (iii) a set of general moral standards.

To avoid misunderstandings about the scope of our subject-matter in this book, I should add here that the principles of natural law, thus understood, are traced out not only in moral philosophy or ethics and 'individual' conduct, but also in political philosophy and jurisprudence, in political action, adjudication, and the life of the citizen. For those principles justify the exercise of authority in community. They require, too, that that authority be exercised, in most circumstances, according to the manner conveniently labelled the Rule of Law, and with due respect for the human rights which embody the requirements of justice, and for the purpose of promoting a common good in which such respect for rights is a component. More particularly, the principles of natural law explain the obligatory force (in the fullest sense of 'obligation') of positive laws, even when those laws cannot be deduced from those principles. And attention to the principles, in the context of these explanations of law and legal obligation, justifies regarding certain positive laws as radically defective, *precisely as laws*, for want of conformity to those principles.

My present purpose, however, is not to anticipate later chapters, but to make some preliminary clarifications. A first essential distinction is that between a theory, doctrine, or account and the subject-matter of that theory, doctrine, or account. There can be a history of theories, doctrines, and accounts of matters that have no history. And principles of natural law, in the sense formulated in the two preceding paragraphs, have no history.

Since I have yet to show that there are indeed any principles of natural law, let me put the point conditionally. Principles of this sort would hold good, as principles, however extensively they were overlooked, misapplied, or defied in practical thinking, and however little they were recognized by those who reflectively theorize about human thinking. That is to say, they would 'hold good' just as the mathematical principles of accounting 'hold good' even when, as in the medieval banking community, they are unknown or misunderstood. So there could be a history of the varying extent to which they have been used by people, explicitly or implicitly, to regulate their personal activities. And there could be a history of the varying extent to which reflective theorists have acknowledged the sets of principles as valid or 'holding good'. And there could be a history of the popularity of the various theories offered to explain the place of those principles in the whole scheme of things. But of natural law itself there could, strictly speaking, be no history.

Natural law could not rise, decline, be revived, or stage 'eternal returns'. It could not have historical achievements to its credit. It could not be held responsible for disasters of the human spirit or atrocities of human practice.

But there is a history of the opinions or set of opinions, theories, and doctrines which assert that there are principles of natural law, a history of origins, rises, declines and falls, revivals and achievements, and of historical responsibilities. Anyone who thinks there really are no such principles will consider that a book about natural law must be a book about mere opinions, and that the principal interest of those opinions is their historical causes and effects. But anyone who considers that there are principles of natural law, in the sense already outlined, ought to see the importance of maintaining a distinction between discourse about natural law and discourse about a doctrine or doctrines of natural law. Unhappily, people often fail to maintain the distinction.[1]

This is a book about natural law. It expounds or sets out a theory of natural law, but is not *about* that theory. Nor is it about other theories. It refers to other theories only to illuminate the theory expounded here, or to explain why some truths about natural law have at various times and in various ways been overlooked or obscured. The book does not enter into discussions about whether natural law doctrines have exerted a conservative or radical influence on Western politics, or about the supposed psychological (infantile)[2] origins of such doctrines, or about the claim that some or all specific natural law doctrines are asserted hypocritically,[3] arrogantly,[4] or as a disguise or vehicle for expressions of ecclesiastical faith. For none of these discussions has any real bearing on the question whether there is a natural law and, if so, what its content is. Equally irrelevant to that question is the claim that disbelief in natural law yields bitter fruit. Nothing in this book is to be interpreted as either advancing or denying such claims; the book simply prescinds from all such matters.

II.2 LEGAL VALIDITY AND MORALITY

The preceding section treated theories of natural law as theories of the rational foundations for moral judgment, and this

---

[1] Notable examples of this failure include A. P. D'Entrèves, *Natural Law* (London: 1951, rev. ed. 1970), e.g. pp. 13, 18, 22, etc.; Julius Stone, *Human Law and Human Justice* (London: 1965), chs. 2 and 7.

[2] See Alf Ross, *On Law and Justice* (London: 1958), pp. 258, 262–3.

[3] See Wolfgang Friedmann, letter (1953) 31 *Canadian Bar Rev.* 1074 at 1075.

[4] See Wolfgang Friedmann, review (1958) 3 *Nat. L.F.* 208 at 210; also Hans Kelsen, *Algemeine Staatslehre* (Berlin: 1925), p. 335, on 'natural law naivety or arrogance' (in the passage, omitted from the 1945 English translation (*General Theory*, cf. p. 300), about the fully legal character of despotism).

will be the primary focus of subsequent sections of this chapter. But in the present section I consider the more restricted and juristic understanding of 'natural law' and 'natural law doctrine(s)'.

Here we have to deal with the image of natural law entertained by jurists such as Kelsen, Hart, and Raz. This image should be reproduced in their own words, since they themselves scarcely identify, let alone quote from, any particular theorist as defending the view that they describe as the view of natural law doctrine. Joseph Raz usefully summarizes and adopts Kelsen's version of this image:

> Kelsen correctly points out that according to natural law theories there is no specific notion of legal validity. The only concept of validity is validity according to natural law, i.e., moral validity. Natural lawyers can only judge a law as morally valid, that is, just or morally invalid, i.e., wrong. They cannot say of a law that it is legally valid but morally wrong. If it is wrong and unjust, it is also invalid in the only sense of validity they recognise.[5]

In his own terms, Raz later defines 'Natural Law theorists' as 'those philosophers who think it a criterion of adequacy for theories of law that they show ... that it is a necessary truth that every law has moral worth'.[6]

For my part, I know of no philosopher who fits, or fitted, such a description, or who would be committed to trying to defend that sort of theoretical or meta-theoretical proposal. Sections IX.2, X.2, X.5, X.6, XI.4, XII.3, and XII.4, below, are devoted to correcting this image. Suffice it here to say that the root of the misunderstanding seems to be the failure of the modern critics to interpret the texts of natural law theorists in accordance with the principles of definition which those theorists have, for the most part, consistently and self-consciously used. I have already given a sketch of those

---

[5] Raz, 'Kelsen's Theory of the Basic Norm' (1974) 19 *Am. J. Juris.* 94 at p. 100.

[6] *Practical Reason*, p. 162. This formulation corresponds to the contradictory of the characterization of 'Legal Positivism' constructed by Hart in order to define 'the issue between Natural Law and Legal Positivism': *Concept of Law*, p. 181. See also *Practical Reason*, pp. 155, 162; all these formulations seem to be intended by Raz to apply equally to 'definitional' and 'derivative approach' theories of natural law. (Since no one uses the 'definitional' approach, there is no need to inquire into the value of the supposed distribution between 'definitional' and 'derivative' approaches.)

principles in section I.3, under the rubric 'central cases and focal meanings'.

The image of natural law theory which we have just been dealing with is closely related, in the mind of Kelsen, with another image. For Kelsen says it is a 'cardinal point of the historical doctrine of natural law ... over two thousand years' that it attempts 'to found positive law upon a natural law delegation'.[7] So far, so good (though the formulation is not classical). But Kelsen regards the attempt as 'logically impossible', on the ground that such a delegation would entail ascribing legal validity to norms not because of their justice but because of their origination by the delegate; and this in turn would entail, he says, that the delegate could override and 're-place' the natural law, 'in view of the fact that positive law is not, on principle, subject to limitations of ... its ... material validity'.[8] The *non sequitur* is Kelsen's, I am afraid, and is not in his sources; the 'principle' to which he appeals is a mere *petitio principii*. If we may translate the relevant portion of, for example, Thomas Aquinas's theory into Kelsenian terminology (as far as possible), it runs as follows: The legal validity (in the focal, moral sense of 'legal validity') of positive law is derived from its rational connection with (i.e. derivation from) natural law, and this connection holds good, normally, if and only if (i) the law originates in a way which is legally valid (in the specially restricted, purely legal sense of 'legal validity') and (ii) the law is not materially unjust either in its content or in relevant circumstances of its positing.[9] Aquinas's discussion of these points is under-elaborated, in relation to the modern jurisprudential debate: see XII.4, below. But it avoids the self-contradiction and/or vacuity of which Kelsen accuses it. To delegate is not to delegate unconditionally.

In view of the foregoing, it is not surprising to find Kelsen

---

[7] *General Theory*, p. 412.

[8] Ibid., pp. 412–13. See also p. 411: 'Any attempt to establish a relationship between the two systems of norms in terms of simultaneously valid orders ultimately leads to their merging in terms of sub- and super-ordination, that is [*non sequitur*] to the recognition of positive as natural law or of natural as positive law.'

[9] See *S.T.* I–II, q. 96, a. 4c; the Thomist equivalent of Kelsen's principal sense of legal validity is the notion of an act of purported law-creation being *infra potestatem commissam*. See X.7 and XII.2, below.

propagating another misleading, and not uncommon, image of
natural law juristic theory:

The natural-law teachers contend, in a version which has remained
a stereotype from the church fathers down to Kant, that positive law
derives its entire validity from natural law; it is essentially a mere
emanation of natural law; the making of statutes or of decisions does
not freely create, it merely reproduces the true law which is already
somehow in existence . . .[10]

Positive law, he says, is thus treated as a mere 'copy' of natural
law. But all this is travesty. We may refer again to Thomas
Aquinas—as always, not because there is any presumption that
whatever he asserts is true, but simply because he is unquestionably a paradigm 'natural law theorist' and dominates
the period 'from the church fathers down to Kant', by synthe-
sizing his patristic and early medieval predecessors and by fixing
the vocabulary and to some extent the doctrine of later
scholastic and, therefore, early modern thought. Now Aquinas
indeed asserts that positive law derives its validity from
natural law; but in the very same breath he shows how it is *not*
a mere emanation from or copy of natural law, and how the
legislator enjoys all the creative freedom of an architect: the
analogy is Aquinas's.[11] Aquinas thinks that positive law is
needed for two reasons, of which one is that the natural law
'already somehow in existence' does *not* itself provide all or even
most of the solutions to the co-ordination problems of
communal life. On any reasonable view, Aquinas's clear
elaborations of these points (based on a hint from Aristotle)[12]
must be considered one of the more successful parts of his not
always successful work on natural law. My own discussion of
the relations between natural law and the content of positive law
is principally in section X.7, below.

Finally we may note that the other of the two justifications
for constructing a system of positive law to supplement the
'natural' requirements of morality, according to Aquinas (who

---

[10] *General Theory*, p. 416.

[11] See *S.T.* I–II, q. 95, a. 2 (q. 91, a. 3 and q. 95, a. 1 must be read in the light of
this very precise article, and of q. 99, a. 3 ad 2, q. 99, a. 5c, q. 100, a. 11c). The analogy
is explained below: X.7.

[12] See *Nic. Eth.* V, 7; 1134b20–24 (reproduced in notes to X.6, below); Aquinas,
in Eth. V, lect. 12, no. 1023; cf. Aristotle, *Rhetoric* I, 13: 1373b.

gives this justification a perhaps excessive prominence), is the need for compulsion, to force selfish people to act reasonably.[13] How strange, then, to read Kelsen finding yet another 'necessary contradiction between positive and natural law', this time 'because the one is a coercive order, while the other, ideally, is not only non-coercive, but actually has to forbid any coercion among men'.[14] This, alas, is yet another distorted image; a sound theory of natural law is an attempt to express reflectively the requirements and ideals of practical reasonableness, not of idealism: see X.1, below.

II.3   THE VARIETY OF HUMAN OPINIONS AND PRACTICES

H. L. A. Hart has said that 'natural law theory in all its protean guises attempts to assert that human beings are equally devoted to and united in their conception of aims (the pursuit of knowledge, justice to their fellow men) other than that of survival.'[15] For my part, I know of no one who has ever asserted this. Certainly the classical theorists of natural law all took for granted, and often enough bluntly asserted, that human beings are not all equally devoted to the pursuit of knowledge or justice, and are far from united in their conception of what constitutes worthwhile knowledge or a demand of justice. There is much to be said for Leo Strauss's judgment that 'knowledge of the indefinitely large variety of notions of right and wrong is so far from being incompatible with the idea of natural right that it is the essential condition for the emergence of the idea: realization of the variety of notions of right is *the* incentive for the quest for natural right.'[16]

Thomas Aquinas frequently tackled the question of the extent of human recognition of the natural law.[17] When his re-

---

[13] *S.T.* I–II q. 90, a. 3 ad 2; q. 95, a. 1c and ad 1; q. 96, a. 5c; see also Plato, *Rep.* 519e; Aristotle, *Nic. Eth.* X, 9: 1180a22.

[14] *General Theory*, p. 411.

[15] Hart, 'Positivism and the Separation of Law and Morals' (1958) 71 *Harv. L. Rev.* 593, reprinted in Dworkin (ed.), *Philosophy of Law* (Oxford: 1977), 17 at p. 36.

[16] Strauss, *Natural Right and History* (Chicago: 1953), p. 10. Likewise H. Rommen, *The Natural Law* (St. Louis and London: 1947), p. 4. For the ancients' awareness of the variety of moral notions see Aristotle, *Nic. Eth.* V, 7: 1134b27–35; I, 3: 1094b14–16; and for sceptical appeals to this variety, see Sextus Empiricus, *Pyrrhonean Hypotyposes* III, xxiv, 198–238.

[17] *S.T.* I–II, q. 93, a. 2c; q. 94, a. 2c, a. 4, a. 5 ad 1, a. 6c; q. 99, a. 2 ad 2; q. 100, a. 1c, a. 3c, a. 6c, a. 11c.

marks are taken together, it can be seen that he is working with a threefold categorization of the principles or precepts of natural law. *First* there are the most general (*communissima*) principles, which are 'not so much precepts as, so to speak, the ends or point of the precepts'; they state the basic forms of human good; at least to the extent that they concern his own good, they are recognized by anyone who reaches the age of reason and who has enough experience to know what they refer to, and in this sense they 'cannot, as general principles [*in universali*], be eliminated from the human heart'.[18] This is the nearest Aquinas gets to making the assertion which Hart suggests is the core of natural law theorizing. It amounts to no more than saying that any sane person is capable of seeing that life, knowledge, fellowship, offspring, and a few other such basic aspects of human existence are, as such, good, i.e. worth having, leaving to one side all particular predicaments and implications, all assessments of relative importance, all moral demands, and in short, all questions of whether and how one is to devote oneself to these goods.

For, *secondly*, even the most elementary and easily recognizable moral implications of those first principles are capable of being obscured or distorted for particular people and, indeed, for whole cultures, by prejudice, oversight, convention, the sway of desire for particular gratifications, etc.;[19] for example, many people (in Aquinas's day, as now) think that morality touches only interpersonal relations and that 'everyone is free to do what he will in those matters that concern only himself', while others cannot see that they have any obligations to other people.[20] And *thirdly*, there are many moral questions which can only be rightly answered by someone who is wise, and who considers them searchingly.[21]

So when Hart objects that the conception of 'the human end or good for man' which was entertained by 'the classical exponents' of natural law was 'complex', 'debatable', and

---

[18] *S.T.* I–II, q. 94, a. 6c; also a. 2c; q. 99, a. 2 ad 2; q. 100, aa. 5 ad 1, 11c; q. 58, a. 5c; q. 77, a. 2c; *De Veritate*, q. 16, a. 3c.

[19] *S.T.* I–II, q. 100, a. 1c (anyone's natural reason can immediately grasp that theft is not to be committed); q. 94, a. 4c, 6c (but whole peoples have failed to see the wrongfulness of theft or brigandage).

[20] *S.T.* I–II, q. 100, a. 5 ad 1; II–II, q. 122, a. 1c.

[21] *S.T.* I–II, q. 100, a. 3c, a. 11c.

'disputable',[22] the classical exponents would have replied that indeed it was complex, debated, and disputed, and that they had made rather extensive contributions to the debate.[23] For the real problem of morality, and of the point or meaning of human existence, is not in discerning the basic aspects of human well-being, but in integrating those various aspects into the intelligent and reasonable commitments, projects, and actions that go to make up one or other of the many admirable forms of human life. And by no means everybody can see these things steadily and whole, let alone put them into practice. The fact that there is controversy is not an argument against one side in that controversy. A genuine requirement of practical reasonableness is not the less a part of natural law (to use the classical phrase) just because it is not universally recognized or is actively disputed.

Julius Stone discerned three 'decisive issues between positivists and natural lawyers', and one of the them was: 'Are [natural lawyers] entitled to claim that what they assert as self-evident must be recognized as self-evident by all?'[24] The formulation of the issue is confused: the pertinent claim would be 'that what they assert to be self-evident is [or should be?] recognized as *true* by all'. For the important thing about a self-evident proposition is that people (with the relevant experience, and understanding of terms) *assent* to it without needing the proof of argument; it matters not at all whether they further recognize it as belonging to the relatively sophisticated philosophical category, 'self-evident'. But even if we correct Stone's formulation accordingly, it remains a non-issue, another imaginary image of natural law theory.

Near the very beginning of the tradition of theorizing about natural right, we find Aristotle quite explicit that ethics can only be usefully discussed with experienced and mature people, and that age is a necessary but not a sufficient condition for the required maturity.[25] He does not explicitly

---

[22] *Concept of Law*, p. 187.

[23] See, e.g., *Nic. Eth.* I, 5: 1095b14–1096a10; *Eud. Eth.* I, 5: 1215b15–1216a10; and *S.T.* I–II, q. 2, aa. 1–6, on the claims of wealth, honour, reputation, power, bodily well-being, and pleasure, respectively, to be the integrating goods of human existence. The existence of 'dispute' and 'debate' about the ultimate ends of human existence is a topic of *S.T.* I–II, q. 1, a. 7; also I, q. 2, a. 1 ad 1.

[24] Stone, *Human Law and Human Justice*, p. 212.

ascribe self-evidence or indemonstrability or axiomatic status
to any ethical or practical principles, though he treats certain
things as beyond question: for example, that no one would wish
to attain 'happiness' at the cost of losing his identity.[26] Aquinas,
on the other hand, has a discussion of self-evidence, if we
translate *propositio per se nota* as 'self-evident proposition'. But,
pace Stone, Aquinas's discussion begins by pointing out that
while some propositions are self-evident to 'everyone', since
everyone understands their terms, other propositions are self-
evident only to 'the wise', since only the relatively wise (or
learned) understand what they mean.[27] He gives two examples
of the latter sort of self-evident propositions, from the field of
speculative philosophy; one is that 'a human being is a rational
being', and the other is that 'a disembodied spirit does not
occupy space'. He then proceeds to speak about the self-
evident pre-moral principles which he later calls *communissima*,
without, unfortunately, indicating which if any of them he
thinks self-evident only to the relatively wise. An example, is
perhaps, the principle 'to know about God is a good'.[28] For
Aquinas denied that the existence of God is self-evident, even
to the relatively wise, in this life.[29]

It does seem to be the case that a good many of the
principles of logic and mathematics employed in natural science
and technology, and in historical and archaeological science,
are such that it would be absurd to say that they either
have been proved or are in need of proof. But what is certain
is that the natural sciences and in general all theoretical
disciplines rest implicitly on epistemic principles, or norms of
theoretical rationality, which are undemonstrated, indemonstrable, but self-evident in a manner strongly analogous to the
self-evidence ascribed by Aquinas to the basic principles of
practical reasonableness: for an identification of some of these

---

[25] *Nic. Eth.* I, 3: 1094b28–a12; 4: 1095a31–b13.

[26] *Nic. Eth.* IX, 4: 1166a20–23; VIII, 7: 1159a9–12.

[27] *S.T.* I–II, q. 94, a. 2c; q. 66, a. 5 ad 4. Note that, like Aristotle (*Post. Anal.* B, 19),
Aquinas vigorously denies that there are any innate ideas; no proposition, however
self-evident, is either formed or assented to by a human mind without an act of
understanding of data of experience: *S.T.* I, q. 79, a. 2c; *De Veritate*, q. 16, a. 1c.

[28] *S.T.* I–II, q. 94, a. 2c

[29] *S.T.* I, q. 2, a. 1.

epistemic principles, see III.4 below; for a use of one of them, see XIII.2.

II.4 THE ILLICIT INFERENCE FROM FACTS TO NORMS

Another of the three 'decisive issues' formulated by Stone was this: 'Have the natural lawyers shown that they can derive ethical norms from facts?'[30] And the answer can be brisk: They have not, nor do they need to, nor did the classical exponents of the theory dream of attempting any such derivation.

This answer will doubtless give widespread dissatisfaction. For if it is correct, the most popular image of natural law has to be abandoned. The corresponding and most popular objection to all theories of natural law has to be abandoned, too, and the whole question of natural law thought through afresh by many.

Thus it is simply not true that 'any form of a natural-law theory of morals entails the belief that propositions about man's duties and obligations can be inferred from propositions about his nature'.[31] Nor is it true that for Aquinas 'good and evil are concepts analysed and fixed in metaphysics before they are applied in morals'.[32] On the contrary, Aquinas asserts as plainly as possible that the first principles of natural law, which specify the basic forms of good and evil and which can be adequately grasped by anyone of the age of reason (and not just by metaphysicians), are *per se nota* (self-evident) and indemonstrable.[33] They are not inferred from speculative principles. They are not inferred from facts. They are not inferred from metaphysical propositions about human nature, or about the nature of good and evil, or about 'the function of a human being',[34] nor are they inferred from a

---

[30] Stone, *Human Law and Human Justice*, p. 212.

[31] D. J. O'Connor, *Aquinas and Natural Law* (London: 1967), p. 68; similarly, amongst countless others, Norberto Bobbio, 'Quelques arguments contre le droit naturel' (1959) 3 *Annales de philosophie politique* 180; *Locke e il Diritto Naturale* (Turin: 1963), pp. 70–1.

[32] O'Connor, op. cit., p. 19.

[33] Aquinas, *in Eth*. V, lect. 12, para. 1018; *S.T*. I–II, q. 94, a. 2: q. 91, a. 3c: q. 58, aa. 4c, 5c.

[34] Cf. the objections of Margaret MacDonald, 'Natural Rights' in P. Laslett (ed.), *Philosophy, Politics and Society* (Oxford: 1956), 35 at p. 44; Kai Nielsen, 'The Myth of Natural Law' in S. Hook (ed.), *Law and Philosophy* (New York: 1964), 122 at p. 132.

teleological conception of nature[35] or any other conception of nature. They are not inferred or derived from anything. They are underived (though not innate). Principles of right and wrong, too, are derived from these first, pre-moral principles of practical reasonableness, and not from any facts, whether metaphysical or otherwise. When discerning what is good, to be pursued (*prosequendum*), intelligence is operating in a different way, yielding a different logic, from when it is discerning what is the case (historically, scientifically, or metaphysically); but there is no good reason for asserting that the latter operations of intelligence are more rational than the former.

Of course, Aquinas would agree that 'were man's nature different, so would be his duties'.[36] The basic forms of good grasped by practical understanding are what is good for human beings with the nature they have. Aquinas considers that practical reasoning begins not by understanding this nature from the outside, as it were, by way of psychological, anthropological, or metaphysical observations and judgments defining human nature,[37] but by experiencing one's nature, so to speak, from the inside, in the form of one's inclinations. But again, there is no process of inference. One does not judge that 'I have [or everybody has] an inclination to find out about things' and then infer that therefore 'knowledge is a good to be pursued'. Rather, by a simple act of non-inferential understanding one grasps that the object of the inclination which one experiences is an instance of a general form of good, for oneself (and others like one).

There are important objections to be made to Aquinas's theory of natural law. O'Connor rightly identifies the main one: Aquinas fails to explain 'just how the specific moral rules which we need to guide our conduct can be shown to be connected with allegedly self-evident principles'.[38] But the objection that Aquinas's account of natural law proposes an illicit inference from 'is' to 'ought' is quite unjustified.

---

[35] *Pace* Strauss, *Natural Right and History*, pp. 7–8; and Hart, *Concept of Law*, pp. 182–7.

[36] O'Connor, *Aquinas and Natural Law*, p. 18.

[37] *Pace* O'Connor who says, ibid., p. 15, that 'the theory of natural law ... turns on the idea that human nature is constituted by a unique set of properties which can be understood and summed up in a definition'.

[38] Ibid., p. 73. For my own attempt to explain this, see Chapter V.

How can this objection have become so popular? There are a number of probable reasons, of which I may mention three. The first is that the very phrase 'natural law' can lead one to suppose that the norms referred to, in any theory of natural law, are based upon judgments about nature (human and/or otherwise).[39] And the second reason is that this supposition is in fact substantially correct in relation to the Stoic theory of natural law (XII.2) and, as we shall shortly see, in relation to some Renaissance theories, including some that claimed the patronage of Thomas Aquinas and have been influential almost to the present day (II.6).

And thirdly, Aquinas himself was a writer not on ethics alone but on the whole of theology. He was keen to show the relationship between his ethics of natural law and his general theory of metaphysics and the world-order. He wished to point out the analogies running through the whole order of being. Thus human virtue is analogous to the 'virtue' that can be predicated of anything which is a fine specimen of things of its nature, in good shape, *bene disposita secundum convenientiam suae naturae*.[40] So he is happy to say that human virtue, too, is in accordance with the nature of human beings, and human vice is *contra naturam*. If we stopped here, the charge against him would seem to be proved, or at least plausible (and certain later philosophical theologians would seem to have been justified in claiming his patronage). But in fact Aquinas takes good care to make his meaning, his order of explanatory priorities, quite clear. The criterion of conformity with or contrariety to human nature is reasonableness.

And so whatever is contrary to the order of reason is contrary to the

---

[39] This sort of *a priori* reasoning from words, without inquiry into their use by particular theorists, is indulged in by those who generalize J. S. Mill's exposé of the confusions of Montesquieu and Combe (between 'is' laws and 'ought' laws) into a general condemnation of natural law theories: cf 'Nature', in Mill, *Three Essays on Religion* (London: 1874). Of the classic theories, the Stoic variety is perhaps exposed to Mill's objection (cf. XIII.2); Plato's is not (as Mill himself points out); and the Aristotelian variety is not (as ought to be clear from the Aristotelian distinction between theoretical and practical reason, from Aristotle's sharp differentiation between the senses of 'necessary' (*Meta.* V, 5: 1015a20), and from Aquinas's willingness to draw, when appropriate, a sharp distinction between the 'natural' and the 'reasonable' (e.g. *S.T.* I–II, q. 1, a. 2c)).

[40] *S.T.* I–II, q. 71, a. 2c.

nature of human beings as such; and what is reasonable is in accordance with human nature as such. *The good of the human being is being in accord with reason, and human evil is being outside the order of reasonableness.* . . . So human virtue, which makes good both the human person and his works, is in accordance with human nature *just* in *so* far as [*tantum . . . inquantum*] it is in accordance with reason; and vice is contrary to human nature just in so far as it is contrary to the order of reasonableness.[41]

In other words, for Aquinas, the way to discover what is morally right (virtue) and wrong (vice) is to ask, not what is in accordance with human nature, but what is reasonable. And this quest will eventually bring one back to the *underived* first principles of practical reasonableness, principles which make no reference at all to human nature, but only to human good. From end to end of his ethical discourses, the primary categories for Aquinas are the 'good' and the 'reasonable'; the 'natural' is, from the point of view of his ethics, a speculative appendage added by way of metaphysical reflection, *not* a counter with which to advance either to or from the practical *prima principia per se nota*.

Since Aquinas's Aristotelian distinction between 'speculative' and practical reason corresponds so neatly with the modern (but not only modern!) distinction which we (roughly!) indicate by contrasting 'fact' and 'norm' or 'is' and 'ought', it will be helpful to examine in greater depth the historical process by which the theory of natural law has come to be associated with a fundamental disregard of this distinction. To this examination the next two sections are devoted; they are, however, no more than an introduction to a much-needed investigation, still to be made.

II.5   HUME AND CLARKE ON 'IS' AND 'OUGHT'

In every system of morality, which I have hitherto met with, I have always remarked, that the author proceeds for some time in the ordinary way of reasoning, and establishes the being of a God, or makes observations concerning human affairs; when of a sudden I am surprised to find, that instead of the usual copulations of propositions,

---

[41] Ibid. (emphasis mine). For similar formulations, see I–II, q. 94, a. 3 ad 3; q. 18, a. 5. The same order of explanatory priorities can be observed in Plato's remarks about acting according to reason and thus according to nature: *Rep.* IV, 444d; IX, 585–6.

is, and *is not*, I meet with no propostion that is not connected with an *ought*, or an *ought not*. This change is imperceptible; but is, however, of the last consequence. For as this *ought*, or *ought not*, expresses some new relation or affirmation, it is necessary that it should be observed and explained; and at the same time that a reason should be given, for what seems altogether inconceivable, how this new relation can be a deduction from others, which are entirely different from it. ... this small attention would ... let us see, that the distinction of vice and virtue is not founded merely on the relations of objects, nor is perceived by reason.[42]

There have been many interpretations of this passage, but it will be safe to attend here only to the two most plausible. The first and standard interpretation treats Hume as announcing the logical truth, widely emphasized since the later part of the nineteenth century, that no set of non-moral (or, more generally, non-evaluative) premisses can entail a moral (or evaluative) conclusion. The second interpretation places the passage in its historical and literary context, and sees it as the tailpiece to Hume's attack on the eighteenth-century rationalists (notably Samuel Clarke), an attack whose centre-piece is the contention that rational perception of the moral qualities of actions could not of itself provide a motivating guide to action. While the second interpretation has more to commend it as an interpretation, there is no harm in accepting the first, since if Hume is not to be credited with announcing the logical principle in question, somebody else is to be; and the important thing is that the principle is true and significant. To the discussion in the preceding section I may here simply add that this principle itself in no way entails or authorizes Hume's conclusion that distinctions between 'vice and virtue' are not 'perceived by reason'.[43] That said, we may consider the second interpretation.

[42] David Hume, *A Treatise of Human Nature* (1740), Book III, Part i, sec. 1 (Raphael, *British Moralists*, para. 504: here as elsewhere I follow Raphael's revision of spelling).

[43] But for the fact that Hume offers, as his own, four or five inconsistent views about the nature and basis of moral propositions (see the careful analysis in Jonathan Harrison, *Hume's Moral Epistemology*, Oxford: 1976, pp. 110–25), I should have to add that Hume himself conspicuously offends against the principle that 'ought' cannot be derived from 'is'. To the extent that his 'predominant' view (Harrison, op. cit., p. 124) is that moral judgments are judgments about what characteristics and actions arouse approval or disapproval in men (so that, as Hume puts it, systems of ethics should be 'founded on fact and observations': *An Enquiry concerning the Principles*

Hume's aim, in the section which concludes with the
is–ought paragraph, is to 'consider, whether it be possible, from
reason alone, to distinguish betwixt moral good and evil, or
whether there must concur some other principles to enable us to
make that distinction'.[44] His arguments are expressly directed
against 'those who affirm that virtue is nothing but a conformity to
reason; that there are eternal fitnesses and unfitnesses of things,
which are the same to every rational being that considers them;
that the immutable measures of right and wrong impose an
obligation, not only on human creatures, but also on the Deity
himself...'.[45]

Who are 'those who affirm' these propositions? It is possible
to point to passages in Joseph Butler's *Fifteen Sermons* (1726)
and Ralph Cudworth's *A Treatise concerning Eternal and Immutable
Morality* (*c.* 1685, first printed 1731). But the obvious source,
identified twice in this connection by Hume himself,[46] is Samuel
Clarke's *A Discourse concerning the Unchangeable Obligations of
Natural Religion* ... (1706, 8th ed. 1732). Clarke's *Discourse*,
popular and influential in its day, is loose, prolix, and re-
petitive; but towards the end of his life, Clarke offered a
summary: 'Thus have I endeavoured to deduce the *original*

---

of Morals (1751), sec. 1 (Raphael, *British Moralists*, para. 563)), Hume plainly
attempts the logically illegitimate derivation. This is certainly some evidence
against the first interpretation of the *is–ought* paragraph of his *Treatise*, qua interpretation: for an interpreter ought not to postulate inconsistencies beyond necessity.
But it is more interesting to observe that many modern epigones of Hume, who
regard him as having laid the basis for a sound ethical theory by discovering
the principle 'no *ought* from an *is*', themselves fall into the same inconsistency as their
master: the *fact* that one has opted for, adopted, chosen, or decided upon some
practical principle is no more a logically legitimate ground for asserting that ϕ ought
to be done than is the fact (which Hume fixed upon) that ϕ arouses sentiments of
approval or disapproval in oneself or in people in general.

[44] *Treatise*, III, i, 1 (*British Moralists*, para. 488). By 'principle' Hume here means
mental factors, such as conscience, moral sense, sentiment, and other passions: see
British Moralists, para. 489, 490, 505, etc.

[45] Ibid.; *British Moralists*, para. 488. For further references to the 'natural fitness and
unfitness of things', see paras. 497 and 500. For the importance to Hume of the problem
whether God could be known to be bound by them, see paras. 500 and 634 (the latter
is Hume's letter of 16 Mar. 1740 to Francis Hutcheson).

[46] See Hume, *A Letter from a Gentleman* (1745), quoted by Raphael in W. B. Todd
(ed.), *Hume and the Enlightenment* (Edinburgh and Austin: 1974), p. 27; and Hume,
An Enquiry concerning the Principles of Morals (1751), sec. III, part ii, para. 158 n.,
mentioning also Cudworth, Malebranche, and Montesquieu's *L'esprit des lois* (which
appeared, however, eight years after Hume's *Treatise*).

obligations of *morality*, from the *necessary and eternal reason* and
proportions of things'.[47] More precisely, we may say that Clarke
has offered to prove that

[i] the same necessary and eternal *different relations*, that different
things bear one to another; with regard to which [ii] the will of God
always and necessarily does determine itself, to choose to act only what
is agreeable to [the eternal rules of] justice, equity, goodness and
truth, in order to the welfare of the whole universe; [iii] *ought*
likewise constantly to determine the wills of all subordinate rational
beings, to govern all their actions by the same rules, for the good of
the public, in their respective stations. That is; [i] these eternal and
necessary differences of things make it *fit and reasonable* for creatures
so to act; they [iii] cause it to be their *duty*, or lay an *obligation* upon
them, so to do; even separate from the consideration of these rules
being the *positive will or command of God* ...[48]

My present interest is in stage (iii) of this argument, the proof
that actions which are fit and reasonable are thereby *obligatory*.
But I may first reproduce one of the examples which Clarke
offers in order to illustrate what he means by an eternal,
unalterable, or absolute proportion or fitness of things: '... in
men's dealing and conversing one with another; it is undeniably
more fit, absolutely and in the nature of the thing itself, that all
men should endeavour to promote the universal good and welfare of all; than that all men should be continually con-
triving the ruin and destruction of all.'[49] Clarke regards such
propositions as 'plain and self-evident',[50] and in need of no
proof. What he wants to *prove* is that the 'eternal reason of

[47] Clarke, op. cit., 8th ed., 225, reproduced in Raphael, *British Moralists*, para. 251
(Clarke's emphases); the passage was added after the 5th ed. (1719). Earlier
(Raphael, para. 244), speaking of the duty of universal benevolence, Clarke says: 'the
obligation to this great duty, may also otherwise be deduced from the *nature of man* ...'
(his emphasis).

[48] Ibid., para. 225 (Clarke's emphases). The numerals in square brackets, which I
have inserted here and in later quotations from Clarke, correspond to the first three
of the seven numbered stages of Clarke's subsequent argument; stages four to seven
overlap with each other and with the first three. The words in square brackets are
taken from the equivalent passage in para. 231; I have inserted them here to make the
passage more readily comprehensible.

[49] Ibid., para. 226. Cf. Hume, *Treatise*, II, iii, 3 (*British Moralists*, para. 483): 'it is
not contrary to reason to prefer the destruction of the whole world to the scratching of
my finger'.

[50] Clarke, op. cit.; *British Moralists*, para. 227.

things',[51] [i] known and expressed in such propositions, [iii] 'ought ... indispensably to govern men's actions', i.e. that it creates (or is) an *obligation*, indeed 'the truest and formallest obligation', 'the original obligation of all'.[52]

Clarke's proof of obligation, so far as it can disentangled from his constant reassertions of the conclusion to be proved, appears to be this: Just as 'it would be absurd and ridiculous for a man in arithmetical matters, [i] ignorantly to believe that twice two is not equal to four; or [iii] wilfully and obstinately to contend, against his own clear knowledge, that the whole is not equal to all its parts', so it is 'absurd and blameworthy, [i] to mistake negligently plain right and wrong, that is, to understand the proportions of things in morality to be what they are not; or [iii] wilfully to act contrary to known justice and equity, that is, to will things to be what they are not and cannot be'.[53] He repeats this argument: the rules of right oblige because those who contravene them 'endeavour (as much as in them is) to make things be what they are not, and cannot be', which is presumptuous, insolent, contrary to understanding, reason, and judgment, an attempt to destroy the order by which the universe subsists, and above all, as *absurd* as 'to pretend to alter the certain proportions of numbers' or to call light darkness.[54]

This argument is a failure. To try to alter the proportions of numbers, or to shut one's eyes to the difference between light and dark, is (where it is not logically impossible) *pointless*, profitless, devoid of potential advantage to oneself or others. But to act contrary to justice is frequently advantageous to oneself and one's friends. (And for that reason alone, such action need not be interpreted as endeavouring to 'make things what they are not and cannot be'.) The demand for a proof of obligation is a demand to be shown the *point* of acting in ways that will certainly sometimes run counter to one's desires and (at least certain of) one's interests. Clarke's argument fails to make the transition from *is* (in this case, 'is reasonable', 'is just', etc.) to

---

[51] Also called by him 'right reason' and 'the law of nature': para. 246.

[52] Ibid., para. 233.

[53] Ibid., para. 232. For my use of bracket numerals, see n. 48 above.

[54] Ibid. See also para. 230, med. In a later reference to this kind of 'absurdity', Clarke cites Cicero, *De Legibus*, I, 44: op. cit., 8th ed., p. 232.

ought because it fails to advert to any desire or interest of the agent's that might be satisfied by acting rightly. His argument does (rather sketchily) attend to human desires, interests, and well-being, but only in order to arrive at the judgment that certain actions are fitting and reasonable. It fails to consider whether acting fittingly and reasonably is an aspect of (or way of realizing) the agent's well-being or is in any other way worth while or desirable.

Now this objection to Clarke is not Hume's, for it treats the problem of obligation as the problem of finding justifying reasons, i.e. adequate point, for acting in certain ways, whereas Hume lacks any clear conception of, or systematic interest in the concept of, justifying reasons. For him, the problem of obligation seems to come down to the problem of finding a motive that *will* move someone to act in certain ways. So the central objection he raises against Clarke's type of argument is this:

It is one thing to know virtue, and another to conform the will to it. In order, therefore, to prove that the measures of right and wrong are eternal laws, *obligatory* on every rational mind, it is not sufficient to show the relations upon which they are founded: we must also point out the connection betwixt the relation and the will; and must prove that this connection is so necessary, that in every well-disposed mind, it must take place and have its influence ... Now ... in human nature no relation can ever alone produce any action ... [W]e cannot prove *a priori*, that these relations [of right and wrong], if they really existed and were perceived, would be universally forcible and obligatory.[55]

Supporters of the 'first', standard interpretation of the *is–ought* paragraph (which follows four paragraphs after that just quoted) should be disconcerted by this manifestation of Hume's indifference to the distinction between the 'forcible' and the 'obligatory', between what ought to move the will and what 'must' (i.e. necessarily does) move it.

Supporters of the second interpretation of the *is–ought* paragraph have no such difficulty. In their view, Hume's concern in the *is–ought* paragraph is essentially the same as his concern in the passage just quoted, where it is clear that the gap which

<hr />

[55] *Treatise*, III, i, 1 (*British Moralists*, para. 500) (Hume's emphasis).

Hume says cannot be bridged is *not* the gap between the factual and the normative, but the gap between *any truth* (even a 'normative truth', a true proposition about what is good or bad, right or wrong) and motivating conclusions about what ought to be done. This interpretation of the *is–ought* paragraph seems to me to be very plausible; it integrates that paragraph with the main thread of thought running right through that section of the *Treatise* which it concludes (viz. the view that morals move one to action but reason does not), and it explains Hume's pervasive indifference to the logical difference between obligation and influence. (This interpretation does not, of course, *defend* Hume against the charge of ignoring that difference; the principle that *ought* is not inferable from *is* retains its validity even if Hume neither announced it nor conformed his arguments to its requirements.)

The problem Clarke set himself was to show that moral truths provide a (conclusive) reason for action. He failed to solve the problem because he ignored the logic of practical reasoning, in which the fundamental category is the good (not necessarily moral) that is to be[56] pursued and realized. Instead he looked exclusively to the logic of speculative or theoretical reasoning, in which the fundamental category is 'what is the case' and the fundamental principle is that contradictions are excluded. Hume saw that Clarke's problem was a real one, and that Clarke was looking in the wrong direction for its solution. Hume himself lacked a viable conception of practical reason and practical principles. So he was able to offer no more than a scatter of notoriously inconsistent and puzzling responses to the problem, some purporting to solve it, others to dissolve it. But his historical importance is that the vigour of his attack brought to an end a line of argument that by then had dominated the main-line theories of natural law for 150 years or more.

II.6 CLARKE'S ANTECEDENTS

The conceptual framework of Clarke's confused and rhetorical

---

[56] I use the phrase 'is to be' as a gerundive, i.e. in the sense it has when we ask 'What is to be done?' ('Quid est *faciendum*.³') Thus it can be understood as equivalent to 'ought to be ...', across a wide range of meanings of 'ought': see II.6, III.2, 3, 5, below.

discourse is to be found, tersely expressed, in Hugo Grotius, *De Jure Belli ac Pacis* (1625) and in Grotius's sources, which certainly included Suarez, *De Legibus* (1612) and probably also Gabriel Vazquez's *Commentary* on Aquinas (1605). Clarke, like all educated men of his time, would have been familiar with Grotius's incomparably influential treatise, and may well have been familiar with the relevant passages of Suarez and Vazquez, either at first hand or through English commentators on their argument such as the Cambridge Platonist, Nathaniel Culverwel.

Grotius is standardly said to have inaugurated a new, modern and secular era in natural law theorizing by his *'etiamsi daremus . . .'*:

what we have been saying would have a degree of validity [*locum aliquem*] even if we should concede [*etiamsi daremus*] that which cannot be conceded without the utmost wickedness, that there is no God, or that the affairs of men are of no concern to him.[57]

But this standard reading of Grotius is a mere misunderstanding. Grotius must be assumed to have known (if only from his reading of Suarez) that, for the purpose of discussing the roots of obligation, the hypothesis of God's non-existence (or indifference) had been a commonplace of theological debate since, at latest, the mid-fourteenth century. And very many of the scholastics used the hypothesis to just the same effect as Grotius. For what had Grotius just 'been saying'? In the preceding sentence but one, he had remarked:

Since ... man has ... judgment, which enables him to determine what things are agreeable or harmful ... and what can lead to either alternative: in such things it is understood, within the limitations of human understanding, to be fitting to human nature [*conveniens humanae naturae*] to follow a well-ordered judgment ... Whatever is clearly repugnant to such judgment is likewise understood to be against the law of nature, that is, of human nature [*contra jus naturae, humanae scilicet*].

And the 'degree of validity' which Grotius would accord the law of nature in the absence of divine command is indicated in the first chapter of the treatise, in a formulation which preserves all the ambiguity of the phrase 'a degree of validity':

[57] *De Jure Belli ac Pacis*, Prolegomena, para. 11 (trans. Kelsey, Oxford: 1925).

The law of nature is a dictate of right reason, pointing out [*indicans*] that an act, according as it is fitting or unfitting [*ex ejus convenientia aut disconvenientia*] to rational nature has in it a quality of moral turpitude or moral necessity; and that, in consequence, such an act is either forbidden or enjoined by the author of nature, God. The acts in regard to which a dictate exists are in themselves either *debiti* or *illiciti*, and so are understood to be necessarily enjoined or forbidden by God.[58]

Translators of the last sentence often render '*debiti*' as 'obligatory'. But this fails to preserve the delicate ambiguity in the thought of Grotius and his sources. The problem that they were uneasily indicating by way of the hypothesis *etiamsi daremus* is essentially the problem so directly confronted later by Clarke and, polemically, by Hume: Granted that we can discern right and wrong, due and undue, by reasoning, what makes it *obligatory* to choose the right and the due and to avoid the wrong and the undue? Grotius himself, of course, had no need to elaborate on this problem in what, after all, is simply the introduction to a law book. But his approach hints at the answer which, by the beginning of the seventeenth century, had become standard among the philosophical theologians: What is right and wrong depends on the nature of things (and what is *conveniens* to such nature), and not on a decree of God; but the normative or motivating significance of moral rightness and wrongness, in particular the obligatoriness of the norm of right and wrong, depends fundamentally upon there being a decree expressing God's will that the right be done (as a matter of obligation) and that the wrong be avoided (likewise): as Grotius put it, 'due and undue acts are therefore understood to be necessarily enjoined or forbidden by God', though they would remain due or undue, even if (*etiamsi daremus*) there were no such divine decrees.

Clarke's difficulties arose from the fact that, while rejecting one part of this twofold thesis, he accepted the other part. Not unreasonably, he rejected the assumption that obligation is

---

[58] *De Jure Belli ac Pacis*, I, c. i, sec. 10, paras. 1, 2. Grotius, like Clarke, regards the 'fundamental conceptions' in the law of nature as so 'manifest and clear, almost as self-evident as are those things which we perceive by the external senses', that 'no one can deny them without doing violence to himself' (ibid., Prolegomena: in the Kelsey trans., para. 39). He also uses the comparison with $2 \times 2 = 4$: ibid. i, 10.

essentially the effect of a superior's act of will. But he remained so firmly within the grip of the thesis that practical reasoning is a matter of discerning relations of fittingness to or consistency with nature that he tried to treat obligation as just one more of the set of relations of consistency.

The ethical theory espoused by Vazquez and Suarez was constructed from terms quarried from the works of Aristotle and, above all, Aquinas. But it differed radically from the ethical theories actually maintained by Aristotle and Aquinas. Vazquez and Suarez maintained, *firstly*, that in discerning the content of the natural law, reason's decisive act consists in discerning precepts of the form 'ϕ is unfitting to human, i.e. rational, nature and thus has the quality of moral wrongfulness' or 'ϕ befits human, i.e. rational nature and thus has the quality of moral rectitude and, if ϕ is the only such act possible in a given context, the additional quality of moral necessity or dueness'.[59] (We can call this thesis 'rationalist'.) For Aquinas, on the other hand, what is decisive, in discerning the content of the natural law, is one's understanding of the basic forms of (not-yet-moral) human well-being as desirable and potentially realizable ends or opportunities and thus as to-be-pursued and realized in one's action, action to which one is already beginning to direct oneself in this very act of practical understanding.[60] *Secondly*, Suarez and (it seems) Vazquez maintained that obligation is essentially the effect of an act of will by a superior, directed to moving the will of an inferior:[61] see also XI.8, XI.9, below. (We can call this thesis 'voluntarist'.) Aquinas, on the other hand, treats obligation as the rational

---

[59] See Vazquez, *in Primam Secundae*, disp. 90, c. 3; disp. 97; c. 3; Suarez, *De Legibus*, Book II, c. 7, paras. 4–7; c. 5, paras. 4–5; c. 6, para. 17.

[60] *S.T.* I–II, q. 94, a. 2. Aquinas would not reject the Vazquez–Suarez formulae, but would give them a subordinate and derivative place in the methodology of ethics.

[61] See Vazquez, *in Primam Secundae*, disp. 49, c. 3; Suarez, *De Legibus*, Book I, c. 5, paras. 12, 15, 16, 24; Book II, c. 6, paras. 6–7, 8, 12, 13, 22. Nothing is more striking than the unquestioned, almost undiscussed assumption of this view amidst the luxuriant subtleties of late scholasticism. Even a writer like Vitoria, who is credited with leading the 'Thomist' revival in the early sixteenth century, says 'it is unintelligible to me how anyone can sin unless he is under some obligation, *and I don't see how anyone can be obligated unless he has a superior*', *De eo ad quod tenetur homo cum primum venit ad usum rationis* (1535; Lyons: 1586), part II, para. 9; and see notes to XI.9, below.

necessity of some means to (or way of realizing) an end or objective (i.e. a good) of a particular sort. What sort? Primarily (i.e. apart from special forms of obligation) the good of a form of life which, by its full and reasonably integrated realization of the basic forms of human well-being, renders one a fitting subject for the friendship of the being whose friendship is a basic good that in its full realization embraces all aspects of human well-being, a friendship indispensable for every person.[62] Aquinas's treatment of all these issues is saturated with the interrelated notions, 'end' and 'good'; the terms 'obligation', 'superior', and 'inferior' scarcely appear, and the notion of conformity to nature is virtually absent. In Suarez and Vazquez the terms 'end' and 'good' are almost entirely gone, replaced by 'right' and 'wrong' and cognate notions.

The reader will ask how Aquinas explained the difference between moral thinking and merely prudential reasoning (in the modern sense of 'prudential'), and how he accounted for the peculiarly conclusory sense of the moral 'ought'. The answer must be that Aquinas's account of these matters is, at best, highly elliptical, scattered, and difficult to grasp, and at worst, seriously underdeveloped; and that these deficiencies occasioned the unsatisfactory responses of those who professed to follow him in the later history of philosophical theology. But to this I must add that the materials for a satisfactory development of the sort of position espoused by Aquinas are available, and that the attempt to put these materials to use is encouraged by the impasse in which the sixteenth- and seventeenth-century theories of natural law manifestly found themselves. The subsequent chapters of this book incorporate such an attempt.

It is not respect for Aquinas that inspires this attempt; after all, the Jesuit theologians of early seventeenth-century Spain did not lack respect for Aquinas, yet felt themselves intellectually compelled to oppose, explicitly, certain strategic theses in his philosophy (see, e.g., XI.8 below, on *imperium*). No; the reason for making the attempt is that a theory of practical reasonableness, of forms of human good, and of practical

[62] See *S.T.* I–II, q. 1, a. 6; q. 4, a. 8c and ad 3; q. 5, a. 7c; q. 90, a. 1c; q. 99, aa. 1c, 2c; II–II, q. 44, a. 1c; q. 47, a. 2 ad 1.

principles, such as the theory Aquinas abumbrated but left insufficiently elaborated, is untouched by the objections which Hume (and after him the whole Enlightenment and post-Enlightenment current of ethics) was able to raise against the tradition of rationalism eked out by voluntarism. That tradition presented itself as the classical or central tradition of natural law theorizing, but in truth it was peculiar to late scholasticism. It was attractive to non-Catholics (like Grotius, Culverwel, and Clarke) who adopted its major concepts not least because of its strong verbal and conceptual resemblances to the Stoicism (XIII.2) so much admired in European culture from the Renaissance to the end of the eighteenth century. The substantive differences between the theory of natural law espoused by Vazquez and Suarez (and most Catholic manuals until the other day) and the theory espoused by Aquinas are scarcely less significant and extensive than the better-known differences between Aristotelian and Stoic ethics. But ecclesiastical deference to a misread Aquinas obscured the former differences until well into this century.

We can put Hume's attack on the ethics of his predecessors into perspective by the following summary remarks: (i) Aristotle and Aquinas would readily grant that *ought* cannot be deduced from *is* (whether or not Hume really formulated and adhered to that principle). (ii) Both would go along with Hume's view that the speculative discernment of 'eternal relations', even relations of 'fitness to human nature', leaves open the question what motive anybody has for regulating his actions accordingly. (iii) Aquinas would deplore both the confusion (shared by Hume and Suarez![63]) of obligation with impulse or influence, and Hume's failure to see that reason is an 'active principle' because one is motivated according to one's *understanding* of the goodness and desirability of human opportunities, including the opportunity of extending intelligence and reasonableness into one's choices and actions. (iv) Aquinas would reject the assumption of Clarke, Grotius, Suarez, and Vazquez that the primary and self-evident principles of natural law are moral principles (in

---

[63] Suarez, *De Legibus*, Book II, c. 6, para. 22: 'obligation is a certain moral impulse [*motio*] to action'; Hume, *Treatise*, Book III, part ii, sec. 5 (*British Moralists*, para. 541): 'promises ... create [a] new motive or obligation.... a sense of interest ... is the first obligation to the performance of promises'.

the modern sense of 'moral'), or that they are initially grasped as principles concerned with self-evident relations of conformity or dis-conformity to human nature. (v) Aquinas, like Clarke and Hume, would reject the view that the will or imperative of a superior accounts for obligation; like Hume he would reject Clarke's view that obligation is essentially a matter of avoiding intellectual inconsistencies; and finally he would reject both Hume's view that it is a matter of, or intrinsically related to, a peculiar sentiment, and equally the recent neo-Humean view that statements of obligation are merely prescriptions expressing a certain sort of commitment or decision.

II.7 THE 'PERVERTED FACULTY' ARGUMENT

A late but traceable descendant of the Vazquez–Suarez conception of natural law is the argument, which looms large among the modern images of natural law theory, that natural functions are never to be frustrated or that human faculties are never to be diverted ('perverted') from their natural ends. But, as a general premiss, in any form strong enough to yield the moral conclusions it has been used to defend, this argument is ridiculous.

II.8 NATURAL LAW AND THE EXISTENCE AND WILL OF GOD

'[T]raditional concepts of natural law are completely dependent for their viability on the soundness of such claims [as that natural theology is intelligible, let alone true, and that God exists]'.[64] It is tempting to dismiss this as yet another phantom. Aquinas, for example, considers that the first principles of natural law are self-evident, but that (i) the existence of God is *not* self-evident to the human mind, (ii) a knowledge that friendship with God is our last end is *not* available by 'natural' reasoning but only by revelation, (iii) attainment of that end is not possible by natural means but only by supernatural grace; and (iv) the will of God, so far as it

---

[64] Kai Nielsen, 'The Myth of Natural Law', in Hook (ed.), *Law and Philosophy*, p. 130.

concerns creatures (such as mankind), cannot be discovered by reasoning. A neo-Suarezian supposes that the first principle of natural law is 'Follow nature' and that this principle has normative significance by being the content of an act of divine will.[65] But neo-Suarezian theory, however widespread it became in Catholic seminaries until the 1960s, is by no means the most important of the 'traditional concepts of natural law'. And Part II of this book offers a rather elaborate sketch of a theory of natural law without needing to advert to the question of God's existence or nature or will.

That perhaps suffices to dispose of the claim which Nielsen actually made. But just as the fact that a good explanation of molecular motion can be provided, without adverting to the existence of an uncreated creator of the whole state of affairs in which molecules and the laws of their motion obtain, does not of itself entail either (i) that no further explanation of that state of affairs is required or (ii) that no such further explanation is available, or (iii) that the existence of an uncreated creator is not that explanation, so too the fact that natural law can be understood, assented to, applied, and reflectively analysed without adverting to the question of the existence of God does not of itself entail either (i) that no further explanation is required for the fact that there are objective standards of good and bad and principles of reasonableness (right and wrong), or (ii) that no such further explanation is available, or (iii) that the existence and nature of God is not that explanation. For this reason, and for others that will appear in the course of our study, Part III of this book undertakes a brief examination of such questions. They are in themselves not practical but theoretical or metaphysical questions. But their exploration, and the answers yielded by it, and the further questions suggested by those answers, all add significance to the integrating good (in itself self-evident) of practical reasonableness and thus to the moral principles involved in the pursuit of that good.

[65] See, among countless examples, Rommen, *The Natural Law*, pp. 49, 63–4. For Suarez himself, see XI.9, below.

NOTES

II.1

History of theories of natural law, and of their influence ... An informative study (rather wider than its subtitle) is C. G. Haines, *The Revival of Natural Law: A study of the establishment and of the interpretation of limits on legislatures with special reference to the development of certain phases of American constitutional law* (Cambridge, Mass.: 1930).

Natural law has no history ... 'But what about changes in human nature?' 'What about the fact that man is a historical being?' 'Does this thesis derive from a theory of eternal or ahistorical essences?' Well, the thesis in the text concerns the basic forms of human flourishing, and the basic requirements of practical reasonableness. So if someone wishes to propose that what, in Chapters III–IV, I identify as basic forms of human flourishing would not have been flourishing for human beings of some epoch, or that what, in Chapters V–VI, I identify as basic requirements of practical reasonableness would not have been applicable to such other human beings (because of some difference between their condition and ours), the onus is on him to show us these beings and those differences. I have read countless proclamations of the historicity, etc., of man, but no serious attempt to meet this challenge. Abstract discussions of the mutability or immutability of human nature are beside the point: the argument of this book does not rely, even implicitly, on the term 'human nature'.

II.2

Natural law theory and legal validity ... Kelsen, Hart, and Raz, to validate their image of natural law theory, could point to Blackstone, I *Comm.* 41: '... no human laws are of any validity, if contrary to this [sc. natural law]'. But Blackstone simply does not mean what he there says; on the very next page, he is saying '... no human laws should be suffered to contradict these [sc. the law of nature and the law of revelation] ... Nay, if any human law should allow or injoin us to commit it [sc. murder, demonstrably forbidden by the natural law], we are bound to transgress *that human law* ...' (emphasis added). The truth is that, though they are not negligible for an understanding of the *Commentaries* (see Finnis, 'Blackstone's Theoretical Intentions' (1967) 12 *Nat. L.F.* 163), Blackstone's remarks in this Introduction to his work cannot be dignified with the title 'a theory'.

'Natural law' and the notion that statutes are merely declaratory ... The mistaken idea that mainstream natural law theories taught that just enactments must be merely declaratory of natural law (or: cannot be identified as enactments without some moral reasoning about their content) has engendered very serious misunderstandings of the history of Western (not least English) law and legal thought. Morris Arnold, 'Statutes as Judgments: the Natural Law Theory of Parliamentary Activity in Medieval England' (1977) 126 *U. Pa. L. Rev.* 329, identifies and refutes the bad history, but not the bad jurisprudence underlying it.

II.3

Variety and conflict in moral opinions ... Weber rightly refused to base his claim that social science is ethically neutral upon the view that the variety of ethical evaluations proves them to be merely subjective: *Methodology*, pp. 12, 55. Why then does Weber maintain that competing values or ideals are all of equal rank in the eye of science? He seems to have three lines of thought. (i) The gap between 'ought' and 'is' proves that value-judgments are inevitably subjective. (This is a *non sequitur*: see

II.4.) (ii) He slides from saying that *empirical science* cannot adjudicate between values to saying that such adjudication is beyond reason and objectivity altogether, and is a matter of faith, demonic decision, radical subjectivity. (But this is just a slide.) (iii) Like Sartre after him, Weber relies mainly upon certain ethical dilemmas, in which it is, he thinks, impossible to show that one of two competing ideals or morally motivated courses of action is superior to the other: for a discussion of Weber's examples, see Strauss, *Natural Right and History*, pp. 67–74; for a discussion of Sartre's main example, see VII.4, below. But all these dilemmas arise from the *complexity* of ethical considerations; they do not show that all value-judgments, or even all ethical value-judgments, are likewise perplexed and beyond rational discrimination (and see III.5, below).

The 'universally acknowledged' first practical principles are not moral principles ... A very frequent misreading of Aquinas, fostered by the main currents of post-Renaissance scholasticism, treats the deliverances of *synderesis* (i.e. the first principles of practical reasonableness: *S.T.* I, q. 79, a. 12; I–II, q. 94, a. 1 ad 2) as already crystallized moral principles (in the form of e.g. the last six of the Ten Commandments). This interpretation finds some support in the wording of occasional passages (e.g. *S.T.* II–II, q. 122, a. 1c). But it makes nonsense of Aquinas's notion of *prudentia*, reducing it to a mere ability to judge when such a crystallized moral rule is applicable, working with such banal 'arguments' as 'murder is wrong; this is an act of murder; therefore this act is wrong and must not be done'. The capacity to make such arguments could never earn the paramount dignity of status accorded to *prudentia* by Aquinas: *S.T.* II–II, q. 47, a. 6 ad 3; I–II, q. 61, a. 2c; q. 66, a. 3 ad 3. Above all, this neo-scholastic theory discards Aquinas's repeated teaching that the first principles of human action are ends (*fines*), so that a man cannot reason rightly in matters of practice, i.e. cannot have *prudentia*, unless he is well disposed towards those ultimate ends: *S.T.* I–II, q. 57, a. 4c; q. 58, a. 5c; II–II, q. 47, a. 6.

Aquinas on self-evidence ... Aquinas is regrettably obscure on the question of which practical principles or precepts are self-evident (whether *per se*, *quoad omnes*, or *quoad sapientes*) and which are deduced conclusions. This is one aspect of his very important failure to discuss the principles which *prudentia* uses to transform the first principles of natural law (which even the most evil of men employ in their practical reasoning: *S.T.* Supp., q. 98, a. 1) into truly moral principles, norms, and judgments. For an effort to fill this gap, see Chapter V, below.

'Intersubjectively transmissible knowledge' ... Arnold Brecht's distinction, in his *Political Theory: the Foundations of Twentieth Century Political Thought* (Princeton: 1959, paperback ed. 1967), between (i) intersubjectively transmissible scientific knowledge, (ii) nontransmissible but genuine knowledge, and (iii) speculation, leans heavily (as he recognizes, p. 181) on neo-positivism or logical positivism, and suffers from the irremediable weakness that it allows no place for, e.g., the philosophical knowledge embodied (purportedly) in the distinction itself. In view of the vagueness and inconsistencies in his set-piece account (pp. 113–16) (*a*) of what is intersubjectively transmissible, and (*b*) of the senses in which 'Scientific Method' is 'exclusive', it is not really surprising to find Brecht advancing (p. 573), as an example of '*scientia transmissibilis*', the 'scientific postulate of adequate proportions' which enables 'science' to 'point to such faults in religious arguing as a gross lack of proportion between ideas of God's greatness, wisdom, and power on one side, and trivial acts, such as table-rapping ...', on the other'. No one who argues that certain basic values are self-evident, and that there are objective basic principles of practical reasonableness, need be concerned about exclusion from a 'science' so elastically and arbitrarily conceived. But he will reject the exclusive equation which Brecht (despite all his protestations

to the contrary) makes between 'according to the method of the natural sciences' and 'rational' (see e.g. ibid., p. 430, quoting and commenting upon Einstein): such an equation is self-refuting. (On self-refutation, see III.6.) The basic principles and requirements of practical reasonableness are intersubjectively transmissible; their transmissibility can be appreciated by anyone who steadily attends to the matter (i.e. to the basic forms of human good) and who is not deflected by the irrelevant objections that not everyone happens to agree in pronouncements on these or related matters, and that the subject-matter and procedures of other disciplines differ from those of practical reasonableness.

For Aquinas, the existence of God is not self-evident ... Still, he thinks that, since the existence and something of the nature of God can be known by demonstration and/or revelation, the principle that God is to be loved is a basic principle of natural law: *S.T.* I–II, q. 100, aa. 3 ad 1, 4 ad 1; cf. q. 100, a. 11c; *De Veritate*, q. 16, a. 1 ad 9. Cf. XIII.5, below.

II.4

Stone on 'the three decisive issues' ... I discussed one of these issues in II.3, above; the remaining one of the three was: 'Have [the natural lawyers] explained how positive law ceases to be law simply by virtue of its violation of natural law?': *Human Law and Human Justice*, p. 212. This presupposes the over-simplified image discussed in II.2, above.

Natural law, or morality, can be understood, assented to and applied without knowledge of metaphysics or anthropology ... Aquinas, *S.T.* I–II, q. 58, a. 4c, is very clear: no one can be morally upright without (*a*) an understanding of the first principles of practical reasoning and (*b*) the practical reasonableness (*prudentia*) which brings those principles to bear, reasonably, on particular commitments, projects, actions; but one can indeed be morally upright without speculative (i.e. theoretical, 'is'-knowledge) wisdom, without the practical knowledge of a craftsmen (art), and without speculative knowledge (*scientia*). As we mentioned in the notes to II.3, Aquinas considered that *prudentia* can exist only in one who is well disposed (*bene dispositus*) towards the basic ends of human existence; but he would have rejected as absurd the view imputed to him by O'Connor, *Aquinas and Natural Law*, p. 29, that 'having "well-disposed affections" (*affectum bene dispositum*) [*sic*] will be a consequence of having a correct insight into the nature of man'.

Natural law and teleological conceptions of nature ... So far as I can see, Strauss, in his exposition of 'classic natural right' (*Natural Right and History*, ch. 4), makes no attempt to justify his prominent but vague assertion (ibid., p. 7) that 'natural right in its classic form is connected with a teleological view of the universe'. Hart too gives much prominence to this claim (*Concept of Law*, pp. 182–7), but actually refers only to such minor figures (for the history of natural law theory) as Montesquieu and Blackstone. It is true that the natural law theory of, say, Aristotle and Aquinas goes along with a teleological conception of nature and, in the case of Aquinas, with a theory of divine providence and eternal law. But what needs to be shown is that the conception of human good entertained by these theorists is *dependent* upon this wider framework. There is much to be said for the view that the order of dependence was precisely the opposite—that the teleological conception of nature was made plausible, indeed conceivable, by analogy with the *intro*spectively luminous, self-evident structure of human well-being, practical reasoning, and human purposive action: read Aristotle, *Physics*, II, 8: 199a9–19. Despite the irrelevance of general teleology to my own argument, two further remarks seem in place: (i) Hart's account of 'the teleological view of nature' is a little extravagant—of what serious writer was it ever true that 'the questions whether [events] *do* occur regularly and whether they *should* occur or whether it is *good* that they occur [were] not regarded as separate questions' (op. cit., p. 185)? In Aristotelian thought 'good' is never used at large, in this fashion, and what is good for the spider is recognized as not good for the fly, while neither spider nor fly is conceived as good for man. (ii) The question of teleology is not philosophically closed, whatever may be the case in the methodology of the natural sciences: see, e.g., Peter Geach, *The Virtues* (Cambridge: 1977), pp. 9–12.

Aquinas on first principles of natural law ... Fundamental for the understanding of Aquinas's widely misunderstood account is G. Grisez, 'The First Principle of Practical Reason: A Commentary on the *Summa Theologiae*, 1–2, Question 94, Article 2' (1965) 10 *Nat. L. F.* 168–96, reprinted in A. Kenny (ed.), *Aquinas: A Collection of Critical Essays* (London: 1970), pp. 340–82 (slightly abbreviated).

'Fact' and 'norm' ... 'Since the term "fact" is properly used as a synonym for "truth" even in its most generic sense, ... we can speak of mathematical and even ethical facts...': Wilfrid Sellars, *Science and Metaphysics* (London and N.Y.: 1968), p. 116. But, since we are accepting that there is *a* distinction to be drawn, relevant to the *justification* of practical (including ethical) judgments, we need not here try to refine the terms in which the distinction of *fact* from *norm* is drawn.

II.5

The gap between 'is' and 'ought' ... A useful history of the growth of explicit attention to this, and of a relativistic conception of ethics as the supposed implication of it, is Arnold Brecht, *Political Theory: the Foundations of Twentieth Century Political Thought*, ch. VI. For explorations of the rational relationship between some sorts of 'facts' and conclusions about what ought to be done, see Jonathan Harrison, *Hume's Moral Espistemology*, pp. 74–82.

Hume's 'is'–'ought' argument(s) ... The structure and arguments of this section of the *Treatise* are carefully disentangled in D. D. Raphael, 'Hume's critique of ethical rationalism' in W. B. Todd (ed.), *Hume and the Enlightenment*, 14 at pp. 20–9; Harrison, op. cit.; and R. David Broiles, *The Moral Philosophy of David Hume* (The Hague: 2nd ed. 1969).

The second interpretation of Hume's 'is'–'ought' paragraph ... is defended by Broiles, op. cit., ch. 6.

Butler and Cudworth on fitnesses and conformity to human nature ... See Joseph Butler, 'Dissertation of the Nature of Virtue', appendix II to *The Analogy of Religion* (1736, 3rd ed. 1740), in Raphael, *British Moralists*, para. 432; *Fifteen Sermons* (1726, 4th ed. 1749), in *British Moralists*, paras. 374, 377, 384, 391 (reference to 'speculative absurdity'), 395, 400, 402, 404, 409 (summary), 423. For Cudworth, see *A Treatise concerning Eternal and Immutable Morality* (c.1685; 1st ed. 1731), Book I, c. ii, paras. 3, 4: Book IV, c. vi, para. 4; in *British Moralists*, paras. 122, 123, 124, 135.

Confusion in Hume between obligation and motivating or necessitating causes ... This accounts for, and is evidenced by, such otherwise surprising remarks in the *Treatise* as: 'the moral obligation, or the sentiment of right and wrong ...' (*British Moralists*, para. 533); 'when the neglect or non-performance of [an action] displeases us after a [certain] manner, we say that we lie under an obligation to perform it. A change of the obligation supposes a change of the sentiment; and a creation of a new obligation supposes some new sentiment to arise' (para. 537); 'No action can be required of us as our duty, unless there be implanted in human nature some actuating passion or motive, capable of producing the action' (para. 538); 'were there no more than a resolution . . ., promises would only declare our former motives, and would not create any new *motive or obligation*' (para. 541, emphasis added); 'interest is the first obligation to performance of promises' (para. 542); 'afterwards a sentiment of morals concurs with interest, and becomes a new obligation upon mankind' (para. 543). Interpretation of some of these passages is complicated by Hume's assumption that the subject-matter of moral assessments is always motives, not actions (except in so far as these reflect motives). A confusion analogous to Hume's is found in Adam Smith (an early Humean moralist), *The Theory of Moral Sentiments* (1776), I, ii, 4, 1; see T. D. Campbell, in A. S. Skinner and T. B. Wilson (eds.), *Essays on Adam Smith* (Oxford: 1975), p. 78.

II.6

Clarke and Grotius ... The connection cannot, I think, and need not be established directly. Available to an English scholar in 1704 were at least fourteen editions, at least two English translations, and at least four additional commentaries on or digests of the *De Jure Belli ac Pacis*. Note that the 'modern' author most cited by Clarke (and very frequently and copiously on the law of nature) is Richard Cumberland *De Legibus Naturae* (1672), and that Cumberland goes out of his way to say on the first page of his Prolegomena that the *De Jure Belli ac Pacis* deserves especially well of mankind, being the first of its kind, truly worthy of its great author and of immortality.

'*Etiamsi daremus* . . .' . . . See J. St. Leger, *The 'Etiamsi Daremus' of Hugo Grotius* (Rome: 1962). For the debate in classical thought, see Plato, *Rep.* II: 365d–e; *Laws* X: 885b; 907b. For the scholastic formulations of the 'etiamsi daremus', see, e.g. Gregory of Rimini, *In Librum Secundum Sententiarum* (c. 1350; Venice: 1503), dist. 34, q. 1, a. 2 (quoted in Pereña's edition of Suarez, *De Legibus*, vol. III, Madrid: 1974, p. 80 n.); Vitoria, op. cit., part II, para. 9; Suarez, *De actibus humanis* ... (1581; first published, in part, by Pereña and Abril, op. cit., p. 210), q. 9 (op. cit., p. 211); Vazquez, *In Primam Secundae*, disp. 97, c. 1. Suarez reports the first of these, and some other scholastic sources where, he says, the hypothesis is raised: *De Legibus*, Book II, c. 6, para. 3. For Culverwel's citations of Vazquez and Suarez, especially on the *etiamsi daremus*, see his *An Elegant and Learned Discourse of the Light of Nature* ([1652, 4th ed. 1669], ed. Brown, 1857), pp. 45, 55, 74–7.

The ethical theory of Vazquez and Suarez ... It is commonly said that Vazquez and Suarez differ as extreme rationalism differs from moderate voluntarism in ethics: see e.g. A.-H. Chroust, 'Hugo Grotius and the Scholastic Natural Law Tradition' (1943) 17 *New Scholasticism* 101 at pp. 114, 117; Rommen, *The Natural Law*, pp. 64, 71, 196; and Suarez himself, *De Legibus*, Book II, c. 5, paras. 2, 5–8. But, *pace* Chroust and Rommen, Vazquez rejected as 'empty' the distinction which they ascribe to him, between *lex praecipiens* and *lex indicans*: see Vazquez, *in Primam Secundae*, disp. 97, c. 1, no. 1. *Pace* Chroust, op. cit., p. 114, he does not say that the natural law is '*compelling* without being expressly commanded'. His theory of obligation is un-developed, but seems to be the same as Suarez's: obligation is the effect of the *imperium* of a superior. Like Suarez, he rejects out of hand Aquinas's theory of *imperium* in the individual human act (see XI.8, below). Vazquez regards law as an act of intellect, rather than of will; but those who seize on this to liken him to Aquinas and oppose him to Suarez altogether overlook that for Vazquez the relevant 'act of intellect' is no more than an *intimatio* to an inferior of the will of his superior: Vazquez, op. cit., disp. 150, c. 3, no. 19; disp. 49, c. 2, no. 6 (and this is essentially the view of Suarez, *De Legibus*, Book I, c. 4, para. 14; c. 5, paras. 21–5). Compare this with Aquinas's reason for saying that law is an act of intellect; this reason has nothing to do with the will of a superior needing to be made known, but only with the fact that it is intelligence that grasps ends, and arranges means to ends, and grasps the necessity of those arranged means; and this is the source of obligation: *S.T.* I–II, q. 90, a. 1c.

Aquinas on 'convenientia' ... For his use of this term and its cognates, in a moral context (but not so as to amount to the Vazquez–Suarez–Grotius *convenientia* to 'rational nature' as such), see particularly *S.T.* I–II, q. 18, aa. 2c, 5c and ad 2, 8c and ad 2, 9c, 10c and ad 3; q. 10, a. 1c; q. 71, a. 2; q. 94, a. 3 ad 3. Vazquez is sometimes said to have originated the later use of the notion, but it is found in a manuscript of Suarez dated 1592, well before the publication of Vazquez's commentary: see vol. III of the Pereña edition of *De Legibus* (op. cit., *supra*), p. 220. For the Stoic use of '*convenientia*', see XIII.1, below.

Stoic influence on post-Renaissance ethical theory ... In considering this influence, note that Cicero's moral works are the most frequently cited of all the works cited or quoted with approval by Clarke, and that all the Ciceronian texts on natural law are translated in the text of Clarke's lectures, as well as referred to and reproduced in his marginal notes: see Clarke, op. cit., 8th ed., pp. 213–17, 221–2. Though Clarke, ibid., p. 210, denounces the 'ranting discourses' of the Stoics on suicide, he praises Cicero, 'that great master', for his knowledge and understanding of the true state of things, and of the original obligations of human nature ...': ibid., p. 209 (*British Moralists*, para. 244).

'*Is*' *and* '*ought*' *in Aristotle and Aquinas* ... Quite unfounded is the notion that 'in its classical formulations, natural law ... asserted ... that there is a connection between morality and the natural order, such that true statements about morality are realized in the actual course of events. What ought to be and what is were believed to be united in a way that contradicts the logical separation that we now maintain between normative and descriptive discourse': Lloyd L. Weinreb, 'Law as Order' (1978) 91 *Harv. L. Rev.* 909 at p. 911; similarly misleading is R. M. Unger, *Law in Modern Society* (New York and London: 1976), p. 79. For Aristotle's account of obligation, see *Nic. Eth.* IX, 8: 1168b29–30, 1169a11–22, an account which needs a supplementation such as is offered below, XIII.5; see also XI.1.

II.7

The '*perverted faculty*' *argument* ... A careful exposition and critique of this argument, adverting to its roots in Suarezian conceptions of natural law, is Germain Grisez, *Contraception and the Natural Law* (Milwaukee: 1964), pp. 19–31. Grisez shows that the argument was tailor-made to meet the demand for a major premiss for arguments against contraception and other sexual vices; he definitively criticizes the inadequate arguments thus yielded (and replaces them). There is room for a deeper historical study of the perverted faculty argument, and for a close study of an argument employed by Aquinas against lying (*S.T.* II–II, q. 110, a. 3c), which can, but need not (and, I think, should not), be read as employing the perverted faculty argument as its general premiss, and was (I imagine) historically important in suggesting the perverted faculty argument to theologians in a hurry.

Part Two

III

A BASIC FORM OF GOOD: KNOWLEDGE

III.1 AN EXAMPLE

NEITHER this chapter nor the next makes or presupposes any moral judgments. Rather, these two chapters concern the evaluative substratum of all moral judgments. That is to say, they concern the acts of practical understanding in which we grasp the basic values of human existence and thus, too, the basic principles of all practical reasoning.

The purpose of this chapter, in particular, is to illustrate (i) what I mean by 'basic value' and 'basic practical principle', (ii) how such values and principles enter into any consideration of good reasons for action and any full description of human conduct, and (iii) the sense in which such basic values are obvious ('self-evident') and even unquestionable. For this purpose, I discuss only one basic value, leaving to the next chapter the identification of the other forms of human good that, so far as I can see, are likewise irreducibly basic.

The example of a basic value to be examined now is: knowledge. Perhaps it would be more accurate to call it 'speculative knowledge', using the term 'speculative' here, not to make the Aristotelian distinction between the *theoretike* and the *praktike*, but to distinguish knowledge as sought for its own sake from knowledge as sought only instrumentally, i.e. as useful in the pursuit of some other objective, such as survival, power, popularity, or a money-saving cup of coffee. Now 'knowledge', unlike 'belief', is an achievement-word; there are true beliefs and false beliefs, but knowledge is of truth. So one could speak of truth as the basic good with which we are here concerned, for one can just as easily speak of 'truth for its own sake' as of 'knowledge for its own sake'. In any event, truth is not a mysterious abstract entity; we want the truth when we want the judgments in which we affirm or deny propositions to be true judgments, or (what comes to the same) want the propositions affirmed or denied, or to be affirmed or denied, to be true propositions. So, to complete the explanation of what is meant by the knowledge under discussion here, as distinct from instrumental knowledge, I can add that the distinction I am drawing is not between one set of propositions and another. It is not a distinction between fields of knowledge. Any proposition, whatever its subject-matter, can be inquired into (with a view to affirming or denying it) in either of the two distinct ways, (i) instrumentally or (ii) out of curiosity, the pure desire to know, to find out the truth about it simply out of an interest in or concern for truth and a desire to avoid ignorance or error as such.

This chapter, then, is an invitation to reflect on one form of human activity, the activity of trying to find out, to understand, and to judge matters correctly. This is not, perhaps, the easiest activity to understand; but it has the advantage of being the activity which the reader himself is actually engaged in. But if it seems too abstruse and tricky to try to understand this form of activity reflectively (i.e. by reflecting on one's attempt to understand and assess the truth of this chapter itself), one can reflect on any other exercise of curiosity. One could consider, for example, the wide-ranging effort of historical inquiry involved in discovering the actual intentions of the principal authors of the Statute of Uses (1536) or of the Fourteenth Amendment of the US Constitution (1866). Or something more humble (like weighing the truth of some gossipy rumour), or more 'scientific' —it makes no difference, for present purposes.

III.2   FROM INCLINATION TO GRASP OF VALUE

Curiosity is a name for the desire or inclination or felt want that we have when, just for the sake of knowing, we want to find out about something. One wants to know the answer to a particular question. Quite apart from my brief or assignment, from the fee or the examination, what does this statutory provision mean? What did the authors of the Fourteenth Amendment care for economic equality? What happened on the night of the murder? Are 'desire', 'inclination', and 'want' as synonymous as the first sentence of this paragraph supposes? Does e = mc²? How does this clock work? *It would be good to find out.* Quite often, of course, the raising of questions is not accompanied by any particular state of feelings. Quite often the inclination is to be described, more colourlessly (and ambiguously), as 'having an interest'.

Commonly one's interest in knowledge, in getting to the truth of the matter, is not bounded by the particular questions that first aroused one's desire to find out. So readily that one notices the transition only by an effort of reflection, it becomes clear that knowledge is a good thing to have (and not merely for its utility), without restriction to the subject-matters that up to now have aroused one's curiosity. In explaining, to oneself and others, what one is up to, one finds oneself able and ready to refer to *finding out, knowledge, truth* as sufficient explanations of the point of one's activity, project, or commitment. One finds oneself reflecting that ignorance and muddle are to be avoided, simply as such and not merely in relation to a closed list of questions that one has raised. One begins to consider the well-informed and clear-headed person as, to that extent, well-off (and not only for the profitable use he can make of his knowledge). 'It's good to find out ...' now seems to be applicable not merely in relation to oneself and the question that currently holds one's attention, but at large—in relation to an inexhaustible range of questions and subject-matters, and for anyone.

To mark this distinction between 'good', referring to some particular objective or goal that one is considering as desirable, and 'good', referring to a general form of good that can be participated in or realized in indefinitely many ways on indefinitely many occasions, it will be useful to reserve the word 'value' so that (for the purposes of this book) it signifies only the latter sense of 'good'. But, to avoid an artificially constricted vocabulary, I will still use the term 'good' to signify both the particular object of a particular person's desire, choice, or action, and the general form, of which that particular object is (or is supposed to be) an instance. For there is typically some general description that makes manifest the aspect under which a particular objective has its interest, attracts desire, choice, and efforts and thus is (or is considered to be) a good thing.

It is important not to allow one's reflection on the value of knowledge to become muddled here. A number of common misunderstandings threaten to short-circuit our understanding of practical reason and its relationship to morality, just at this point. So we should bracket out these misunderstandings one by one: the reasons for doing so will appear more fully in the next chapter. (i) To think of knowledge as a value is not to think that every true proposition is equally worth knowing, that every form of learning is equally valuable, that every subject-matter is equally worth investigating. Except for some exceptional purpose, it is more worth while to know whether the contentions in this book are true or false than to know how many milligrams of printer's ink are used in a copy of it. (ii) To think of knowledge as a basic form of good is not to think that knowledge, for example, of the truth about these contentions, would be equally valuable for every person. (iii) Nor is it to think that such knowledge, or indeed any particular item of knowledge, has any priority of value even for the reader or writer at this moment; perhaps the reader would be better off busying himself with something else, even for the rest of his life . . . (iv) Just as 'knowledge is good' does not mean that knowledge is to be pursued by everybody, at all times, in all circumstances, so too it does not mean that knowledge is the only general form of good, or the supreme form of good. (v) To think of knowledge as a value is not, as such, to think of it as a 'moral' value; 'truth is a good' is not, here, to be understood as a moral proposition, and 'knowledge is to be pursued' is not to be understood, here, as stating a moral obligation, requirement, prescription, or recommendation. In our reflective analysis of practical reasonableness, morality comes later. (vi) At the same time, finally, it is to be recalled that the knowledge we here have in mind as a value is the knowledge that one can call an *intrinsic* good, i.e. that is considered to be desirable for its own sake and not merely as something sought after under some such description as 'what will enable me to impress my audience' or 'what will confirm my instinctive beliefs' or 'what will contribute to my survival'. In sum, (vii) to say that such knowledge is a value is simply to say that reference to the pursuit of knowledge makes intelligible (though not necessarily reasonable-all-things-considered) any particular instance of the human activity and commitment involved in such pursuit.

III.3   PRACTICAL PRINCIPLE AND PARTICIPATION IN VALUE

'Knowledge is something good to have.' 'Being well-informed and clear-headed is a good way to be.' 'Muddle and ignorance are to be avoided.' These are formulations of a practical principle. Any such expression of our understanding of a value can provide the starting-point (in Latin, *principium*) for reasoning about what to do, and thus is a principle of practical reasonableness.

For example: '(i) It would be good to find out the truth about the alleged principles of natural law; (ii) reading this book critically seems likely to help me find out what I want to find out about these matters; (iii) so, despite its tedium, I'll read it right through and think its main arguments out.' The first premiss is expressed as a practical principle; it formulates a want but makes the want more than a blind urge by referring its object (one's finding-out about natural law) to the intelligible and general form of good which that object is one possible way of participating in or instantiating. When combined with the second premiss, which is a straightforward factual judgment about the relevance, coherence, etc., of a particular book, the first premiss or practical principle expresses a reason for acting in the manner signified in the conclusion, the third step in the train of reasoning. The force of this reason varies, of course, depending on how much one values these matters in particular (and in one's particular circumstances), and on the certainty or uncertainty of one's factual estimate of the appropriateness of the proposed means for realizing that value in this particular case.

Basic practical principles, such as that knowledge is a good to be pursued and ignorance is to be avoided, do not play the same role as rules do, in practical reasoning or the explanation and description of intelligent action. A basic practical principle serves to orient one's practical reasoning, and can be instantiated (rather than 'applied') in indefinitely many, more specific, practical principles and premisses. Rather than restrict, it suggests new horizons for human activity.

The basic practical principle that knowledge is good need

hardly ever be formulated as the premiss for anyone's actual practical reasoning. Particular practical premisses (such as that knowledge about natural law would be good to have) are not usually adopted as the conclusions of an inferential train of reasoning from the more general and basic principle. In this respect, practical reasoning is like 'theoretical' reasoning, which has its own basic and usually tacit presuppositions and principles. We often say 'Too late!'; but how often do we formulate the presupposition on which our conclusion rests, the guiding presupposition that time cannot be reversed?

Yet such presuppositions and principles can be disengaged and identified, by reflection not only on our own thinking but also on the words and deeds of others. In trying to make sense of someone's commitments, projects, and actions over a period, we may say that he acted 'on the basis that' knowledge is a good worthy of a life-shaping devotion. The good of knowledge was not for him an 'end' external to the 'means' by which he 'pursued' it or sought to 'attain' it. Rather, it was a good in which, we may say, he *participated*, through or in those of his commitments, projects, and actions which are explicable by reference to that basic practical principle, that basic form of good. A particular action (say, reading a book) and a particular project (such as understanding a certain body of theory) can be more or less completely attained, completed, finished off. But it may be helpful to reserve the word 'commitment' for that sort of participation-in-a-value which is never finished and done with (except by abandonment of the commitment) and which takes shape in a potentially inexhaustible variety of particular projects and actions, each with its particularized first premiss of practical reasoning.

III.4   THE SELF-EVIDENCE OF THE GOOD OF KNOWLEDGE

Is it not the case that knowledge is really a good, an aspect of authentic human flourishing, and that the principle which expresses its value formulates a real (intelligent) reason for action? It seems clear that such indeed is the case, and that there are no sufficient reasons for doubting it to be so. The good of knowledge is self-evident, obvious. It cannot be demonstrated, but equally it needs no demonstration.

This is not to say that everyone actually does recognize the value of knowledge, or that there are no pre-conditions for recognizing that value. The principle that truth (and knowledge) is worth pursuing is not somehow innate, inscribed on the mind at birth. On the contrary, the value of truth becomes obvious only to one who has experienced the urge to question, who has grasped the connection between question and answer, who understands that knowledge is constituted by correct answers to particular questions, and who is aware of the possibility of further questions and of other questioners who like himself could enjoy the advantage of attaining correct answers. A new-born child, for example, has presumably not had any such set of felt inclinations, memories, understandings, and (in short) experiences.

In asking oneself whether knowledge is indeed a value (for its own sake: thus, a basic value), one should not be deflected by the fact that one's inclination to seek truth has psychological roots. It may well be that at an early stage in the life of the mind the urge to know is scarcely differentiated from other urges, such as the sexual drive. This early lack of differentiation may be never wholly surmounted, so that the one urge remains capable not only of deflecting but also of reinforcing the other. Such facts, interesting and important as they may be in some contexts, are not relevant to the question 'Is knowledge indeed a good, objectively worth pursuing?'. In considering the question: 'Is the psychologist's opinion that curiosity is a form of sexuality a true or at least a warranted opinion?', it is relevant to attend to the coherence of the psychologist's hypothesis, to the pertinence of his evidence, to the soundness of his inferences. But it is *not* relevant to ask whether the psychologist's opinion emerged in his psyche at the call of his sexuality or as a reflection of his organic constitution or under the influence of any other such sub-rational cause. The soundness of an answer to a particular question is never established or disconfirmed by the answer to the *entirely different* question of what are the physical, biological, and psychological pre-conditions and concomitants of the raising of that question (or any question) and of the proposing of that answer (or any answer).

And all this holds true of the answer 'Yes, obviously' to the question 'Is knowledge worth having?'.

Just as we should not appeal to causes, pre-conditions, and concomitants in order to raise an illegitimate doubt about the self-evidence of the value of knowledge, so we should not seek a deduction or inference of that value from facts. If one is to go beyond the felt urge of curiosity to an understanding grasp of the value of knowledge, one certainly must know at least the fact that some questions can be answered. Moreover, one certainly will be assisted if one also knows such facts as that answers tend to hang together in systems that tend to be illuminating over as wide a range as the data which stimulate one's questions. But one who, thus knowing the possibility of attaining truth, is enabled thereby to grasp the value of that possible object and attainment is not inferring the value from the possibility. No such inference is possible. No value can be deduced or otherwise inferred from a fact or set of facts.

Nor can one validly infer the value of knowledge from the fact (if fact it be) that 'all men desire to know'. The *universality* of a desire is not a sufficient basis for inferring that the object of that desire is really desirable, objectively good. Nor is such a basis afforded by the fact that the desire or inclination manifests, or is part of, a *deep* structure shaping the human mind, or by the fact that the desire, or the structure, is *ineradicable*, or by the fact that in whole or part the desire is (or is not) *common* to all animals, or by the fact that it is (or is not) *peculiar* to human beings.

Nor would it be logically decisive to establish that all human persons not only desire to know (have the urge of curiosity) but also affirm the value of knowledge and respect and pursue it in their lives. (Conversely, the fact that not all men pursue or admit to pursuing or even give lip-service to the value of knowledge does not give sufficient ground for denying or rejecting that value.) To know that and how other persons have valued knowledge is *relevant*, for it serves as a disclosure or intimation or reminder of the range of opportunities open to one. The life and death of a Socrates, and the disciplined, exact, profound, and illuminating investigations of a Plato (or a Galileo or a Maitland), reveal an aspect of human possibility only vaguely prefigured by one's own relatively feeble or fickle curiosity: IV.1. But to say that knowledge *must* be a real value, because intelligent men, or great men, or mature men have regarded it as a value and as an aspect of their own flourishing, is not to make what could be called an inference. For one's assessment of a person as flourishing, mature, great, or, in the relevant respect, intelligent is made possible only by one's own underived understanding that what that person is and does is really good (in the relevant respects). The 'premiss' of the apparent inference thus rests on its 'conclusion'.

But is there not something fishy about appeal to self-evidence? Do modern sciences and other theoretical disciplines rest on self-evident concepts or principles? Or is it not rather the case that appeal to allegedly self-evident principles is a relic of the discredited Aristotelian conception of axiomatized sciences of nature?

A proper discussion of self-evidence would have to be embarrassingly complex, not only because almost every controverted question in epistemology is here brought to a focus, but also because the modern conception of an axiom is not the conception taken for granted by Aristotle and Aquinas. For the axioms of, say, modern geometries are not selected, as those of Euclid apparently were, for their purported self-evidence, but rather for their capacity to generate a system of theorems, proofs, etc. which is consistent and complete. We may observe in passing that appeal to self-evidence does seem to be made (though without much advertisement) in a modern geometry (i) in establishing the meaning of at least some of the 'primitive' terms employed to formulate the axioms and theorems (e.g., in Hilbert's or Veblen's postulates for Euclidean geometry, the term 'between', as in 'C is between A and B'); (ii) in generating the theorems and proofs, by employing as inference rules a logic which (as geometers rather freely admit) is imported into geometry without too much scrutiny; (iii) at some point in the assessment of consistency, and (iv) at some point in the assessment of completeness. Still, someone may ask whether a modern pure geometry is intended to state truths or to amount to knowledge at all. So, leaving that question to one side, it may be more pertinent to observe that the natural sciences (not to mention the historical sciences, and the disciplined common sense of forensic assessment of evidence) certainly rest, implicitly but thoroughly, on the principles of elementary formal logic (though those principles are far from exhausting the rational principles on which the elaboration of such sciences and disciplines proceeds).

It may be still more helpful, for the purposes of this brief reflection on self-evidence, to consider some of the principles or norms of sound judgment in every empirical discipline. These principles might be described as methodological; in this respect they resemble the basic requirements of practical reasonableness to be discussed in Chapter V, rather than the principles of practical reasonableness considered in this chapter and the next, principles identifying substantive forms of human good. But reflection on what it means to say that the principles or norms of sound empirical judgment are self-evident will help to eliminate some misunderstandings of what it means to say that the substantive principles of practical reasonableness are self-evident. In particular, it will help to show that the self-evidence of a principle entails neither (a) that it is formulated reflectively or at all explicitly by those who are guided by it, nor (b) that when it is so formulated by somebody his formulation will invariably be found to be accurate or acceptably refined and sufficiently qualified, nor (c) that it is arrived at, even only implicitly, without experience of the field to which it relates.

There are indeed many principles of sound empirical judgment or, more generally, of rationality in theoretical inquiries. One such principle is that the principles of logic, for example the forms of deductive inference, are to be used and adhered to in all one's thinking, even though no non-circular proof of their validity is possible (since any proof would employ them). Another is that an adequate reason why anything is so rather than otherwise is to be expected, unless one has a reason not to expect such a reason: cf. XIII.2, below. A third is that self-defeating theses are to be abandoned: see III.6. A fourth is that phenomena are to be regarded as real unless there is some reason to distinguish between appearance and reality. A fifth is that a full description of data is to be preferred to partial descriptions, and that an account or explanation of phenomena is not to be accepted if it requires or postulates something inconsistent with the data for which it is supposed to account. A sixth is that a method of interpretation which is successful is to be relied upon in further similar cases until contrary reason appears. A seventh is that theoretical accounts which are simple, predictively successful, and explanatorily powerful are to be accepted in preference to other accounts. And there are many others: XIII.2.

Such principles of theoretical rationality are not demonstrable, for they are presupposed or deployed in anything that we would count as a demonstration. They do not describe the world. But although they cannot be verified by opening one's eyes and taking a look, they are obvious—obviously valid—to anyone who has experience of inquiry into matters of fact or of theoretical (including historical and philosophical) judgment; they do not stand in need of demonstration. They are objective; their validity is not a matter of convention, nor is it relative to anybody's individual purposes. They can be meaningfully denied, for they are not principles of logic conformity to which is essential if one is to *mean* anything. But to defy them is to disqualify oneself from the pursuit of knowledge, and to deny them is as straightforwardly unreasonable as anything can be. In all these respects, the principles of *theoretical* rationality are self-evident. And it is in these respects that we are asserting that the basic *practical* principle that knowledge is a good to be pursued is self-evident.

Nowadays, any claim that something is self-evident is commonly misunderstood by philosophers. They think that any such claim either asserts or presupposes that the criterion of the truth of the allegedly self-evident principle, proposition, or fact is one's *feeling of certitude* about it. This is indeed a misunderstanding. Self-evident principles such as those I have been discussing are not validated by feelings. On the contrary, they are themselves the criteria whereby we discriminate between feelings, and discount some of our feelings (including feelings of certitude), however intense, as irrational or unwarranted, misleading or delusive.

III.5 'OBJECT OF DESIRE' AND OBJECTIVITY

The principle that truth is worth pursuing, knowledge is worth having, is thus an underived principle. Neither its intelligibility nor its force rests on any further principle.

This may tempt us to say that knowledge is a good *because* we desire it, are interested in it, value it, pursue it. But the temptation has plausibility only if we abandon the effort to understand the value of knowledge. And we are tempted to abandon that effort only when, for bad philosophical reasons, we confuse a principle's lack of derivation with a lack of justification or lack of objectivity. Non-derivability in some cases amounts to lack of justification and of objectivity. But in other cases it betokens self-evidence; and these cases are to be found in every field of inquiry. For in every field there is and must be, at some point or points, an end to derivation and inference. At that point or points we find ourselves in face of the self-evident, which makes possible all subsequent inferences in that field.

In the next section I look to see what can be said in defence of the underived and underivable principle that knowledge is an intrinsic value. For the moment let us reflect on the fact that, for one who considers something like knowledge to be a good, the true expression of his opinion and attitude is *not* 'it is good because or in so far as I desire it', *but* 'I desire it because and in so far as it is good'.

It is easy to be confused by the Aristotelian tag that 'the good is what all things desire'—as if the goodness were consequential on the desires. But, as it applies to human good and human desire, this tag was intended to affirm simply that (i) our primary use of the term 'good' (and related terms) is to express our practical thinking, i.e. our thinking, in terms of reasons for action, towards decision and action; and that (ii) we would not bother with such thinking, or such action, unless we were in fact interested in (*desirous* of . . .) whatever it is we are calling good. Those who used the tag were equally insistent that one's human desire is a pursuit of something in so far as it seems desirable, and that things seem desirable to one in so far as they (appear to) promise to make one better-off (not necessarily 'materially', or instrumentally).

Other people, sceptical about the objectivity of value judgments, do grant that, from the 'internal' or 'practical' viewpoint of one who is judging something to be good and desirable, his desire and decision to pursue the object are consequential on his judgments (i) that the object *is* good and (ii) that he will *really* be better-off for getting or doing or effecting it. But, in their philosophizing, these sceptics argue that the internal view-point or practical mode of thinking is systematically delusory, precisely in this respect. Our practical judgments of value, they say, are ultimately no more than expressions of our feelings and desires; we *project* our desires on to objects, and *objectify* our feelings about objects by mistakenly ascribing to those objects such 'qualities' as goodness, value, desirability, perfection, etc. One who says 'knowledge is good and ignorance is bad' may think he is affirming something objective, something that is correct and would be so even if he were not aware of the value of knowledge and were content with ignorance. Indeed (the sceptics grant), some such beliefs are built into our ordinary thought and language. But anyone who thinks this about what he is affirming is, they say, in error. Really his affirmations express only a subjective concern. He can affirm, correctly or truly, no more than that he regards knowledge as something satisfying an aim or desire which he happens to have (and which he has, probably, because it is an aim widely shared or com-mended in his community).

It is important to see both how much such sceptics are claiming, and how precise must be their grounds for claiming it. They are claiming much, because their claim, if true, would render mysterious the rational characteristics of the principle that knowledge is a good worth pursuing. These rational characteristics can be summed up as self-evidence or obvious-ness, and peremptoriness. As to self-evidence we said enough already: to someone who fixes his attention on the possibilities of attaining knowledge, and on the character of the open-minded, clear-headed, and wise man, the value of knowledge is obvious. Indeed, the sceptic does not really deny this. How could he? What he does instead is invite us to shift our atten-tion, away from the relevant subject-matter, to other features of the world and of human understanding.

Now understanding the value of truth, grasping a practical principle, is not just like understanding a principle of logic, or mathematics, or physical science. It is not just like opening one's eyes and perceiving the black marks on this page, or even like 'seeing' those marks as words with meanings. Judging that a man is well-off because he is wise is not like judging that he is a bearer of infection because he has tuberculosis. By referring us to these differences between evaluation and other forms of human understanding, the sceptic hopes to raise a philosophical doubt about what seems beyond doubt when one is considering the relevant subject-matter itself. He argues that our belief in the objectivity of values amounts to a belief in very queer 'things', perceived by a very queer faculty of 'intuition': all very fishy.

But we should not be deflected. It is obvious that a man who is well informed, etc., simply *is* better-off (other things being equal) than a man who is muddled, deluded, and ignorant, that the state of the one is better than the state of the other, not just in this particular case or that, but in all cases, as such, universally, and *whether I like it or not*. Knowledge is better than ignorance. Am I not compelled to admit it, willy-nilly? It matters not that I may be feeling incurious myself. For the understanding affirmation of the practical principle is neither a reference to nor an expression of any desire or urge or inclination of mine. Nor is it merely a reference to (or implied presupposition of) any desires that my fellows happen to have. It goes beyond the desires and inclinations which may first have aroused my interest in the possibility of knowledge and which may remain a necessary substratum of any interest in truth sufficient to *move* me to pursue it *for myself*. It is a rational judgment about a general form of human well-being, about the fulfilment of a human potentiality. As such, it has (in its own way) the peremptoriness of all other rational judgments. It constitutes a critique of my passing likes and dislikes. The practical principle is hard to play fast and loose with; I may ignore it or reject it, but again and again it will come to mind, and be implicit in my deliberations and my discourse, catching me out in inconsistency. To avoid it, I have to be arbitrary.

To gainsay the rational force or objectivity of this practical principle, it is not enough for the sceptic to point to the diversity of moral opinions. For the principle that truth is worth knowing and that ignorance is to be avoided is not itself a moral principle. In due course we shall see that it is a principle relevant to the making of moral judgments, in the sense that it is a necessary condition of the truth or validity of certain moral norms: V.3, V.7, V.10. But at the moment we are assuming or asserting nothing about 'morality' or 'ethics', and are ascribing no 'moral' force to the value judgment under consideration. Problems about morality and moralities are therefore beside the point.

It is equally irrelevant for the sceptic to argue that values cannot be derived from facts. For my contention is that, while awareness of certain 'factual' possibilities is a necessary condition for the reasonable judgment that truth is a value, still that judgment itself is derived from no other judgment whatsoever.

Moreover, it is insufficient for the sceptic to point out that not everyone who might be asked would affirm that truth is a value worth pursuing. For I am saying nothing about whether the principle happens to be universally affirmed, or will be in the future. I am contending only (i) that if one attends carefully and honestly to the relevant human possibilities one can understand, without reasoning from any other judgment, that the realization of those possibilities is, as such, good and desirable for the human person; and (ii) that one's understanding needs no further justification. To refer, at this point, to the opinions of other men is simply to change the subject.

Thus the usual general arguments of sceptics in ethics give no support to the sceptic's denial of the objectivity of the value of knowledge. Much more precise grounds for his claim can rightly be demanded of the sceptic. Can they be forthcoming?

III.6   SCEPTICISM ABOUT THIS BASIC VALUE IS
INDEFENSIBLE

In the case of the basic values and practical principles to be identified in the next chapter, the discussion of their self-evidence and objectivity would have to rest at this point. But in the case of the basic value of knowledge we can go one step further. We can show that *any* argument raised by the sceptic is going to be self-defeating. To show this is not to show that the basic value of knowledge is self-evident or objective; it is only to show that counter-arguments are invalid. But to make even this limited defensive point, in relation to only one basic value, may help to undermine sceptical doubts about all and any of the basic principles of practical reasoning.

Some propositions refute themselves either because they are directly self-contradictory or because they logically entail their contradictory: for example, 'I know that I know nothing'; 'It can be proved that nothing can be proved'; 'All propositions are false'.

Then again, there are some statements whose occurrence *happens* to refute their content. An example of this pragmatic self-refutation is afforded by someone singing 'I am not singing'. Here there is what we may call performative inconsistency, that is, inconsistency between what is asserted by a statement and facts that are given in and by the making of the statement.

Thirdly, there are propositions which cannot be coherently asserted, because they are *inevitably* falsified by any assertion of them. The proposition 'I am not singing' is not such a proposition, for it can be asserted in writing. But the proposition 'I do not exist' is inevitably falsified by an assertion of it. Another example of this operational self-refutation is 'No one can put words (or other symbols) together to form a sentence'. Operationally self-refuting propositions are not logically incoherent. Nor are they meaningless or empty or semantically paradoxical, as are 'This sentence is false' or 'This provision shall come into effect on 1st January' (where 'this sentence' or 'this provision' in each case is not a colloquial reference to some other sentence or norm but is self-referential and fails to establish any definite reference). Operationally self-refuting propositions have a quite definite reference and so can be (and inevitably are) false. They have a type of performative inconsistency; that is, they are inconsistent with the facts that are given in and by *any* assertion of them. An operationally self-refuting proposition cannot be coherently asserted, for it contradicts either the proposition that someone is asserting it or some proposition entailed by the proposition that someone is asserting it.

The sceptical assertion that knowledge is not a good is operationally self-refuting. For one who makes such an assertion, intending it as a serious contribution to rational discussion, is implicitly committed to the proposition that he believes his assertion is worth making, and worth making *qua* true; he thus is committed to the proposition that he believes that truth is a good worth pursuing or knowing. But the sense of his original assertion was precisely that truth is not a good worth pursuing or knowing. Thus he is implicitly committed to formally contradictory beliefs.

One can certainly toy with the notion that knowledge is not a good worth pursuing. But the fact that to *assert* this (whether to an audience, or as the judgment concluding one's own inner cogitations) would be operationally self-refuting should persuade the sceptic to cut short idle doubting. Self-defeating positions should be abandoned. The sceptic, on this as on other matters, can maintain coherence by *asserting* nothing; but coherence is not the only requirement of rationality.

A judgment or belief is objective if it is correct. A proposition is objective if one is warranted in asserting it, whether because there is sufficient evidence for it, or compelling grounds, or because (to one who has the experience and intelligence to understand the terms in which it is expressed) it is obvious or self-evidently correct. And if a proposition *seems* to be correct *and* could never be coherently denied, we are certainly justified in affirming it and in considering that what we are affirming is indeed objectively the case (in the relevant sense of 'what is the case'). But all this is true of the proposition we have been considering, viz. that knowledge is a good to be pursued. We do not thereby directly demonstrate that knowledge is a good to be pursued; that principle remains indemonstrable, self-evident. What we demonstrate is simply that it is presupposed in all demonstrations, indeed in all serious assertions, whatsoever, and has as much title to be called 'objective' as any other proposition whose contradictory is inevitably falsified by the act of asserting it.

NOTES

III.2

'*Value*' as a general form of good, the aspect or description under which particular objects are (or are regarded as) good ... Aquinas's exposition of his ethics particularly suffers for want of a term reserved for signifying this. He has to make do with *bonum commune* (which has other quite different meanings in his work) or *bonum generale* or *bonum universale* or plain *bonum*. Endless confusion has resulted, notwithstanding that Aquinas himself was quite clear that, while the object of intelligent desire is always a particular (thing, action, state of affairs), nevertheless that particular is always so desired *secundum aliquam rationem universalem* or *sub communi ratione boni*: see *S.T.* I. q. 80, a. 2 ad 2;

II–II, q. 24, a. 1c. For the notion of value (as contrasted with particular objective) used here, see G. Grisez and R. Shaw, *Beyond the New Morality* (Notre Dame and London: 1974), ch. 2 and 7.

The shift of interest from urge or inclination to concern for value ... Hence, at this second level, 'something's being good is its having the properties that it is *rational to* want in things of its kind ... the criteria of evaluation differ from one kind of thing to another. Since we want things for different purposes, it is obviously rational to assess them by different features': Rawls, *Theory of Justice*, pp. 405–6 (emphasis added). But intelligence or reason also evaluates the various 'different purposes', by reference to *basic* values ('things' which it is 'rational to want' simply for one's 'well-being'), such as truth (and knowledge of it).

Knowledge is an intrinsic and basic form of good ... Thus knowledge is a *bonum honestum*, in the classical distinction between *bonum honestum, bonum utile* and *bonum delectabile*: see Aquinas, *S.T.* I–II, q. 94, a. 2; q. 100, a. 5 ad 5. For *honestum* does not necessarily mean *morally* worthy, as many English translations suggest. A *bonum honestum* is simply a good that is worth while having or doing or effecting for its own sake, and not just for the sake of any utility it may have as a means to some other good, nor just for the pleasure it may afford. Moral good is thus just one sort of *bonum honestum*. For the threefold distinction, see Aquinas, *in Eth.* para. 58 (on 1095b17–18); *S.T.* I, q. 5, a. 6; I–II, q. 34, a. 2 ad 1; II–II, q. 145, a. 3; following Ambrose, *De Officiis*, I, c. 9, following Cicero, *De Officiis*, II, c. 3. See also Aristotle, *Nic. Eth.* VIII, 2: 1155b18–20; II, 2: 1104b31–32 with *Gauthier–Jolif*, ad loc., which points out that Aristotle is simply adopting a commonplace and is not ascribing great importance to it; also *Topics*, I, 13: 105a28; III, 3: 118b28. See notes to VI. 3–4, below, on the three types of *philia* (friendship).

Knowledge is good but can be inappropriately pursued ... See Aquinas, *S.T.* II–II, q. 167, a. 1c on the vice of *curiositas*.

III.3

'Knowledge is a good to be pursued ...' ... This is the mode of formulation of each of the first principles of natural law (of which this principle about truth and knowledge is one), according to Aquinas, *S.T.* I–II, q. 94, a. 2. For the sense of the formula, and sound exegesis of the whole article, see G. Grisez, 'The First Principle of Practical Reason: A Commentary on the *Summa Theologiae*, 1–2, Question 94, Article 2' (1965) 10 *Nat. L.F.* 168, also (abbreviated) in A. Kenny (ed.), *Aquinas: A Collection of Critical Essays* (London: 1970), pp. 340–82.

One's objective constitutes a principle in one's practical reasoning ... See Aristotle, *Nic. Eth.* VI, 5: 1140b17; VI, 12: 1144a31–33; VII, 8: 1151a15–20, with Aquinas, *in Eth.* on the same passages (i.e. paras. 1170, 1273, 1431) and para. 286.

Trains of practical reasoning (the 'practical syllogism') ... See Aristotle, *Nic. Eth.* VI, 9, 12: 1142b22–26, 1144a31–36; VII, 3: 1146b34–1147a36; *de Anima* III, 11: 434a16–21; *de Motu Animalium*, 7: 701a7–33; W. F. R. Hardie, *Aristotle's Ethical Theory* (Oxford: 1968), ch. XII; J. Donald Monan, *Moral Knowledge and its Methodology in Aristotle* (Oxford: 1968), pp. 61–3, 68–72; *Gauthier–Jolif*, II, 209–12, 605–14; David Shwayder, *The Stratification of Behaviour* (London: 1965), pp. 92–104; G. E. M. Anscombe, *Intention* (Oxford: 1958), pp. 57–79.

'Principles' and 'rules' ... '"Principles" and "rules" are often used interchangeably, though the word "principle" usually carries an implication of greater generality and greater

importance than the word "rules". Many of the features which mark the distinction between rules and principles in common discourse are devoid of philosophical importance ... It should be mentioned, however, that the word "principle" is sometimes used to assert an ultimate value or to assert that a value is a reason for action ...': Raz, *Practical Reason*, p. 49. It is the latter use of 'principle', not the 'rule'-like use, that concerns us here. For the more 'rule'-like use of 'principle', see e.g. X.7 below.

Ends and Means ... It is hazardous to use the terms 'ends' and 'means'; the reader must take care lest his thought about ends and means be dominated by any one instance of the relationship. A useful introduction to the different sorts of ends and means is Shwayder, op. cit., pp. 144-8. All the discussions of practical reasoning cited in the preceding note underline the necessity, as a minimum, of distinguishing between (i) actions which are means materially (spatially or temporally ...) *external* to that-to-which-they-are-means (as drawing money from the bank is external to buying this book, and buying this book is external to reading it ...), and (ii) actions which are means *constitutive* of, or *components* or *ingredients* in, or *materially identified* with that-to-which-they-are-means (as reading this book is a way of thinking about certain important matters, which in turn is a way of realizing, actualizing, or instantiating the value of knowledge). To the above citations add, likewise, J. L. Ackrill, 'Aristotle on *Eudaimonia*' (1974) 60 *Proc. Brit. Acad.* 339 at pp. 342-4.

'Participation in value' and 'commitment' ... These notions, as I use them, are rather similar to the existentialist concept of *project*, as explained by George Kateb, 'Freedom and Worldliness in the Thought of Hannah Arendt' (1977) 5 *Political Theory* 141 at 153: 'The project is a task without boundaries; one can never say that it is done, yet the whole meaning of it is found in every action done for its sake. ("For the sake of" does not mean "in order to" [Arendt, *The Human Condition*, Chicago and London: 1958, pp. 154, 156-7]). It is never realized. The fact that I adopt a principle prevents no one else from adopting it; it is inexhaustible ... A principle is not a consideration external to the act and reachable by a neutral method.' Of course, as a matter of *words*, this is precisely *not* my concept of project.

III.4

Self-evidence and having no reason to doubt what seems to be the case ... See Roy Edgley, *Reason in Theory and Practice* (London: 1969), p. 156.

First principles are indemonstrable and self-evident but not innate ... See Aristotle, *Post. Anal.* II, 15: 100a; *Meta.* I, 1: 980b–981a (these texts relate to speculative or theoretical indemonstrable principles, and Aristotle seems to lack any explicit concept of indemonstrable *practical* first principles). Aquinas followed Aristotle's theory of the 'induction' of indemonstrable first principles by insight working on observation, memory, and experience, but extended the account to a parallel 'induction' of indemonstrable first principles of practical reason (i.e. of natural law) by insight working on felt inclinations and a knowledge of possibilities: *S.T.* I–II, q. 94, a. 2 (first principles, naturally known, of natural law); I, q. 79, a. 12 (our natural disposition to know these first practical principles: *synderesis*); I–II, q. 94, a. 1 ad 2 (*synderesis* is the habit of mind which holds the precepts of natural law, which are the first principles of human actions); I–II, q. 10, a. 1c; II–II, q. 47, a. 6c; II–II, q. 79, a. 2 ad 2; *In 2 Sent.*, d. 24, q. 2, a. 3. (for any definite knowledge of first principles we need both sense-experience and memory); d. 39, q. 3, a. 1; *de Veritate*, q. 16, a. 1; *in Eth.* VI, lect. 12 (para. 1249).

Sexuality and curiosity ... Charles Fried, *An Anatomy of Values* (Cambridge, Mass.: 1970), pp. 88–9, suggests reasons for setting aside the psychologists' hypotheses when considering the *value* of truth.

Self-evident principles of theoretical rationality ... See Michael Slote, *Reason and Scepticism* (London and New York: 1970), p. 220 ('Index of Principles'); G. Grisez, *Beyond the New Theism* (Notre Dame and London: 1975), pp. 76–81, 114, 134–5, 168–72, 392; J. Boyle, G. Grisez, and O. Tollefsen, *Free Choice: A Self-Referential Argument* (Notre Dame and London: 1976), pp. 144–52, 168–77.

Principles of formal logic in scientific reasoning ... See, e.g., R. Harré, *The Principles of Scientific Thinking* (London: 1970), pp. 140–1; W. Sellars, *Science, Perception and Reality* (London and New York: 1963), p. 295; and generally Henry E. Kyburg, *Philosophy of Science: A Formal Approach* (New York and London: 1968).

III.5

'*The good is what all things desire*' ... See Aristotle, *Topics*, III, 1: 116a19–20; *Rhet*. I, 6: 1362a23; *Nic. Eth*. I, 1: 1094a3. As Aquinas points out in his commentary on this last-mentioned passage, Aristotle is not asserting that there is some one good thing which everything is tending towards; rather he is indicating the general conception of good (*bonum communiter sumptum*). As Aquinas also points out, 'desire' here really means 'tend towards', such 'tending' being unconscious, instinctive, conscious, or truly volitional depending on the nature of the subject of the tendency. It is only by an extended analogy that our notions of desire or *appetitus*, and even of good, are applied to beings which act without awareness of objectives and without freedom to choose to pursue or reject them: see Aquinas, *in Meta*. paras. 999–1000 (on *Meta*. V, 14: 1020b26). True, as metaphysicians both Aristotle and Aquinas hold a 'teleological view of the world' something like that described by Hart, *Concept of Law*, pp. 184–7 (but see note to II.4, above). But both would have regarded as a false contrast the view, ascribed to them by Hart (ibid., p. 186), that man's 'optimum state is not man's good or end because he desires it; rather he desires it because it is already his natural end.' Metaphysically, in their view, desire is explained by end *in one explanatory perspective* (see the next note, below), while end is explained by desire *in another explanatory perspective* (see, e.g. *S.T*. I–II, q. 94, a. 2c); and in a third explanatory perspective (equally legitimate, in their view), both desire and end are accounted for by the essence or nature of the being (here, man) (see, e.g., *S.T*. I, q. 77, a. 6; and see XIII.4, below). But both Aristotle and Aquinas consider that 'practical philosophy' (including ethics) is a rational inquiry distinct from metaphysics; both are clear that in ethics one looks not for explanations of the form 'A desires X because it is his natural end'; rather, one is looking for reasons for action that are good as reasons. And Aquinas, at least, is quite explicit that the search for good reasons for desiring and choosing and acting comes to an end not in the speculative (i.e. theoretical) propositions of metaphysics but in indemonstrable *practical* principles which are self-evident (*per se nota*) and in need of no further explanation: such as '*truth* is a good to be pursued ...': see *S.T*. I–II, q. 94, a. 2; see also notes to III.4, above.

Objects are desired as desirable, and considered desirable as making one better-off ... This is implicit throughout Aristotle's ethics and is made explicit in sympathetic commentaries such as Aquinas, *in Eth*. paras. 1552 (on 1155b20) and 257 (on 1103b31–33). The tersest formulations are in Aquinas, *S. T*. I, q. 5, a. 1c and ad 1: 'The goodness of something consists in its being desirable [*appetibile*]; hence Aristotle's dictum that *good is what all things desire*. Now desirability is consequent upon completion (or fulfilment) for things always desire their completion ... The term "good" expresses the idea of desirable completion [*bonum dicit rationem perfecti quod est appetibile*]'; see also I, q. 5, a. 3c; q. 48, a. 1c; q. 6, a. 3c: '... a thing is called "good" in so far as it is [considered by the speaker to be] complete ...'. In the present instance, one's being well informed etc. is the relevant 'completion', and knowledge and the means involved in acquiring and retaining it are good and desirable as 'completing' ('perfecting'). Thus Aquinas himself remarks, commenting on Aristotle: 'All knowledge is obviously good, because the good of anything is that which belongs to the fullness of being which all things seek after and desire; and man as man reaches fullness of being through knowledge'; *in De Anima*, intro., s. 3; cf., as to 'good' and 'fulness of being', *S.T.* I–II, q. 18, a. 1c. Or again: 'by the fact that they [persons] know something, they are completed by the true': *De Veritate*, q. 21, a. 3c. On the relation between the desired, the desirable, and the perfective in Aquinas's notion of good, see Ronald Duska, 'Aquinas's Definition of Good: Ethical-Theoretical Notes on *De Veritate*, Q. 21' (1974) 58 *The Monist* 151 at pp. 152–8 (only).

'*Value judgments seem to those who make them to be objective but really succeed in saying nothing more about the world than that the speakers have certain desires*' ... J. L. Mackie, *Ethics: Inventing Right and Wrong* (Harmondsworth: 1977), ch. 1, lucidly argues for a sceptical thesis like this; he mentions 'objectification', in order to explain why people are under the delusion (as he deems it) that their practical principles are fundamentally objective and rational; similar, in both respects, is E. Westermarck, *Ethical Relativity* (London: 1932), p. 143 and *passim*. Both Mackie's main arguments (the one from 'queerness', the other from the diversity of human opinions about value) are briefly attended to in the text, above. Fundamental to such positions as Mackie's (and explicit on pp. 39–40 of his book) is a metaphysics and epistemology of a philosophical doctrine (which can be more or less subtle) of empiricism. For a fundamental critique of empiricism and of its conception of objectivity, see B. J. Lonergan, *Insight: A Study of Human Understanding* (London: 1957), chs. I–V, VIII–XIV, esp. pp. 411–16. In assessing Mackie's difficulties with the notion of 'objective prescriptivity' (op. cit., p. 47) (e.g. with the notion that knowledge really is a good and really is to be pursued), observe that he considers that, while the prescriptivity (to-be-pursuedness) of a way of being is *not* self-evident even for one who understands correctly that that way of being is thoroughly appropriate for human beings (because it fully develops their capacities and gives deepest satisfaction), nevertheless the *objective* prescriptivity of a way of being *would* be established by the fact that God (if there were a God) had issued a command requiring men to live in that way: ibid., pp. 230–2. For a critique of this and other 'will' theories of prescriptivity, normativity, and obligation, see XI.8 (excursus to notes), XI.9; and cf. XIII.5, below.

The significance of the variety of ethical opinions ... See notes to II.3, above; see also V.10 below. Bear in mind the remark of Wilfrid Sellars, *Science and Metaphysics* (London and New York: 1968), p. 223: '... reasoning from the moral point of view proceeds in a context of ignorance and diversity of opinion. But, then, the same is true of consensus on matters of fact, scientific laws and theoretical principles.' To like effect, see Alan Gewirth, 'Positive "Ethics" and Normative "Science"' (1960) 69 *Philosophical Review* 311–330, reprinted in Thomson and Dworkin (eds.), *Ethics* (New York: 1968), 27–47, at ibid., p. 32; and P. T. Geach, *The Virtues* (Cambridge: 1977), pp. 14–15.

III.6

Self-refutation ... For a much fuller statement of the argument of this section, including explanation of my use of terms such as 'proposition', 'statement', 'sentence', etc., see Finnis, 'Scepticism, Self-Refutation and the Good of Truth', in *Essays*, 247 at pp. 250–4, 258–66. To the references to the literature given there, add (more recent), Boyle, Grisez, and Tollefsen, *Free Choice: A Self-Referential Argument*, pp. 122–38.

IV

THE OTHER BASIC VALUES

IV.1 THEORETICAL STUDIES OF 'UNIVERSAL' VALUES

CURIOSITY is not the only basic urge, inclination, or interest. Knowledge is not the only basic aspect of human well-being. The last chapter was devoted to a reflection on the value of knowledge, not because that value is more important or basic than all other values, but simply because the materials for an analysis were so readily available, in a form substantially common to each reader, in the shape of his own commitment to understanding (including understanding that chapter itself). So we may now widen our reflections on our interests and commitments, and ask whether there are other basic values besides knowledge, other indemonstrable but self-evident principles shaping our practical reasoning.

Such a course of reflection is, in a way, an attempt to understand one's own character, or nature. The attempt thus parallels attempts made, in quite another way, by those anthropologists and psychologists who ask (in effect) whether there is a human nature and what are its characteristics. The anthropological and psychological studies ought to be regarded as an aid in answering our own present question—not, indeed, by way of any 'inference' from universality or 'human nature' to values (an inference that would be merely fallacious), but by way of an assemblage of reminders of the range of possibly worthwhile activities and orientations open to one.

To anyone who surveys the literature, whether on ethics (or other practical modes of thinking about values) or on anthropology (or other 'theoretical' modes of investigating what humans value) it is obvious that investigation of the basic aspects of human well-being (real or supposed) is not easy. The difficulty manifests itself (a) in arbitrary and implausible reductions of the many basic values to one (or two, or three) values, or of the many basic inclinations or interests to one (or two, or three) basic inclinations or interests; (*b*) in lists of basic tendencies (or values, or features of human nature) which as lists are incoherent because drawn up on shifting criteria; and (*c*) in short-winded analyses which mention a few tendencies, values, or features, and then tail off into 'etc.' or 'and other basic values' ... etc. (not for convenience, as in this sentence, but for want of sustained attention to the problem).

Reductionism, cross-categorization, and the daunting variety of the lists offered by investigators, can be overcome by steady attention to distinctions drawn and emphasized in the preceding chapter. Recall, first of all, the distinction between the brute fact of an urge (or drive or inclination or tendency) and the forms of good which one who has such urges can think it worth while to pursue and realize, on the ground not that he has the urges but that he can see the good of such pursuit and realization. Secondly, and *a fortiori*, recall the distinction between the material conditions for, or affecting, the pursuit of a value and the value itself. A sound brain and intelligence are necessary conditions for the understanding, pursuit, and realization of truth, but neither brainpower nor intelligence should appear in a list of basic values: knowledge is the relevant value. Or again, H. L. A. Hart's 'natural facts and aims',[1] or 'truisms' about human beings, concern the material and psychological conditions ('the setting') under which persons seek their various ends (and his list of universally recognized or 'indisputable' ends contains only one entry: survival). Thirdly, in listing the basic values in which human beings may participate, recall the distinctions between general value and particular goal, and between ends and the means for attaining, realizing, or participating in those ends. Amongst these means are to be included the many intermediate and subordinate ends involved in such wide-ranging, long-lasting, and fecund means as languages, institutions like laws or property, or an economy. Thus, for example, John Rawls's 'primary goods' (liberty, opportunity, wealth, and self-respect) are primary, in his view, not because they are the basic *ends* of human life but because 'it is rational to want these goods whatever else is wanted, *since* they are in general *necessary for* the

---

[1] *Concept of Law*, pp. 190, 191, 195.

framing and the execution of a rational plan of life';[2] see V.3, VIII.5, below.

Students of ethics and of human cultures very commonly assume that cultures manifest preferences, motivations, and evaluations so wide and chaotic in their variety that no values or practical principles can be said to be self-evident to human beings, since no value or practical principle is recognized in all times and all places: cf. II.3, above. But those philosophers who have recently sought to test this assumption, by surveying the anthropological literature (including the similar general surveys made by professional anthropologists), have found with striking unanimity that this assumption is unwarranted.

These surveys entitle us, indeed, to make some rather confident assertions. All human societies show a concern for the value of human life; in all, self-preservation is generally accepted as a proper motive for action, and in none is the killing of other human beings permitted without some fairly definite justification. All human societies regard the procreation of a new human life as in itself a good thing unless there are special circumstances. No human society fails to restrict sexual activity; in all societies there is some prohibition of incest, some opposition to boundless promiscuity and to rape, some favour for stability and permanence in sexual relations. All human societies display a concern for truth, through education of the young in matters not only practical (e.g. avoidance of dangers) but also speculative or theoretical (e.g. religion). Human beings, who can survive infancy only by nurture, live in or on the margins of some society which invariably extends beyond the nuclear family, and all societies display a favour for the values of co-operation, of common over individual good, of obligation between individuals, and of justice within groups. All know friendship. All have some conception of *meum* and *tuum*, title or property, and of reciprocity. All value play, serious and formalized, or relaxed and recreational. All treat the bodies of dead members of the group in some traditional and ritual fashion different from their procedures for rubbish disposal. All display a concern for powers or principles which

---

[2] *Theory of Justice*, p. 433 (emphasis added).

are to be respected as suprahuman; in one form or another, religion is universal.

Certainly, there seems to be no practical principle which has the specificity we expect of a 'moral rule' and which is accepted, even 'in principle' or 'in theory', amongst all human beings. But my present concern is not at all with 'morals' or 'ethics'. The emergence of ethical judgment as a mode of practical judgment is treated in the next chapter. My present concern is the universality of those basic value judgments that are manifested not only in various moral requirements and restrictions but also in the many forms of human culture, institutions, and initiative. For in so far as we can 'see the point' of a human institution, art, or endeavour, even one very remote from us and open to our criticism or distaste, there is put before us a revelation or reminder of the range of opportunities open to us in shaping our own life through the free and selective pursuit of the basic values: III.4. The universality of a few basic values in a vast diversity of realizations emphasizes *both* the connection between a basic human urge/drive/inclination/tendency and the corresponding basic form of human good, *and* at the same time the great difference between following an urge and intelligently pursuing a particular realization of a form of human good that is never completely realized and exhausted by any one action, or lifetime, or institution, or culture (nor by any finite number of them): III.3.

This plasticity of human inclinations, which correlates with the generality or universality of the corresponding values understood by one's practical intelligence, is important for an accurate grasp not only of human anthropology and history but also of the human virtues and vices, conscience and ethics (the subjects of the next chapter). So it is worth dwelling upon.

Consider again the drive of curiosity. It finds its response and satisfaction in the intellectual cathedrals of science, mathematics, and philosophy, whose ramifications and sophistications are beyond the grasp of even the most dedicated individual. But equally it finds a response and satisfaction in detective stories, daily newspapers, and gossip. Universally the practical principle that truth is a good worth attaining (and that mistake, muddle, and misinformation are to be avoided) is applied by human beings to whatever form of knowledge-gathering they choose to interest themselves in or commit themselves to. The unity of practical principle is as important as the immense diversity of method.

Besides limitless diversity in such forms of pursuit, there is diversity in the depth, intensity, duration of commitment, in the extent to which the pursuit of a given value is given priority in the shaping of one's life and character. One man's recognition of the value of truth may elicit from him the response of a lifetime of austere self-discipline and intellectual grind; another's may evoke a commitment sufficient only to enjoy the intellectual play of a good argument; another's may carry him no further than a disposition to grumble at the lying propaganda on his television set ... This diversity results not only from the fact that truth is not the only basic value, but also from the fact that human beings (and thus whole cultures) differ in their determination, enthusiasm, sobriety, far-sightedness, sensitivity, steadfastness, and all the other modalities of response to *any* value.

IV.2 THE BASIC FORMS OF HUMAN GOOD: A PRACTICAL REFLECTION

It is now time to revert, from the descriptive or 'speculative' findings of anthropology and psychology, to the critical and essentially practical discipline in which each reader must ask himself: What *are* the basic aspects of my well-being? Here each one of us, however extensive his knowledge of the interests of other people and other cultures, is alone with his own intelligent grasp of the indemonstrable (because self-evident) first principles of his own practical reasoning. From one's capacity to grasp intelligently the basic forms of good as 'to-be-pursued' one gets one's ability, in the descriptive disciplines of history and anthropology, to sympathetically (though not uncritically) see the point of actions, life-styles, characters, and cultures that one would not choose for oneself. And one's speculative knowledge of other people's interests and achievements does not leave unaffected one's practical understanding of the forms of good that lie open to one's choice. But there is no inference from fact to value. At this point in our discourse (or private meditation), inference and proof are left behind (or left until later), and the proper form of discourse is: '... is a good, in itself, don't you think?'.

Remember: by 'good', 'basic good', 'value', 'well-being', etc. I do *not* yet mean 'moral good', etc.

What, then, are the basic forms of good for us?

A. *Life*

A first basic value, corresponding to the drive for self-preservation, is the value of life. The term 'life' here signifies every aspect of the vitality (*vita*, life) which puts a human being in good shape for self-determination. Hence, life here includes bodily (including cerebral) health, and freedom from the pain that betokens organic malfunctioning or injury. And the recognition, pursuit, and realization of this basic human purpose (or internally related group of purposes) are as various as the crafty struggle and prayer of a man overboard seeking to stay afloat until his ship turns back for him; the team-work of surgeons and the whole network of supporting staff, ancillary services, medical schools, etc.; road safety laws and programmes; famine relief expeditions; farming and rearing and fishing; food marketing; the resuscitation of suicides; watching out as one steps off the kerb ...

Perhaps we should include in this category the transmission of life by procreation of children. Certainly it is tempting to treat procreation as a distinct, irreducibly basic value, corresponding to the inclination to mate/reproduce/rear. But while there are good reasons for distinguishing the urge to copulate from both the urge to self-preservation and the maternal or paternal instincts, the analytical situation is different when we shift from the level of urges/instincts/drives to the level of intelligently grasped forms of good. There may be said to be one drive (say, to copulate) and one physical release for that drive (or a range of such physical forms); but as a human action, pursuit and realization of value, sexual intercourse may be play, and/or expression of love or friendship, and/or an effort to procreate. So, likewise, we need not be analytically content with an anthropological convention which treats sexuality, mating, and family life as a single category or unit of investigation; nor with an ethical judgment that treats the family, and the procreation and education of children, as an indistinguishable cluster of moral responsibilities. We can distinguish the desire and decision to have a child, simply for the sake of bearing a child, from the desire and decision to cherish and to educate the child. The former desire and decision is a pursuit of the good of life, in this case life-in-its-transmission; the latter desires and decisions are aspects of the pursuit of the distinct basic values of sociability (or friendship) and truth (truth-in-its-communication), running alongside the continued pursuit of the value of life that is involved in simply keeping the child alive and well until it can fend for itself.

B. Knowledge

The second basic value I have already discussed: it is knowledge, considered as desirable for its own sake, not merely instrumentally.

C. Play

The third basic aspect of human well-being is play. A certain sort of moralist analysing human goods may overlook this basic value, but an anthropologist will not fail to observe this large and irreducible element in human culture. More importantly, each one of us can see the point of engaging in performances which have no point beyond the performance itself, enjoyed for its own sake. The performance may be solitary or social, intellectual or physical, strenuous or relaxed, highly structured or relatively informal, conventional or *ad hoc* in its pattern ... An element of play can enter into any human activity, even the drafting of enactments, but is always analytically distinguishable from its 'serious' context; and some activities, enterprises, and institutions are entirely or primarily pure play. Play, then, has and is its own value.

D. Aesthetic experience

The fourth basic component in our flourishing is aesthetic experience. Many forms of play, such as dance or song or football, are the matrix or occasion of aesthetic experience. But beauty is not an indispensable element of play. Moreover, beautiful form can be found and enjoyed in nature. Aesthetic experience, unlike play, need not involve an action of one's own;

what is sought after and valued for its own sake may simply
be the beautiful form 'outside' one, and the 'inner' experience of
appreciation of its beauty. But often enough the valued
experience is found in the creation and/or active appreciation
of some *work* of significant and satisfying form.

E. *Sociability* (*friendship*)

Fifthly, there is the value of that sociability which in its
weakest form is realized by a minimum of peace and harmony
amongst men, and which ranges through the forms of human
community to its strongest form in the flowering of full friendship. Some of the collaboration between one person and another
is no more than instrumental to the realization by each of his
own individual purposes. But friendship involves acting for the
sake of one's friend's purposes, one's friend's well-being. To be in
a relationship of friendship with at least one other person is
a fundamental form of good, is it not?

Friendship and, to a lesser degree, the other forms of
sociability are of special significance for the theme of this
book, and so are more amply discussed later: VI.2–4.

F. *Practical reasonableness*

Sixthly, there is the basic good of being able to bring one's own
intelligence to bear effectively (in practical reasoning that issues
in action) on the problems of choosing one's actions and life-
style and shaping one's own character. Negatively, this involves
that one has a measure of effective freedom; positively, it
involves that one seeks to bring an intelligent and reasonable
order into one's own actions and habits and practical attitudes.
This order in turn has (i) an internal aspect, as when one strives
to bring one's emotions and dispositions into the harmony of an
inner peace of mind that is not merely the product of drugs or
indoctrination nor merely passive in its orientation; and (ii) an
external aspect, as when one strives to make one's actions
(which are external in that they change states of affairs in
the world and often enough affect the relations between persons)
authentic, that is to say, genuine realizations of one's own freely
ordered evaluations, preferences, hopes, and self-determination. This value is thus complex, involving freedom and reason,
integrity and authenticity. But it has a sufficient unity to be

treated as one; and for a label I choose 'practical reasonableness'. This value is the theme of Chapter V.

G. 'Religion'

Seventhly, and finally in this list, there is the value of what,
since Cicero, we summarily and lamely call 'religion'. For, as
there is the order of means to ends, and the pursuit of life, truth,
play, and aesthetic experience in some individually selected
order of priorities and pattern of specialization, and the
order that can be brought into human relations through
collaboration, community, and friendship, and the order that is
to be brought into one's character and activity through inner
integrity and outer authenticity, so, finally there arise such
questions as: (a) How are all these orders, which have their
immediate origin in human initiative and pass away in death,
related to the lasting order of the whole cosmos and to the
origin, if any, of that order? (b) Is it not perhaps the case that
human freedom, in which one rises above the determinism of
instinct and impulse to an intelligent grasp of worthwhile forms
of good, and through which one shapes and masters one's
environment but also one's own character, is itself somehow
subordinate to something which makes that human freedom,
human intelligence, and human mastery possible (not just 'originally' but from moment to moment) and which is free, intelligent, and sovereign in a way (and over a range) no human
being can be?

Misgivings may be aroused by the notion that one of the
basic human values is the establishment and maintenance of
proper relationships between oneself (and the orders one can
create and maintain) and the divine. For there are, always,
those who doubt or deny that the universal order-of-things
has any origin beyond the 'origins' known to the natural
sciences, and who answer question (b) negatively. But is it
reasonable to deny that it is, at any rate, peculiarly important
to have thought reasonably and (where possible) correctly
about these questions of the origins of cosmic order and of
human freedom and reason—whatever the answer to those
questions turns out to be, and even if the answers have to be
agnostic or negative? And does not that importance in large
part consist in this: that if there is a transcendent origin of the

universal order-of-things and of human freedom and reason,
then one's life and actions are in fundamental disorder if they
are not brought, as best one can, into some sort of harmony
with whatever can be known or surmised about that transcendent other and its lasting order? More important for us than
the ubiquity of expressions of religious concerns, in all human
cultures, is the question: Does not one's own sense of 'responsibility', in choosing what one is to be and do, amount to a
concern that is not reducible to the concern to live, play,
procreate, relate to others, and be intelligent? Does not even a
Sartre, taking as his *point de départ* that God does not exist (and
that therefore 'everything is permitted'), none the less
appreciate that he is 'responsible'—obliged to act with freedom
and authenticity, and to will the liberty of other persons
equally with his own—in choosing what he is to be; and all this,
because, *prior to* any choice of his, 'man' is and is-to-be
free?[3] And is this not a recognition (however residual) of, and
concern about, an order of things 'beyond' each and every man?
And so, without wishing to beg any question, may we not for
convenience call that concern, which is concern for a good
consisting in an irreducibly distinct form of order, 'religious'?
The present remarks are no more than place-holders; I discuss
the issue on its merits in Chapter XIII.5.

IV.3   AN EXHAUSTIVE LIST?

Now besides life, knowledge, play, aesthetic experience, friendship, practical reasonableness, and religion, there are countless
objectives and forms of good. But I suggest that these other
objectives and forms of good will be found, on analysis, to be
ways or combinations of ways of pursuing (not always sensibly)
and realizing (not always successfully) one of the seven basic
forms of good, or some combination of them.

Moreover, there are countless aspects of human self-determination and self-realization besides the seven basic aspects
which I have listed. But these other aspects, such as courage,
generosity, moderation, gentleness, and so on, are not themselves basic values; rather, they are ways (not means, but

---

[3] J.-P. Sartre, *L'Existentialisme est un humanisme* (Paris: 1946), pp. 36, 83–4.

modes) of pursuing the basic values, and fit (or are deemed by some individual, or group, or culture, to fit) a man for their pursuit.

In this way we can analytically unravel even very 'peculiar' conventions, norms, institutions, and orders of preference, such as the aristocratic code of honour that demanded direct attacks on life in duelling.

Again, though the pursuit of the basic values is made psychologically possible by the corresponding inclinations and urges of one's nature, still there are many inclinations and urges that do not correspond to or support any basic value: for example, the inclination to take more than one's share, or the urge to gratuitous cruelty. There is no need to consider whether these urges are more, or less, 'natural' (in terms of frequency, universality, intensity, etc.) than those urges which correspond to the basic values. For I am not trying to justify our recognition and pursuit of basic values by deducing from, or even by pointing to, any set of inclinations. The point, rather, is that selfishness, cruelty, and the like, simply do not stand to something self-evidently good as the urge to self-preservation stands to the self-evident good of human life. Selfishness, cruelty, etc., stand in need of some explanation, in a way that curiosity, friendliness, etc., do not. (This is not to say that physiologists and psychologists should not investigate the physical and psychosomatic substructure of curiosity, friendliness, etc.) Often enough the explanation will be that the pursuit of a value (say, truth), or of a standard material means to sustaining a value (say, food), becomes locked into a pattern of exclusiveness or inversion—producing selfish indifference to the inclusive realization of that same value in the lives of others, and to the intrinsic value of sharing goods in friendship. Or again, cruelty may be found to be an inverted form of pursuit of the value of freedom and self-determination and authenticity: a man may make himself 'feel real' to himself by subjecting others to his utter mastery. In the absence of such explanations, and of psychosomatic disease, we find these urges as baffling as persistent illogicality, as opaque and pointless as, say, a demand for a plate of mud for no reason at all.

But are there just seven basic values, no more and no less? And what is meant by calling them basic?

There is no magic in the number seven, and others who have reflected on these matters have produced slightly different lists, usually slightly longer. There is no need for the reader to accept the present list, just as it stands, still less its nomenclature (which simply gestures towards categories of human purpose that are each, though unified, nevertheless multi-faceted). My brief discussion of the problem of whether procreation should be treated as an analytically distinct category of human good illustrates the scope that exists for modification of the details of the list. Still, it seems to me that those seven purposes are all of the basic purposes of human action, and that any other purpose which you or I might recognize and pursue will turn out to represent, or be constituted of, some aspect(s) of some or all of them.

VI.4 ALL EQUALLY FUNDAMENTAL

More important than the precise number and description of these values is the sense in which each is basic. First, each is equally self-evidently a form of good. Secondly, none can be analytically reduced to being merely an aspect of any of the others, or to being merely instrumental in the pursuit of any of the others. Thirdly, each one, when we focus on it, can reasonably be regarded as the most important. Hence there is no objective hierarchy amongst them. Let me amplify this third point, which includes the other two.

If one focuses on the value of speculative truth, it can reasonably be regarded as more important than anything; knowledge can be regarded as the most important thing to acquire; life can be regarded as merely a pre-condition, of lesser or no intrinsic value; play can be regarded as frivolous; one's concern about 'religious' questions can seem just an aspect of the struggle against error, superstition, and ignorance; friendship can seem worth forgoing, or be found exclusively in sharing and enhancing knowledge; and so on. But one can shift one's focus. If one is drowning, or, again, if one is thinking about one's child who died soon after birth, one is inclined to shift one's focus to the value of life simply as such. The life will not be regarded as a mere pre-condition of anything else; rather, play and knowledge and religion will seem secondary, even rather optional extras. But one can shift one's focus, in this way, one-by-one right round the circle of basic values that constitute the horizon of our opportunities. We can focus on play, and reflect that we spend most of our time working simply in order to afford leisure; play is performances enjoyed for their own sake as performances and thus can seem to be the point of everything; knowledge and religion and friendship can seem pointless unless they issue in the playful mastery of wisdom, or participation in the play of the divine puppetmaster (as Plato said),[4] or in the playful intercourse of mind or body that friends can most enjoy.

Thus I have illustrated this point in relation to life, truth, and play; the reader can easily test and confirm it in relation to each of the other basic values. Each is fundamental. None is more fundamental than any of the others, for each can reasonably be focused upon, and each, when focused upon, claims a priority of value. Hence there is no objective priority of value amongst them.

Of course, each one of us can reasonably *choose* to treat one or some of the values as of more importance in *his* life. A scholar chooses to dedicate himself to the pursuit of knowledge, and thus gives its demands priority, to a greater or lesser degree (and perhaps for a whole lifetime), over the friendships, the worship, the games, the art and beauty that he might otherwise enjoy. He might have been out saving lives through medicine or famine relief, but he chooses not to. But he may change his priorities; he may risk his life to save a drowning man, or give up his career to nurse a sick wife or to fight for his community. The change is not in the relation between the basic values as that relation might reasonably have seemed to him before he chose his life-plan (and as it should always seem to him when he is considering human opportunity and flourishing in general); rather, the change is in his chosen life-plan. That chosen plan *made* truth more important and fundamental for him. His new choice changes the status of that value *for him*; the change is in him. Each of us has a subjective order of priority amongst the basic values; this ranking is no doubt partly shifting and partly stable, but is in any case essential if we are to

---

[4] *Laws*, VII: 685, 803–4; see XIII.5, below.

act at all to some purpose. But one's reasons for choosing the particular ranking that one does choose are reasons that properly relate to one's temperament, upbringing, capacities, and opportunities, not to differences of rank of intrinsic value between the basic values.

Thomas Aquinas, in his formal discussion of the basic forms of good and self-evident primary principles of practical reasoning—which he calls the first principles and most general precepts of natural law[5]—sets a questionable example. For he arranges the precepts in a threefold order: (i) human life is a good to be sustained, and what threatens it is to be prevented; (ii) the coupling of man and woman, and the education of their young, etc., is to be favoured, and what opposes it is to be avoided; (iii) knowledge (especially of the truth about God), sociable life, and practical reasonableness are goods, and ignorance, offence to others, and practical unreasonableness are to be avoided. And his rationale for this threefold ordering (which all too easily is interpreted as a ranking) is that the self-preservative inclinations corresponding to the first category are common not just to all men but to all things which have a definite nature; that the sexual-reproductive inclinations corresponding to the second category of goods are shared by human beings with all other animate life; and that the inclinations corresponding to the third category are peculiar to mankind. Now all this is no doubt true, and quite pertinent in a metaphysical meditation on the continuity of human order with the universal order-of-things (of which human nature is a microcosmos, incorporating all levels of being: inorganic, organic, ... mental ...). But is it relevant to a meditation on the *value* of the various basic aspects of human well-being? Are not speculative considerations intruding into a reconstruction of principles that are practical and that, being primary, indemonstrable, and self-evident, are not derivable (nor sought by Aquinas to be derived) from any speculative considerations? As it happens, Aquinas's threefold ordering quite properly plays no part in his practical (ethical) elaboration of the significance and consequences of the primary precepts of natural law: for example, the 'first-order' good of life may not, in his view, be deliberately attacked

[5] *S.T.* I–II, q. 94, a. 2c.

even in order to preserve the 'third-order' good of friendship with God.[6] In ethical reflection the threefold order should be set aside as an irrelevant schematization.

IV.5 IS PLEASURE THE POINT OF IT ALL?

At the opposite extreme, so to speak, from Thomas Aquinas's injection of metaphysical considerations into the reconstruction of practical discourse, is the characteristically modern mistake of trying to find a form of human well-being yet more basic and important to man than any of the seven basic values— namely some form of experience (such as 'pleasure', or 'peace of mind', or 'freedom' considered as an experience of 'floating', etc.) or set of experiences (such as 'happiness', in the common, casual sense of that word, or 'bliss'). But this notion that pleasure, or any other real or imagined internal feeling, is the point of everything is mistaken. It makes nonsense of human history and anthropology. More importantly, it simply mislocates what is really worth while.

Carry out the thought-experiment skilfully proposed by Robert Nozick.[7] Suppose you could be plugged into an 'experience machine' which, by stimulating your brain while you lay floating in a tank, would afford you all the experiences you choose, with all the variety (if any) you could want: but you must plug in for a lifetime or not at all. On reflection, is it not clear, first, that you would not choose a lifetime of 'thrills' or 'pleasurable tingles' or other experiences of that type? But, secondly, is it not clear that one would not choose the *experiences* of discovering an important theorem, or of winning an exciting game, or of sharing a satisfying friendship, or of reading or writing a great novel, or even of seeing God ... or any combination of such experiences? The fact is, is it not, that if one were sensible one would not choose to plug into the experience machine *at all*. For, as Nozick rightly concludes, one wants to *do* certain things (not just have the experience of doing them); one wants to *be* a certain sort of person, through one's own authentic, free self-determination and self-realization; one

---

[6] *S.T.* II–II, q. 64, a. 5 ad 2; a. 6 ad 2; III, q. 68, a. 11 ad 3.

[7] *Anarchy, State and Utopia* (Oxford: 1974), pp. 42–5. See also Aristotle, *Eud. Eth.* I, 5: 1216a.

wants to *live* (in the active sense) oneself, making a real world through that real pursuit of values that inevitably involves making one's personality in and through one's free commitment to those values.

The pursuit and realization of any of the basic values is effected partly through physical routines (many of which, when successfully consummated, give more-or-less physical pleasure); and partly through programmes, schemes, and courses of action (each of which includes physical routines, has a more-or-less specific goal, and gives satisfaction when successfully completed). But one's self-determination and self-realization is never consummated, never successfully and finally completed. And none of the basic aspects of one's well-being is ever fully realized or finally completed. Nor does a basic value lie at the end of one's choice, activity, and life in the way that the culmination of a physical performance and the goal of a definite course of action typically lie at the end of the performance or course of action. So 'pursuit' and 'realization' are rather misleading in their connotations here, and it is convenient to say that one *participates* in the basic values: III.3. By participating in them in the way one chooses to, one hopes not only for the pleasure of successfully consummated physical performance and the satisfaction of successfully completed projects, but also for 'happiness' in the deeper, less usual sense of that word in which it signifies, roughly, a fullness of life, a certain development as a person, a meaningfulness of one's existence.

The experiences of discovery ('Eureka!') or creative play or living through danger are pleasurable, satisfying, and valuable; but it is because we want to make the discovery or to create or to 'survive' that we want the experiences. What matters to us, in the final analysis, is knowledge, significantly patterned or testing performances (and performing them), beautiful form (and appreciating it), friendship (and being a friend), freedom, self-direction, integrity, and authenticity, and (if such there be) the transcendent origin, ground, and end of all things (and *being* in accord with it). If these give pleasure, this experience is one aspect of their reality as human goods, which are not participated in fully unless their goodness is experienced as such. But a participation in basic goods which is emotionally dry,

subjectively unsatisfying, nevertheless is good and meaningful
as far as it goes.

So it is that the practical principles which enjoin one to participate in those basic forms of good, through the practically
intelligent decisions and free actions that constitute one the
person one is and is to be, have been called in the Western
philosophical tradition the first principles of natural law,
because they lay down for us the outlines of everything one
could reasonably want to do, to have, and to be.

NOTES

IV.1

Lists of basic tendencies, or values, or features of human nature ... Thomas E. Davitt, 'The
Basic Values in Law: A Study of the Ethicolegal Implications of Psychology and
Anthropology' (1968) 58 *Trans. Amer. Phil. Soc.* (NS), Part 5, surveys the anthropological, psychological, and philosophical literature and reports: 'Some have said there
is only one basic drive be it regarding sex, economics, will-to-power, or inquiry. Some
have claimed that there are two drives, feeding and breeding. Some have said there
are three drives, self-preservation, reproduction, and gregariousness; or feeding, breeding and inquiring. Others have said there are four fundamental drives, hunger, thirst,
sex and seeking physical wellbeing; or self-maintenance, self-perpetuation, self-
gratification and religion; or self-preservation, procreation, organized co-operation,
and religion; or the visceral, the active, the esthetic, the emotional; or the avoidance
of injury, maintenance, reproduction, and creativity; or self-preservation, nutrition,
sex and gregariousness. Still others have maintained that there are five basic drives
which stand in hierarchical relation to each other, namely, the physical, safety, love,
esteem and self-actualization ... Still others, relating drives to values, list as many
as twelve drives and fourteen values' (pp. 13–14, where Davitt provides bibliographical
references, criticisms, and a list of his own).

Universally recognized values ... Surveys, by philosophers, of the anthropological evidence
and the testimony of general anthropologists include the following (each of which
affirms the universality or virtual universality of the values and norms mentioned in
this section): E. Westermarck, *Ethical Relativity* (London: 1932), ch. VII (Westermarck
was defending ethical relativism but found that all the important 'differences of moral
opinion' between 'savage peoples' and 'civilized nations' 'depend on knowledge or
ignorance of facts, on specific religious or superstitious beliefs, on different degrees of
reflection, or on different conditions of life or other external circumstances' (p. 196)
with the exception of differences of opinion concerning the range of persons to whom
moral duties might be owed); Alexander MacBeath, *Experiments in Living: A Study of
the Nature and Foundations of Ethics or Morals in the Light of Recent Work in Social
Anthropology* (London: 1952); Morris Ginsberg, *On the Diversity of Morals* (London: 1956),
chs. VII and VIII; M. Edel and A. Edel, *Anthropology and Ethics* (Springfield: 1959).
For the most detailed bibliography, see Richard H. Beis, 'Some Contributions of
Anthropology to Ethics' (1964) 28 *Thomist* 174; and Davitt, op. cit.

IV.2

The basic forms of good for us ... My account is substantially similar to G. Grisez and R. Shaw, *Beyond the New Morality: The Responsibilities of Freedom* (Notre Dame and London: 1974), ch. 7. See also (i) the list assembled from philosophical accounts of the 'sorts of things it is rational to desire for their own sakes', in W. K. Frankena, *Ethics* (2nd ed., Englewood Cliffs, New Jersey: 1973), pp. 87–8; (ii) A. H. Maslow's psychological account of basic human needs, in *Motivation and Personality* (New York: 1954), pp. 80–106; (iii) the chapter headings in Robert H. Lowrie, *An Introduction to Cultural Anthropology* (London: 1934). Morris Ginsberg, 'Basic Needs and Moral Ideals' in *The Diversity of Morals*, ch. VII, gives a shorter list, but analyses the relation between self-evident values ('ideals') and corresponding inclinations ('needs') in a manner similar to mine. Cf. Aquinas's rather similar, short but explicitly open-ended lists: *S.T.* I–II, q. 10, a. 1c; q. 94, a. 2c.

Play as a basic aspect of human well-being ... See Johan Huizinga, *Homo Ludens: A Study of the Play-Element in Culture* ([1938] London: 1949; paperback 1970); Josef Pieper, *Leisure, the Basis of Culture* (London: 1952); Hugo Rahner, *Man at Play* ([1949] London: 1965). Huizinga (1970 ed., p. 32) says: 'Summing up the formal characteristics of play, we might call it a free activity standing quite consciously outside "ordinary" life as being "not serious", but at the same time absorbing the player intensely and utterly. It is an activity connected with no material interest, and no profit can be gained by it. It proceeds within its own proper boundaries of time and space according to fixed rules and in an orderly manner ...'. For a reminder that not every element in such a definition is to be found literally obtaining in every instance of what we call games, see L. Wittgenstein, *Philosophical Investigations* (London: 1953), secs. 66–71, 75, 83–4.

Play in drafting enactments ... See the beautiful examples from Old Frisian and Old Icelandic law, quoted in Huizinga, *Homo Ludens* (1970 ed.), pp. 149–51.

Aesthetic experience ... See further the discussion and citations in Finnis, 'Reason and Passion: The Constitutional Dialectic of Free Speech and Obscenity' (1967) 116 *U.Pa. L. Rev.* 222 at pp. 232–7.

Practical intelligence is a basic form of good to be cultivated ... See Aquinas, *S.T.* I–II, q. 94, a. 3c; *De Veritate*, q. 16, a. 1 ad 9. Grisez and Shaw, op. cit., pp. 67–8, prefer to speak here of two basic human purposes, which they label 'integrity' and 'authenticity'.

'Religion' as a basic form of human good ... I follow Grisez in using this label, but am aware that *'religion* is not an analytical concept of anything, but a topical response to certain problems in the Roman subsection of an ecumenic–imperial society': Eric Voegelin, *Order and History*, vol. 4, *The Ecumenic Age* (Baton Rouge: 1974), p. 45; cf. also ibid., vol. I, *Israel and Revelation* (1956), p. 288 n. 47 and p. 376. See Cicero, *De Natura Deorum*, I, 2–4, II, 70–2, analysed by Voegelin, op. cit., vol. 4, at pp. 44–5. On the universality of (i) the search for ultimate explanations of the universal order-of-things and of human life and destiny, and (ii) the attempt to bring human affairs into harmony, actual or ritualistic, with the source of such explanations, see e.g. Davitt, op. cit., pp. 70–4, citing many anthropologists' affirmations of this universality, e.g. Ruth Benedict, 'Religion' in F. Boas (ed.), *General Anthropology* (Boston: 1938), p. 628.

IV.3

Reputation, though not a mere 'means', is not a basic end or value ... A good short exposition of the classical analysis of the worth of reputation is Henry B. Veatch, *Rational Man* (Bloomington, Ind.: 1962), pp. 60–1, showing that reputation is valuable only as a reassuring sign or mark of one's own real achievements and perfections (as measured by the basic values). An intelligent concern for one's reputation is in fact a very complex and close weave of aspects of one's concern for truth, one's concern to be in harmony with other persons, and one's concern for practical reasonableness (an authentic realization of one's basic concerns).

V

THE BASIC REQUIREMENTS OF
PRACTICAL REASONABLENESS

V.1 THE GOOD OF PRACTICAL
REASONABLENESS STRUCTURES OUR
PURSUIT OF GOODS

THERE is no reason to doubt that each of the basic aspects of
human well-being is worth seeking to realize. But there are
many such basic forms of human good; I identified seven. And
each of them can be participated in, and promoted, in an
inexhaustible variety of ways and with an inexhaustible variety
of combinations of emphasis, concentration, and specialization.
To participate thoroughly in any basic value calls for skill, or
at least a thoroughgoing commitment. But our life is short.

By disclosing a horizon of attractive possibilities for us, our
grasp of the basic values thus creates, not answers, the problem
for intelligent decision: What is to be done? What may be left
undone? What is not to be done? We have, in the abstract,
no reason to leave any of the basic goods out of account. But
we do have good reason to choose commitments, projects, and
actions, knowing that choice effectively rules out many alternative reasonable or possible commitment(s), project(s), and
action(s).

To have this choice between commitment to concentration
upon one value (say, speculative truth) and commitment to
others, and between one intelligent and reasonable project (say,
understanding this book) and other eligible projects for giving
definite shape to one's participation in one's selected value, and
between one way of carrying out that project and other
appropriate ways, is the primary respect in which we can call
ourselves both free and responsible.

For amongst the basic forms of good that we have no good
reason to leave out of account is the good of practical
reasonableness, which is participated in precisely by shaping
one's participation in the other basic goods, by guiding one's
commitments, one's selection of projects, and what one does
in carrying them out.

The principles that express the general ends of human life do not acquire what would nowadays be called a 'moral' force until they are brought to bear upon definite ranges of project, disposition, or action, or upon particular projects, dispositions, or actions. How they are thus to be brought to bear *is* the problem for practical reasonableness. 'Ethics', as classically conceived, is simply a recollectively and/or prospectively reflective expression of this problem and of the general lines of solutions which have been thought reasonable.

How does one tell that a decision is practically reasonable? This question is the subject-matter of the present chapter. The classical exponents of ethics (and of theories of natural law) were well aware of this problem of criteria and standards of judgment. They emphasize that an adequate response to that problem can be made only by one who has experience (both of human wants and passions and of the conditions of human life) and intelligence and a desire for reasonableness stronger than the desires that might overwhelm it. Even when, later, Thomas Aquinas clearly distinguished a class of practical principles which he considered self-evident to anyone with enough experience and intelligence to understand the words by which they are formulated, he emphasized that moral principles such as those in the Ten Commandments are *conclusions from* the primary self-evident principles, that reasoning to such conclusions requires good judgment, and that there are many other more complex and particular moral norms to be followed and moral judgments and decisions to be made, all requiring a degree of practical wisdom which (he says) few men in fact possess: II.3, above.

Now, you may say, it is all very well for Aristotle to assert that ethics can be satisfactorily expounded only by and to those who are experienced and wise and indeed of good habits,[1] and that these characteristics are only likely to be found in societies that already have sufficiently sound standards of conduct,[2] and that the popular morality of such societies (as crystallized and detectable in their language of praise and blame, and their lore) is a generally sound pointer in the

---

[1] *Nic. Eth.* I, 3: 1095a7–11; 4: 1095b5–13; X, 9: 1179b27–30.
[2] *Nic. Eth.* X, 9: 1179b27–1180a5.

elaboration of ethics.[3] He may assert that what is right and morally good is simply *seen* by the man (the *phronimos*, or again the *spoudaios*) who is right-minded and morally good,[4] and that what such a man thinks and does *is* the criterion of sound terminology and correct conclusions in ethics (and politics).[5] Such assertions can scarcely be denied. But they are scarcely helpful to those who are wondering whether their own view of what is to be done is a reasonable view *or not*. The notion of 'the mean', for which Aristotle is perhaps too well known, seems likewise to be accurate but not very helpful (though its classification of value-words doubtless serves as a reminder of the dimensions of the moral problem). For what is 'the mean and best, that is characteristic of virtue'? It is 'to feel [anger, pity, appetite, etc.] when one ought to, and in relation to the objects and persons that one ought to, and with the motives and in the manner that one ought to ...'.[6] Have we no more determinate guide than this?

In the two millennia since Plato and Aristotle initiated formal inquiry into the content of practical reasonableness, philosophical reflection has identified a considerable number of requirements of *method* in practical reasoning. Each of these requirements has, indeed, been treated by some philosopher with exaggerated respect, as if it were the exclusive controlling and shaping requirement. For, as with each of the basic forms of good, each of these requirements is fundamental, underived, irreducible, and hence is capable when focused upon of seeming the most important.

Each of these requirements concerns what one *must* do, or think, or be if one is to participate in the basic value of practical reasonableness. Someone who lives up to these requirements is thus Aristotle's *phronimos*; he has Aquinas's *prudentia*; they are requirements of reasonableness or practical wisdom, and to fail to live up to them is irrational. But, secondly, reasonableness both *is* a basic aspect of human well-being and

[3] See *Nic. Eth.* VI, 5: 1140a24–25; II, 5: 1105b30–31; III, 6: 1115a20; III, 10: 1117b32; cf. X, 2: 1173a1.

[4] *Nic. Eth.* VI, 11: 1143a35–1143b17.

[5] *Nic. Eth.* X, 10: 1176a17–18; cf. III, 6: 1113a33; IX, 4: 1166a12–13: see also I.4, above.

[6] *Nic. Eth.* II, 6: 1106b21–24.

concerns one's participation in all the (other) basic aspects of human well-being. Hence its requirements concern fullness of well-being (in the measure in which any one person can enjoy such fullness of well-being in the circumstances of his lifetime). So someone who lives up to these requirements is also Aristotle's *spoudaios* (mature man), his life is *eu zen* (well-living) and, unless circumstances are quite against him, we can say that he has Aristotle's *eudaimonia* (the inclusive all-round flourishing or well-being—not safely translated as 'happiness'). But, thirdly, the basic forms of good are opportunities of *being*; the more fully a man participates in them the more he is what he can be. And for this state of being fully what one can be, Aristotle appropriated the word *physis*, which was translated into Latin as *natura* (cf. XIII.1, below). So Aquinas will say that these requirements are requirements not only of reason, and of goodness, but also (by entailment) of (human) nature: II.4, above.

Thus, speaking very summarily, we could say that the requirements to which we now turn express the 'natural law method' of working out the (moral) 'natural law' from the first (pre-moral) 'principles of natural law'. Using only the modern terminology (itself of uncertain import) of 'morality', we can say that the following sections of this chapter concern the sorts of reasons why (and thus the ways in which) there are things that morally ought (not) to be done.

V.2 A COHERENT PLAN OF LIFE

First, then, we should recall that, though they correspond to urges and inclinations which can make themselves felt prior to any intelligent consideration of what is worth pursuing, the basic aspects of human well-being are discernible only to one who things about his opportunities, and thus are realizable only by one who intelligently directs, focuses, and controls his urges, inclinations, and impulses. In its fullest form, therefore, the first requirement of practical reasonableness is what John Rawls calls a rational plan of life.[7] Implicitly or explicitly one must have a harmonious set of purposes and orientations, not as the

---

[7] *Theory of Justice*, pp. 408–23, adopting the terminology of W. F. R. Hardie, 'The Final Good in Aristotle's Ethics' (1965) 60 *Philosophy* 277.

'plans' or 'blueprints' of a pipe-dream, but as effective commitments. (Do not confuse the adoption of a set of basic personal or social commitments with the process, imagined by some contemporary philosophers, of 'choosing basic values'!) It is unreasonable to live merely from moment to moment, following immediate cravings, or just drifting. It is also irrational to devote one's attention exclusively to specific projects which can be carried out completely by simply deploying defined means to defined objectives. Commitment to the practice of medicine (for the sake of human life), or to scholarship (for the sake of truth), or to any profession, or to a marriage (for the sake of friendship and children) ... all require both direction and control of impulses, and the undertaking of specific projects; but they also require the redirection of inclinations, the reformation of habits, the abandonment of old and adoption of new projects, as circumstances require, and, overall, the harmonization of all one's deep commitments—for which there is no recipe or blueprint, since basic aspects of human good are not like the definite objectives of particular projects, but are *participated in* (see III.3, above).

As Rawls says, this first requirement is that we should 'see our life as one whole, the activities of one rational subject spread out in time. Mere temporal position, or distance from the present, is not a reason for favouring one moment over another.'[8] But since human life is in fact subject to all manner of unforeseeable contingencies, this effort to 'see' our life as one whole is a rational effort only if it remains on the level of general commitments, and the harmonizing of them. Still, generality is not emptiness (as one can confirm for oneself by contrasting any of the basic forms of good, which as formulated in the 'substantive' practical principles are quite general, with their opposites). So, in every age, wise men have counselled 'in whatever you do remember your last days' (Ecclesiasticus 7:36), not so much to emphasize the importance of the hour of death in relation to a life hereafter, but rather to establish the proper perspective for choosing how to live one's present life. For, from the imagined and heuristically postulated standpoint of the still unknown time of one's death, one can see that many sorts of choices would be irrational, a waste of opportunities, meaning-

[8] *Theory of Justice*, p. 420.

less, a failure, a shame. So the Christian parable of the man who devoted all his energies to gathering riches, with a view to nothing more than drinking and eating them up, makes its 'moral' point by appealing to the intelligence by which we discern folly: 'You *fool*! This night your life shall be required of you. Then whose shall that wealth be which you have heaped together?' (Luke 12:20.)

The content and significance of this first requirement will be better understood in the light of the other requirements. For indeed, all the requirements are interrelated and capable of being regarded as aspects one of another.

V.3   NO ARBITRARY PREFERENCES AMONGST VALUES

Next, there must be no leaving out of account, or arbitrary discounting or exaggeration, of any of the basic human values. Any commitment to a coherent plan of life is going to involve some degree of concentration on one or some of the basic forms of good, at the expense, temporarily or permanently, of other forms of good: IV.4. But the commitment will be rational only if it is on the basis of one's assessment of one's capacities, circumstances, and even of one's tastes. It will be unreasonable if it is on the basis of a devaluation of any of the basic forms of human excellence, or if it is on the basis of an over-valuation of such merely derivative and supporting or instrumental goods as wealth or 'opportunity' or of such merely secondary and conditionally valuable goods as reputation or (in a different sense of secondariness) pleasure.

A certain scholar may have little taste or capacity for friendship, and may feel that life for him would have no savour if he were prevented from pursuing his commitment to knowledge. None the less, it would be unreasonable for him to deny that, objectively, human life (quite apart from truth-seeking and knowledge) and friendship are good in themselves. It is one thing to have little capacity and even no 'taste' for scholarship, or friendship, or physical heroism, or sanctity; it is quite another thing, and stupid or arbitrary, to think or speak or act as if these were not real forms of good.

So, in committing oneself to a rational plan of life, and in interacting with other people (with their own plans of life), one must not use Rawls's 'thin theory of the good'. For the sake of a 'democratic'[9] impartiality between differing conceptions of human good, Rawls insists that, in selecting principles of justice, one must threat as primary goods only liberty, opportunity, wealth, and self-respect, and that one must not attribute intrinsic value to such basic forms of good as truth, or play, or art, or friendship. Rawls gives no satisfactory reason for this radical emaciation of human good, and no satisfactory reason is available: the 'thin theory' is arbitrary. It is quite reasonable for many men to choose not to commit themselves to any real pursuit of knowledge, and it is quite unreasonable for a scholar-statesman or scholar-father to demand that all his subjects or children should conform themselves willy-nilly to the modes and standards of excellence that he chooses and sets for himself. But it is even more unreasonable for anyone to deny that knowledge *is* (and is to be treated as) a form of excellence, and that error, illusion, muddle, superstition, and ignorance are evils that no one should wish for, or plan for, or encourage in himself or in others. If a statesman (VIII.5) or father or any self-directing individual treats truth or friendship or play or any of the other basic forms of good as of no account, and never asks himself whether his life-plan(s) makes reasonable allowance for participation in those intrinsic human values (and for avoidance of their opposites), then he can be properly accused both of irrationality and of stunting or mutilating himself and those in his care.

V.4   NO ARBITRARY PREFERENCES AMONGST PERSONS

Next, the basic goods are human goods, and can in principle be pursued, realized, and participated in by any human being. Another person's survival, his coming to know, his creativity, his all-round flourishing, may not interest me, may not concern me, may in any event be beyond my power to affect. But have I any *reason* to deny that they are really good, or that they are fit matters of interest, concern, and favour by that man and by all those who have to do with him? The questions of friendship, collaboration, mutual assistance, and justice are the subject of the next chapters. Here we need not ask just who

[9] Cf. *Theory of Justice*, p. 527.

is responsible for whose well-being: see VII.4. But we can add, to the second requirement of fundamental impartiality of recognition of each of the basic forms of good, a third requirement: of fundamental impartiality among the human subjects who are or may be partakers of those goods.

My own well-being (which, as we shall see, includes a concern for the well-being of others, my friends: VI.4; but ignore this for the moment) is reasonably the first claim on my interest, concern, and effort. Why can I so regard it? Not because it is of more value than the well-being of others, simply because it is mine: intelligence and reasonableness can find no basis in the mere fact that A is A and is not B (that I am I and am not you) for evaluating his (our) well-being differentially. No: the only *reason* for me to prefer my well-being is that it is through *my* self-determined and self-realizing participation in the basic goods that I can do what reasonableness suggests and requires, viz. favour and realize the forms of human good indicated in the first principles of practical reason.

There is, therefore, reasonable scope for self-preference. But when all allowance is made for that, this third requirement remains, a pungent critique of selfishness, special pleading, double standards, hypocrisy, indifference to the good of others whom one could easily help ('passing by on the other side'), and all the other manifold forms of egoistic and group bias. So much so that many have sought to found ethics virtually entirely on this principle of impartiality between persons. In the modern philosophical discussion, the principle regularly is expressed as a requirement that one's moral judgments and preferences be *universalizable*.

The classical non-philosophical expression of the requirement is, of course, the so-called Golden Rule formulated not only in the Christian gospel but also in the sacred books of the Jews, and not only in didactic formulae but also in the moral appeal of sacred history and parable. It needed no drawing of the moral, no special traditions of moral education, for King David (and every reader of the story of his confrontation with Nathan the prophet) to feel the rational conclusiveness of Nathan's analogy between the rich man's appropriation of the poor man's ewe and the King's appropriation of Uriah the Hittite's wife, and thus the rational necessity for the King to extend his condemnation of the rich man to himself. 'You are the man' (2 Samuel 12:7).

'Do to (or for) others what you would have them do to (or for) you.' Put yourself in your neighbour's shoes. Do not condemn others for what you are willing to do yourself. Do not (without special reason) prevent others getting for themselves what you are trying to get for yourself. These are requirements of reason, because to ignore them is to be arbitrary as between individuals.

But what are the bounds of reasonable self-preference, of reasonable discrimination in favour of myself, my family, my group(s)? In the Greek, Roman, and Christian traditions of reflection, this question was approached via the heuristic device of adopting the viewpoint, the standards, the principles of justice, of one who sees the whole arena of human affairs and who has the interests of each participant in those affairs equally at heart and equally in mind—the 'ideal observer'. Such an impartially benevolent 'spectator' would condemn some but not all forms of self-preference, and some but not all forms of competition: VII.3–4, below. The heuristic device helps one to attain impartiality as between the possible subjects of human well-being (persons) and to exclude mere bias in one's practical reasoning. It permits one to be impartial, too, among inexhaustibly many of the life-plans that differing individuals may choose. But, of course, it does not suggest 'impartiality' about the basic aspects of human good. It does not authorize one to set aside the second requirement of practical reason by indifference to death and disease, by preferring trash to art, by favouring the comforts of ignorance and illusion, by repressing all play as unworthy of man, by praising the ideal of self-aggrandizement and contemning the ideal of friendship, or by treating the search for the ultimate source and destiny of things as of no account or as an instrument of statecraft or a plaything reserved for leisured folk . . .

Therein lies the contrast between the classical heuristic device of the benevolently divine viewpoint and the equivalent modern devices for eliminating mere bias, notably the heuristic concept of the social contract. Consider Rawls's elaboration of the social contract strategy, an elaboration which most readily discloses the purpose of that strategy as a measure and instrument of practical reason's requirement of interpersonal impartiality. Every feature of Rawls's construction is designed to guarantee that if a supposed principle of justice is one that would be unanimously agreed on, behind the 'veil of ignorance', in the 'Original Position', then it must be a principle that is fair and unbiased as between persons. Rawls's heuristic device is thus of some use to anyone who is concerned for the third requirement of practical reasonableness, and in testing its implications. Unfortunately, Rawls disregards the second requirement of practical reasonableness, viz. that each basic or intrinsic human good be treated as a basic and intrinsic good. The conditions of the Original Position are designed by Rawls to guarantee that no principle of justice will systematically favour any life-plan simply because that life-plan participates more fully in human well-being in any or all of its basic aspects (e.g. by favouring knowledge over ignorance and illusion, art over trash, etc.).

And it simply does not follow, from the fact that a principle chosen in the Original Position would be unbiased and fair as between individuals, that a principle which would *not* be chosen in the Original Position must be unfair or not a proper principle of justice in the real world. For in the real world, as Rawls himself admits, intelligence can discern intrinsic basic values and their contraries.[10] Provided we make the distinctions mentioned in the previous section, between basic practical principles and mere matters of taste, inclination, ability, etc., we are able (and are required in reason) to favour the basic forms of good and to avoid and discourage their contraries. In doing so we are showing no improper favour to individuals as such, no unreasonable 'respect of persons', no egoistic or group bias, no partiality opposed to the Golden Rule or to any other aspect of this third requirement of practical reason: see VIII.5–6, below.

V.5   DETACHMENT AND COMMITMENT

The fourth and fifth requirements of practical reasonableness are closely complementary both to each other and to the first requirement of adopting a coherent plan of life, order of priorities, set of basic commitments.

[10] *Theory of Justice*, p. 328.

In order to be sufficiently open to all the basic forms of good in all the changing circumstances of a lifetime, and in all one's relations, often unforeseeable, with other persons, and in all one's opportunities of effecting their well-being or relieving hardship, one must have a certain detachment from all the specific and limited projects which one undertakes. There is no good reason to take up an attitude to any of one's particular objectives, such that if one's project failed and one's objective eluded one, one would consider one's life drained of meaning. Such an attitude irrationally devalues and treats as meaningless the basic human good of authentic and reasonable self-determination, a good in which one meaningfully participates simply by trying to do something sensible and worth while, whether or not that sensible and worthwhile project comes to nothing. Moreover, there are often straightforward and evil consequences of succumbing to the temptation to give one's particular project the overriding and unconditional significance which only a basic value and a general commitment can claim: they are the evil consequences that we call to mind when we think of fanaticism. So the fourth requirement of practical reasonableness can be called detachment.

The fifth requirement establishes the balance between fanaticism and dropping out, apathy, unreasonable failure or refusal to 'get involved' with anything. It is simply the requirement that having made one's general commitments one must not abandon them lightly (for to do so would mean, in the extreme case, that one would fail ever to really participate in any of the basic values). And this requirement of fidelity has a positive aspect. One should be looking creatively for new and better ways of carrying out one's commitments, rather than restricting one's horizon and one's effort to the projects, methods, and routines with which one is familiar. Such creativity and development shows that a person, or a society, is really living on the level of practical *principle*, not merely on the level of conventional rules of conduct, rules of thumb, rules of method, etc., whose real appeal is not to reason (which would show up their inadequacies) but to the sub-rational complacency of habit, mere urge to conformity, etc.

V.6 THE (LIMITED) RELEVANCE OF CONSEQUENCES: EFFICIENCY, WITHIN REASON

The sixth requirement has obvious connections with the fifth, but introduces a new range of problems for practical reason, problems which go to the heart of 'morality'. For this is the requirement that one bring about good in the world (in one's own life and the lives of others) by actions that are efficient for their (reasonable) purpose(s). One must not waste one's opportunities by using inefficient methods. One's actions should be judged by their effectiveness, by their fitness for their purpose, by their utility, their consequences . . .

There is a wide range of contexts in which it is possible and only reasonable to calculate, measure, compare, weigh, and assess the consequences of alternative decisions. Where a choice must be made it is reasonable to prefer human good to the good of animals. Where a choice must be made it is reasonable to prefer basic human goods (such as life) to merely instrumental goods (such as property). Where damage is inevitable, it is reasonable to prefer stunning to wounding, wounding to maiming, maiming to death: i.e. lesser rather than greater damage to one-and-the-same basic good in one-and-the-same instantiation. Where one way of participating in a human good includes *both* all the good aspects and effects of its alternative, *and* more, it is reasonable to prefer that way: a remedy that both relieves pain and heals is to be preferred to the one that merely relieves pain. Where a person or a society has created a personal or social hierarchy of practical norms and orientations, through reasonable choice of commitments, one can in many cases reasonably measure the benefits and disadvantages of alternatives. (Consider a man who has decided to become a scholar, or a society that has decided to go to war.) Where one is considering objects or activities in which there is reasonably a market, the market provides a common denominator (currency) and enables a comparison to be made of prices, costs, and profits. Where there are alternative techniques or facilities for achieving definite objectives, cost–benefit analysis will make possible a certain range of reasonable comparisons between techniques or facilities. Over a wide range of preferences and wants, it is reasonable for an individual or society to seek to maximize the satisfaction of those preferences or wants.

But this sixth requirement is only one requirement among a number. The first, second, and third requirements require that in seeking to maximize the satisfaction of preferences one should discount the preferences of, for example, sadists (who follow the impulses of the moment, and/or do not respect the value of life, and/or do not universalize their principles of action with impartiality). The first, third, and (as we shall see) seventh and eighth requirements require that cost–benefit analysis be contained within a framework that excludes any project involving certain intentional killings, frauds, manipulations of personality, etc. And the second requirement requires that one recognize that each of the basic aspects of human well-being is equally basic, that none is objectively more important than any of the others, and thus that none can provide a common denominator or single yardstick for assessing the utility of all projects: they are incommensurable, and any calculus of consequences that pretends to commensurate them is irrational.

As a general strategy of moral reasoning, utilitarianism or consequentialism is irrational. The utilitarian or (more generally) the consequentialist claims that (i) one should always choose the act that, so far as one can see, will yield the greatest net good on the whole and in the long run ('act-utilitarianism'), or that (ii) one should always choose according to a principle or rule the adoption of which will yield the greatest net good on the whole and in the long run ('rule-utilitarianism'). Each of these claims is not so much false as senseless (in a sense of 'senseless' that will shortly be explained). For no plausible sense can be given, here, to the notion of a 'greatest net good', or to any analogous alternative notions such as 'best consequences', 'lesser evil', 'smallest net harm', or 'greater balance of good over bad than could be expected from any available alternative action'.

Of course, modern ethical theories are most obviously distinguished from earlier theories precisely by their adoption of consequentialist method. So the claim that any such method is irrational may arouse the reader's misgivings. Now there are many features of consequentialist method which are arbitrary or unworkable; I mention some of these briefly, later in this section. But the fundamental problem is that the methodological injunction to maximize good(s) is irrational. And it is important to see that this irrationality is not merely the unreasonableness of adopting a practically unworkable method. Consequentialist method is indeed unworkable, and notoriously so. But more than that, its methodological injunction to maximize good is *senseless*. That is to say, it is senseless in the way that it is senseless to try to sum together the size of this page, the number six, and the mass of this book.

'Good(s)' could be measured and computed in the manner required by consequentialist ethics only if (*a*) human beings had some single, well-defined goal or function (a 'dominant end'), or (*b*) the differing goals which men in fact pursue had some common factor, such as 'satisfaction of desire'. But neither of these conditions obtains. Only an inhumane fanatic thinks that man is made to flourish in only one way or for only one purpose. If a religious person says that man is made simply for the glory of God, or simply for eternal life in friendship with God, we must reply by asking whether the glory of God may not be manifested in *any* of the many aspects of human flourishing, whether these aspects are not all equally fundamental, whether love of God may not thus take, and be expressed in, any of the inexhaustibly many life-plans which conform to the requirements set out in this chapter, which are requirements of a reason-loving love of those things that can be humanly (humanely) loved: see XIII.5, below. If, at the other extreme, someone asserts that each and every human desire has the same prima-facie entitlement to satisfaction, so that the univocal meaning of 'good' (in the consequentialist methodological injunction) is 'satisfaction of desire', we must repeat that this has no plausibility at all to anyone who steadily reflects on the basic principles of his practical intelligence. What reason can you find to deny that truth (and knowledge) is a good? What reason, then, can be found for treating the desire of someone who wants to keep people ignorant as a desire that even prima facie is just as much entitled to satisfaction as the desire of someone who loves knowledge? Why should anyone who desires (as consequentialists obviously do) to regulate his conduct by practical reasonableness treat as of equal value the desire (which he may find in himself or in others) to live according to sheer whim, or according to a programme adopted and loved for its sheer arbitrariness? And we can ask the same question in relation to all those desires that focus on death, pain, joylessness, trash, hatred and destruction of others, incoherence, and any other form of human ruin. These evils can be embraced, as if they were intrinsic goods, by persons who once accepted them only as means to ends and whose personalities were skewed by their wrongdoing. To say that one who gives vent to these desires is 'mentally sick' (and hence not to be counted in the grand calculus of satisfactions) is, often enough, a mere form of words disguising a moral evaluation made tacitly on non-consequentialist lines.

I have already (IV.5) discussed and rejected the view that pleasure or any other definable form of experience can provide the homogeneous and complete human good that the consequentialist needs to be able to identify before he begins computing a maximum net good. To my earlier discussion I add the following two points. Firstly: attempts to define 'good' (for the purposes of the calculus) in terms of enjoyment, satisfaction, happiness, and desire have to assume that 'disvalues' such as pain and frustration stand to their valued opposites as cold stands to heat, viz. as just a low level of the value, on one and the same scale. But this assumption of commensurability is quite implausible. So some consequentialists have been concerned to maximize enjoyments, etc., while others have been concerned to minimize pains, etc. It is rash to assume that these two approaches can be harmonized by subtracting the disvalues from the values, to arrive at a 'net maximum (or greater) good' or 'net minimum (or lesser) evil'. Some consequentialists were so well aware of this awkward incommensurability of good and evil that they argued that *good* results were morally irrelevant: their ('negative utilitarian') methodological injunction was to choose the act (or rule) that will bring about least evil. Secondly: desires, enjoyments, and satisfactions, even when sieved to exclude those opposed to the basic forms of human good, seem to differ in kind, as well as degree. One can compare the strength and degree of one's desire to have a cup of tea now with one's desire to have a cup of coffee now, and the degree of the respective enjoyment or satisfactions. But how can either of those desires and their satisfaction be compared with one's desire to be a fine scholar, a craftsmanlike lawyer, a good father, a true friend ... ?

In short, no determinate meaning can be found for the term 'good' that would allow any commensurating and calculus of good to be made in order to settle those basic questions of practical reason which we call 'moral' questions. Hence, as I said, the consequentialist methodological injunction to maximize net good is senseless, in the way that it is senseless to try to sum up the quantity of the size of this page, the quantity of the number six, and the quantity of the mass of this book. Each of these quantities *is* a quantity and thus has in common with the others the feature that, of it, one can sensibly ask 'How much?' Similarly, each of the basic aspects of human good *is* a good and thus has in common with the others the feature that, of it, one can sensibly ask 'Is this something I should rather be getting/doing/being?' But the different forms of goods, like the different kinds of quantities, are objectively incommensurable. One can *adopt* a system of weights and measures that will *bring* the three kinds of quantity into a relation with each other (there might be six times as many square inches to this page as there are ounces of weight in this book, or 600 times as many square millimetres as kilograms, or ...). But adopting a system of weights and measures is *nothing like* carrying out a computation in terms of the system. Similarly, one can *adopt* a set of commitments that will *bring* the basic values into a relation with each other sufficient to enable one to choose projects and, in some cases, to undertake a cost–benefit analysis (or preference-maximizing or other like analysis) with some prospect of a determinate 'best solution'. But the adoption of a set of commitments, by an individual or a society, is *nothing like* carrying out a calculus of commensurable goods, though it should be controlled by all the rational requirements which we are discussing in this chapter, and so is far from being blind, arbitrary, directionless, or indiscriminate.

Consequentialism is arbitrary in a number of other respects. And again this arbitrariness is not a matter of mere 'unworkability' that can be surmounted 'in principle', i.e. if human limitations could be surmounted.

For example, consequentialism provides no reason for preferring altruism to egoism or to exclusive concern for one's family or party or class or country or church. Jeremy Bentham oscillated and equivocated for sixty years about whether his utilitarianism was to maximize his own happiness or the happiness of 'everybody'. A given consequentialist may *happen* to find (or think he finds) his own good in maximizing the good of others or of 'all'; but his consequentialist analysis and method of practical reasoning affords him no principle by reference to which he could criticize as unreasonable or immoral those who set out to maximize their own happiness regardless of the welfare of others.

Again, consequentialism that goes beyond pure egoism requires a principle of distribution of goods. Supposing (what is in fact logically impossible) that human goods could be commensurated and summed, and supposing (what is for consequentialism an arbitrary importation of a principle of universalization not explicable by appeal to consequences) that 'everyone's' good is to be counted impartially, it remains that the methodological injunction to maximize good still yields no determinate result. No determinate result will follow until we further specify whether maximized good means (*a*) maximum amounts of good regardless of distribution ('over-all utility': a minority, or even a majority, can be enslaved, tortured, or exterminated if that will increase over-all net satisfaction/ happiness/good), or (*b*) maximum *average* amounts of good ('average utility': any number of people can be enslaved, etc., if that will increase the average net satisfaction, etc.), or (*c*) maximum amounts of good for those worst-off ('maximin' or 'minimax' utility: whatever is chosen must increase the well-being of those worst-off more than any alternative choice), or (*d*) equal amounts of good for 'everyone' (notwithstanding that *almost* everyone might be *much* better-off in a society regulated in accordance with specifications (*a*), (*b*), or (*c*)). Some such specification is logically necessary: as it stands, any principle containing a term such as 'the greatest good of the greatest number' is as logically senseless as offering a prize for 'writing the most essays in the shortest time' (Who wins?—the person who turns up tomorrow with three essays, or the person who turns up in a week with twelve, or … ?). But there is no *consequentialist* reason for preferring any particular one of the eligible specifications. The ambition to maximize goods logically cannot be a sufficient principle of practical reasoning.

Again, consequentialist method enjoins us to make the choice that would produce greater net good than could be expected to be produced by any alternative choice. But the alternatives that are in fact 'open' or 'available' to one are innumerable. A genuine consequentialist assessment of alternative possibilities could never end, and could begin anywhere. So it should never begin at all, in reason. (To say this is not at all to say that one should ever disregard or shut one's eyes to foreseeable consequences, or look no further than one's 'good intentions'.)

Now individuals and societies do in fact 'solve' these problems for themselves, and so make the consequentialist injunctions *seem* workable. They focus on something which they have already set their hearts on (an increase in national wealth by collectivizing farming, an end to the war, the detection of those heretics or criminals, re-election as President, an end to that young woman's suffering . . .). 'The' good consequences of this, and 'the' bad consequences of omitting or failing to get it, are dwelt upon. Such requirements as interpersonal impartiality of focus, fidelity to commitments, etc., are brushed aside. Thus the 'calculus' is forced through to provide a determinate solution (the quickest, cheapest way of getting what was first focused upon: hence the forced collectivization and liquidation of the farmers, the nuclear or fire-storm bombing of the enemy's hostage civilians, the inquisitorial torture of suspects or informers, the fraudulent cover-up and obstruction of legal process, the abortion of unborn and 'exposure' of newly-born children . . .). Of course, by focusing on some other alternatives, and on some other long-term or over-all consequences of choosing the favoured alternative, and on the life-possibilities of the proposed victims, and so on, one can in every case find reasons to condemn the favoured action 'on consequentialist grounds'. But in truth both sets of calculations, in such cases, are equally senseless. What generates the 'conclusions' is always something other than the calculus: an overpowering desire, a predetermined objective, the traditions or conventions of the group, or the requirements of practical reason discussed in this chapter.

The limits of the 'reasonable foresight' demanded by our law, and *a fortiori* the nature of the choices ('reasonable care' etc.) demanded, by our law, in view of what was 'reasonably foreseeable', are manifestly fixed almost entirely by (tacit) appeal to social commitments and moral evaluations made, not by consequentialist method, but by following out (with greater or less integrity and success) the requirements of practical reason discussed in this chapter.

The sixth requirement—of efficiency in pursuing the definite goals which we adopt for ourselves and in avoiding the definite harms which we choose to regard as unacceptable—is a real requirement, with indefinitely many applications in 'moral' (and hence in legal) thinking. But its sphere of proper application has limits, and every attempt to make it the exclusive or supreme or even the central principle of practical thinking is irrational and hence immoral. Still, we ought not to disguise from ourselves the *ultimate* (and hence inexplicable, even 'strange'[11]) character of the basic principles and requirements of reasonableness (like the basic aspects of the world ...) once we go beyond the intellectual routines of calculating cost–benefit and efficiency.

V.7 RESPECT FOR EVERY BASIC VALUE IN EVERY ACT

The seventh requirement of practical reasonableness can be formulated in several ways. A first formulation is that one should not choose to do any act which *of itself does nothing but* damage or impede a realization or participation of any one or more of the basic forms of human good. For the only 'reason' for doing such an act, other than the non-reason of some impelling desire, could be that the good *consequences* of the act *outweigh* the damage done in and through the act itself. But, outside

[11] Thus Brian Barry rightly begins his 'Justice Between Generations', *Essays*, pp. 269–84, by asking (quoting Wilfred Beckerman) 'Suppose that, as a result of using up all the world's resources, human life did come to an end. So what?' and concludes a thorough analysis of the issues for practical reasonableness by saying '... the continuation of human life into the future is something to be sought (or at least not sabotaged) even if it does not make for the maximum total happiness. Certainly, if I try to analyse the source of my own strong conviction that we should be wrong to take risks with the continuation of human life, I find that it does not lie in any sense of injury to the interests of people who will not get born but rather in a sense of its cosmic impertinence—that we should be grossly abusing our position by taking it upon ourselves to put a term on human life and its possibilities' (p. 284).

merely technical contexts, consequentialist 'weighing' is always and necessarily arbitrary and delusive for the reasons indicated in the preceding section.

Now an act of the sort we are considering will always be done (if it is done intelligently at all) as a means of promoting or protecting, directly or indirectly, one or more of the basic goods, in one or more of their aspects. For anyone who rises above the level of impulse and acts deliberately must be seeking to promote some form of good (even if only the good of authentically powerful self-expression and self-integration which he seeks through sadistic assaults or through malicious treachery or deception, with 'no ulterior motives'). Hence, if consequentialist reasoning were reasonable, acts which themselves do nothing but damage or impede a human good could often be justified as parts of, or steps on the way to carrying out, some project for the promotion or protection of some form(s) of good. For example, if consequentialist reasoning were reasonable, one might sometimes reasonably kill some innocent person to save the lives of some hostages. But consequentialist reasoning is arbitrary and senseless, not just in one respect but in many. So we are left with the fact that such a killing is an act which of itself does nothing but damage the basic value of life. The goods that are expected to be secured in and through the consequential release of the hostages (if it takes place) would be secured not in or as an aspect of the killing of the innocent man but in or as an aspect of a distinct, subsequent act, an act which would be one 'consequence' amongst the innumerable multitude of incommensurable consequences of the act of killing. Once we have excluded consequentialist reasoning, with its humanly understandable but in truth naïvely arbitrary limitation of focus to the purported calculus 'one life versus many', the seventh requirement is self-evident. (The following paragraphs, therefore, seek not to demonstrate, but to clarify the sense of this requirement; on self-evidence, see III.4.)

The basic values, and the practical principles expressing them, are the only guides we have. Each is objectively basic, primary, incommensurable with the others in point of objective importance. If one is to act intelligently at all one must choose to realize and participate in some basic value or values rather than others, and this inevitable concentration of effort will indirectly impoverish, inhibit, or interfere with the realization of those other values. If I commit myself to truthful scholarship, then I fail to save the lives I could save as a doctor, I inhibit the growth of the production of material goods, I limit my opportunities for serving the community through politics, entertainment, art, or preaching. And within the field of science and scholarship, my research into K means that L and M go as yet undiscovered. These unsought but unavoidable side-effects accompany every human choice, and their consequences are incalculable. But it is always reasonable to leave some of them, and often reasonable to leave all of them, out of account. Let us for brevity use the word 'damage' to signify also impoverishment, inhibition, or interference, and the word 'promote' to signify also pursuit or protection. Then we can say this: to indirectly damage any basic good (by choosing an act that directly and immediately promotes either that basic good in some other aspect or participation, or some other basic good or goods) is obviously quite different, rationally and thus morally, from directly and immediately damaging a basic good in some aspect or participation by choosing an act which in and of itself simply (or, we should now add, primarily) damages that good in some aspect or participation but which indirectly, *via* the mediation of expected consequences, is to promote either that good in some other aspect or participation, or some other basic good(s).

To choose an act which in itself simply (or primarily) damages a basic good is thereby to engage oneself willy-nilly (but directly) in an act of opposition to an incommensurable value (an aspect of human personality) which one treats as if it were an object of measurable worth that could be outweighed by commensurable objects of greater (or cumulatively greater) worth. To do this will often accord with our feelings, our generosity, our sympathy, and with our commitments and projects in the forms in which we undertook them. But it can never be justified in reason. We must choose rationally (and this rational judgment can often promote a shift in our perspective and consequently a realignment of initial feelings and thus of our commitments and projects). Reason requires that every basic value be at least respected in each and every action. If one could ever rightly choose a single act which *itself* damages and *itself* does not promote some basic good, then one could rightly choose whole programmes and institutions and enterprises that themselves damage and do not promote basic aspects of human well-being, for the sake of their 'net beneficial consequences'. Now we have already seen that consequences, even to the extent that they can be 'foreseen as certain', cannot be commensurably *evaluated*, which means that 'net beneficial consequences' is a literally absurd general objective or criterion. It only remains to note that a man who thinks that his rational responsibility to be always doing and pursuing good is satisfied by a commitment to act always for best consequences is a man who treats every aspect of human personality (and indeed, therefore, treats himself) as a utensil. He holds himself ready to do *anything* (and thus makes himself a tool for all those willing to threaten sufficiently bad consequences if he does not co-operate with them).

But the objection I am making to such choices is not that programmes of mass killing, mass deception, etc. would then be morally eligible (though they would) and indeed morally required (though they would), but that no sufficient reason can be found for treating any act as immune from the only direction which we have, viz. the direction afforded by the basic practical principles. These each direct that a form of good is to be pursued and done; and each of them bears not only on all our large-scale choices of general orientations and commitments, and on all our medium-scale choices of projects (in which attainment of the objective will indeed be the good consequence of successful deployment of effective means), but also on each and every choice of an act which itself is a complete act (whether or not it is also a step in a plan or phase in a project). The incommensurable value of an aspect of personal full-being (and its corresponding primary principle) can never be rightly subordinated to any project or commitment. But such an act of subordination inescapably occurs at least whenever a distinct choice-of-act has in *itself* no meaning save that of damaging that basic value (thus violating that primary principle).

Such, in highly abstract terms, is the seventh requirement, the principle on which alone rests (as we shall later see) the strict inviolability of basic human rights: VIII.7. There is no human right that will not be overridden if feelings (whether

generous and unselfish, or mean and self-centred) are allowed
to govern choice, or if cost–benefit considerations are taken outside their appropriate technical sphere and allowed to govern
one's direct engagement (whether at the level of commitment,
project, or individual act) with basic goods. And the perhaps
unfamiliar formulation which we have been considering should
not obscure the fact that this 'seventh requirement' is well
recognized, in other formulations: most loosely, as 'the end does
not justify the means'; more precisely, though still ambiguously,
as 'evil may not be done that good might follow therefrom';
and with a special Enlightenment flavour, as Kant's 'categorical
imperative': 'Act so that you treat humanity, whether in your
own person or in that of another, always as an end and never
as a means only'.[12]

Obviously, the principal problem in considering the implications of this requirement is the problem of individuating and
characterizing actions, to determine what is one complete act-
that-itself-does-nothing-but-damage-a-basic-good. Human acts
are to be individuated primarily in terms of those factors which
we gesture towards with the word 'intention'. Fundamentally,
a human act is a that-which-is-decided-upon (or -chosen) and
its primary proper description is as what-is-chosen. A human
action, to be humanly regarded, is to be characterized in the
way it was characterized in the conclusion to the relevant train
of practical reasoning of the man who chose to do it (cf. III.3).
On the other hand, the world with its material (including our
bodily selves) and its structures of physical and psycho-physical
causality is not indefinitely malleable by human intention. The
man who is deciding what to do cannot reasonably shut his
eyes to the causal structure of his project; he cannot characterize
his plans *ad lib*. One can be engaged willy-nilly but directly,
in act, with a basic good, such as human life.

Perhaps the consequences of one's act seem likely to be very
good and would themselves directly promote further basic
human good. Still, these expected goods will be realized (if at
all) not as aspects of one-and-the-same act, but as aspects or
consequences of other acts (by another person, at another time
and place, as the upshot of another free decision ...). So,

[12] Kant, *Foundations of the Metaphysics of Morals* (1785; trans. Beck, Indianapolis: 1959), p. 47.

however 'certainly foreseeable' they may be, they cannot be used to characterize the act itself as, *in and of itself*, anything other than an intentional act of, say, man-killing. This is especially obvious when a blackmailer's price for sparing his hostages is 'killing that man'; the person who complies with the demand, in order to save the lives of the many, cannot deny that he is choosing an act which of itself does nothing but kill.

Sometimes, however, the 'good effects' are really aspects of one-and-the-same act, and can form part of the description of what it is in and of itself. Then we cannot characterize the act as in and of itself *nothing but* damaging to human good. But is it rationally justifiable? Not necessarily; the seventh requirement is not an isolated requirement, and such a choice may flout the second, third, fourth, and fifth requirements. The choice a man makes may be one he would not make if he were sufficiently detached from his impulses and his peculiar project to avoid treating a particular act or project as if it were itself a basic aspect of human well-being; or if he were *creatively* open to all the basic goods and thus careful to adjust his projects so as to minimize their damaging 'side-effects' and to avoid substantial and irreparable harms to persons. The third requirement here provides a convenient test of respect for good: would the person acting have thought the act reasonable had *he* been the person harmed? Considerations such as these are woven into the notion of *directly* choosing against a basic value. And for most practical purposes this seventh requirement can be summarized as: Do not choose directly against a basic value.

For indeed the pattern of our reflections on particular, often tragic, problem situations (*casus*) can be generalized, by lawyers and professional moralists, into 'doctrines' (such as the so-called doctrine of double effect) which press to their limit the implications of such common notions as 'direct/indirect', 'side-effect', 'intention', 'permission', etc. Such doctrines have their use as summary reminders of analogies and differences across a vast range of human affairs, many of which are hard to think straight about, both because of their complexity and because they include such factors as differential 'risks'. But the doctrines of the legal (legislative, judicial, or academic) or moral casuists are not themselves the principles of practical reasonableness— i.e. the 'substantive' principles discussed in Chapter IV and the 'methodological' requirements of reasonableness discussed in this chapter. In many problematic circumstances, the implications of the seventh requirement are clear: such-and-such an action, for all that it has such-and-such desirable expected consequences, is unreasonable. But in many *casus* the characterization of the actions calls for the 'judgment' that wisely good persons have (more or less) and other persons have not (more or less). In abstract discussions, we ought not to expect more precision than the subject-matter will bear. Still, recognition of this need for judgment is not to be confused with sliding into the morass of arbitrariness which we call consequentialism. And recognition of the tragic implications of some circumstances and decisions is not a rational ground for undertaking the heroic but absurd burden self-imposed by consequentialism—the burden of being responsible for 'over-all net good' (cf. notes to VII.4 and VIII.7).

Finally, a note about terminology. The principal bearer of an explicit theory about natural law happens, in our civilization, to have been the Roman Catholic Church. Without committing itself to any explanation of the sort attempted in this chapter and the last, that Church has stringently elaborated the implications of the seventh requirement, as those implications concern the basic values of life (including the procreative transmission of life), truth (including truth in communication), and religion. And it has formulated those implications in strict negative principles such as those declaring wrongful any killing of the innocent, any anti-procreative sexual acts, and lying and blasphemy. (The ecclesiastical formulations are more complex; but that is their gist.) Those strict negative principles have thus become popularly regarded as the distinctive content of natural law doctrine. But in fact, as the term 'natural law' is used both in this book and, it seems to me, in the pronouncements of the Roman Catholic Church, *everything* required by virtue of *any* of the requirements discussed in this chapter is required by natural law. In this use of the term, if *anything* can be said to be required by or contrary to natural law, then *everything* that is morally (i.e. reasonably) required to be done is required (either mediately or immediately: cf. X.7) by natural law, and everything that is reasonably (i.e. morally) required not to be done is contrary to natural law. The seventh requirement of practical reasonableness is no more and no less a 'natural law principle' than any of the other requirements.

V.8 THE REQUIREMENTS OF THE COMMON GOOD

Very many, perhaps even most, of our concrete moral responsibilities, obligations, and duties have their basis in the eighth requirement. We can label this the requirement of favouring and fostering the common good of one's communities. The sense and implications of this requirement are complex and manifold: see especially VI.8, VII.2–5, IX.1, XI.2, XII.2–3.

V.9 FOLLOWING ONE'S CONSCIENCE

The ninth requirement might be regarded as a particular aspect of the seventh (that no basic good may be directly attacked in any act), or even as a summary of all the requirements. But it is quite distinctive. It is the requirement that one should not do what one judges or thinks or 'feels'-all-in-all should not be done. That is to say one must act 'in accordance with one's conscience'.

This chapter has been in effect a reflection on the workings of conscience. If one were by inclination generous, open, fair, and steady in one's love of human good, or if one's milieu happened to have settled on reasonable *mores*, then one would be able, without solemnity, rigmarole, abstract reasoning, or casuistry, to make the particular practical judgments (i.e. judgments of conscience) that reason requires. If one is not so fortunate in one's inclinations or upbringing, then one's conscience will mislead one, unless one strives to be reasonable and is blessed with a pertinacious intelligence alert to the forms of human good yet undeflected by the sophistries which intelligence so readily generates to rationalize indulgence, time-serving, and self-love. (The stringency of these conditions is the permanent ground for the possibility of authority in morals, i.e. of authoritative guidance, by one who meets those conditions, acknowledged willingly by persons of conscience.)

The first theorist to formulate this ninth requirement in all its unconditional strictness seems to have been Thomas Aquinas: if one chooses to do what one judges to be in the last analysis unreasonable, or if one chooses not to do what one judges to be in the last analysis required by reason, then one's choice is unreasonable (wrongful), however erroneous one's judgments of conscience may happen to be. (A *logically* necessary feature of such a situation is, of course, that one is ignorant of one's mistake.)

This dignity of even the mistaken conscience is what is expressed in the ninth requirement. It flows from the fact that practical reasonableness is not simply a mechanism for producing correct judgments, but an aspect of personal full-being, to be respected (like all the other aspects) in every act as well as 'over-all'—whatever the consequences.

V.10 THE PRODUCT OF THESE REQUIREMENTS: MORALITY

Now we can see why some philosophers have located the essence of 'morality' in the reduction of harm, others in the increase of well-being, some in social harmony, some in universalizability of practical judgment, some in the all-round flourishing of the individual, others in the preservation of freedom and personal authenticity. Each of these has a place in rational choice of commitments, projects, and particular actions. Each, moreover, contributes to the sense, significance, and force of terms such as 'moral', '[morally] ought', and 'right'; not every one of the nine requirements has a direct role in every moral judgment, but some moral judgments do sum up the bearing of each and all of the nine on the questions in hand, and every moral judgment sums up the bearing of one or more of the requirements.

Obligation and related notions come up for discussion later (XI.1–2, XI.4, XIII.5). Suffice it to say here that each of the requirements can be thought of as a mode of moral obligation or responsibility. For each plays its part in reasonable deciding, by generating arguments of the form (roughly):

1. Harmony of purposes/recognition of goods/absence of arbitrariness between persons/detachment from particular realizations of good/fidelity to commitments/efficiency in the technical sphere/respect in act for every basic value/

community/authenticity in following one's reason ... are (all) aspects of the real basic good of freedom and reason;
2. That harmony of purposes, or ..., can in such-and-such circumstances be achieved/done/expressed/etc. only (or best, or more fittingly) by (not) doing act ϕ; so
3. Act ϕ should (not)/must (not)/ought (not) to ... be done.

Such a train of practical reasoning is not to be found on the surface of every piece of moral discourse. This chapter and the last have been explorations not of the surface but of the deep structure of practical thinking, more particularly, of moral thought. The requirements of practical reasonableness generate a moral language utilizing and appealing to moral distinctions employed more or less spontaneously. The sources of these distinctions have to be discerned by an effort of reflection which, as the history of philosophy demonstrates, is not too easy.

If, finally, we look back over the complex of basic principles and basic requirements of practical reasonableness, we can see how 'natural' is that diversity of moral opinion which the sceptic makes such play of. It is a diversity which has its source in too exclusive attention to some of the basic value(s) and/or some basic requirement(s), and inattention to others. Sometimes, no doubt, the distortion or deflection is most immediately explicable by reference to an uncritical, unintelligent spontaneity; sometimes, by reference to the bias and oversight induced by conventions of language, social structure, and social practice; and sometimes (and always, perhaps, most radically) by the bias of self-love or of other emotions and inclinations that resist the concern to be simply reasonable.

NOTES

V.1

Freedom of choice ... The notion of freedom of choice, as the matrix in which human responsibility for good is set, first becomes an explicit theme in Christian writings. It is given great prominence by Thomas Aquinas, who opens the part of his *Summa Theologiae* which deals with human action and morality by stating: 'Man is made in the image of God, and this implies, as St. John of Damascus said, that man is intelligent and free in judgment and master of himself. So, having considered both the exemplar of that image, namely God, and the things that proceed by divine power and the will of God, it remains for us now to consider the image itself, i.e. man, precisely insofar as he is the source of his own actions and has freedom of judgment and power over his own works and deeds': *S.T.* I–II, Prologue. For a vindication of the reality of freedom of choice, see J. Boyle, G. Grisez, and O. Tollefsen, *Free Choice: A Self-Referential Argument* (Notre Dame and London: 1976).

Ethics as the reflective account of practical reasonableness ... There is no clearly settled meaning of 'ethics' in modern philosophical discussion. But there is substantial agreement that one can usefully distinguish between (i) descriptive empirical enquiries about people's moral judgments, (ii) 'moral', 'normative', or (practically) 'critical' questions, for one's own judgment, about what is to be done, and (iii) 'analytical', 'meta-ethical', (theoretically) 'critical' questions about the language and logic used in discourse of the two preceding kinds. Still, 'meta-ethics' cannot well proceed without assuming that some 'normative' judgments are more worthy of attention than others, while normative moral judgment cannot be made with full rationality without critical reflection on itself to clarify its terms and its logic. Hence there is no good reason to *separate* (ii) from (iii); the classical conjunction of the two, as 'ethics' or 'moral philosophy', was fully justified. For modern discussion, see e.g. R. M. Hare, 'Ethics' in his *Essays on the Moral Concepts* (London: 1972), pp. 39–40; William K. Frankena, *Ethics* (2nd ed., Englewood Cliffs, New Jersey: 1973), pp. 4–5 (taking 'the more traditional view' that 'ethics' should rightly include both 'meta-ethics' and 'normative ethics').

'Moral principles' are conclusions from primary practical principles ... In Aquinas's view, most of the Ten Commandments are (*a*) moral principles, and (*b*) secondary principles of natural law, *conclusions* drawn from the primary principles by a rational elaboration which most men find easy but which can be perverted by passion and convention: *S.T.* I–II, q. 100, a. 3c and ad 1; a. 6c; a. 11c and ad 1; cf. also q. 94, a. 5c; a. 6c and ad 3; and see next note.

Elaboration of moral principles, and particular moral decisions, both require wisdom that is far from universal ... see, e.g., *S.T.* I–II, q. 100, aa. 1, 3, 11; this wisdom is *prudentia* (II–II, q. 47, a. 2c and ad 1; aa. 6, 15; and notes to II.3 above). On the folly of the many see I–II, q. 9, a. 5 ad 3; q. 14, a. 1 ad 3. On the corruption of practical reasonableness in various cultures and people(s), see I, q. 113, a. 1; I–II, q. 58, a. 5; q. 94, a. 4; q. 99, a. 2 ad 2; and II.3 above.

'The mean' ... Aristotle's account is circular: right action is action according to right principle (or right reason) (*Nic. Eth.* II, 2: 1103b31–32); the criterion of right principle is the mean between the vices of excess and deficiency (*Nic. Eth.* II, 2: 1104a12–27; II, 6: 1106a25–1107a8); but the mean is itself determined by reference to the practical wisdom of the *phronimos* [as to whom see the next note, below] and (which comes to the same thing) to the right principle (*Nic. Eth.* II, 6: 1107a1; VI, 1: 1133b20). The importance of this idea of the mean in Aristotle's ethics is often exaggerated.

The 'phronimos' in Aristotle ... He is the man who has *phronesis*, practical wisdom, full reasonableness (in the Latin writings, *prudentia*). He *is* the norm of action: *Nic. Eth.* II, 6: 1107a1; VI, 11: 1143b15. 'Men like Pericles are considered to be *phronimoi* because they have the faculty of discerning what things are good for themselves and for mankind': *Nic. Eth.* VI, 5: 1140b8–10. *Phronesis* is 'a truth-attaining rational quality, concerned with action in relation to things that are good and bad for human beings': *Nic. Eth.* VI, 5: 1140b6–8.

Aquinas's notion of 'prudentia' ... For Aquinas, the virtue of *prudentia* is what enables one to reason well towards choice of commitments, projects, and actions, to apply the most general practical principles concretely, to choose rightly, to find the right mean, to be virtuous, to be a good man: *S.T.* II–II, q. 47, aa. 1–7; notes to II.3 above.

The 'spoudaios' in Aristotle ... The term is often translated 'good man' or 'virtuous man'. But a richer translation is 'mature man' (by contrast with the young and inexperienced who can scarcely, if at all, do ethics: *Nic. Eth.* I, 3: 1095a3). He it is who judges practical affairs correctly, and he it is 'who *is* the standard and measure [*kanon kai metron*, in Latin *regula et mensura*: Aquinas will take these terms into the heart of his definition of *lex*, law: *S.T.* I–II, q. 90, a. 1c] of what is noble [or upright: *kalon*] and pleasant': *Nic. Eth.* III, 5: 1113a32. What the *spoudaios* does is done well and properly: I, 7: 1098a15. 'Those things are actually valuable and pleasant which appear so to the spoudaios': X, 6: 1176b26. So the central case of friendship is the friendship of *spoudaioi*, who can reasonably find each other lovable simply as such (IX, 9: 1170a13–15; cf. IX, 4: 1166a13); and the central case of the *polis* is the *spoudaia polis* (*Pol.* VII, 12: 1332a33). See I.4 above, XII.4 below.

Aristotle's notion of 'eudaimonia' ... See John M. Cooper, *Reason and Human Good in Aristotle* (Cambridge, Mass., and London: 1975), and note to V.2, below, on 'rational plans of life'.

'Physis' *and* 'natura' *as fullness of being* ... See Aristotle, *Meta.* XII. 3: 1070a12; V. 4: 1015a14–15.

Morality, for Aquinas, is fullness of reasonableness, goodness, and human nature ... See especially *S.T.* I–II, q. 18, a. 1c; q. 71, a. 2.

The modern notion(s) of morality ... 'Morality' and cognate words have connotations and overtones that no single word (or standard set of words) has either in Plato and Aristotle's Greek or in Aquinas's Latin (though for examples of a use similar to the modern, see *S.T.* I–II, q. 18; q. 99, a. 2; q. 100 . A useful description of aspects of the modern concept is Hart, *Concept of Law*, pp. 163–76.

The basic requirements of practical reasonableness ... The differentiation and analysis of these requirements is largely the work of Germain Grisez, and marks a major advance in the philosophical analysis of natural law. He calls these guidelines 'modes of obligation' ('Methods of Ethical Inquiry' (1967) 41 *Proc. Amer. Cath. Philosophical Ass.* 160) or 'modes of responsibility' (*Beyond the New Morality: The Responsibilities of Freedom*, Notre Dame and London, 1974, pp. 108–36, 213). His list numbers eight, rather than nine, and differs in some details.

V.2

Rational plans of life ... Besides Rawls, *Theory of Justice*, pp. 408–23, see Charles Fried, *An Anatomy of Values: Problems of Personal and Social Choice* (Cambridge, Mass.: 1970), pp. 97–101 (the 'life plan'). Like Grisez, both Rawls and Fried are drawing on Josiah Royce, *The Philosophy of Loyalty* (New York: 1908), who argued, at p. 168, that 'a person, an individual self, may be defined as a human life lived according to a plan' (a definition which makes its point by the paradox of metonymy). The term 'plan' has the serious drawback that it suggests, too much, that participation in human fullness and reasonableness is just like pursuit of a definite objective, and that commitments to basic values 'for good' (i.e. with a view to a lifetime, or 'indefinitely') are just like settling on particular concrete projects and taking efficient steps to carry them out. Nevertheless, the idea of a plan of life expresses in modern terms the rational requirement (viz. of an over-all *unity* and harmony of purpose, of an *integration* of commitments, projects, actions, habits, feelings) that the ancients preferred to express in terms of a unity of *end*. This notion ('end') has much the same drawbacks as its modern counterpart, 'plan'; hence the constant temptation to treat what is really an 'inclusive end' as if it were a 'dominant end', a temptation which not only Aristotle's interpreters (often) but also Aristotle himself (occasionally) find hard to resist. See J. L. Ackrill, 'Aristotle on *Eudaimonia*' (1975) 60 *Proc. Brit. Acad.* 339, and notes to III.3, above; and further, below, notes to V.7, concerning 'dominant end' theories. In any event, Cooper, *Reason and Human Good in Aristotle*, pp. 96–7, 121–5, and *passim*, has suggested that in Aristotle *eudaimonia* can be regarded as the effective possession-in-action of a rational over-all plan of life. If the matter were further investigated I think it would emerge that Aristotle's implicit conception of *eudaimonia* is of that condition in which a man is (or tends to be: see next note) when he satisfies-in-action not merely this first requirement of practical reasonableness but all nine requirements traced in this chapter.

Unforeseeable contingencies in human life ... The subjection of human reasonableness and fulfilment to chance and hazard is emphasized by Aristotle: see P. Aubenque, *La Prudence chez Aristote* (Paris: 1963), pp. 64–91. Christian, like Stoic, reflection, introduced the notion of providence rejected by Aristotle (but not by Plato: see *Laws* X, 903–4): human affairs are subject to divine *prudentia*, which makes everything contribute to the good of the universe: Aquinas, *S.T.* I, q. 22, aa. 1, 2; I–II, q. 19, a. 10c; XIII.3 below. But: that 'we *do not know* what God concretely [or in particular] wills' remains a central tenet of Aquinas's theory of natural law: I–II, q. 19, a. 10 ad 1; q. 91, a. 3 ad 1; XIII.5 below; so we have to cling to the general principles of reason, the general forms of good, the general structure of our nature: I–II, q. 19, a. 10 ad 1 and ad 2. Moreover, on the view of Aquinas (unlike both Aristotle and the Stoics), the good of the universe includes and is in part realized by the good of creatures 'made in God's image', i.e. creatures whose good includes and is realized by their own intelligent creativity and free self-determination: I–II, prol. (quoted in notes to V.1, above). Divine providence, on this view, works itself out through, *inter alia*, human choices that are really free and self-constituting (not merely blind).

Seeing one's life from the imagined standpoint of one's death ... So Plato's Socrates teaches that philosophy (which for him is always contemplatively practical) is the practice of dying: *Phaedo* 64a.

V.3

Wealth, reputation, 'opportunity' (power), and pleasure as secondary forms of good ... See Aristotle, *Nic. Eth.* 1, 5; X, 1–3; Aquinas, *S.T.* I–II, q. 2, aa. 1–6; notes to IV.3 above. Cf. the notes on Rawls's 'primary goods', below.

Rawls's 'thin theory' of good ... Good, in this 'thin' sense, is what it is rational for *any* man to want *whatever else* his preferences, wants, aims, etc. See *Theory of Justice*, pp. 396–407, 433–4.

Rawls's 'primary goods' ... These are the goods which 'it is rational to want ... whatever else is wanted, since they are in general necessary for the framing and the execution of a rational plan of life', and are 'liberty and opportunity, income and wealth, and above all self-respect': *Theory of Justice*, p. 433; also 253, 260, 328. Rawls will not permit a theorist of justice to treat real primary goods (in our sense), such as truth, art, culture, religion, or friendship, as having an *intrinsic* value or as being *objective* final ends of human life (see ibid., pp. 419, 527): to do so would be out of line with his 'rejection of the principle of perfection and the acceptance of democracy in the assessment of one another's excellences': ibid., p. 527.

Rawls on intrinsic goods, excellences, and perfections ... Rawls expressly does *not* contend that 'criteria of excellence lack a rational basis from the standpoint of everyday life', and he grants that 'the freedom and well-being of individuals, when measured by the excellence of their activities and works, is vastly different in value' and that 'comparisons of intrinsic value can obviously be made': *Theory of Justice*, pp. 328, 329. But he will not allow such differentiations (e.g. of the intrinsic value of [having] true beliefs and the intrinsic disvalue of [having] false beliefs) to enter at all into the rational determination of the basic principles of justice: see ibid., pp. 327–32.

V.4

The rationality of priority of concern for one's own good ... On the proper priority of self-love—a principle that must be understood with precision—see *Nic. Eth.* IX, 4: 1166a1–1166b29; *S.T.* II–II, q. 26, aa. 3–5; VI.1, VI.4, and XIII.5, below.

'Passing by on the other side' ... See Luke 10:32. On the 'Good Samaritan' principle in modern societies, see James Ratcliffe (ed.), *The Good Samaritan and the Law* (New York: 1966).

The Golden Rule ... See Tobit 4:16; Matthew 7:12; Luke 6:31. Kelsen's contention (*What is Justice?* Berkeley: 1957, pp. 16–18) that the Golden Rule is empty overlooks the fact that it is only one amongst (say) nine basic requirements of practical reason, which itself is only one amongst (say) seven basic practical principles. In fact, the Golden Rule is a potent solvent and determinant in moral matters.

The heuristic device of the 'ideal observer' ... Plato's formulation is implicit, but central to his thought: both the Myth of the Cave (*Rep.* VII: 514a–521b) and the image of the divine puppet-master whose tug we are to follow (*Laws*, VII: 804b; see XIII.5, below) are to be understood as insisting on the need to raise one's mind's eye to this viewpoint in judging human affairs. For the modern discussion, initiated by David Hume and elaborated by Adam Smith, see e.g. D. D. Raphael, 'The Impartial Spectator' (1972) 58 *Proc. Brit. Acad.* 335.

The 'social contract' as a heuristic device for excluding bias ... Rawls is particularly clear that his notion of the Original Position (which includes a requirement that the parties in it agree together, i.e. 'contract' on principles of justice) is a device for excluding bias, for guaranteeing objectivity, and for seeing the whole human situation *sub specie aeternitatis*: see especially the last page of *Theory of Justice*, p. 587; also p. 516.

V.5

The requirement of reasonable detachment ... Epictetus' version of Stoicism (*c.*AD 100) elevates this requirement to a dominant position: see especially Arrian's *Encheiridion of Epictetus, passim*. For balance, see Josiah Royce, *The Philosophy of Loyalty* (New York: 1908), especially Lecture V, sec. 1.

The requirement of 'commitment' ... See Gabriel Marcel (much influenced by Royce), e.g. *Homo Viator* (London: 1951), pp. 125–34, 155–6.

V.6

The rational limitations of cost–benefit analysis ... See E. J. Mishan, *Cost–Benefit Analysis: An Introduction* (London: 1971), pp. 108, 307–21.

Problems of utilitarianism or consequentialism ... See D. H. Hodgson, *Consequences of Utilitarianism* (Oxford: 1967), chs. II–III; Dan W. Brock, 'Recent Work in Utilitarianism' (1973) 10 *Amer. Philosophical Q.* 245; Germain Grisez, 'Against Consequentialism' (1978) 23 *Am. J. Juris.* 21. Notice that what I describe as irrational is consequentialism as a general method in ethics (i.e. in open-ended practical reasoning), and *not* what Neil MacCormick, *Legal Reasoning and Legal Theory* (Oxford: 1978), pp. 105–6 and ch. VI, calls 'consequentialist' reasoning by judges, viz. (to summarize his valuable analysis) (i) examining the *types* of decision which would 'have to be given' in other cases if a certain decision is given in the case before them, and (ii) asking about the acceptability or unacceptability of such 'consequences' of the proposed decision in that case. As MacCormick notes (ibid., p. 105), 'there is ... no reason to assume that [this mode of argument] involves evaluation in terms of a single scale ...'. In fact, the evaluation will be by reference to the established commitments of a society.

Consequentialism: irrational and arbitrary, or merely 'unworkable'? ... G. J. Warnock, *The Object of Morality* (London: 1971), pp. 28–30, recites some objections to utilitarianism, not explicitly distinguishing 'practical' difficulties of unworkability from problems that go to the very sense (intelligibility) of the utilitarian method. He remarks that objections 'of this sort are not really, I think, all that impressive'. For moral problems *are* difficult. 'And as to the difficulty in comparison and computation of "happinesses", it is at any rate clear that such comparisons do somehow get made ...' Warnock thus misses the point; some approximate commensuration of some goods is, of course, possible and commonplace within a 'moral' framework established by commitments, relationships, etc., which have been adopted reasonably-in-terms-of-the-nine-requirements-of-practical-reasonableness; just as some more precise commensuration of costs with benefits is possible in relation to some concrete operational goal. The trouble with utilitarianism is that it offers to replace the nine criteria of practical reasonableness with one that is in truth rationally applicable only in a subordinate, contained element of practical thinking: the recommendation could be called a sort of category mistake.

Critique of 'dominant end' theories of ethics ... See Rawls, *Theory of Justice*, pp. 548–60, esp. 554; see also Cooper, *Reason and Human Good in Aristotle*, pp. 94–100.

'Every desire has an equal claim to satisfaction' ... See William James, *The Will to Believe* (New York: 1897), pp. 195 ff.; Bertrand Russell, *Human Society in Ethics and Politics* (London: 1954), pp. 56–9, 84. For the importation of this view into jurisprudence by Roscoe Pound, see VII.6, below. In a muted form this view, at least as a methodological postulate, lies at the root of Rawls's *Theory of Justice*. In a more or less straightforward way it underpins most modern versions of utilitarianism and indeed most modern ethics. John Stuart Mill rebelled against Jeremy Bentham's version of it: *Utilitarianism* (1863), ch. 1. But the utilitarian has no choice but to adopt either a strict dominant end theory or a strict equality of desires (or preferences) theory. Hence Mill's utilitarian criterion is incoherent, as is shown e.g. by Anthony Quinton, *Utilitarian Ethics* (London: 1973), pp. 39–47.

Maximization of good (pleasure) or minimization of evil (pain)? ... See the vigorous exploration of the problem by Cicero, *De Finibus*, II, 6–25, esp. 17. For critique of the view that pain and pleasure are commensurable, see Robinson A. Grover, 'The Ranking Assumption' (1974) 4 *Theory and Decision* 277–99.

'Greatest good of the greatest number' ... For the logical problems caused by the double superlative, see P. T. Geach, *The Virtues* (Cambridge: 1977), pp. 91–4.

V.7

The seventh requirement ... This is clearly and variously formulated in Germain Grisez's works, e.g. (with R. Shaw), *Beyond the New Morality*, ch. 13; *Contraception and the Natural Law* (Milwaukee: 1964), pp. 68–71, 110–14; *Abortion: the Myths, the Realities and the Arguments* (New York: 1970), pp. 318–19. For the classic formulation, see Romans 3:8.

'Intention' and the characterization of action ... See Germain Grisez, 'Toward a Consistent Natural-Law Ethics of Killing' (1970) 15 *Am. J. Juris.* 64; J. M. Finnis, 'The Rights and Wrongs of Abortion: A Reply to Judith Thomson' (1973) 2 *Phil. Pub. Aff.* 117–45 (reprinted in, e.g., Dworking, *Philosophy of Law*, Oxford: 1977); H. L. A. Hart, *Punishment and Responsibility* (Oxford: 1968), ch. 5; G. E. M. Anscombe, 'War and Murder' in W. Stein (ed.), *Nuclear Weapons and Christian Conscience* (London: 1961),

pp. 57–9; Charles Fried, 'Right and Wrong—Preliminary Considerations' (1976) 5 *J. Legal Studies* 165–200.

The 'doctrine' of 'double-effect' ... See, e.g., J. T. Mangan, 'An Historical Account of the Principle of the Double Effect' (1949) 10 *Theological Studies* 40–61.

'Natural law' in Roman Catholic pronouncements of strict negative principles ... A recent example is Vatican Council II's declaration that it is a 'principle of universal natural law' that 'every act of war which tends indiscriminately to the destruction of entire cities or extensive areas along with their population is a crime': Pastoral Constitution *Gaudium et Spes* (1965) 79, 80. As to some of the ecclesiastically recognized implications of the seventh requirement, briefly listed in the text, see Finnis, 'Natural Law and Unnatural Acts' (1970) 11 *Heythrop J.* 365; 'The Rights and Wrongs of Abortion: A Reply to Judith Thomson' (1973) 2 *Phil. Pub. Aff.* 117–45.

V.9

Conscience (practical reasonableness) and the obligation to follow it ... See Eric D'Arcy, *Conscience and its Right to Freedom* (London: 1961), pp. 76–125. Aquinas's discussion is clear: *S.T.* I–II, q. 19, a. 5. It scarcely needs to be added that (i) if my conscience is erroneous, what I do will be unreasonable, and (ii) if my conscience is erroneous because of my negligence and indifference in forming it, in doing what I do I will be acting culpably (notwithstanding that *I* am required by the ninth requirement of reasonableness to do it): see *S.T.* I–II, q. 19, a. 6; and (iii) that if I am aware that I have formed my practical judgment inadequately it will be reasonable of me to bow to contrary advice or instructions or norms. Of course, it by no means follows (as D'Arcy's own argument too easily assumed) that if, because of this ninth requirement, I have an obligation to φ, others have no liberty to prevent me from doing φ, or to punish me from doing φ; indeed, often enough they have not only the liberty but also an obligation to do so: see X.1, below.

VI
COMMUNITY, COMMUNITIES, AND COMMON GOOD

VI.1 REASONABLENESS AND SELF-INTEREST

THE previous chapter, on the requirements of reasonable self-constitution, will have aroused misgivings. Certainly the discussion overlooked neither the requirement of impartiality between persons, nor the requirement that basic values be always respected not only in one's own but also in others' participation in them. But are these and all the other requirements really in the service of one's own self, one's own self-constitution, self-realization, self-fulfilment? Rather than expounding morality in terms of the 'practical reason' and 'well-being' of the moral actor, should we not be *contrasting* the requirements of morality with those of rational self-interest?

The preceding sentence plays on the terms 'rational' and 'self-interest'. The ambiguities of 'reason', 'rational', and cognate terms, are well understood. Everyone knows about the rationality, often very finely turned, of mass-murderers or drug-addicts, or of one's own egoistic little schemes; and equally, everyone knows that by shifting one's focus of attention, one can criticize these schemes as arbitrary (though not whimsical), short-sighted (though cunning), unreasonable and indeed irrational (though not without a certain, sometimes rather overwhelming rationality). But not everyone is so much at ease with 'self-interest', which is sliding away from the dignity of 'self-constitution' towards the moral indignity of 'self-centredness' and 'selfishness'. And does not the analysis of morality as reasonableness in self-constitution overlook the fact that moral responsibilities can require one to sacrifice not merely one's selfishness, and one's self-interest, but even, on occasion, *oneself*?

So this chapter undertakes a fuller analysis of the proper relationship between one's own well-being and the well-being of others. It does not complete that analysis, even in outline. The question just raised, about the reasonableness of self-sacrifice, and the related question whether the effort to be reasonable is in the end just a pursuit of self-perfection, are questions to be tackled and resolved only in Chapter XIII. Conversely, the present chapter's exploration of the network of overlapping relationships in which and for which all individual lives are to be lived is an indispensable foundation for all the subsequent explorations of justice, rights, authority, law, and obligation—explorations of practical reasonableness which finally demand the venture of speculative reason undertaken in Chapter XIII.

VI.2   TYPES OF UNIFYING RELATIONSHIP

Who has not noticed the peculiar vagueness of the term 'social'? Who has not felt slightly baffled about the 'communities', and 'societies', which are spoken of sometimes as (lots of) individuals, sometimes as if they were themselves individuals with interests, well-being, etc., and sometimes as extremely abstract 'systems' (of what?)? Little progress can be made by talking about social life, social responsibilities, social rules, etc., until what it is to be involved in community is quite particularly and concretely understood.

Two preliminary remarks may be made. First: what is here said of 'community' might equally be said of 'society'. The two words have slightly different ranges and flavours in ordinary usage; but the differences themselves differ from one European language to another, and there seems no advantage in following here the fashion, initiated by Tönnies, of appropriating the two words to signify extremes or poles in the range of forms of human community/society/friendship which we are about to study. The second preliminary point is that it is helpful to begin by thinking of community or association not as *a* community or *an* association (an 'entity' or 'substance' or 'thing' which 'exists', acts, etc.) but rather as community or association, an ongoing state of affairs, a sharing of life or of action or of interests, an associating or coming-together. Community in this sense is a matter of relationship and interaction. So, in the title of this chapter, I distinguish between community and communities; and in the development of the chapter the discussion of what it is to say that communities (groups ...) *exist* is left to section VI.7.

Whatever else it is, community is a form of unifying relationship between human beings. Now such relationships in part are, and in part are not, the outcome of human intelligence, practical reasonableness, and effort. We can indeed identify four basic ways in which human understanding stands to unifying relationships, and can show that human community involves relationships in all four 'orders'. ('Order' means simply a set of unifying relationships.) My purpose in referring to these four orders is not metaphysical or epistemological; still less is it to suggest some hierarchy of value or importance. It is to give some concreteness to our discussion of human community by assembling conveniently some reminders of the complexity of human community. This complexity is often lost sight of by those who attempt to explain one order of reality using exclusively techniques of analysis suitable for another order (i.e. who try to reduce one order to another). When we are considering the connection between the basic principles of practical reasonableness and the intelligible order and existence of reality as a whole, it will be useful to recall these reminders of the ordered complexity of things (including human affairs): XIII.2.

There is first the order which we can understand but which we do not ourselves bring about: the order which is studied by the 'natural sciences'. A simple example of this order is the unifying relationship that exists between lecturer and listener when the listener *hears the sounds* made by the lecturer's vocal chords; the interrelated movements of vocal chords, sound waves, air, eardrums, etc. are subjects for natural scientific study. Part of our unity in human community, then, is physical and biological. An aspect of human community is the genetic unity of the race: human beings can (and have the physical and psychological urge to) interbreed with each other and not with other animals. A family has a special physical unity of close genetic interrelationship, sexual intercourse between parents, the feeding of the unborn infant children from their mother's body, a certain degree of compatibility of blood groups and tissues, inherited similarities of physique and perhaps of feeling, temperament, intelligence ...

Secondly, there is the unity or order which we can bring

into our understanding itself: the order which is studied reflectively in logic, epistemology, methodology, and similar disciplines, and which is manifested more straightforwardly in the internal coherence of each body of knowledge, each field of discourse. A simple example of this order is the relationship that exists between lecturer and listener when the listener *hears expositions, arguments, and explanations*; the listener brings his understanding into line with the lecturer's even if only to the degree needed to disagree with the lecturer's views. (In order to disagree with each other, we must each be thinking of the same proposition.) Part of our unity in human community, then, is unity of intelligence in its capacities, its workings, and its product, knowledge. Thus, for example, we can speak of 'what science has established', notwithstanding that no one person knows all science (or even all of 'a science'). A family can have a special unity in this order of relationships, inasmuch as its members think and learn together, acquiring a common fund of experience and insight, and even knowing how much the others know ...

Thirdly, there is the unity or order which we bring into, or impose upon, whatever matter is subject to our powers. This order is studied in the arts (such as cooking, shipbuilding, sailing), in technology and all the applied sciences, but also in studies of human symbol-making (such as linguistics, and even some aspects of literary criticism). A simple example of this order is the relationship that exists between lecturer and listener when the listener *hears the English language* and a pedagogical technique; the listener shares with the lecturer in making and decoding the formalized symbols of a language and the less formalized symbols, signs, and expressions (e.g. gestures and smiles) which, by pedagogical or rhetorical art, can be made the bearers of meanings. Part of our unity in human community, then, is the cultural unity of shared language, common technology, common technique (as in an orchestra), a common capital stock, and so on. A family can have a special unity in this order of relationships, inasmuch as its members share not only house and property and possessions but also a range of especially subtle modes of communication with one another ...

Fourthly, there is the unity or order which we bring into

our own actions and dispositions by intelligently deliberating and choosing: the order which is studied in one way by psychology (in one of its branches), in another way by biography and the history of human affairs, and in another way by ethics, political philosophy, and the like. A simple example of this order is the relationship that exists between lecturer and listener when the listener *hears the lecturer*, as a person and a teacher; the listener shares with the lecturer in making a self-constituting decision; the lecturer's decision is to devote part of his life to trying to communicate knowledge to another person (perhaps for the sake of truth and a kind of friendship, perhaps only to earn a living), while the listener's is to commit part of his life to trying to acquire knowledge from another person (perhaps for the sake of truth, perhaps only to gain a qualification which in turn will enable him to . . .). Part of our unity in human community, then, is the unity of common action. A family can have a special unity in this order of relationships, inasmuch as each of its members (especially the one(s) directing and shaping the common life) is devoted to finding his or her own self-fulfilment (at least in part) in helping the other members to fulfil themselves, by caring for them and helping them to grow in freedom and responsibility and other basic aspects of human flourishing.

Obviously, human community as we are concerned with it in this book's exploration of practical reasonableness is primarily a matter of community in the fourth order. Some degree of unity of the other three sorts is clearly needed if there is to be the community of joint action or of mutual commitment to the pursuit of some common good. But no degree of unity in those other three orders can substitute for such co-operation and common commitment; the most united family can just fall apart. So in the following section we consider more closely the main types of co-ordination of action. Throughout the analysis, 'collaboration', 'co-operation', and 'co-ordination' are used more or less synonymously and are to be understood without the flavour of effort or formality that they often have in ordinary usage. Where I refer to 'negative co-ordination' I mean mutual non-interference (e.g. abstaining from assault, theft, etc.); and 'co-ordination' without qualification is normally to be taken as including this negative co-ordination. Much of the analysis is in terms of two individuals; this is merely for the sake of simplicity and can be understood as 'two or more'.

VI.3   'BUSINESS' COMMUNITY AND 'PLAY' COMMUNITY

Consider first the pursuit, by each of two individuals, of some particular objective which each has in view, and which each can attain only by collaborating or at least co-ordinating with the other. For example, A wants to learn what tutor X has to say about 'natural law', and so does B. Tutor X gives tutorials only to pairs of students. So A and B must collaborate with each other to some (rather minimal) degree, co-ordinating their arrival, settling on the tutor's chairs without fighting, abstaining from incessant interruptions of each other, and so on. Each may be entirely indifferent to the other's success in pursuing his objective; indeed, their projects may to some degree conflict: they may be competing with each other for a prize or a position. But each has an interest in the maintenance of the ensemble of conditions (e.g. quiet, fresh air in the room, holding the tutor's attention to the subject, etc.) for successful pursuit of his own objective; and since that pursuit is required (by the tutor) to be co-ordinated, the interest of A and B in that ensemble of conditions can be said to be a common interest; and the ensemble of conditions, being a state of affairs which A and B each consider worth maintaining as a means to his objective, can be said to be a good common to A and B, a common good; and A's and B's pursuit (their effort and care to maintain that ensemble of conditions) can be said, notwithstanding the indifference of each to the other's objective, to be a common pursuit (common effort, care, etc.).

The relationship between A and B, here, is one of collaboration or co-ordination without contract. The relationships between A and X, and B and X are, on the other hand, contractual (in form, if not in legal effect). A wants to learn something and X wants (say) to earn his living; each, in order to attain his *own* objective, can agree to assist the other to attain *his* objective, but the condition of such assistance is that it shall be reciprocal: A will pay X if and only if X will teach, and X will teach if and only if A will pay. The performance of the contract between A and X (and, likewise, between B and X) thus becomes a common interest, a common pursuit, a common good, for A and X (and B and X), notwithstanding that A and X, apart from the contract, may have no interest in each other's objective, and notwithstanding that the reciprocity of interest between A and X is significantly different from the likeness of interest between A and B.

Aristotle classed all such relationships between A and B, A and X, and B and X, as relationships of utility. In such relationships there is some common interest, some common good and some common (co-ordinated) action—but all in the service of each attaining his own objective. The objective of each remains individual and private, not only in the sense that the success of other parties in attaining their objectives is a matter of indifference to each party (save to the extent, if any, that such success assists him to attain his own success), but also in the sense that the co-ordination of action is not valued by any of the parties as a component or aspect of his objective.

This last-mentioned feature of business or 'utility' relationships serves to distinguish them from relationships in which the co-ordination of action is what the parties value, i.e. *is* the objective (or a substantial component of the objective) of each of the parties. Aristotle named this class of relationships relationships of 'pleasure', and we can see what he was getting at: we engage in these relationships 'for fun'. But a better name would be relationships of *play*. For, as we saw in Chapter IV.2, the central feature and good of play is that the activity or performance is valued by the participants for its own sake, and is itself the source of their pleasure or satisfaction. (We ought here to understand 'participant' in a broad sense: the audience at an entertainment are really 'part of the game', as is shown by the interest that both entertainers and audience have in the quality of audience-reaction.)

The common good in play relationships is, thus, that there be a 'good play of the game' (in a broad sense of 'game'). Beyond that, neither of the participants need have any interest in the other participant, even when, as in *some* games or play relationships (e.g. swopping jokes), one party's envincing pleasure or satisfaction is a necessary condition of the other party's finding the game satisfying.

Thus the community of action and interest that exists between business associates (in the broad sense that includes workmates, partners, and contracting parties), and between play-partners, is to be distinguished from the community of action and interest that exists between *friends* in the full sense. Aristotle thought that the three sorts of community of action and interest are sufficiently similar to warrant applying a common name to all these relationships, which he therefore called three sorts of *philia*. And he was willing to analyse types of constitutional order in terms of these types of *philia*. But he was, of course, insistent that what we call friendship in the full sense is the central case of *philia*.

VI.4   FRIENDSHIP

For if A and B are friends, then the collaboration of each is for the sake (at least in part) *of the other*, and there is community between them not only in that there is a common interest in the conditions, and common pursuit of the means, whereby each will get what he wants for himself, but also in that what A wants for himself he wants (at least in part) under the description 'that-which-B-wants-for-himself', and vice versa. Indeed, the good that is common between friends is not simply the good of successful collaboration or co-ordination, nor is it simply the good of two successfully achieved coinciding projects or objectives; it is the common good of mutual self-constitution, self-fulfilment, self-realization.

The preceding paragraph was very summary, indeed rapid. Since our understanding of the significance of community for individual well-being and practical reasonableness will hardly be complete if only half-hearted forms of community remain in the foreground of our analysis, we need a clear and precise understanding of the most intense form of community, the friendship of true friends. This is more often treated as a matter for sentimental appreciation than for clear and precise analysis. But certainly there is no possibility of understanding the classical tradition of 'natural law' theorizing, or my own later explorations of obligation, without first appropriating the analysis of friendship in its full sense. Perhaps you or I have no real friends, in this full sense? But we can see the good of real friendships, in the lives perhaps of some of our acquaintances, and in our aspirations, or as reflected in our language, poetry, tragedy ... And in real life, outside the confines of our reflections, the boundaries between business, play, and full friendship are not too clear. Many relationships initiated merely for business and private need or advantage, or for play and individual pleasure, ripen into relationships of more or less intense friendship. Conversely, friendships can readily degenerate into mutual exploitation.

In the fullest sense of 'friendship', A is the friend of B when (i) A acts (or is willing to act) for B's well-being, for the sake of B, while (ii) B acts (or is willing to act) for A's well-being, for the sake of A, (iii) each of them knows of the other's activity and willingness and of the other's knowledge, and (iv) each of them co-ordinates (at least some of) his activity with the activity (including acts of friendship) of the other so that there is a sharing, community, mutuality, and reciprocity not only of knowledge but also of activity (and thus, normally, of enjoyment and satisfaction). And when we say that A and B act 'for the sake of each other', we mean that the concern of each for the other is founded, not in devotion to some principle according to which the other (as a member of a class picked out by that principle) is entitled to concern, but in regard or affection for that individual person as such.

The core of friendship is the following dialectic:

1. Having a friend is a basic form of good. That is to say, for any person, A, to have a friend, B, is a basic aspect of A's well-being. He can scarcely think of himself as really well-off if he has no friends. The intrinsic value of having a true friend does not consist precisely in the services the friend may render him (though they may be valuable), or precisely in the pleasure the friend may give him (though who would not welcome that?), but in the state of affairs itself that we call friendship. That state of affairs itself is the source of the deep satisfaction which normally accompanies it and which is a manifestation of the intrinsic value of the state of affairs.

2. But if A treats his relationship with B as being for his (A's) own sake, then the relationship will not be one of friendship and the benefits (if any) that A derives from it will not include the benefit of real friendship. For A to be B's friend, A must

act (at least in substantial part) for the sake of B's well-being, and must value B's well-being for the sake of B. A must treat B's well-being as an aspect of his (A's) own well-being.

3. On the other hand, what is said of A in steps (1) and (2) is true equally of B. That is to say: (1') for B to be a friend of A is a constitutive element in B's well-being, and requires (2') that B value A's well-being for the sake of A, and treat A's well-being as an aspect of his (B's) own well-being. It follows that A must value his (A's) own well-being for the sake of B, while B must value his (B's) own well-being for the sake of A. And so on. The reciprocity of love does not come to rest at either pole.

Thus self-love (the desire to participate fully, oneself, in the basic aspects of human flourishing) requires that one go beyond self-love (self-interest, self-preference, the imperfect rationality of egoism ...). This requirement is not only in its content a component of the requirement of practical reasonableness; in its form, too, it is a parallel or analogue, for the requirement in both cases is that one's inclinations to self-preference be subject to a critique in thought and a subordination in deed. The demands of friendship thus can powerfully reinforce the other demands of practical reasonableness, not least the demands of impartiality as between persons (though it is obvious that friendship complicates those demands and can, if unmeasured, compete with and distort them).

Just as the unknown time of one's prospective death is, in thought, a vantage point from which to distinguish some reasonable alternative plans of life, so friendship establishes an analogous vantage point. In friendship one is not thinking and choosing 'from one's own point of view', nor from one's friends's point of view. Rather, one is acting from a third point of view, the unique perspective from which one's own good and one's friend's good are equally 'in view' and 'in play'. Thus the heuristic postulate of the impartially benevolent 'ideal observer', as a device for ensuring impartiality or fairness in practical reasoning, is simply an extension of what comes naturally to friends.

Finally, to return to the analysis of community, we can say that friendship is the most communal though not the most extended or elaborated form of human community. There is

community in a full sense when (i) A makes B's well-being and
self-constituting participation in human goods one of his (A's)
own self-constituting commitments, and (ii) B makes A's well-
being likewise one of his (B's) basic commitments, and (iii) A
and B collaborate in pursuance of these commitments. ('Commitment' does not here refer to contracts or agreements, but
to commitment in the sense that a scholar commits himself to
scholarship; some but by no means all commitments to the well-
being of another person or persons are expressed by bilateral
agreement or unilateral promise or vow.)

VI.5 'COMMUNISM' AND 'SUBSIDIARITY'

Plato proposed a sharing of women and children, and of goods
and possessions, throughout the political community (*polis*).
And in every age, enthusiasm for community, for the widest
sharing in friendship, has inspired the dream of a 'state of
nature' (a golden age in the past, a utopia beyond the seas,
or a millennial realm of the future) in which sexual partners,
and their offspring, and the whole stock of land and chattels
and everything else contributing to the material matrix of
human life, all would be held in common, so that no one could
treat any of them as 'mine and not thine'.

So Aristotle had to begin his *Politics* with some reminders.
Friendship is nothing if it is not willing the good of one's friend,
committing oneself to helping him in his self-constituting participation in any or all of the basic aspects of human flourishing.
In the first place, then, there will be no friendship if there is
no commitment, and to commit oneself is, in this finite life,
to turn aside from an inexhaustible multitude of alternative
commitments that one might have made. In the second place,
one can give nothing to a friend unless one has something of
one's own to give. One cannot even have him to dinner if one
has no food save one's own ration. You say, let him bring his
own food, it is the sharing that counts. But what am I sharing
with him? *My* shelter, warmth, living-space. You say, have
dinner together in the communal eating place. But still I have
to give him *my* company, my attention and interest, which I
thereby deny to someone else. In the third place, much that
I have to give can only be given to a few and can only be

fully given to a few who are specified by a relationship to me
that is intrinsically permanent (e.g. genetic) or deliberately
made quasi-permanent. A woman can give her maternal affection only to a child that is hers (or that she can treat as hers). Only
a family or quasi-family can build up over time that common
stock—of uncalculated affection, physical and psychological
rapport, of shelter and means of support and material bases
for new projects, of memories and experience, of symbols, signs,
and gestures to bear moods and meanings, of knowledge of each
other's strengths and weaknesses, loves and detestations, and
of formal and informal but reliable commitment and devotion
—which each member holds at the others' disposal, and which,
being rich in all four orders of reality, constitutes an incomparably fine thing for a friend to give or to receive. To
cut the whole matter short, we must bluntly say that Plato's
proposal, made in the name of friendship, is tantamount to a
drastic dilution, 'watering-down',[1] of friendship—a radical
emaciation of a basic aspect of human well-being. (Notice that
none of this argument goes to the justice of common or private
ownership of property; this is considered in the next chapter,
VII.3.)

Still, as Aristotle also points out, if the family is thus to contribute to this growth of its members in freedom, friendship, and
all-round good, it must be liberated from the requirement of
unremitting toil by all its members for material necessities.
Things will be better for everyone if there is a division of
labour between families, specialization, technology, joint or
co-operative enterprises in production and marketing, a market
and a medium of exchange, in short, an economy that is more
than domestic. And the same goes for the other goods participated in by the family. The resources not only of material
goods and of technology, but also of language, of knowledge,
of aesthetic experience, of interpersonal concern and religious
aspiration, are all more ample than any family can mediate
to its members by itself. Hence, the members of a family will
flourish more fully if, without dissolving their family, they enter
into a whole network of associations with their neighbours.
Aristotle speaks of this level of associations as essentially the

---

[1] Aristotle, *Pol.* II, 1: 1262b17.

community of neighbourhood. But neighbourhood, we must add, need not be merely geographical.

To Aristotle's whole analysis of this vastly ramified level of forms of community intermediate between the family and the political community, we must also add that just as the dissolution of family and property would water down human friendship, so the complete absorption by the family of its members would radically emaciate their personal freedom and authenticity, which also are basic aspects of human full-being. One who treats his or her spouse as a sheer possession, or who, when his or her children have been nurtured to the threshold of maturity, seeks to make those children's basic commitments for them, robs that spouse or those children of a basic good, just as surely as Plato's republic would rob its members of another basic good. In face of the perennial dream of a general communism in friendship, the justification for the family, for its contractual or quasi-contractual permanence and exclusiveness, for its possessiveness and its possessions, is a justification which holds good only to the extent that each member of the family is enabled to grow in self-possession (of which self-giving in friendship is one basic aspect).

To say this is to formulate, in relation to the family, a principle which in fact holds good for all other forms of human community (though only in a modified form for full friendship itself). Some recent political thinkers have given this principle the name 'subsidiarity', and this name will be convenient provided we note that it signifies not secondariness or subordination but assistance; the Latin for help or assistance is *subsidium*. As we shall see (VII.3), the principle is one of justice. It affirms that the proper function of association is to help the participants in the association to help themselves or, more precisely, to constitute themselves through the individual initiatives of choosing commitments (including commitments to friendship and other forms of association) and of realizing these commitments through personal inventiveness and effort in projects (many of which will, of course, be co-operative in execution and even communal in purpose). And since in large organizations the process of decision-making is more remote from the initiative of most of those many members who will carry out the decision, the same principle requires that larger associations should not assume functions which can be performed efficiently by smaller associations.

What is the source of this principle? I touched on it when I discussed the 'experience machine': IV.5. Human good requires not only that one *receive* and *experience* benefits or desirable states; it requires that one *do* certain things, that one should *act*, with integrity and authenticity; if one can obtain the desirable objects and experiences through one's own action, so much the better. Only in action (in the broad sense that includes the investigation and contemplation of truth) does one fully participate in human goods. No one can spend all his time, in all his associations, leading and taking initiatives; but one who is never more than a cog in big wheels turned by others is denied participation in one important aspect of human well-being.

VI.6 COMPLETE COMMUNITY

Family is a very thoroughgoing form of association, controlling or influencing every corner of the lives of its members for a considerable proportion of their lifetime. But it is incomplete and inadequate. Indeed, it cannot even properly provide for the unimpaired transmission of its own genetic basis; a family that breeds within itself is headed for physical self-destruction. And its weakness as an economic unit, capable of supporting the health and culture of its members, has already been mentioned and needs no elaboration here. Economic, cultural, and sporting associations, in turn, are more or less explicitly specialized in their concerns. And as for friendship in its full sense, if the friendship of husband and wife is an incomplete basis for ample well-being, so is any other. So there emerges the desirability of a 'complete community', an all-round association in which would be co-ordinated the initiatives and activities of individuals, of families, and of the vast network of intermediate associations. The point of this all-round association would be to secure the whole ensemble of material and other conditions, including forms of collaboration, that tend to favour, facilitate, and foster the realization by each individual of his or her personal development. (Remember: this personal development includes, as an integral element and not merely as a means or pre-condition, both individual self-direction and community with others in family, friendship, work, and play.)

Such an ensemble of conditions includes some co-ordination (at least the negative co-ordination of establishing restraints against interferences) of any and every individual life-plan and any and every form of association. So there is no aspect of human affairs that as such is outside the range of such a complete community. Now Aristotle, by a premature generalization from incomplete empirical data, declared that the Greek *polis* was the paradigmatic form of complete and self-sufficient community for securing the all-round good of its members. So the form of community that today claims to be complete and self-sufficient, the territorial state, retains the label 'political community' or 'body politic'; for though it does not fit Aristotle's descriptions of paradigmatic forms of *polis*, it claims the all-embracing function which Aristotle (after Plato) ascribed to the *polis*. There can be 'parish pump politics', 'College politics', and so on; but 'politics' without qualification signifies the field of action and discourse to do with the affairs of complete communities.

Nor is 'politics' the only term whose focal meaning concerns complete community. 'Law' is another such term. We can certainly speak intelligibly and usefully of the law of some lesser group, even of a gang. But, as the common understanding of the unqualified expressions 'law' and 'the law' indicates, the central case of law and legal system is the law and legal system of a complete community. That is why it is characteristic of legal systems that (i) they claim authority to regulate all forms of human behaviour (a claim which in the hands of the lawyer becomes the artificial postulate that legal systems are gapless); (ii) they therefore claim to be the supreme authority for their respective community, and to regulate the conditions under which the members of that community can participate in any other normative system or association; (iii) they characteristically purport to 'adopt' rules and normative arrangements (e.g. contracts) from other associations within and without the complete community, thereby 'giving them legal force' for that community; they thus maintain the notion of completeness and supremacy without pretending to be either the only association to which their members may reasonably belong or the only complete community with whom their members may have dealings, and without striving to foresee and provide substantively for every activity and arrangement in which their members may wish to engage.

All these defining features, devices, and postulates of law have their foundation, from the viewpoint of practical reasonableness, in the requirement that the activities of individuals, families, and specialized associations be co-ordinated. This requirement itself derives partly from the requirements of impartiality as between persons, and of impartiality as between the basic values and openness to all of them, given certain facts about the ensemble of empirical conditions under which basic goods such as health, education, science, and art can be realized and realized in the lives of each person according to the measure of his own inclinations and capacities. I shall have more to say of this when I explicitly turn to study justice: VII.1, VII.3.

Suffice it for the moment to say that, like other forms of community, political community exists partially (and sometimes primarily) as a kind of business arrangement between self-interested associates (the kind of mutual insurance association or 'social contract' derided by Aristotle and all the classics for it meagreness as a form [or account] of community); partially (and sometimes primarily) as a form of play, in which the participants enjoy the give-and-take, the dissension, bargaining, and compromise, for its own sake as a vastly complex and absorbing performance; partially (and sometimes primarily) as an expression of disinterested benevolence, reinforced by grateful recognition of what one owes to the community in which one has been brought up and in which one finds and founds one's family and one's life-plan, and further reinforced by a determination not to be a 'free rider' who arbitrarily seeks to retain the benefits without accepting the burdens of communal interdependence; and characteristically by some admixture of all these rationales.

But we must not take the pretensions of the modern state at face value. Its legal claims are founded, as I remarked, on its self-interpretation as a complete and self-sufficient community. But there are relationships between men which transcend the boundaries of all *poleis*, realms, or states. These relationships exist willy-nilly, in manifold and multiplying ways, in three of the four orders: for there is physical, biological, ecological interdependence, there is a vast common stock of knowledge (including knowledge of each other's existence, concerns, and conditions), and there is a vast common stock of technology, systems of intercommunication, ideological symbolisms, universal religions ... Thus there is no reason to deny the good of international community in the fourth order, the order of reciprocal interactions, mutual commitments, collaboration, friendship, competition, rivalry ... If it now appears that the good of individuals can only be fully secured and realized in the context of international community, we must conclude that the claim of the national state to be a complete community is unwarranted and the postulate of the national legal order, that it is supreme and comprehensive and an exclusive source of legal obligation, is increasingly what lawyers would call a 'legal fiction'.

VI.7   THE EXISTENCE OF A COMMUNITY

Thus far I have been speaking about the rationale(s) of community or association, as forms of relationship. It is now time to explain what is meant by saying that *a* community, or *an* association, exists, or acts, or has members or rules that belong to it. It will be convenient to frame this explanation in terms of 'a group', since that word lacks the ambiguity of 'community' and 'association' to which I have referred. In common usage, however, 'group' has some distracting connotations. So what I now have to say about groups applies as well to two-member teams, couples or pairs (which are not usually called groups), but is not intended to apply to any group in the sense of a mere aggregation, i.e. a class whose members have something important in common, but which is not spoken of as acting, and in and for which there is no authority (e.g. the group comprised of all English-speakers, or all aunts; or perhaps such groups as a rush-hour crowd).

In solving the obvious mystery about what it means to say that a group exists, many modern thinkers hoped to be able to do without reference to the practical reasoning ('internal attitudes') of its members. Thus, for A, B, and C to constitute a group, it was said to be sufficient that, over a given period of time, A interacts with B and C *more often* than he does with P, Q, and R (who are outsiders or members of other groups), while B similarly interacts more often with A and C than he does with outsiders, and so on.[2] But this analysis will not do. Suppose that (i) in the library A has more interactions with B than with any other reader while B has more interactions with A than with any other reader, and (ii) in the tavern A sees more of C than of anyone else, while C sees more of A there than of anyone else, and (iii) at the sportsground B plays more often with C, while C plays more often with B, than either of them plays with anyone else. Yet C never goes to the library, B never goes to the tavern, and A has no interest in sport. A, B, and C then may interact more often with one another than with anyone else. But why should they be called a group?

When the inadequacy of simply counting interactions became apparent, an attempt was made to rescue the behaviouristic analytical strategy by stipulating that, to constitute a group, the persons in question must interact with one another more than they interact with anyone else, *in a given context.*[3] But what constitutes a different context? Obviously, it cannot be merely geographical location. Members of a family, or of a secret police service, may be scattered all over the world; or the circus may be simply on the move. Consider the employee who opens and shuts a factory gate for incoming and outgoing lorries of independent contractors who bring supplies for the factory through that gate. He may interact with lorry drivers, or even with particular lorry drivers, more frequently than he interacts with other employees or with the management; indeed he may interact almost exclusively with the lorry drivers at the gate. Yet he is a member of the factory business, and conversely there is no point in talking of a group comprising himself and those outside lorry drivers. What makes him a member of the factory business? It is that his *purpose* in being there, opening and shutting the gate, is to work for the business (to increase its profits, or to earn his wage, or both); he is therefore prepared to adjust his conduct to the needs of the factory, as he perceives

---

[2] See G. C. Homans, *The Human Group* (London: 1951), p. 84; he adds 'It is possible just by counting interactions to map out a group quantitatively distinct from others.'

[3] See e.g. W. J. H. Sprott, *Human Groups* (Harmondsworth: 1958), p. 9.

them (e.g. if he sees it catch fire) or as the factory management direct him. Though his purposes or aims and those of the lorry drivers are (normally) co-ordinated, they are not shared; they are tangential or coincidental aims. Conversely, he and the lorry drivers become a group as soon as they begin to share an aim; if he conspires with them, even by a nod and a wink, to open the gates to let them burgle the factory and make a get-away, then he has teamed up with them, even if only temporarily, and is associating himself with their gang ...

In short, sharing of aim rather than multiplicity of interaction is constitutive of human groups, communities, societies.[4] (This is fortunate for our understanding of human groups; for if we take no account of the practical reasonings of the actors, which allow us to individuate *actions*, there is in fact no way of individuating *interactions* other than by *ad hoc* stipulation. How many interactions are there between a lecturer and his audience in an hour?) Outside the 'given context' of a sharing (i.e. in the active sense, community) of purpose, interactions have no significance as constitutive of a group. This remains the case even when the purpose in view is materially identical with the interaction or shared activity, as is the case with games and all forms of play (the shared objective being a good play of the game). Interactions between persons may be unilateral (as where A's act is intended to and does prompt B's) or reciprocal (as where A's prompts B's and B's prompts A's). No doubt reciprocal interactions are apt to constitute a sustained group existence. But far more important than the form of interaction is the shared purpose of A and B that their activities be co-ordinated, either for the sake of the co-ordinated interaction itself (as in a game) or for the sake of some further shared objective. (To see the importance of this shared intention to co-ordinate or co-operate, in the constituting of a group, consider the reciprocal interactions of the submarine commander and the destroyer captain who is hunting him down, or of the evasive witness and cross-examining counsel.)

Notice that in this section we have been considering what would be said by men of common sense, historians, sociologists, and the like; we are not considering the quite different problem

---

[4] Despite his initial definition, Sprott concedes that a group, in his sense, only exists when it has a 'purpose collectively pursued': ibid., p. 11.

of analysing and accounting for settled rules or propositions of law which ascribe existence, rights, liabilities, etc., to corporations, funds, idols, or other 'legal persons' or legal institutions. On the other hand, my analysis of the existence of a group can be relevant when the question is not how such rules are to be analysed, but is whether such rules *should* be extended to such-and-such an alleged group, or conversely whether the protection of such rules *should* be removed by 'lifting the veil' of legal personality to disclose the 'real' group or individuals who *ought* to be held responsible for certain actions or states of affairs.

To summarize: a group, in the relevant sense, whether team, club, society, enterprise, corporation, or community, is to be said to exist wherever there is, over an appreciable span of time, a co-ordination of activity by a number of persons, in the form of interactions, and with a view to a shared objective.

If we ask why common sense tends to require co-ordination over some space of time before being willing to speak of a group existing, the answer is not far to seek. The more the co-ordination of the relevant persons is pursuant to some value or open-ended commitment, or, if directed to some definite and fully realizable project, is nevertheless controlled by concern for some value(s) that requires adaptation of the co-ordination in response to contingencies, the more likely we are to be willing to think of the participants as constituting a group. And, as we shall see, the more likely it is that the participants themselves will think of themselves as a group, and look about for practices, usages, conventions, or 'norms' for solving their co-ordination problems, and/or for someone with authority to select among available solutions. Such norms will then be thought of as norms *of* and *for* the group, and the leader(s) will be thought of as having authority *in* and *over* the group. The 'existence' of the group, the 'existence' of social rules, and the 'existence' of authority tend to go together. And what makes sense of these ascriptions of existence is in each case the presence of some more or less shared objective or, more precisely, some shared conception of the point of continuing co-operation. This point we may call the common good.

VI.8   THE COMMON GOOD

Confronted by the term 'the common good', one is first inclined to think of the utilitarian 'greatest good of the greatest number'. When one is persuaded that, outside limited technical contexts, that notion is not merely practically unworkable but intrinsically incoherent and senseless (V.6), one is inclined to think that reference to the common good must inevitably be empty. But if the reader looks back at the uses of the term in earlier sections of this chapter, he will see that it need not be vacuous. In the case of the pair of students (VI.3), their common good (some conception of which could guide their co-ordination of actions) was the ensemble of conditions which would enable each to pursue his own objective. In the case of a game (VI.3), the common good for the participants was that there should be a good play of the game, which requires not only a substratum of material conditions but also a certain quality (rule-conformity, sportsmanship, etc.) in the co-ordination itself. In the case of friendship (VI.4), the common good was identified as the self-fulfilment of each of the friends through the sharing of life and affection and activity and material goods (which of course also requires the maintenance of a certain ensemble of material conditions, for intercommunication, etc.). Finally, in the case of political community (VI.6), the point or common good of such an all-round association was said to be the securing of a whole ensemble of material and other conditions that tend to favour the realization, by each individual in the community, of his or her personal development. In each case, therefore, 'the common good' referred to the factor or set of factors (whether a value, a concrete operational objective, or the conditions for realizing a value or attaining an objective) which, as considerations in someone's practical reasoning, would make sense of or give reason for his collaboration with others and would likewise, from their point of view, give reason for their collaboration with each other and with him.

The classical analogy of the 'ship of state', i.e. between governing a political community and navigating a ship, though it is by no means as unwarranted as many have claimed, is indeed misleading in one important respect. Since passengers normally board ships because they wish to get to an advertised destination (or to some set of ports of call), the analogy suggests that the political community, too, has some definite and completely attainable objective. But here, as so often, we must recall the distinction between, on the one hand, values in which we participate but which we do not exhaust and, on the other hand, the particular projects we undertake and objectives we pursue (normally, if we are reasonable, as ways of participating in values) and which can at a given point of time be said to have been fully attained, or not, as the case may be: III.2–3. There is no reason to suppose that political community has any aim or destination of the latter sort. Equally there is no reason to suppose that the members of a political community each have, or ought to have, any one such aim or determinable set of aims which political community does or should seek to support. Committing oneself to a life-plan is not at all like setting oneself to bake a cake. Nor is there only one reasonable life-plan or determinable set of reasonable life-plans, which the state should seek to get its citizens to commit themselves to. Yet there is a common good of the political community, and it is definite enough to exclude a considerable number of types of political arrangement, laws, etc.

For there is a 'common good' for human beings, inasmuch as life, knowledge, play, aesthetic experience, friendship, religion, and freedom in practical reasonableness are good for any and every person. And each of these human values is itself a 'common good' inasmuch as it can be participated in by an inexhaustible number of persons in an inexhaustible variety of ways or on an inexhaustible variety of occasions. These two senses of 'common good' are to be distinguished from a third, from which, however, they are not radically separate. This third sense of 'common good' is the one commonly intended throughout this book, and it is: a set of conditions which enables the members of a community to attain for themselves reasonable objectives, or to realize reasonably for themselves the value(s), for the sake of which they have reason to collaborate with each other (positively and/or negatively) in a community. The community referred to in this definition may be specialized, partial, or complete; when I speak simply of 'the common good' hereafter, I normally mean the all-round or complete community, the political community subject to my caveat about the incompleteness of the nation state in the modern world: VI.5. The common good in this sense is a frequent or at least a justified meaning of the phrases 'the general welfare' or 'the public interest'.

Notice that this definition neither asserts nor entails that the members of a community must all have the same values or objectives (or set of values or objectives); it implies only that there be some set (or set of sets) of conditions which needs to obtain if each of the members is to attain his own objectives. And that there is, in human communities, some such set (or set of sets) of conditions is no doubt made possible by the fact that human beings have a 'common good' in the first sense mentioned in the last paragraph. The common good in the first sense thus explains the availability and relevance of a common good in the third sense. In this respect we can speak of the common good on different explanatory levels.

What, then, is the content of the common good of the political community, or of the international community that ought to (but in practice cannot yet) assume some though not all of the present justified functions and aspects of the political communities we call states? That is the subject-matter of the following chapters on justice, authority, and law.

NOTES

VI.1

An individual who acts for any common good is rejecting the claims of 'self-interest' but is not ignoring his own interests ... For useful preliminary clarifications see B. J. Diggs, 'The Common Good as Reason for Political Action' (1973) 83 *Ethics* 283–93.

VI.2

'Community' and 'society' ... Much that Aristotle said or might have said in terms of *koinonia* is said by Augustine in relation to *societas* and *vita socialis*: see, e.g., *De Civitate Dei*, XIX, 5–9. Ferdinand Tönnies, *Gemeinschaft und Gesellschaft* (1887; trans. C. P. Loomis, *Community and Association*, London: 1957), proposed a broad distinction, rather similar to that made earlier by Maine (in terms of 'status' and 'contract') and later by Durkheim (in terms of 'mechanical solidarity' and 'organic solidarity'), between *community*, in which instinct and tradition are the basis of social union, and *society*, in which rational self-interest prevails. On the other hand, Thomas Gilby, *Between Community and Society: A Philosophy and Theology of the State* (London: 1953), contrasts community (rooted in instinct, natural affections, mass-pressures, etc.), not with the 'rational' order of contractual and similar relations, but with the *communicatio amicorum*,

i.e. friendship in the full sense. (*Communicatio* is the Latin for *koinonia*.) The fact is that the two words have no settled resonance or connotation, and thus can either be put to stipulative use to make a contrast, or else (as here) be left undifferentiated in the analysis.

Unifying relationships ... In Aristotle, *taxis* (see e.g. *Pol.* III, 4: 1278b9; 1: 1274b9; VII, 4: 1326a30); in Augustine, *ordo* (see e.g. *De Civitate Dei*, XIX, 1; *De Libero Arbitrio*, I, 6, 15); in much modern writing, 'system'—as in the common usage of 'the social system', 'the legal system' ...

The four orders ... See Aquinas, *in Eth.* I, 1 (introduction): 'Order stands to reason in four ways ...'. The reintroduction of Aquinas's taxonomy into the modern debate is the work of Germain Grisez, *Beyond the New Theism: A Philosophy of Religion* (Notre Dame and London: 1975), pp. 230–40, 353–6, who adjusts Aquinas's account by recognizing that language is an artefact. The account in the text, above, follows Grisez closely.

Family relationships ... The reference, throughout the analysis, is primarily but not exclusively to the 'nuclear family', the procreative community of two parents living in the same household and co-operating in the care of their own children. References in this chapter and elsewhere are not intended to express any judgment on proposed alternatives to the rearing of children in families (e.g. communes, kibbutzim, etc.). The point here is to discuss 'community' in relation to a context very familiar to most readers of this book.

VI.3

Aristotle on three types of 'friendship' ... Aristotle's distinction between friendships of utility, friendships of pleasure, and the 'perfect friendship' of those who love each other for their own sake is expressly based on the already traditional threefold distinction between types of good or objective (see notes to Chapter III.2, above): *Nic. Eth.* VIII, 2: 1155b17–20; 3–4: 1156a6–1157b6; and it is carefully linked to the classic threefold distinction between types of political constitution: *Nic. Eth.* VIII, 9–11; 1159b25–1161b11. In using an analogous threefold distinction between types of co-ordination and community, I do not intend to import all the results of Aristotle's analysis, e.g. that 'friendships of utility seem to occur most frequently amongst the old' (1156a25), etc., etc. For Aristotle's analysis itself, see John M. Cooper, 'Aristotle on the Forms of Friendship' (1977) 30 *Rev. Metaphysics* 619.

'A good play of the game' ... See Rawls, *Theory of Justice*, pp. 525–6. I agree with Rawls that the shared end of a social union (such as a family or a state) is 'clearly not merely a common desire for the same particular thing' (ibid., p. 526), but I do not agree with him that the 'shared final end of all the members of [a well-ordered society]' is 'the successful carrying out of just institutions' (ibid., p. 527). The latter view assimilates communities such as the family and the state too closely to games in which 'a good play of the game' *is* the shared final end. In a really well-ordered society the shared final end of each is the well-being of all, to which end the 'carrying-out of just institutions' (an odd phrase, which I interpret very broadly, for the sake of the argument) is the proximate means.

VI.4

Friendship as the central case of community ... The classic analysis is by Aristotle, who opens his *Politics* with the statement that the *polis* is a *koinonia* (*Pol.* I, 1: 1252a1; see also the little treatise on politics in *Nic. Eth.* VIII, 9–11: 1160a8–1161b11) and who then makes *koinonia* (which ranges in meaning from any degree of common interest, e.g. between businessmen, to the deepest intimacy and communion of minds in real friendship) the pivot in his analysis of *philia* (roughly, friendship in its various forms): see *Nic. Eth.* VIII, 9: 1159b32; IX, 12: 1171b33. On *koinonia*, see W. L. Newman, *The Politics of Aristotle*, vol. I (Oxford: 1887), pp. 41–2; *Gauthier–Jolif*, II, 2, pp. 696–7, 768.

Friendship in the full sense ... Although 'friendship' has lost some of its resonance and become rather cool and narrow in modern English, it lends itself better to analysis for present purposes than 'love', which is too charged with special Christian (agapeistic) or, more usually, erotic or merely sentimental overtones. Thomas Aquinas did well to begin his treatise on love (*caritas*, in Greek *agape*) by showing that *caritas* is a friendship (*amicitia*): *S.T.* II–II, q. 23, a. 1. Much of what is said by Aristotle in relation to *philia* and by Aquinas in relation to *amicitia* or *amor amicitiae* is said by Augustine in relation to *amor* and *concordia*. With the intention of superseding this entire range of classical philosophical and theological meanings, Auguste Comte invented the term 'altruism' (in French, *altruisme*): Comte, *Système de politique positive*, vol. I (1851), Introduction, and ch. III (see *System of Positive Polity*, trans. J. H. Bridges, London: 1875, vol. I, pp. 502, 558, 564–70; cf. pp. 10–18). This word has made its way in the world; it has a peculiar thinness, however, related to the important fact that it means 'willingness to live [act, etc.] for the sake of another [person]' ('vivre pour autrui'), and lacks the mutuality, and hence the special 'third viewpoint' and sense of *common* good, that are intrinsic to friendship, as the text of this section shows. For a modern discussion close to mine, as far as it goes, see Rawls on 'the idea of social union' and 'the good of community', *Theory of Justice*, pp. 520–9.

Friendship as the central case (focal meaning) of 'philia' ... Aristotle says: 'But since people do apply the term "friends" [*philoi*] to persons whose regard for each other is based on utility, just as states can be "friends" (since expediency is generally recognised as the motive of international alliances), or on pleasure, as children make friends, perhaps we too must call such relaionships friendships; but then we must say that there are several sorts of friendship, that between good men, as good, being friendship [*philia*] in the primary and proper [*protos ... kai kyrios*: in Latin, *primo et principaliter*] meaning of the term, while the other kinds are friendships in an analogical sense [or: by way of resemblance to true friendship: *kath homoioteta*: in Latin, *secundum similitudinem*]': *Nic. Eth.* VIII, 4: 1157a26–33, trans. Rackham (Loeb). Hence the intimacy (*suzen*) of true friends is the central case of *koinonia*: cf. *Nic. Eth.* IX, 12: 1171b32–33 with *Gauthier–Jolif*, II, 2, pp. 768–9.

The dialectic of self-love and love of the friend ... See Aristotle, *Nic. Eth.* VIII, 2: 1156a1–5; IX, 4: 1166a2–33; 8: 1168b15–1169b2; 9: 1170b5–19; 12: 1171b33–1172a1; *Rhet.* II, 4: 1380b36; also Cicero, *De Legibus*, I, xii, 34; xviii, 49; Aquinas, *S.T.* II–II, q. 25, a. 4; q. 26, aa. 4, 5.

VI.5

Plato's communism of women, children, and property ... See *Rep.* V: 457c–465a, where the communizing (*koinoneo*) seems to be restricted to the class of guardians of the *polis*; *Laws*, V: 739 b-d, where the proposal extends to the whole *polis*. As to the motivations of the proposal, see Eric Voegelin, *Order and History*, vol. 3, *Plato and Aristotle* (Baton Rouge: 1957), pp. 47, 49, 118–19.

Aristotle's critique of Plato's communism ... See *Pol.* II, 1–2: 1260b37–1264b3; for outline and summary, see Newman, op. cit., vol. I pp. 160–8; for the interpretation followed here, see Voegelin, op. cit., pp. 319–22.

Aristotle on the family, domestic management, and the economy of the 'polis' ... See *Pol.* I, 3–4: 1256a1–1259a38. There are many deficiencies in his analysis. The neighbourhood association, having been introduced as the intermediate association between family and *polis*, immediately drops out of view altogether.

'Subsidiarity' ... This principle is one important development of the Aristotelian political science, drawing on but going well beyond Aristotle's critique of Plato's communism. It has been popularized by recent Popes under the name of 'subsidiary function' or 'subsidiarity'. Pius XI first referred to it as such in his encyclical letter *Quadragesimo Anno* (1931) [para. 79]: '... just as it is wrong to withdraw from the individual and commit to a group what private initiative and effort can accomplish, so too it is an injustice ... for a larger and higher association to arrogate to itself functions which can be performed efficiently by smaller and lower associations. This is a fundamental principle of social philosophy ... Of its very nature the true aim of all social activity should be to help [*subsidium afferre*] members of a social body, and never to destroy or absorb them ...'. Later pronouncements of the Roman Catholic authorities have applied the principle to relationships of production in the economy (1961, 1967), to world political order (1963) and world economic order (1965), to the relationships between families, schools, and the state (1965), to the ecclesiastical community (1969), and to politics at all levels (1971). Being a matter of right (justice), not merely efficiency, it is obviously closely related to what many people refer to as the right to *liberty*.

VI.6

Aristotle and the 'natural' progression from family through neighbourhood association to political community ... See *Pol.* I, 2: 1252a15–1253a29; Ernest Barker, *The Politics of Aristotle* (Oxford: 1946), p. 7; for penetrating analysis and critique, see Voegelin, op. cit., pp. 315–17, concluding that 'the polis is a premature generalization from insufficient materials' (p. 317; see also pp. 310–14). My discussion goes beyond Aristotle in a number of respects, and rejects both his fundamental assumption (*Pol.* I, 1: 1252b13–30) that the family is merely an association for the sake of life [survival and reproduction] (while the *polis* is an association for the sake of the good life) and the conclusions which he draws from that assumption, notably that education is exclusively the function of the *polis* and not primarily or at all the responsibility of parents (see *Pol.* VIII, 1: 1337a23–32). Nor does my analysis make any claims about the historical priority of one form of association over others.

Comprehensiveness, purported supremacy, and absorptive capacity ('openness') of legal systems ... For these characteristics of the central cases of legal systems, see Raz, *Practical Reason*, pp. 150–4.

The state as merely a mutual insurance society: the classical critique ... See Aristotle, *Pol.* III, 5: 1280a31–1281a5: '... the *polis* was formed not for the sake of life only but rather for the good life ... and ... its purpose is not [merely] military alliance for defence ... and it does not exist [merely] for the sake of trade and of business relations ... any *polis* which is truly so called, and is not one merely in name, must devote itself to the aim of encouraging excellence [*arete*]. Otherwise a *polis* sinks into a mere alliance, which only differs in space from other forms of alliance where the members live at a distance from each other. Otherwise, too, the law becomes a mere covenant—or (in the phrase of the sophist Lycophron) "a guarantor of justice as between one man and another"—instead of being, as it should be, such as will make the members of the *polis* good and just ... The *polis* is not merely the sharing of a common locality for the purpose of preventing mutual injury and exchanging goods. These are necessary pre-conditions of the existence of a *polis* ... but a *polis* is a *koinonia* of families and clans [and neighbourhoods] in living well, with the object of a full and self-sufficient life [and for the sake of truly good (*kalon*) actions, not merely of living together] ...'. In short, analysis of political community should not be based on a view of what would be reasonable in Hobbes's 'state of nature' or in the game-theorist's 'prisoners' dilemma' (cf. E. Ullmann-Margalit, *The Emergence of Norms* (Oxford: 1977), ch. II). On the political theory of the sophists, see Voegelin, *Order and History*, vol. 2, *The World of the Polis* (Baton Rouge: 1957), pp. 305–31.

Aristotle on the complete sufficiency of the 'polis' ... For Aristotle the *polis* is a complete and self-sufficient community because it provides context and resources completely adequate for the full and complete development of a man. On this *autarkeia*, see *Nic. Eth.* I, 6–7: 1097b7–17; *Pol.* I, 1: 1252b29; III, 5: 1281a1. See Voegelin's critique, cited above, of this 'premature generalization'. Aristotle envisages neither the spiritual community of a universal Church nor the international community of all mankind.

VI.7

The existence of a group and the number of interactions between its members ... I follow the lucid critique of this theory by A. M. Honoré, 'What is a Group?' (1975) 61 *Arch. R. S. P.* 161 at pp. 167–76.

Sharing of aim as constitutive of human groups ... See Honoré, op. cit., at pp. 168–70; Rawls, *Theory of Justice*, p. 525; Aristotle, *Pol.* I, 1: 1252a1–4: 'Observation shows us, first, that every *polis* is a species of association [*koinonia*], and, secondly, that all associations are instituted with a view to some good—for all men do all their acts with a view to something which is, in their view, good'.

Analysis of the existence, as a matter of law, of corporations and other legal institutions ... See H. L. A. Hart, 'Definition and Theory in Jurisprudence' (1954) 70 *L.Q.R.* 37 at 49–59; D. N. MacCormick, 'Law as Institutional Fact' (1974) 90 *L.Q.R.* 102 at 106–10.

VI.8

Community to be analysed in terms of common good ... Cf. Aristotle, *Pol.* I, 1: 1252a2: 'every *koinonia* is formed with a view to some good (since all the actions of all men are done with a view to what they think to be good)'. This good Aristotle usually calls 'common interest' (*koinon sympheron*) but sometimes calls 'common good' (*koinon agathon*): e.g. *Pol.* III, 8: 1284b6.

The common good of the political community ... The definition here given is similar to that worked out by French commentators on Aquinas: see J. T. Delos in *Saint Thomas d'Aquin, Somme théologique: La Justice*, vol. I [II–II, qq. 63–6] (1932), pp. 209, 242.

VII
JUSTICE

VII.1 ELEMENTS OF JUSTICE

THE preceding chapter's examination of community enables
me to turn to the requirement of practical reasonableness held
over from Chapter V (V.8), the requirement of justice—an
ensemble of requirements of practical reasonableness that hold
because the human person must seek to realize and respect
human goods not merely in himself and for his own sake but
also in common, in community. (Something of the sense of this
'must', this rational necessity, was indicated in VI.4, above.)
This being my purpose, I use the concept of justice with all
the breadth that that concept has had in academic discussion
since Aristotle first treated it as an academic topic. That is to
say, I set aside all the special and limiting shades of meaning
that the word 'justice' may have acquired in common parlance,
as in the expression 'courts of justice', or in the contrast that
might be drawn by saying that a perfectly *fair* lottery does not
necessarily produce a *just* result.

In its full generality, the complex concept of justice embraces
three elements, and is applicable to all situations where these
elements are found together. The first element might be called
other-directedness: justice has to do with one's relations and
dealings with other persons; it is 'inter-subjective' or interpersonal. There is a question of justice and injustice only where
there is a plurality of individuals and some practical question
concerning their situation and/or interactions *vis-à-vis* each
other. Of course, by a kind of metaphorical extension, we can
speak of 'doing oneself justice' (e.g. by performing well in a
game or examination, not necessarily competitive): here we
preserve the element of other-directedness by implicitly relating
the subject and his actual performance to the subject and his
performance as they should be. Plato capitalized on another
quasi-metaphorical extension by treating justice as concerned

essentially with the relation between three aspects of the soul (reasonableness, desire, and the spiritedness which normally allies itself to reason to master desire):[1] justice as order in the soul then becomes the model for and cause of justice as right order in society.[2] I shall not follow Plato in this extension. Suffice it to note, first, that he preserves the element of other-directed-ness by treating the aspects of the soul as if they were (or could be compared to) distinct individuals; and second, that modern European languages are still more liberal than Plato in their word-play. They embody an immensely complex and extensive web of overlapping notions which shift and play in and between the field of human society (our present concern) and quite other fields: consider the sequence, '*le mot juste*', 'just so', 'correct', 'rectify', '*Recht*', 'right', '*dirritto*', '*droit*', 'direct', 'regular', 'regulate', 'rule' ... So we must let our discussion be ruled by the substantive questions we have in mind (about what is reasonable and unreasonable in human conduct), not by the conventions and associations of our language (which provide, nevertheless, a useful assemblage of reminders).

The second element in the relevant concept of justice is that of *duty*, of what is owed (*debitum*) or due to another, and correspondingly of what that other person has a right to (viz. roughly, to what is his 'own' or at least his 'due' by right). To the complexities of this element I devote the next chapter, and to the roots of all obligation or duty I devote Chapter XI. For the present, suffice it to say that justice concerns not every reasonable relationship or dealing between one person and another, but only those relations and dealings which are necessary or appropriate for the avoiding of a wrong. (There may, of course, be more than one way of avoiding the relevant sort of wrong; but in calling something 'just' we are not asserting that it is the *only* way of avoiding a wrong, and are not assessing it by comparison with other possible ways, but are asserting that it is a way of avoiding something that in reason *must* not be or be done in the relevant, i.e. inter-subjective, field.)

The third element in the relevant concept of justice can be called *equality*. But, even more than in the case of the other two elements, this must be taken in an analogical sense: that

[1] *Rep.* IV, 439c–441b.
[2] *Rep.* IV, 441c–444a; and *passim*.

is to say, it can be present in quite various ways. There is, for example, the 'arithmetical' equality of $2 = 2$, and there is also the 'geometrical' equality of $1:1 = 2:2$, or of $3:2 = 6:4$; to feed a large man the same rations as a small child both is and is not to treat the two 'equally'. To avoid misunderstandings and over-simplifications, therefore, it may be better to think of *proportionality*,[3] or even of *equilibrium* or balance. Even so, there remains the question of the terms of the comparison in any assessment of proportions; we may be interested in comparing the large man's rations with the small child's rations as shares of some available supply, or we may be interested in comparing the large man's rations with what he needs or with what it is *fitting* for him to have if he is to remain alive and well, regardless of questions of supply and shares. Given the analogical nature of the concept of justice and of each of its three main conceptual components, either sort of comparison suffices to supply the equality/inequality or proportion/disproportion that must enter, at least implicitly, into any assessment in terms of justice/injustice.

By treating these three elements, thus understood, as necessary and sufficient for an assessment to be an assessment of justice, I am seeking to give the concept of justice sufficient precision to be useful in an analysis of practical reasonableness, and sufficient breadth for it to be worthy of its classical and popular prominence in that analysis. My theory of justice, then, is not restricted (like Rawls's) to the 'basic institutions of society'.[4] Nor is it restricted (as Aristotle was tempted to restrict his[5]) to relations between mature and free equals in political community. In my theory a parent can treat his child with straightforward injustice. Nor are the requirements of justice in my account restricted (like Hart's) to what can be drawn from the principle 'Treat like cases alike and different cases differently'.[6] My theory includes principles for assessing how one person ought to treat another (or how one person has a right to be treated), regardless of whether or not others are

---

[3] 'Proportion being equality of ratios': Aristotle, *Nic. Eth.* V, 3: 1131a31.

[4] See *Theory of Justice*, pp. 4, 7, 84; see also the diagram, ibid., p. 109: justice as treated in the present chapter would appear not only where Rawls places it in that diagram but also at the foot of arms III, II(b) and both limbs of II(a).

[5] See *Nic. Eth.* V, 6: 1134a25–b17.

[6] See *Concept of Law*, pp. 155–6. On the principle, see VII.4, below.

being so treated; in my usage, a principle forbidding torture
in *all* cases is a principle of justice. Finally, it goes without saying
that my theory is not restricted (like Rawls's) to the ideal
conditions of a society in which everyone complies fully with
the principles and institutions of justice.[7] So my theory incorporates theses about war, about punishment, about civil
obligation in face of unjust legislation, and about other
situations of social breakdown and individual recalcitrance.
Many parts of the theory are only mentioned (if that) in this
chapter; some others are treated in the chapters on rights
(VIII), authority (IX), law (X), and obligation (XI).

VII.2   GENERAL JUSTICE

The requirements of justice, then, are the concrete implications
of the basic requirement of practical reasonableness that one
is to favour and foster the common good of one's communities.
That principle is closely related both to the basic value of friendship and to the principle of practical reasonableness which
excludes arbitrary self-preference in the pursuit of good; but
it may not be reducible to either or both without remainder, so
I referred to it in Chapter V.8 as a distinct eighth principle
of practical reasonableness. The principle contains, in other
terminology, all three elements discussed in the preceding
section: other-directedness, in the reference to the community
or communities of which one is a member, and whose other
members (as well as oneself) one assists in serving the common
good; duty, by virtue of the fact that this is a *requirement* of
practical reasonableness; and equality or proportionality, since
(*a*) the principle looks to the *common* good of the relevant
community, not to the good of any individual or group in
disregard of the well-being of the others, and (*b*) the principle
looks to the common *good*, which entails a reference to standards
of fittingness or appropriateness relative to the basic aspects
of human flourishing, which are pertinent whether or not an
interpersonal comparison is being made.

Now to live up to this principle fully would obviously require
that one lived up fully to all the other principles of practical
reasonableness; for though one's personal failings do not all on

[7] See *Theory of Justice*, pp. 4–5, 8, 454.

every occasion implicate one in injustice, still, any form of personal failing is liable to implicate one in a failure of justice, by act or omission. That is why Aristotle, partly under the influence of Plato's ambitious extension of the analogy of justice, began his treatise on justice by identifying a general sense of 'justice' in which the word signifies *comprehensive* virtue (in my terminology, full practical reasonableness) as displayed in relation to other persons.[8] Since Aristotle wanted to introduce into academic discourse a technical distinction between two connotations of *dikaion*, the Greek word for that which is just— namely, just *qua* lawful (conforming to standard) and just *qua* equal (taking no more than one's share)—the Aristotelian name for justice in this general sense is 'legal justice'.[9] Since we, on the other hand, are equipped with two technical notions which, as technical notions, Aristotle lacked—namely, the common good and the distinct and enumerable requirements of practical reasonableness—we can discard the confusing term 'legal justice' while retaining the fundamental notion (which I formulated as a principle at the beginning of this section) as an orientation in the subsequent discussion. Justice, as a quality of character, is in its general sense always a practical willingness to favour and foster the common good of one's communities, and the theory of justice is, in all its parts, the theory of what in outline is required for that common good.

VII.3   DISTRIBUTIVE JUSTICE

The requirement of practical reasonableness is not satisfied by a general disposition, in one or all, to favour the well-being of other members of the community or communities in question. Few will flourish, and no one will flourish securely, unless there is an effective collaboration of persons, and co-ordination of resources and of enterprises (including always, in the notion of collaboration and co-ordination, patterns of mutual restraint and non-interference). Such an ensemble of conditions of collaboration which enhance the well-being (or at least the opportunity of flourishing) of all members of a community is, indeed, often called the common good (VI.8). And when we

8 *Nic. Eth.* V, 1: 1129b26–1130a13.
9 Ibid., 1130b10, 21–5.

wish to consider the concrete requirements of justice ('particular' as distinct from the 'general' justice discussed in the
preceding section), we need to consider the term 'common
good', used in formulating the general principle of justice, as
taking on now this more concrete meaning.

A full analysis of what is for the common good is, of course,
far beyond the scope of this chapter or indeed this book. But
we can at least orient ourselves in a bafflingly complex field,
by observing that the problems of realizing the common good
through a co-ordinated ensemble of conditions for individual
well-being in community can be divided into two very broad
classes. *First*, there are problems of *distributing* resources,
opportunities, profits and advantages, roles and offices, responsibilities, taxes and burdens—in general, the *common stock* and
the *incidents of communal enterprise*, which do not serve the common
good unless and until they are appropriated to particular
individuals. The theory of distributive justice outlines the range
of reasonable responses to these problems. *Second*, there are all
the other problems, concerning what is required for individual
well-being in community, which arise in relations and dealings
between individuals and/or groups, where the common stock
and what is required for communal enterprise are not directly
in question. The range of reasonable responses to these problems
is outlined in what I shall call (for reasons that will appear)
the theory of *commutative* justice.

The intentions of this classification should not be misunderstood. On the one hand, the classification is intended as
exhaustive, in the sense that all problems of justice, and all the
specific requirements generated by the requirement of 'general
justice', are intended to find a place in one or other or (under
different aspects) both of these two classes of 'particular justice'.
On the other hand, it is not denied that other classifications,
and certainly sub-classifications, could be found. But, as will
be seen in section VII.4, the classification here adopted, though
academic in inspiration and philosophical in origin, can help
towards understanding certain perennial tensions in sophisticated legal systems.

A disposition is *distributively just*, then, if it is a reasonable
resolution of a problem of allocating some subject-matter that
is essentially common but that needs (for the sake of the common

good) to be appropriated to individuals. Now subject-matters may be common in a variety of ways.

(A) A subject-matter is common, in the sense relevant to distributive justice, if it is part of no individual person and has not been created by anybody, but is apt for use for the benefit of anyone or everyone: for example, solar energy and light, the sea, its bed and its contents, land and its contents, rivers, air and airspace, the moon ...

(B) Another sort of common subject-matter arises out of the willingness of individuals to collaborate to improve their position. For example, a set of individuals may come under attack by others or by the sea or pestilence or famine. None of them can secure his safety by his own uncoordinated efforts, but all may be saved by collaboration. Such collaboration involves (B1) the task of deciding what is to be done and how; the task of participating in particular aspects of determinate projects; the responsibility of contributing necessary resources or funds; etc. Such collaboration also yields (B2) a city-wall and stock of weapons; a sea-wall or dyke; a drainage system and hospitals; a harvest in communal granaries; etc. Both the roles, responsibilities, offices, and burdens mentioned in (B1) and the products in (B2) are intrinsically common. In the general characterization of problems of distributive justice, earlier in this section, I compendiously called the natural resources in (A) and the products in (B2) *common stock*, while the subject-matters in (B1) I called *incidents of communal enterprise*. All these subject-matters are essentially common, and none of them fulfils its beneficial potentialities for anyone or everyone without some appropriation, conditionally or unconditionally, to particular persons (in the limiting case, to everyone in the community, including passing strangers). The problem of distributive justice is: to whom and on what conditions to make this necessary appropriation.

Some of the problems of distributing the responsibilities mentioned in (B1) above are to be treated later, in our discussion of authority: IX.4. But here we may notice that, as human experience shows, very many common enterprises are best conducted by charging particular individuals with the responsibility of settling co-ordination problems which *must* be settled if the enterprise is to go forward and which could otherwise be settled only by a unanimity which is in practice impossible to attain or to attain in time. Few are the armies, few indeed the victorious armies, without any officers.

Some who hold office in common ('public') enterprises, civil or military, have responsibilities clearly definable and regulated by rules which require little more than application or administration. Other responsibilities cannot be discharged adequately unless the officer who bears them is permitted to exercise a wide and even unreviewable discretion. Such discretionary authority remains, however, public; it is the good of the common enterprise that the officer is conscientiously to pursue, not his own ('private') advantage. A government that appoints unworthy party hacks to public office violates distributive justice, as does a biased licensing magistrate.

At this point we must recall that the common good is fundamentally the good of individuals (an aspect of whose good is friendship in community). The common good, which is the object of all justice and which all reasonable life in community must respect and favour, is not to be confused with the common stock, or the common enterprises, that are among the means of realizing the common good. Common enterprises and the exploitation and creation of a common stock of assets are alike for the common good because they are for the benefit of the individual members of the community: talk about benefiting 'the community' is no more than a shorthand (not without dangers) for benefiting the members of that community. And here we must further recall that the fundamental task of practical reasonableness is self-constitution or self-possession; inner integrity of character and outer authenticity of action are aspects of the basic good of practical reasonableness, as are freedom from the automatism of habit and from subjection to unintegrated impulses and compulsions; even friendship, in its ordinary sense, and the intense community of family require and entail a certain specialization and limitation of one's attentions; in short, no common enterprise can itself bring about the all-round flourishing of any individual. An attempt, for the sake of the common good, to absorb the individual altogether into common enterprises would thus be disastrous for the common good, however much the common enterprises might prosper (see also VI.5, above).

It is therefore a fundamental aspect of general justice that common enterprises should be regarded, and practically conducted, not as ends in themselves but as means of assistance, as ways of helping individuals to 'help themselves' or, more precisely, to constitute themselves. And in all those fields of activity, including economic activity, where individuals, or families, or other relatively small groups, can help themselves by their own private efforts and initiatives without thereby injuring (either by act or omission) the common good, they are entitled in justice to be allowed to do so, and it is unjust to require them to sacrifice their private initiative by demanding that they participate instead in a public enterprise; it remains unjust even if the material dividend they receive from the public enterprise is as great as or even somewhat greater than the material product of their own private efforts would have been. The principle of subsidiarity (VI.5) is a principle of justice.

All this has implications in many fields of activity, not least in that field of work and enterprise which we call economic activity. The implications concern, for example, the proper conditions of employment for wage or salary, i.e. of service which is a *proprium*—something of his own—of the person who renders it, but is not within the focal meaning of 'property'. But to illustrate the interrelation of 'private' and 'common' in the notion of justice, I will say something about private ownership.

The good of personal autonomy in community, as we have just traced it in outline, suggests that the opportunity of exercising some form of private ownership, including of means of production, is in most times and places a requirement of justice.[10] It is a requirement that strongly conditions, but also is conditioned by, the concrete application of the general principles and criteria of distributive justice. Clearly, the term 'private property' calls for some explanation. But that explana-

[10] All requirements of general justice are specifically requirements either of distributive justice or of commutative justice or of both. The present requirement (i) is a requirement of distributive justice in so far as it is unfair if the opportunity to control the use of natural resources, or of products of, claims to or means of claiming such resources, is not distributed to some but is to others, for inadequate reason, and (ii) is a requirement of commutative justice in so far as, if everyone in a community is deprived of the opportunity of private ownership, for inadequate reasons, then *each* is being treated unfairly, regardless of the like treatment of the others. See the end of VII.6, below.

tion will be easier if we look first at a second (alternative) basis
in justice for establishing a regime of private property. (As
always, the explanation of social institutions, and of the terms
appropriate for talking about them, is primarily a matter of
grasping their rationale.) This second basis rests on a 'rule' of
human experience: natural resources, and the capital resources
and consumer durables derivable therefrom, are more produc-
tively exploited and more carefully maintained by private
enterprise, management, husbandry, and housekeeping than
by the 'officials' (including all employees) of public enterprises.
At least for the times and places and the classes of resources
for which this rule of experience holds true, a regime of private
ownership will be a requirement of justice, provided that the
increased stock of goods yielded by such a regime is not hoarded
by a class of successful private owners but is made available
by appropriate mechanisms (e.g. profit-sharing; trade under
competitive market conditions; redistributive taxation; full
employment through productive investment; etc.) to all members of the community, in due measure. Of course, *if* the active
members of the community were more detached from considerations of private advantage, from love of 'their own', etc., then
common ownership and enterprise *would* be more productive
of benefits for all. But a theory of justice is to establish what
is due to a person in the circumstances in which he is, not in
the circumstances of some other, 'ideal' world. And those many
members of the community who reasonably[11] depend for their
livelihood upon the productive efforts and good husbandry of
other members can rightly complain of injustice[12] if a regime
of property (exploitation, production, and management of
resources) is adopted, on the basis that it *would* enhance their
well-being if the non-dependent members of the community
had characters different from those that in fact they have, but
which *actually* yields them (and everyone else) a lower standard

[11] In testing the justice of a social arrangement by considering it from the viewpoint of the 'worst-off member of the community' (which is certainly a relevant
viewpoint), we ought ordinarily to exclude from the class of 'worst-off' those who
unreasonably *refuse* to contribute by work or otherwise to the common good. In the
pithy phrase of St. Paul (2 Thess. 3:10), quoted (without acknowledgement) in Art. 10
of the Constitution of the Chinese People's Republic (1978): 'He who will not work,
let him not eat'; likewise Art. 13 of the Constitution of Albania (1946).

[12] Certainly commutative and usually also distributive; cf. above, p. 169, n. 10.

of living than they would enjoy under a different regime of
property operated by the non-dependent members as they
actually are.

Having mentioned two independent reasons why a system
of private ownership (which may coexist in the same community
with more or less extensive public ownership, i.e. management
of resources by officials) is typically required for the common
good and thus by justice, it remains to clarify what is meant
by 'private ownership'. What I mean is summed up in the
apparent paradox which Aristotle uses to sum up his rather
similar discussion: 'property ought to be common in a sense,
but private speaking generally . . . possessions should be privately owned, but common in use; and to train the citizens to this
is the special task of the legislator'.[13] I cite Aristotle partly in
order to emphasize that the analyses put forward in this section,
even where they are applicable to issues of current political
debate in the reader's community, are not to be taken as if
they were intended as a contribution to any particular such
debate.

For regimes of property are very various and, usually,
complex; and not unreasonably so, since what combinations
of private and public ownership reasonably answer to the
requirements of general justice varies with time, place, and
many different circumstances: indeed, the very distinction
between 'public' and 'private' may reasonably be treated in
some systems as not exhaustive. (See also X.7, below.) Hence
there is no question here of setting out some model or 'pure
case' of private ownership as the relevant demand of justice
in all or even in most political communities. Suffice it to say
that the two arguments put forward above suggest that
individuals, singly or in combination, should have access either
directly or (as, for example, in the case of a shareholder in a
joint-stock company) indirectly to natural resources, capital
goods, and/or consumer durables, such access being more or
less exclusive (in that he or they are entitled to exclude other

---

[13] *Pol.* II, 2: 1263a26, 38–9; see likewise Aquinas, *S. T.* II–II, q. 66, a. 2c; q. 32, a. 5 ad 2.
Cf. Basic Law of the Federal Republic of Germany (1949), Art. 14: '(1) Property and
the right of inheritance are guaranteed. Their content and limits shall be determined
by law. (2) Property imposes duties. Its use should also serve the common weal. (3) . . .'.
Likewise, Art. 24 of the Constitution of the German Democratic Republic (1949).

individuals from access), more or less immune from divestment by or at the instance of other individuals, and more or less transmissible by him at his choice. The purpose of these rights of exclusion and transmission and immunity from divestment is to give the private owner freedom to expend his own creativity, inventiveness, and undeflected care and attention upon the goods in question, to give him security in enjoying them or investing or developing them, and to afford him the opportunity of exchanging them for some alternative item(s) of property seeming to him more suitable to his life-plan. These are the principal features required to meet the demands of the common good referred to in the two arguments put forward above for the justice of private ownership.

Those arguments in no way suggest that private ownership, thus understood, is unconditionally just. On the contrary, by starting from the general notion of the common good, and by emphasizing that natural resources are essentially common stock (though apt for distribution, including distribution as private property), the arguments themselves suggest the conditions which private owners must conform to if their ownership is to be distributively just.

The private owner of a natural resource or capital good has a duty in justice to put it to productive use or, if he lacks the further resources required to do so, to dispose of it to someone willing and able to do so. The undeveloped *latifundia* of the rich (as in the Roman Empire and in various regions today) are a sign of injustice, whether or not they are tolerated by law. Similarly, speculative acquisition and disposition of property, for the purposes of merely financial gain uncorrelated with any economically productive development or use, is contrary to distributive justice. So, typically, is the hoarding of gold and in general the withholding of liquid assets from capital markets in which they might be mobilized for productive use. So too are dilapidations and failures of reasonable conservation of consumer durables, such as houses. So is the development of monopolistic and oligopolistic positions or arrangements which, for the profit and power of a restricted class of individuals, restrict the availability of property to other individuals, and prevent the working of a competitive market system which would encourage the unwasteful production and distribution of goods, more widely, in larger quantities and less expensively than is otherwise possible. So, likewise, are various (not all!) privately devised restrictions on alienation and/or on the future use of property.

The point, in justice, of private property is to give the owner first use and enjoyment of it and its fruits (including rents and profits), for it is this availability that enhances his reasonable autonomy and stimulates his productivity and care. But beyond a reasonable measure and degree of such use for his and his dependants' or co-owners' needs, he holds the remainder of his property and its fruits as part (in justice if not in law) of the common stock. In other words, beyond a certain point, what was commonly available but was justly made private, for the common good, becomes again, in justice, part of the common stock; though appropriated to his management and control, it is now not for his private benefit but is held by him immediately for common benefit (as Aristotle, we saw, more tersely said). From this point, the owner has, in justice, duties not altogether unlike those of a trustee in English law. He may fulfil them in various ways—by investing his surplus in production of more goods for later distribution and consumption; by providing gainful employment to people looking for work; by grants or loans for hospitals, schools, cultural centres, orphanages, etc., or directly for the relief of the poor. Where owners will not perform these duties, or cannot effectively co-ordinate their respective efforts to perform them, then public authority may rightly help them to perform them by devising and implementing schemes of distribution, e.g. by 'redistributive' taxation for purposes of 'social welfare', or by a measure of expropriation.

VII.4   CRITERIA OF DISTRIBUTIVE JUSTICE

Equality is a fundamental element in the notion of justice and thus of distributive justice. In particular, *all* members of a community *equally* have the right to respectful consideration when the problem of distribution arises: see further VIII.6. This is the moral relevance of the so-called 'formal' principle of justice: 'Treat like cases alike'. But, for resolving problems of distributive justice, equality is a residual principle, outweighed by other criteria and applicable only when those other criteria are inapplicable or fail to yield any conclusion. For the objective of justice is not equality but the common good, the flourishing of all members of the community, and there is no reason to suppose that this flourishing of all is enhanced by treating everyone identically when distributing roles, opportunities, and resources. Thus, to revert to the question of private ownership: what is unjust about large disparities of wealth in a community is not the inequality as such but the fact that (as the inequality suggests) the rich have failed to redistribute that portion of their wealth which could be better used by others for the realization of basic values in their own lives. If redistribution means no more than that more beer is going to be consumed morosely before television sets by the relatively many, and less fine wine consumed by the relatively few at salon concerts by select musicians, then it can scarcely be said to be a demand of justice. But if redistribution means that, at the expense of the wine, etc., more people can be preserved from (non-self-inflicted) illness, educated to the point where genuine self-direction becomes possible for them, defended against the enemies of justice, etc., then such redistribution is a requirement of justice.

There are, of course, no very precise yardsticks for assessing these questions. The all-round flourishing of human beings in community is indefinitely many-sided. There is no one criterion universally applicable for resolving questions of distribution. In respect of the realization of basic human goods, up to a certain threshold level in each member of the community, the primary criterion is *need*. For here we are dealing with the fundamental component of the common good. Even this is, however, subject to considerable discounting in the case of those whose indigence either results from their own unreasonable unwillingness to exert themselves for their own good, or is imposed upon them as lawful punishment for their culpable self-preference and harmful indifference to the good of others (see X.1, below). And, apart from that, the priority of need as a criterion for distribution is not a straightforwardly 'lexicographical' priority; in situations of emergency, which are not too uncommon, a few or even many may rightly be deprived of much in order that those who can defend the whole community against its dangers may be enabled and encouraged to do so.

For a second criterion of just distribution is *function*, that is to say, need relative not directly to basic human good but to roles and responsibilities in the community. And since this book is not a treatise on justice, I may be summary in mentioning the other reasonable criteria. Thirdly, then, there is *capacity*, relative not only to roles in communal enterprises but also to opportunities for individual advancement. 'Flutes to flute-players': if higher education is to be made available (whether by private or by public initiative) it should go only to those capable of benefiting from it. Fourthly, *deserts and contributions*, whether deriving from self-sacrifice or from meritorious use of effort and ability, are a proper criterion of distribution; for the friendliness that is expressed by manifested gratitude is a great human good, for both giver and receiver. Fifthly, in the distribution of the costs and losses of communal enterprise fairness will often turn on whether some parties have *created* or at least *foreseen and accepted avoidable risks* while others have neither created them nor had opportunity of foreseeing or of avoiding or insuring against them: this is a problem familiar to lawyers but rather overlooked by philosophers and (so?) lacks a convenient short label.

Finally, in considering and employing criteria of distributive justice we must not lose sight of the fact that in speaking of justice we are not trying to assess states of affairs and their consequences. Rather, we are trying to assess what practical reasonableness *requires* of particular people (in their dealings with other people). And what is thus required of a particular person depends essentially on what responsibilities he has, whether by virtue of his own voluntary commitments (e.g. his assumption of rulership) or by virtue of his past or present receipt of benefits from another (e.g. as a child, in relation to his parents), or by virtue of the dependence of others upon him (e.g. as a parent, in relation to his children), or by virtue of a network of relationships of actual and potential inter-dependencies (such as exist strongly, for one set of reasons, amongst members of a family living unit, and strongly, for another set of reasons, amongst members of a sound political community, and to a lesser but increasing extent between the communities that together make up the whole community of mankind).

Here Aristotle's famous and often overworked dictum about not demanding too much precision in ascertaining the demands of practical reasonableness[14] has an important application. The claim of Weber, Sartre, and many others, that objective or rational judgements are impossible in the field of values (ethics and politics), has been based partly upon the difficulty ('impossibility') of resolving certain problems of conflicting claims of responsibility. Sartre, for example, proposes the case of a young man trying to decide whether he ought to stay at home to care for his aged and dependent mother or leave home to fight against Nazi occupation of France.[15] But such arguments lack the force ascribed to them by Sartre and Weber. Neither of the courses of action contemplated by the young man need be regarded as incompatible with justice. His dilemma cannot be solved by declaring one of his two prima-facie responsibilities to be the exclusive requirement of practical reasonableness. But practical reasonableness certainly convicts of irrational irresponsibility someone who in such a situation decides to do whatever the first person he meets suggests, whether it be to shoot his mother, join the occupying forces, drink himself to stupefaction, commit suicide, or whatever—all of these being possibilities that Sartre simply overlooks.

But the inappropriate demand for precise and unqualified directives of reason in assessing responsibilities also seems to lie behind a quite different development in contemporary thought. For it is becoming common, at least in academic discussion, to propose, in effect, that 'everyone of us is responsible for everyone else in every way'.[16] Here the feeling that it is difficult or impossible to find norms for definitively apportioning one's effort in differing degrees amongst different potential beneficiaries seems to link up with the assumption that justice is primarily a property of states of affairs and only derivatively a property of particular decisions of ascertained persons; and this combination of unformulated assumptions yields the

---

[14] *Nic. Eth.* I, 3: 1094b12–14.

[15] J.-P. Sartre, *L'Existentialisme est un humanisme* (Paris: 1946), pp. 40–1.

[16] Cf. Father Zossima's brother, in Dostoyevsky's *The Brothers Karamazov*, quoted by Johathan Glover, *Causing Death and Saving Lives* (Harmondsworth: 1977), p. 104, as bearing 'an obvious resemblance to what has been argued' by Glover himself. Perhaps the resemblance is only apparent; cf. Herbert Morris, *On Guilt and Innocence* (Berkeley and London: 1976), ch. 4.

peculiarly utilitarian concept of justice. Here the principle 'Treat like cases alike' becomes, specifically, 'each person counts for one and only one': indeed, the new view is simply drawing out the conclusions of the logic of classic utilitarianism.[17] And a principal conclusion is: each of us is morally bound to devote his wealth and energy (which he might otherwise have devoted to the interests of himself, his 'dependants', his own local and political communities, etc.,) to the interests of the most dis-advantaged persons whom he can find anywhere in the world, up to the point where his (marginal) sacrifice of wealth and energy would render himself and his 'dependants' worse off than those most disadvantaged persons.[18] Any other use of one's wealth and energy is, on this view, simply unjust.

In so far as this view is a version of utilitarianism, it is subject to the general critique which shows that its substratum of principle is incoherent (V.6). But, in thinking about justice, we should go further and reject the principle, so plausible prima facie, that 'each person counts for one and only one'; for this principle is not reasonable as a principle for the practical deliberations of anyone. Of everyone it is true that, because of his promises, and/or his parenthood, and/or his debts of gratitude, and/or his relations of interdependence with or assumption of authority in relation to ascertained persons or communities, he cannot reasonably give equal 'weight', or equal concern, to the interests of every person anywhere whose interests he could ascertain and affect.

To say this is not to deny that the problem of assessing the extent of one's responsibilities in reason for the welfare of persons in other political communities (the problem of 'international justice') is one of the most difficult of all practical problems; and its resolution, by each of us (for our situations and thus our responsibilities differ), is constantly threatened by the pull of unreasonable self-preference, group bias, and lukewarmness about human good.

VII.5 COMMUTATIVE JUSTICE

There is a vast range of relationships and dealings between persons (including dealings between officials and individuals)

---

[17] Cf. J. S. Mill, *Utilitarianism* (1863), ch. 5 (ad fin.).
[18] See Glover, op. cit., pp. 109–10.

in which neither the requirements or incidents of communal enterprise nor the distribution (whether by public or private owners) of a common stock are directly at stake, but in which there can be question of what is fitting, fair, or just as between the parties to the relationship. A theory of justice must respond to this range of questions, and as I have used the name 'distributive' for the justice whereby one gives and puts into practice reasonable solutions to the problems discussed in the preceding section, so it will be convenient to have a single name for the justice that responds to the present range of problems. For want of a satisfactory term from common English, I adopt a traditional academic term, 'commutative justice'.

This term has a definite origin. Aristotle, too, wished to divide the whole field of problems of justice into two broad classes. The first class he named problems of *distributive* justice (*dianemetikon dikaion*),[19] and he characterized these problems much as I have: they deal with whatever pertains to the community as common but divisible by allotment amongst its members. The second class of problems he named problems of *corrective* justice (*diorthotikon dikaion*),[20] the justice that rectifies or remedies inequalities which arise in dealings (*synallagmata*) between individuals. These 'dealings' may be either voluntary, as in sale, hire, and other business transactions, or involuntary, as where one man 'deals with' another by stealing from him, murdering him, or defaming him.[21] *Synallagmata* in Aristotle's account must therefore be understood very broadly, and not restricted (as in modern Roman law systems) to reciprocal 'exchanges'; the terms 'dealings' and 'deals with' have several irrelevantly narrow connotations, but I intend their most general meaning. The real problem with Aristotle's account is its emphasis on correction, on the *remedying* of the inequality that arises when one person injures or takes from another, or when one party fulfils his side of a bargain while the other does not. This is certainly one field of problems of justice, but even when added to the field of distributive justice it leaves untouched a wide range of problems. 'Correction' and 'restitution' are notions parasitic on some prior determination of what

[19] *Nic. Eth.* V, 3: 1131b28; 1132b24, 32.
[20] *Nic. Eth.* V, 2: 1131a1; 3: 1131b25; 4: 1132b25.
[21] *Nic. Eth.* V, 2: 1131a1–9.

is to count as a crime, a tort, a binding agreement, etc.

So it was that Thomas Aquinas, purporting to interpret Aristotle faithfully, silently shifted the meaning of Aristotle's second class of particular justice, and invented a new term for it: 'commutative justice'. Many followers of Aquinas have understood *commutativa* as 'pertaining to exchanges'. But the advantage of Aquinas's new term is precisely that, in his usage, it is limited neither to correction nor to voluntary or business transactions, but is almost as extensive as the term *commutatio* in classical Latin (= 'change'), limited only by its contextual restriction here to the field of human interaction. With this term, then, we can cover the whole field in which, problems of allocation of common stock and the like apart, the problem is to determine what dealings are proper between persons (including groups).

The distinction between distributive and commutative justice is no more than an analytical convenience, an aid to orderly consideration of problems. Many actions are both distributively and commutatively just (or unjust). Consider the act of the judge in giving judgment. The subject-matter of his judgment may be a matter of distributive justice (whether that justice has been assessed by the legislator, as with rules of succession on intestacy, or is left to be assessed by the judge, as in apportionment of damages where there is contributory negligence or of the costs of litigation), or again the subject-matter for adjudication may be a matter of commutative justice (as in an action for the price of goods sold and delivered, or for damages for trespass to goods). But, whether the subject-matter of his act of adjudication be a problem of distributive or of commutative justice, the act of adjudication itself is always matter for distributive justice. For the submission of an issue to the judge itself creates a kind of *common* subject-matter, the *lis inter partes*, which must be allocated between parties, the gain of one party being the loss of the other. The biased or careless judge violates distributive justice by using an irrelevant criterion (or by inappropriately using a relevant criterion) in apportioning the merits and awarding judgment and/or costs. But, finally, we can also consider the judge's duty simply in so far as it is a duty to apply the relevant legal rules; in this respect his duty is one of commutative justice: faithful application of the law

is simply what is fitting and required of him in his official
dealings with others.

Moreover, to revert to the question of the subject-matter of
litigation, mentioned in the preceding paragraph, there may
be fields of law of which it is difficult to say (or at least a matter
of controversial interpretation) whether the rules are intended
to secure distributive or, rather, commutative justice. The
modern law of liability in tort for non-intentionally inflicted
personal injuries is such a field, and so, perhaps, is the modern
law of frustration of contracts.

Consider the common law of torts. In its 'classical' period
(say, between 1850 and 1950) this set of rules and principles
was regarded as an instrument of commutative justice, indeed
of corrective justice in Aristotle's sense. One party was bound
to make payment or restitution to another if and (with
'marginal' exceptions) only if he had conducted himself wrong-
fully in relation to that other (e.g. by carelessly running him
down on the road). But in recent times, in some places more
than in others, this view of the function of the law has been
challenged by another view which implicitly represents the
proper function of the law about compensation for personal
injuries as an essentially distributive one. In this view, the
question is not 'What are the standards of conduct which one
person must live up to in relation to his "neighbours"?', or
'What should be the extent of liability of one who fails to live
up to those standards of conduct?', or even 'How should someone injured by the wrong of another be restored to his former
condition?'. Those are questions central to the theory of
commutative justice. But in the newer view, the question is held
to be 'How should the risks of *common life* be apportioned,
especially the risks of such essentially *collaborative* enterprises as
travel and traffic by road?'. Injury to one of the participants is
then treated as an incidental loss to be set against the gains
which accrue to all who participate in this sphere of common
life. The costs of this loss should then, as a matter of distributive
justice, be shared amongst those who gain most from their part
in the whole 'enterprise' and/or who are able to pay with least
injury to their own interests or position in it; or should even be
shared amongst *all* the participants. The question whether the
injury was caused by any fault becomes substantially irrelevant.

Mutual participation, bringing common gains, thus calls for mutual insurance. By the same token, the claims of the injured party for compensation, being now treated as incidents in a kind of common enterprise, are treated as claims upon the common resources; and all such claims must therefore be measured by reference not to the fault and ability to pay of any individual wrongdoer, but to all the other claims, of every sort, on public funds or (if the scheme of compensation is funded wholly by the participants in that particular sphere of life) by reference to all the other claims, public and private, on the funds of the participants.

Such a legal scheme for securing distributive justice seeks, then, to compensate *all* who suffer injury in the relevant course of common life, whereas the scheme for securing commutative justice seeks to compensate *only* those who were injured by the act of one who failed to live up to his duties (in commutative justice) of care and respect for the well-being of others, and who is therefore required to make reparation. On the other hand, the distributive scheme will typically be limited by the resources of the common funds, so that *none* of those compensated will receive as much as *some* of them might have received under the commutative scheme. The duties of wrongdoers in commutative justice no doubt remain, discounted to allow for the compensation received by the injured party from the distributive scheme; but they are no longer enforced by law. Hence, if a pure distributive scheme is adopted in a context in which it is inappropriate, some injured parties can rightly say that the law fails to secure them justice.

A similar tension between the perspectives of distributive and commutative justice has long been developing within the common law of contract. In one perspective, which informs much of that law, the parties to a contract are treated as individuals dealing with one another at arm's length, each pursuing his own interests which remain entirely individual and are merely juxtaposed, so to speak, to the other party's interests by and to the extent defined by the contract. Thus if one party fails to perform as he promised, he ought (subject to any contrary provisions of the contract itself) to restore the other party (so far as money can) to a position *equivalent* to that which he, the promisee, would have enjoyed but for the promisor's non-performance; in short, a promise is a guarantee of performance or its equivalent in damages. Such is a perspective characteristic of the theory of commutative justice. But as early as *Hadley* v. *Baxendale* (1854),[22] which settled the English law on quantum of damages for breach of contract, we can discern an alternative perspective which sees non-performance as one of the risks that *both* parties accept when they enter upon their mutual agreement, and that therefore can reasonably be *shared* between them, so that neither bears the risk of having to compensate for *all* the losses that the other may suffer through non-performance. As this perspective has won acceptance, so the rules of frustration of contract have been developed to relieve contracting parties of their obligations of performance or compensation in circumstances where the contractual arrangement, viewed (usually implicitly) by reference to its 'point', *rather as if it were a kind of partnership or common enterprise,* has been frustrated by unforeseen external contingencies. Contemporary English law provides that on frustration of a contract a party who has paid money may recover it, and a party who owed money due under the contract before frustration is relieved from payment, while a party who has incurred expenses may, 'as the court considers just', be allowed to recover them, and a party who has received benefits under the contract before frustration may, 'as the court considers just', be required to share their monetary value with, or hand it over to, the other party.[23] The distributive perspective is carried yet further by recent proposals under which every party to a frustrated contract would be entitled to restitution for any performance of any part of his contractual obligations, while losses would be apportioned equally between the parties making and receiving restitution.

There is no need here to take sides for or against any of these changes in perspective. Often enough, legislative debate concerning them turns on matters only mediately related to the criteria of justice, for example on the efficiency with which alternative schemes or perspectives can be implemented and their expense. But the fundamental issue is really: How reasonable is it to regard the persons whose activities are in question

---

[22] 9 Ex. 341.
[23] Law Reform (Frustrated Contracts) Act 1943 (Eng.), s. 1.

as engaged in a common enterprise? The modern developments in relation to compensation for personal injuries spring from schemes for compensating industrial accidents, where the employees who are injured and the employers who are bound to contribute to the scheme are manifestly engaged in a kind of common enterprise (notwithstanding that the form of their relationship is not that of a legal partnership but envisages only the limited participation that pertains to wage-labour). Can this conception of participation in a common enterprise, in which risk of loss should be shared amongst all participants, reasonably be extended to encompass the whole of the national community? It seems not, at least in respect of certain causes and certain forms of loss.

Having stressed at some length the complex relations that hold between the theory of distributive and the theory of commutative justice, it remains to indicate some of the matters securely located within the province of the latter theory. There are, of course, innumerable aspects of commutative justice: so the following examples are intended only to illustrate some outlines.

Firstly, then, commutative justice may concern relations between ascertained individuals. If A fails, without good reason, to perform his contract with B, he is commutatively unjust; and in English (unlike French) law he is required in commutative justice to pay damages to B even when his failure was not culpable (subject to the limitations on liability introduced by the doctrines of remoteness and frustration, already mentioned). If A defames B, being careless of the true facts, or communicating his defamation to persons who have no purposeful and good reason to hear ill of B, he wrongs B in commutative justice, even if a particular legal system (as in the USA) in certain contexts denies B a remedy lest political debate be chilled. (Observe, from the two preceding observations about particular laws, that the relation between law and justice is not symmetrical; the existence of a certain legal regime, say of contract, may create legal duties which are also 'moral' duties in justice because of the other party's reliance upon performance according to *that* legal regime, but which would not be duties in justice under another reasonable legal regime; yet it does not follow that, where the law reasonably abstains from enforcing a duty in justice, that duty is cancelled in justice.)

Again, if A perjures himself in litigation against B, he wrongs B in commutative justice; so, too, if he appeals against judgment, not in the belief that he has a good case in law or justice, but to delay satisfaction of the judgment debt. The reader will think of very many other instances. Having done so, it will be useful to reflect that adherence to these duties of commutative justice between one *individual* and another is an integral and indispensable aspect of respect and favour for the *common* good. How can a society be said to be well-off in which individuals do not respect each other's rights?

Secondly, an individual may have a duty in commutative justice to many more or less ascertained individuals. One's duty of care in the modern law of tort embodies such a duty.

Thirdly, an individual may have duties in commutative justice to many more or less unascertained individuals. An individual who abuses, exploits, or 'free-rides' on some system which is advantageous to himself and to others, knowing that his abuse may bring about the limitation or abandonment of the scheme (*après moi le déluge*), is commutatively unjust to all those who might in future have enjoyed the benefits of the original scheme.

Fourthly, an individual has duties in commutative justice to the governing authorities of his community. (The 'duties to the State' which are violated, say, by treason are a complex amalgam of duties of the second, third, and fourth kind here listed.) So perjury and contempt of court offend against commutative justice in this respect as well as others. The general duty of both officials and private citizens to conform to just (and even, sometimes, to unjust) laws is a duty of commutative justice. (I shall return to this topic at length: XI.7 and XII.1–3.)

Finally, persons holding public authority (in the lax terminology of recent centuries, 'the State') owe duties of commutative justice to those subject to their authority. A scheme of taxation and social welfare may be distributively just; its lawful and regular administration is a matter of commutative justice owed to all those who have ascertainable rights, powers, immunities, or duties under it.

VII.6 JUSTICE AND THE STATE

The foregoing enumeration, like much else in the preceding

sections, was tacitly directed against an analysis of justice which became so widespread after the sixteenth century that many people consider it the 'classical' analysis. Much discussion, even outside the confines of this 'traditional' analysis, is significantly moulded by assumptions drawn from it.

The origins of the analysis in question can be traced to Cardinal Cajetan's famous commentary on Aquinas's *Summa Theologiae*. Aquinas had devoted an article to the question whether it is proper to divide justice into two species, distributive and commutative, and had argued that it is.[24] In his commentary on this article, Cajetan introduced a novel interpretation of the whole Aristotelian–Thomist schema which had classified justice into 'general' (or 'legal') and 'particular', and had subdivided particular justice between distributive and commutative. The charm of Cajetan's new analysis of justice was that it used all the language of the old, and indeed appeared at first glance to be based on some reasoning of Aquinas's—but above all, its abiding attraction was its appearance of symmetry:

There are three species of justice, as there are three types of relationships in any 'whole': the relations of the parts amongst themselves, the relations of the whole to the parts, and the relations of the parts to the whole. And likewise there are three justices: legal, distributive and commutative. For legal justice orients the parts to the whole, distributive the whole to the parts, while commutative orients the parts one to another.[25]

In a very short time, certainly by the time of Dominic Soto's treatise *De Justitia et Jure* (1556), the inner logic of Cajetan's synthesis was being worked out. A modern representative of the post-Cajetan tradition puts it thus:

There are three sorts of relationship: that of the parts to the whole, that of the whole to the parts, that of one part to another. Legal justice pertains to the first sort, since it relates the citizens to the State. Distributive justice pertains to the second sort, since it relates the State to the citizens. Commutative justice pertains to the third, relating one private citizen to another.[26]

[24] *S.T.* II–II, q. 61, a. 1.

[25] *Commentaria in Secundam Secundae Divi Thomae de Aquino* (1518), *in* II–II, q. 61, a. 1.

[26] 'Triplex exigitur ordo: ordo partium ad totum, ordo totius ad partes, ordo partis ad partem. Primum respicit justitia legalis quae ordinat subditos ad rempublicam; secundum, justitia distributiva, quae ordinat rempublicam ad subditos; tertium, justitia commutativa quae ordinat privatum ad privatum': B.-H. Merkelbach, *Summa theologiae moralis* (Paris: 1938), vol. II, no. 252, p. 253.

On Aquinas's view, anyone in charge of an item of 'common stock' will have duties of distributive justice; hence any property-holder can have such duties, since the goods of this earth are to be exploited and used for the good of all. In the newer view (now thought of as traditional), the duties of distributive justice belong only to the State or the personified 'whole' (community). On Aquinas's view, the State and its officials have duties in commutative justice to the subjects of the State; punishment, for instance, is fundamentally though not exclusively a matter of commutative justice,[27] and the framing of an innocent person is a denial of commutative justice.[28] In the newer view, commutative justice concerns only private transactions. On Aquinas's view (though he is not explicit enough about it), 'legal justice' is the fundamental form of *all* justice, the basis of all obligations, distributive or commutative; for it is the underlying duty to respect and advance the common good. In the newer view, legal justice is little more than the citizen's duty of allegiance to the State and its laws.

The historical success of the new, symmetrically triadic schema is of more than merely historical significance. Particularly influential has been, and is, the notion that it is the State or 'the community as a whole' that is responsible for distributive justice. This drastic limitation of perspective helps along the argument (to take only one contemporary instance) which Robert Nozick directs against redistributive taxation. A primary concern of Nozick's *Anarchy, State and Utopia* is to argue that once anyone has justly acquired capacities, endowments, or holdings (property, etc.), it is unjust for anyone, including the State, to deprive him of any of those holdings, or to conscript any of his capacities, for the purpose of aiding other persons. Systems of taxation for purposes of redistribution and social welfare are therefore unjust; they amount to the imposition of forced labour, an unwarrantable infringement of a man's rights over his own body, effort, and property, his rights not to be forced to do certain things.[29]

[27] *S.T.* II–II, q. 62, a. 3c; q. 80, a. un. ad 1; q. 108, a. 2 ad 1.
[28] *S.T.* II–II, q. 64, introduction; q. 68, a. 3.
[29] See *Anarchy, State and Utopia* (Oxford: 1974), pp. ix, 167–74 (in the chapter entitled 'Distributive Justice').

Nozick is far indeed from the tradition of the scholastic textbooks, pre- or post-Cajetan. But the plausibility of his argument comes entirely from its focus on the coercive nature of the State's intervention as the agent of (re)distributive justice. Suppose we abandon this perspective. That is to say: leave the State out of consideration for a moment, and ask instead whether a private property-holder has duties of (re)distributive justice. (The question is strictly inconceivable in the post-Cajetan tradition.) Then we will find that Nozick has little indeed to say in favour of his assumption that what one has justly acquired one can justly hold without regard for the needs, deserts, or other claims of others (except such claims as one has actually created, e.g. by contract, which one has a duty to satisfy in what I, not Nozick, would call commutative justice). If we see no reason to adopt his assumption that the goods of the earth can reasonably be appropriated by a few to the substantial exclusion of all others, and if we prefer instead the principle[30] that they are to be treated by all as for the benefit of all according to the criteria of distributive justice though partly through the mediation of private holdings, then the question of State coercion, which dominated Nozick's argument, becomes in principle of very secondary importance. For in establishing a scheme of redistributive taxation, etc., the State need be doing no more than crystallize and enforce duties that the property-holder *already* had. Coercion, then, comes into play only in the event of recalcitrance that is wrongful not only in law but also in justice. Distributive justice is here, as in most contexts, a relation between citizens, or groups and associations

[30] On what is this principle based? Well, in a nicely ironical passage on p. 160 of *Anarchy, State and Utopia*, Nozick remarks: 'Things come into the world already attached to people having entitlements over them. From the point of view of the historical entitlement conception of justice in holdings [which Nozick favours], those who start afresh to complete "to each according to his—" treat objects as if they appeared from nowhere, out of nothing. A complete theory of justice might cover this limit case [which, in the attached end-note, he says is not 'our own' case]; perhaps here is a use for the usual conceptions of distributive justice.' But, whether or not my theory of distributive justice is one of the 'usual conceptions' that Nozick had in mind, it is clear that his irony is misdirected. The decisive fact is that in 'our own' world the natural resources from which all 'things' or 'objects' are made *did* appear 'from nowhere, out of nothing' and did *not* 'come into the world already attached to people having entitlements over them'. This basic fact conditions all the entitlements subsequently derived from labour, contribution, purchase, or other just sources of private title. And see pp. 170–3, above.

within the community, and is the responsibility of those citizens and groups. The role of the governing authorities and the law in determining, for particular political communities, the particular requirements of distributive justice is a decisive but subsidiary (see VI.5) role.

VII.7   AN EXAMPLE OF JUSTICE: BANKRUPTCY

In this final section I try to consolidate, illustrate, and extend the foregoing analysis by reference to some elements of the English law of bankruptcy, a characteristic modern legal regulation of insolvency.

Bankruptcy is a legal process whereby someone who is insolvent (i.e. cannot discharge his financial liabilities) is judicially declared bankrupt, whereupon his property vests in a trustee who holds it solely for the purpose of division amongst the bankrupt's creditors. During bankruptcy the opportunities and rights of the bankrupt to engage in business are severely limited. Upon satisfactory division of the property, he may be judicially discharged from bankruptcy, whereupon he is relieved for all further liability in respect of his former debts.

The first thing to observe about the legal provisions thus roughly described is that they replace provisions under which an unsatisfied creditor could have a debtor imprisoned. The old provisions were unsatisfactory. For they imposed a condition of servitude upon one who might be innocent of any contempt of law or justice. And, by allowing the debtor to be removed, by one of his creditors, into prison where (unlike a free man or even a slave) he could do nothing to improve his financial position or work off his debts, the old provisions tended to frustrate the commutatively just claims of his other creditors.

Next, observe that the bankruptcy law both gives effect to the commutatively just claims of the insolvent's creditors and at the same time subjects all those claims to a principle of distributive justice. Without a law of bankruptcy, and indeed before the provisions of such law are applied to a particular debtor, each of his creditors is entitled to satisfy the whole of his claim from the whole of the debtor's property, regardless of the claims of any other creditor. Bankruptcy law pools all the claims, and treats the debtor's property as if it were now the common propery of the creditors (put technically, the legal ownership vests in the trustee in bankruptcy but the beneficial interest vests in the creditors in common, subject to a division according to law by the trustee). Bankruptcy law thus departs radically from the fundamental principle of Nozick's 'historical entitlement theory' of justice: 'Whatever arises from a just situation by just steps is itself just'.[31] For if a creditor enforces his commutatively just claim, by the normal processes of law (which are themselves quite just), and thereby swallows up the wherewithal for satisfying any of the equally just claims of other creditors, the situation that has thus 'arisen' cannot (so the law of bankruptcy assumes, quite reasonably) be properly regarded as 'itself just'.[32]

Thirdly, in dividing the debtor's property amongst his creditors, the bankruptcy law uses more than one criterion of distributive justice. (i) It recognizes above all the bankrupt's *need* to be preserved from outlawry, slavery,[33] or helpless indigence; excluded, therefore, from the common pool of assets for division among creditors are the bankrupt's tools of trade, the 'necessary wearing apparel and bedding of himself, his wife and his children', and such earnings of his (after adjudication as a bankrupt and before discharge) as are necessary for maintenance of that family. (ii) The law recognizes the similar *need* of those who were presumably wholly dependent on the debtor for their livelihood; high in the list of preferential claims, which must be satisfied in full before further division of the pooled assets, are the wages or salaries of the debtor's 'clerks or servants, labourers or workmen', earned during the four months before bankruptcy.[34] (iii) The law gives preference, over all other claims upon the pooled assets, to those whose claims are *not* based on their having entered into a business arrangement with the debtor: (*a*) the expenses and remuneration of those who have

---

[31] Nozick, *Anarchy, State and Utopia*, p. 151.

[32] Indeed, any attempt by an actually insolvent person (even before he is legally bankrupted) to give one of his creditors preference over the others is treated by English law as a 'fraudulent preference' (notwithstanding that the debtor could truthfully say 'I am simply paying off one of my just debts'); see Bankruptcy Act 1914, s. 44(1).

[33] See *Re Wilson, ex parte Vine* (1878) 8 Ch. D. 364 at p. 366 (C.A.).

[34] Even higher, rightly or wrongly, is ranked the claim of an apprentice or articled clerk to be released from his obligations to the bankrupt master or principal, and to be repaid a proper proportion of his fee for apprenticeship or articles.

to administer the law of bankruptcy and apply it to the debtor's affairs; (*b*) claims to money or property belonging to a Friendly Society or Trustee Savings Bank where the bankrupt was an officer of the Society or Bank and had these assets in his possession (for these are essentially the funds of persons who dealt with the Society or Bank, not with the bankrupt); (*c*) the claims of central and local governments to one year's unpaid taxes or rates. (iv) Conversely, where someone has entered into an arrangement with the debtor that partakes of the nature of partnership as such, that person's claims under that arrangement are deferred or postponed to the claims of all the ordinary business creditors: such arrangements include loans between spouses, and loans on the basis that the lender will share in profits. (v) Finally, as between all the ordinary creditors, who are neither preferred nor deferred under the law and who have no realizable security (mortgage, charge, or lien over the debtor's property), 'equality is equity'. The debts they prove are paid to them *pari passu*. That is to say, each receives, from the pool remaining after payment of preferred creditors, the same percentage of the debt owed *to him* (not the same percentage of that pool); if the pool is insufficient, the claim of each abates proportionately. This is, then, another instance of the 'geometrical' equality which, as opposed to 'arithmetical' equality, is (as Aristotle said) characteristic of distributive justice. In other words, within this class of creditors, the criterion of distributive justice is: 'to each according to his (legally recognized) claim upon the debtor in commutative justice'.

Fourthly, as even the foregoing incomplete list of principles for treating the property in the possession of the debtor may have suggested to the reader, the English law of bankruptcy applies principles of justice in ways which are reasonable but not necessarily or always the only reasonable, or even most reasonable, amongst possible ways. Doubts have reasonably, if not compellingly, been raised about, for example, the priority accorded to claims to unpaid taxes, and about the doctrine (expanded by the courts in both England and the USA) that 'traceable' property held by the insolvent on an actual or even a constructive trust can be claimed directly by the 'beneficiary' and is exempted from the common pool.

Fifthly, many features of the law of bankruptcy are devices

to deter and/or to circumvent the effects of fraud, i.e. of attempts by the debtor to evade his debts or the process of bankruptcy, or to live beyond his means at the expense of his creditors, or to enter into new debts with unsuspecting persons, or to prefer one of his creditors to others without lawful reason. The law has to determine the requirements of justice in a society where persons are only partially compliant and imperfectly just.

Sixthly, the law of bankruptcy itself can be made the instrument of injustice, above all by the bankrupt himself. For it is certainly possible, and in some places not uncommon, that someone who could pay his just debts if he were so minded may choose instead to have them cancelled by bankruptcy, submitting himself to temporary inconvenience for the sake of a future freedom from financial difficulty, a freedom which his own action may deny to his defeated creditors (say, small shopkeepers) or to others (say, fellow students to whom valuable sources of credit may now be closed). No system of law can secure justice if its subjects, let alone its officials, are themselves careless of justice.

Seventhly, any law about insolvency must effect an adjustment between aspects of justice which, in particular circumstances, compete. The whole idea of bankruptcy is to make such an adjustment between commutative and distributive justice in the peculiar circumstances of insolvency. But in detail, too, there are numerous compromises between, for example, speed (for it is an aspect of justice that just debts be paid at the time promised and that distribution to the needy be made at the time of their need) and certainty (for it is an aspect of justice that persons who have just claims should not lose them through momentary oversight or temporary absence, and that persons who have no just claim should not be paid on some inadequately tested story). *General* and clear rules about procedure, proof, notification, time, appeals, etc., must be adopted, notwithstanding that their very generality and clarity—the source of their value in the effort to do justice—will sometimes occasion the failure of particular parties to secure the satisfaction of their just claims. It is not that such contingencies were unforeseen, but that to provide exhaustively against them would 'for practical purposes' defeat the just claims of many more.

Finally, the law of bankruptcy is worth attending to, as one of the relatively few instances in which a formal distribution of a common stock or pool is carried out. More commonly, in societies which for the all-round well-being of their members have grown complex and which recognize the value of individual autonomy both as an aspect of human flourishing and as a cause of economic advancement, the claims of distributive justice are met by establishing schemes of property-holding, inheritance, contract, taxation, etc., which *tend* to check the growth of *de facto* inequalities (whether arising from catastrophic loss or from unlimited accumulation) within a framework which, since it looks formally to a *process* of piecemeal satisfaction of particular claims of commutative justice, would otherwise permit unlimited inequalities. This is reasonable, both (*a*) because the reasonable criteria for assessing distributive justice do not yield any one pattern of distribution (or even any determinable set of patterns) on which all reasonable men would be bound to agree, and more fundamentally (*b*) because to secure and maintain a pattern of distribution without reference to any of the commutatively just claims, gifts, and liabilities which individuals, families, or other groups create for themselves would be possible only if every individual initiative were stifled *and* every individual's acts of injustice overlooked. No mutually exclusive distinction between 'end-states' which can be assessed as distributively just and 'processes' which create and satisfy claims and liabilities in commutative justice can reasonably be maintained except in relation to very limited projects. On the scale of the full community which seeks the common good of the all-round flourishing of all its members the distinction fails (i) because the flourishing of persons has among its intrinsic aspects (as distinct from mere extrinsic means) the opportunity of engaging in certain processes (such as giving and being given, choosing one's own commitments and investments of skill or effort, etc.), and (ii) because the existence of such a community is radically open-ended, members continually being born into it, departing and dying, so that no one slice of time (by reference to which a pattern could be assessed as just, purely distributively) has the privileged status of an 'end-state'.

Recalling an earlier discussion (Chapter V.6), we can now

add: the dream of a purely distributive justice shares with
utilitarian consequentialism the illusion that human good is
adequately quantifiable, the illusion that pursuit of the common
good is pursuit of a once-for-all attainable objective, like
making an omelette, and the illusion that it is reasonable to
postulate a privileged point or slice of time by reference to
which the consequences of actions could notionally be summed
and evaluated, apportioned and distributed.

NOTES

VII.1

'Justice to oneself' and 'justice in the soul' ... I follow Aristotle in discounting these
metaphorical extensions and in focusing on relations between distinct persons: see *Nic.
Eth.* V, 11: 1138a4–b13.

Word-play about right, rights, etc. ... This is not restricted to modern European
languages. See the analysis of the Barotse word *tukelo* and its cognates, meaning 'right',
'a right', 'straight', 'upright (just)', 'duty', and 'justice': Max Gluckman, *The Judicial
Process among the Barotse* (Manchester: 1955), p. 66.

Other-directedness, duty, and equality ... The excavation of these elements from the quarry
of Aristotle's treatise on justice (which was itself an excavation from Plato and from
common language) is the work of Aquinas: on other-directedness, see *S.T.* II–II, q. 57,
a. 1c; q. 58, aa. 1c, 2; q. 80, a. un. c; on equality, see I–II, q. 114, a. 1c; II–II, q. 57,
a. 1 ad 3, a. 2c; q. 61, a. 2 ad 2; q. 157, a. 3c; on the *debitum*, which Aquinas owes
to both the Latin language and the Roman law, see I, q. 21, a. 1 ad 3; I–II, q. 60,
a. 3c; II–II, q. 58, aa. 10c, 11c; also q. 58, a. 1 ad 6 and a. 3 ad 2; q. 122, a. 1c. At
the head of his analysis of justice, Aquinas places the Roman jurists' tag 'justitia est
constans et perpetua voluntas jus suum [uni]cuique tribue[ndi]', *Digest* I, 1, de Justitia
et Jure, 10; also *Institutes* I, 1, 1. Close to Aquinas's analysis is Cicero's eclectic synthesis,
De Finibus. V, xxiii, 65–7.

'Arithmetical' and 'geometrical' equality ... This is the *differentia* which Aristotle most
emphasizes in distinguishing distributive from corrective justice: *Nic. Eth.* V, 3–4:
1131a10–1132b20, esp. 1131b12, 1132a2.

VII.2

From 'legal' to 'general' justice ... On the importance of Aristotle's effort to clarify the
connotations of *dikaion*, see *Gauthier–Jolif*, II, 1, pp. 335–6. Aristotle comes close to
calling his 'legal justice' also 'general justice': *Nic. Eth.* V, 1: 1130b15–16. The
terminological emphasis is somewhat shifted by Aquinas from 'legal' towards 'general
justice', but 'legal justice' is retained: *S.T.* II–II, q. 58, aa. 5c, 6c; a. 7, tit. and obj.
3; I–II, q. 60, a. 3 ad 2. On the unfortunate later consequences of Aquinas's retention of the term 'legal justice' see section VII.6. Beyond matters of terminology, however, it is important to recognize that Aristotle uses the term 'legal justice' (*dikaion* ...
nomimon) above all because his whole analysis is focused on the *polis*, in which the whole
of human life is regulated by posited law: see *Pol.* I, 1: 1253a38–40; *Nic. Eth.* V, 1:
1129b12, 18–19; 6: 1134a30–36, b13–15; this leads to the notorious unclarity of his

discussion of natural as distinct from conventional (*nomikon*) justice: 7: 1134b18–1135a6; for all this see Eric Voegelin, 'Das Rechte von Natur' in his *Anamnesis* (Munich: 1966), pp. 116 ff. In Aquinas's account of legal or general justice the restriction to the political community and posited law is clearly transcended: the 'law' that is the *ratio* of the *jus* which is the object of justice is primarily the *lex naturalis* and only secondarily the *lex positiva* which is 'derived' from *lex naturalis*: see, e.g., *S.T.* II–II, q. 57, a. 1 ad 2; I–II, q. 95, a. 2; X.7, below. Notice, finally, the link between Aquinas's adoption of the Aristotelian term 'legal justice' and his own fundamental definition of law as 'an ordinance of reason *for the common good* . . .': I–II, q. 90, aa. 1c, 2c, 4c, explicitly recalled in II–II, q. 58, a. 5; also I–II, q. 100, a. 8c. On 'general justice' between Plato and the seventeenth century, see G. Del Vecchio, *Justice* (ed. A. H. Campbell, Edinburgh: 1952), ch. II, esp. the notes.

VII.3

Distributive justice concerns the appropriation to individuals of what is 'common' . . . See *Nic. Eth.* V, 2: 1130b31–33; 4: 1131b27–32; *S.T.* II–II, q. 61, a. 1c and ad 5. On the importance of not confusing this divisible 'id quod est commune' (common stock, incidents of common enterprise, etc.) with 'the common good', see P.-D. Dognin, 'La notion thomiste de justice face aux exigences modernes' (1961) 45 *Rev. des Sc. Phil. et Théol.* 601, 615, 620, 627; 'La justice particulière comporte-t-elle deux espèces?' (1965) 65 *Rev. Thom.* 398, 403, 408. The common good which is the object(ive) of all justice logically cannot be distributed.

The common good requires that individuality not be absorbed in common enterprises . . . This is no more paradoxical than the related principles that privacy is a good which the organs of the community should defend, or that there is a public interest in maintaining the confidentiality of certain sorts of personal communication.

Common enterprises should be to help individuals to help themselves . . . On this principle of justice, see the note on 'subsidiarity', appended to Chapter VI.5, above. For its application to the question of property, in the 'natural law' teaching of the Catholic Church, see e.g. Second Vatican Council, *Gaudium et Spes: Pastoral Constitution on the Church in the Modern World* (1965), paras. 65, 69, and citations.

Private property . . . For an analysis of the elements of the focal meaning of 'private property', see A. M. Honoré, 'Ownership' in A. G. Guest (ed.), *Oxford Essays in Jurisprudence* (Oxford: 1961), pp. 107–47. For an ample treatment of the place of private property and enterprise in a just social economy, see J. Messner, *Social Ethics: Natural Law in the Modern World* (St. Louis: 1949), pp. 697–947, esp. 785–800.

VII.4

Equal right of all to respectful consideration in distribution . . . See R. M. Dworkin, *Taking Rights Seriously* (London: 1977), pp. 180, 227, and (with some ambiguous gloss, and questionable conclusions from a 'thin theory' of human good) 273. Note, moreover, that if it is to be treated as 'the formal principle of *justice*', the injunction 'Treat like cases alike' must be taken in a more than merely formal sense; it must, for example, implicitly treat all human beings as alike in their humanity and in their basic entitlement to be treated differently from animals and to be treated by the agent, to whom the injunction is addressed, as 'like' him in their fundamental capacity to be subjects of human flourishing: see, with reservations, Del Vecchio, *Justice*, ch. 8; see also Finnis, 'The Value of the Human Person' (1972) 27 *Twentieth Century* (Australia), 126–37. Those who propose that animals have rights have a deficient appreciation of the basic forms of human good. At the root of their contention is the conception that good consists essentially in sentience (cf. IV.5); for it is only sentience that is common to human beings and the animals which are said to have rights. (For they do not have regard to life as such, or even to animal life as such: they do not propose to stop the phagocytes in their blood from destroying alien life.) Even if we consider the bodily human goods, and those simply as experienced, we see that the quality of this experience is very different from a merely animal consciousness, since it is experienced as expressive of decision, choice, reflectiveness, commitment, as fruition of purpose, or of self-discipline or self-abandonment, and as the action of a responsible personality. The basic human goods are not abstract forms, such as 'life' or 'conscious life': they are good as aspects of the flourishing of a person. And if the proponents of animal rights point to very young babies, or very old and decayed or mentally defective persons (or to someone asleep?), and ask how their state differs empirically from that of a flourishing, friendly, and clever dog, and demand to know why the former are accorded the respect due to right-holders while the latter is not, we must reply that respect for human good reasonably extends as far as human being, and is not to be extinguished by the circumstance that the incidents or 'accidents' of affairs have deprived a particular human being of the opportunity of a full flourishing.

Does justice demand that we give up virtually everything to feed the starving anywhere in the world? ... For the suggestion that it does ('perhaps to the point of marginal utility'), see P. Singer, 'Famine, Affluence and Morality' (1972) 1 *Phil. Pub. Aff.* 229 at p. 234. Many strands of ethical methodology and of *Weltanschauung* are involved in any discussion of this question. So far as the suggestion rests on a denial of the moral relevance of the distinction between actions and omissions, note that the implications of the denial do not all have the 'edifying' quality of the suggestion itself. Thus Glover, *Causing Death and Saving Lives*, pp. 104–6, qualifies Father Zossima's claim that 'everyone of us is responsible in every way' (VII.4, fn. 16), by observing that our time is limited, so that selection of priorities is inevitable. From here he argues that his denial of the action–omission distinction 'does not *entail* the view that ... parents playing with their children ought to be trying to raise money for Oxfam instead. (But it does make us ask the disturbing question: would we kill people if it were necessary for our pursuit of [such] activities? ... (There is always the disturbing question, for those of us who reject the acts and omissions doctrine, of the extent to which we would think it legitimate to kill people, in order to bring about things that make life interesting for the rest of us ... This Dostoyevskian question, when taken seriously, is likely to force us to reconsider *both* how justifiable it is for us to spend time playing with our children rather than helping fight starvation *and* the matter of whether positive acts of killing are quite as hard to justify as we usually suppose ...)' Leaving to one side Glover's odd procedure of framing questions for practical reasonableness in terms of what 'we *would*' do or think, and what we are 'likely' to do or think, it cannot be said that his very frank book even sketches an answer to *these* questions. This is not to say that the distinction between action and omission is *always* morally decisive or important; nor is it to say that the following maxim, adopted by the Vatican Council II, *Gaudium et Spes* (1965), para. 69, from Gratian's *Decretum* (*c*.1140), c. 21, dist. 86, has no application: 'Feed the man dying of hunger, because if you do not feed him you are killing him'.

Classic and latter-day utilitarianism ... In assessing the new utilitarian conception of justice developed in Glover's book, and in other recent writings, bear in mind G. E. M. Anscombe's comment on an earlier phase in the development of utilitarianism: 'we may state the thesis thus: it does not make any difference to a man's responsibility for an effect of his action which he can foresee, that he does not intend it. Now this sounds rather edifying; it is I think quite characteristic of very bad degenerations of thought on such questions that they sound edifying' ('Modern Moral Philosophy' (1958)

33 *Philosophy* 1 at p. 11). The difference between the thesis there mentioned and the new thesis is simply that the new utilitarians condemn as morally irrelevant the distinction between actions and omissions, which the older utilitarians retained from the non-utilitarian moral culture of their upbringing. See Glover, op. cit., p. 94.

VII.5

'Synallagmata' *not limited to exchanges* ... See *Gauthier–Jolif*, II, 1, p. 350.

'*Corrective justice*' ... For the translation of *diorthotikon*, and for critique of Aristotle's restriction of this second category of particular justice, see *Gauthier–Jolif*, II, 1, pp. 358–9; also pp. 369–72; cf. Del Vecchio, *Justice*, p. 61. The fascination of Aristotle's restriction can be seen in Hart, *Concept of Law*, pp. 154–5, where the 'primary application of justice' is said to be 'to matters of distribution and compensation'. For Hart's ingenious relating of 'redress' to his 'general principle ... of justice' ('Treat like cases alike and treat different cases differently'), see *Concept of Law*, pp. 160–1.

Aquinas's invention: 'commutative justice' ... Gauthier and Jolif, op. cit., p. 370, argue that the invention rests on a misunderstanding occasioned by the ambiguous Latin translation of Aristotle that Aquinas used. This seems unlikely, in view of the extremely elaborate treatment of commutative justice that Aquinas undertook in *S.T.* II–II, qq. 64–78, and in view of the conceptual gaps left by Aristotle's emphasis on correction. For an example of Aquinas's wide use of *commutatio*, see e.g. II–II, q. 80, a. un. ad 4; but the real proof is the range of topics he treats under the heading of commutative justice, outlined II–II, q. 61, a. 3c.

Distributive justice, commutative justice, and the act of judicial judgment ... See Aquinas, *S.T.* II–II, q. 63, a. 4 ad 1.

Compensation for personal injuries ... See P. S. Atiyah, *Accidents, Compensation and the Law* (London: 1970). For the conceptual shift of the modern law of torts towards an attempt to 'distribute risks and losses', see e.g. J. G. Fleming, *Law of Torts* (5th ed., Sydney: 1977), pp. 9–10.

Limitation of liability in law of contract ... For suggestive analysis along the lines adopted here, see F. H. Lawson, *Remedies of English Law* (Harmondsworth: 1972), pp. 336–8, 104–9, 177–9. For a criticism of recent developments, from the perspective of commutative justice, and linking the developments to a 'risk' theory of contractual obligation (itself linked to Holmes's analysis of contractual obligation, criticized below, XI.5), see Roscoe Pound, *An Introduction to the Philosophy of Law* (rev. ed. 1954), pp. 164–8.

VII.6

The triadic schema: distributive–commutative–legal ... For one of the countless expositions adopting this schema, see H. Rommen, *The Natural Law* (St. Louis and London: 1947), p. 67. For references to some sources, and a recognition that the schema falsifies both Aristotle and Aquinas, see Del Vecchio, *Justice*, pp. 35–6; also pp. 37–9, suggesting rightly that the term 'social justice' used in recent Catholic social teaching is equivalent to Aquinas's 'legal justice', and is used to fill the gap left by the mislocation of legal justice by the triadic schema. To like effect, and more fundamentally, see P.-D. Dognin, 'La notion thomiste de justice face aux exigences modernes' (1961) 45 *Rev. des Sc. Phil. et Théol.* 601–40; 'La justice particulière comporte-t-elle deux espèces?' (1965) *Rev. Thom.* 398–425. For the priority of Cajetan, see ibid. (1965) pp. 415–16; (1961) pp. 624–38. For attempts to interpret Aristotle 'triadically' for the purpose (not shared by Cajetan) of assimilating him to the threefold principle of justice proposed by *Digest*

I, 1, 10 (Ulpian) ('honeste vivere, neminem laedere, suum cuique tribuere'), see citations in Del Vecchio, *Justice*, pp. 25–6, 63–4; and G. Grua, *La justice humaine selon Leibniz* (Paris: 1956). pp. 80–3.

Nozick on redistribution of property ... For criticism of Nozick's position on other grounds, compatible with those advanced here (though too doubtful of the justice of private property), see A. M. Honoré, 'Property, Title and Redistribution' (1977) 10 *Arch. R. S. P.* 107–15.

VII.7

Doubts about the order of priority in distribution in bankruptcy ... See e.g. Lawson, *Remedies of English Law*, pp. 181–94, 338–41.

'End-states' and 'processes' ... Nozick's discussion in *Anarchy, State and Utopia*, pp. 153–64, is valuable, but fails to reach the fundamental point made here in the text. This fundamental point is expressed by Aristotle in his important distinction between practical reasonableness (*phronesis*) and technical ability (*techne*) (in other words, between 'doing something' and 'making something'): 'making aims at an end distinct from the end of making, whereas in doing the end cannot be other than the act itself: doing well [*eupraxia*] is in itself the end [*telos*]': *Nic. Eth.* VI, 4: 1140b3–6; see also II, 4: 1105a32; and John M. Cooper, *Reason and Human Good in Aristotle* (Cambridge, Mass.: 1975), pp. 2, 78, 111. More vivid, perhaps, is Cicero, *De Finibus* III, vii, 24: 'Wisdom is not like seamanship or medicine, but like the arts of acting and of dancing—for its end, being the actual exercise of the art, is contained within the art, and is not something extraneous to it.' This is the root of the principle of the *subsidiary* function of communal enterprise (a principle of justice: VII.3, above).

VIII

RIGHTS

ALMOST everything in this book is about human rights ('human rights' being a contemporary idiom for 'natural rights': I use the terms synonymously). For, as we shall see, the modern grammar of rights provides a way of expressing virtually all the requirements of practical reasonableness. Indeed, this grammar of rights is so extensive and supple in its reach that its structure is generally rather poorly understood; misunderstandings in discussions about rights, and about particular (alleged) rights and their extent, are consequently rather frequent. For this reason, and also because both the explanatory *justification* of claims of right and the resolution of many conflicting claims of right require us to identify values and principles which need not be expressed in terms of rights, the explicit discussion of rights occupies only this one chapter. But the reader who follows the argument of this chapter will readily be able to translate most of the previous discussions of community and justice, and the subsequent discussions of authority, law, and obligation, into the vocabulary and grammar of rights (whether 'natural' or 'legal').

This vocabulary and grammar of rights is derived from the language of lawyers and jurists, and is strongly influenced by its origins. So, although our own concern is primarily with the human or natural rights that may be appealed to whether or not embodied in the law of any community, it will be useful to devote the next section to a résumé of the results of contemporary juristic analysis of rights-talk. For the logic that we can uncover in legal uses of the term 'a right' and its cognates will be found largely applicable for an understanding of 'moral' rights-talk. (Human or natural rights are the fundamental and general moral rights; particular or concrete moral rights—for example, James's right not to have his private correspondence read by John during his absence from the office today—can be spoken of as 'human' or 'natural', but it is more usual to speak of them as 'moral' rights, derived, of course, from the general forms of moral, i.e. human rights: the distinction thus drawn by usage is not, however, very firm or clear.)

VIII.2   AN ANALYSIS OF RIGHTS-TALK

The American jurist Hohfeld, building on earlier juristic work, published an analysis of rights which, though poorly understood by many of its exponents, satisfactorily accommodates a wide range of lawyers' uses of the term 'a right' and its cognates— though not, as we shall see, all such uses. Departing from Hohfeld's own style of exposition, we may say that the fundamental postulates of his system are: (i) that all assertions or ascriptions of rights can be reduced without remainder to ascriptions of one or some combination of the following four 'Hohfeldian rights': (*a*) 'claim-right' (called by Hohfeld 'right *stricto sensu*'), (*b*) 'liberty' (called by Hohfeld 'privilege'), (*c*) 'power', and (*d*) 'immunity'; and (ii) that to assert a Hohfeldian right is to assert a three-term relation between one person, one act-description, and one other person. These two postulates, supplemented by a vocabulary partly in current use and partly devised *ad hoc*, generate the following logical relations (where A and B signify persons, natural or legal, and ϕ stands for an act-description signifying some act):

(1) A has a *claim-right* that B should ϕ, if and only if B has a *duty* to A to ϕ.

(2) B has a *liberty* (relative to A) to ϕ, if and only if A has *no-claim-right* ('a no-right') that B should not ϕ.

(2') B has a *liberty* (relative to A) not to ϕ, if and only if A has *no-claim-right* ('a no-right') that B should ϕ.

(3) A has a *power* (relative to B) to ϕ, if and only if B has a *liability* to have his legal position changed by A's ϕ-ing.

(4) B has an *immunity* (relative to A's ϕ-ing), if and only if A has no power (i.e. a *disability*) to change B's legal position by ϕ-ing.

It will be observed that the reference of 'ϕ' in (3) and (4) is

to some act (a 'juridical act')[1] which is defined at least partly
by reference to its effect upon juridical relationships, whereas,
in (1), (2), and (2'), 'ϕ' may denote either juridical acts or, more
commonly, acts ('natural acts')[2] fully definable without reference to their effect upon juridical relationships (even though
the act may entail such an effect under a given legal regime
and may accordingly be the subject of legal definition in that
regime). It may be thought that in discussion of human rights,
outside the context of particular legal regimes, relations on the
model of (3) and (4) will play little or no part. But, although
powers and immunities from the exercise of powers do indeed
play a less prominent role in such discussions than claim-
rights and liberties, it would be a mistake to overlook them.
For wherever A can grant B permission to do something that
otherwise he (B) would have the (moral) duty not to do, A
can be said to have a right of much the same character as a
Hohfeldian legal power; and wherever A's moral claim-rights,
liberties, and powers cannot be affected merely by B's purported
grants of permission to C, A's rights can be said to involve or
be buttressed by a right of the same character as a Hohfeldian
immunity.

Still, the most important of the aids to clear thinking provided
by Hohfeld's schema is the distinction between A's *claim-right*
(which has as its correlative B's duty) and A's *liberty* (which
is A's freedom from duty and thus has as its correlative the
absence or negation of the claim-right that B would otherwise
have). A claim-right is always either, positively, a right to be
given something (or assisted in a certain way) by someone else,
or, negatively, a right *not* to be interfered with or dealt with
or treated in a certain way, by someone else. When the subject-
matter of one's claim of right is one's own act(s), forbearance(s),
or omission(s), that claim cannot be to a claim-right, but can
only be to a liberty (or, in the case of juridical acts, to a power).
Of course, one's liberty to act in the specified way may be
enhanced and protected by a *further* right or set of rights, viz.
the claim-right(s) not to be interfered with by B, C, D ... in
exercising one's liberty. But a liberty thus protected by a claim-

---

[1] For example, buying, selling, leasing, granting, marrying, paying, adjudicating,
enacting ...

[2] For example, walking, hitting, travelling by aeroplane, defaming ...

right is not a distinct type of Hohfeldian right; it is a conjunction, never logically necessary but always beneficial to the
liberty-holder, of two distinct Hohfeldian relationships (each
of which, of course, may be and normally is 'multital', i.e.
obtains in identical form not only between A and B but also
between A and C, A and D, A and ...). In the law, such
conjunctions of a liberty with a claim-right are often supplemented by further conjoined rights, for example, by the claim-
right to compensation in the event of wrongful (i.e. duty-
breaking) interference with the liberty, and/or by the ancillary
liberty to resort to self-help or to approach the courts in defence
of one's substantive liberty, and/or by the power to institute
legal proceedings or to waive compliance with the duty, etc.
Most 'legal rights', even when not multital, are in fact
combinations, often very complex, of Hohfeldian rights;
Hohfeld's ambition was to enable any legal right, such as the
undifferentiated legal 'right of A to £10 under this contract',
to be resolved or translated without remainder into its component Hohfeldian rights.

It has, recently, however, been demonstrated that such a
translation, while it may always be possible (at least in
principle), may none the less fail to provide a full elucidation
of lawyers' ascriptions of rights. Lawyers frequently talk about
rights, not as three-term relations between two persons and an
act of a certain type, but as two-term relations between persons
and one subject-matter or (in a broad sense) *thing*: for example,
someone's right to £10 under a contract, or to (a share in)
a specified estate, or to the performing rights of an opera. The
reason why such a two-term ascription of rights is preferred
by lawyers, in many contexts, is this: it gives an intelligible unity
to a temporal series of the many and varying *sets of* Hohfeldian
rights which at different times one and the same set of rules
provides in order to secure and give substance to one *subsisting*
objective. To take the simplest example: if A has the right to
£10 under a contract, he may at one time have a Hohfeldian
claim-right to be paid £10 by B, and at a later time (B's debt
having been assumed by C) another Hohfeldian claim-right,
to be paid £10 by C; and the procedural rights (Hohfeldian
claim-rights, powers, etc.) that A enjoys to enforce his right
may be shifting, either in step or out of step with the shift

between the earlier claim-right to be paid £10 and the later.
Yet this series of differing sets of Hohfeldian rights is intelligibly
unified; for the shifting applications of the various relevant legal
rules all relate to one topic, the 'right to £10 under that
contract', a non-Hohfeldian right of which the benefit, the
burden, and the procedural props and incidents can all be
shifted more or less independently of each other without affecting
the 'right itself' which is the constant focus of the law's concern.

This explanation of the persistence of 'two-term' 'thing-
oriented' rights-talk, amongst lawyers familiar with Hohfeld's
'three-term' 'act-oriented' schema of rights, will be worth
bearing in mind when we turn to consider natural rights such
as 'the right to life' (VIII.5). At the moment, however, it will
be useful to conclude this short account of the logic of contemporary legal rights-talk by referring briefly to the jurisprudential debate about the proper *explanation* of rights and of
the logic of rights-talk. This debate is provoked by two different
problems, but the principal opposing answers to each of these
problems overlap (as if there were only one problem evoking
the opposing theses).

The first problem is technical. Before the Hohfeldian schema
can be applied to any rule or to the translation of any non-
Hohfeldian rights-talk, it is necessary to stipulate at least one
further definitional postulate which Hohfeld omitted (at least,
expressly) to supply. For, granted that B has a *duty* when, in
virtue of a certain rule, he is required to act in a certain way,

when shall we say that there is, correlative with this duty, a
claim-right? And in whom does the claim-right vest? To these
questions there are two opposing answers. The first answer is
that there is a claim-right correlative to B's duty if and only
if there is some ascertainable person A for whose benefit the
duty has been imposed, in the sense that he is to be the recipient
of the (presumable) advantage of B's performance of or compliance with his duty; and that that person A has the claim-
right correlative to B's duty. The alternative answer is that there
is some person A with a claim-right correlative to B's duty,
if and only if there is some person A who has the power to
take appropriate remedial action at law in the event of B's
failure to comply with his duty. It seems that Hohfeld himself
would have favoured the latter answer had he squarely faced

the question. But neither answer is consistently reflected in legal discourse. Consider, for example, a body of law which (like English law) provides that, where B and C enter into a contract that C shall pay a sum to A, A has no power to enforce C's duty or to take any remedial action at law in the event of C's non-performance. On the first approach, we could express the purport of this law by saying that, under such a contract, A has a claim-right correlative to C's duty but cannot himself enforce or uphold his claim-right at law.[3] On the second approach, we would be bound to say that, in this state of the law, A simply has no rights under the contract made for his benefit. English lawyers, while agreed about the content of the relevant rules, in fact waver between these two approaches. Most state brusquely that in English law a third party (A) has no rights under a contract. Others, of high authority, say that such a third party does indeed have rights (meaning legal rights) which, however, he himself is unable to enforce at law.[4]

Someone, therefore, who wishes to apply the Hohfeldian analysis must first *stipulate* which of these two meanings of 'claim-right' he is going to adopt, and must bear in mind that, whichever one he adopts, his subsequent ascriptions of claim-rights will not always correspond with legal usage. But beyond this first, technical problem, which is thus to be solved by simply stipulating how one will use the term 'claim-right', there is a philosophical problem not to be solved by stipulation. This is the question: What, if any, is the underlying principle, unifying the various types of relationships that are reasonably said to concern 'rights'? Or, more crudely: Is there some general explanation of what it is to have a right?

The principal competing answers to this broad question parallel and overlap with the above two proposals for providing a specific meaning for 'claim-right'. On the one hand, rights of all forms are said to be <u>benefits secured for persons by rules</u> regulating the relationships between those persons and other

---

[3] We could add, on this approach, that (i) B, too, has a claim-right correlative to C's duty (so that, formally, C has a legal duty comprising two Hohfeldian duties of identical form), since it is always (presumably) for the benefit of a promisee that his promisor should honour his promise (even when the material benefits of the promise go to someone other than the promisee); and (ii) B, unlike A, can enforce his claim-right.

[4] See *Beswick* v. *Beswick* [1968] A.C. 58 at 71 (Lord Reid), 89 (Lord Pearce).

persons subject to those rules. These benefits are various: there is the advantage of being the recipient of other persons' acts of service or forbearances; the advantage of being legally or morally free to act; the advantage of being able to change one's own or others' legal position, and of being immune from such change (when of a form characteristically disadvantageous to anyone subject to the change) at the hands of others; the advantage of being able to secure any or all of the foregoing advantages by action at law, or at least compensation for wrongful denial of any of them; and finally, if we shift to the two-term thing-focused rights of lawyers' talk, there are the various advantages constituted by the things or states of affairs which are the subject-matter of such rights.

On the other hand, it has been argued that the foregoing 'benefit' or 'interest' theory of rights treats rights too un-discriminatingly, as if they were no more than the 'reflex' of rules which impose duties, or relieve from duties, or enable duties to be created, shifted, or annulled. This, it is said, is to miss the point of rights. For, it is said, the point and unifying characteristic of rules which entail or create rights is that such rules specifically recognize and respect a person's *choice*, either negatively by not impeding or obstructing it (liberty and immunity) or affirmatively by giving legal or moral effect to it (claim-right and power). Indeed, in this view, moral rights are said to belong to a 'branch of morality which is specifically concerned to determine when one person's freedom may be limited *by another's* [freedom]'. Just as the 'benefit' theory gives reason for adopting the first approach to fixing the meaning of Hohfeld's claim-right, so the 'choice' theory gives reason for adopting the second approach. As Hart puts it: 'The case of a right correlative to obligation then emerges as only a special case of legal power in which the right-holder is at liberty to waive or extinguish or to enforce or leave unenforced another's obligation.'[5]

---

[5] H. L. A. Hart, 'Bentham on Legal Rights' in *Oxford Essays II*, 171 at pp. 196–7: also p. 192: 'The idea is that of one individual being given by the law exclusive control, more or less extensive, over another person's duty so that in the area of conduct covered by that duty the individual who has the right is a small-scale sovereign to whom the duty is owed.' This image of 'temporary authority or sovereignty' is already present in Hart, 'Are there any Natural Rights?' (1955) 64 *Philosophical Rev.*, reprinted in A. M. Quinton, *Political Philosophy* (Oxford: 1967), at p. 70.

But Hart, the principal contemporary exponent of the 'choice' or 'will' theory of rights, has recently conceded (in the course of a firm defence of it as an explanation of lawyers' talk about 'ordinary' law) that that theory is inadequate to explain how the language of rights is deployed by those who, in assessing the justice or constitutionality of laws, treat 'certain freedoms and benefits ... as essential for the maintenance of the life, the security, the development, and the dignity of the individual' and thus speak of these freedoms and benefits as rights. In such discourse, 'the core of the notion of rights is neither individual choice nor individual benefit but basic or fundamental individual needs':[6] in my terminology, basic aspects of human flourishing. In the light of this concession, it is not necessary here to settle the dispute between the 'benefit' and the 'choice' theories, as regards strictly legal rights. It suffices that, for the less restricted purposes of this chapter, we may safely speak of rights wherever a basic principle or requirement of practical reasonableness, or a rule derived therefrom, gives to A, and to each and every other member of a class to which A belongs, the benefit of (i) a positive or negative requirement (obligation) imposed upon B (including, *inter alia*, any requirement not to interfere with A's activity or with A's enjoyment of some other form of good) or of (ii) the ability to bring it about that B is subject to such a requirement, or of (iii) the immunity from being himself subjected by B to any such requirement.

VIII. 3   ARE DUTIES 'PRIOR TO' RIGHTS?

In short, the modern vocabulary and grammar of rights is a many-faceted instrument for reporting and asserting the requirements or other implications of a relationship of justice *from the point of view of the person(s) who benefit(s) from* that relationship. It provides a way of talking about 'what is just' from a special angle: the viewpoint of the 'other(s)' to whom something (including, *inter alia*, freedom of choice) is owed or due, and who would be wronged if denied that something. And the contemporary debate shows that there is a strong though not irresistible tendency to specialize that viewpoint still further, so that the peculiar advantage implied (on any view) by any

[6] Hart, in *Oxford Essays II*, at pp. 200–1.

ascription of rights is taken to be the advantage of *freedom* of action, and/or *power* to affect the freedom of action of others.

All this can be better understood if we review the history of the word 'right(s)' and its antecedent in the classical language of European culture, viz. '*jus*'. For this history has a watershed, and it is essentially the same watershed as we saw in the classification of types of justice (VII.6) and as we shall see again in the explanation of authority (IX.4) and of the source or justification of obligation (XI.6, XI.8).

The word '*jus*' ('*ius*') begins its academic career in the Roman law. But its meaning in the Roman texts has become an object of controversy, particularly since scholars became aware of the watershed. (The Roman lawyers did not attempt a linguistic analysis of their framework juristic concepts.) So it is more convenient to begin this historical sketch by asking what '*jus*' was taken to mean by Thomas Aquinas, a philosophical theologian but fairly well acquainted with the Roman law systems of his day (especially the canon law of his Church). Here there is little ambiguity. Aquinas prefaces his elaborate study of justice with an analysis of '*jus*', at the forefront of which he gives a list of meanings of '*jus*'. The primary meaning, he says, is 'the just thing itself' (and by 'thing', as the context makes clear, he means acts, objects, and states of affairs, considered as subject-matters of relationships of justice). One could say that for Aquinas '*jus*' primarily means 'the fair' or 'the what's fair'; indeed, if one could use the adverb 'aright' as a noun, one could say that his primary account is of 'arights' (rather than of rights). He then goes on to list secondary and derivative meanings of '*jus*' (relationships of justice): 'the art by which one knows or determines what is just' (and the principles and rules of this art, he adds, are the law), 'the place in which what is just is awarded' (i.e. in modern legal systems, the court), and finally 'the award (even if unjust) of the judge, whose role it is to do justice'.[7]

If we now jump about 340 years to the treatise on law by the Spanish Jesuit Francisco Suarez, written *c*.1610, we find another analysis of the meanings of '*jus*'. Here the 'true, strict and proper meaning' of '*jus*' is said to be: 'a kind of moral power [*facultas*] which every man has, either over his own property

[7] *S.T.* II–II, q. 57, a. 1c, ad 1 and ad 2.

or with respect to that which is due to him'.[8] The meaning which for Aquinas was primary is rather vaguely mentioned by Suarez and then drops out of sight; conversely, the meaning which for Suarez is primary does not appear in Aquinas's discussion at all. Somewhere between the two men we have crossed the watershed.

A few years after Suarez (and not altogether independently of him), Hugo Grotius begins his *De Jure Belli ac Pacis* (1625) by explaining that the meaning of the term *jus* (*jure*) in his title is 'that which is just';[9] but he then offers an elaborate exposition of 'another meaning of *jus* . . . which has reference to the person; this meaning of *jus* is: a moral quality of the person enabling [*competens*] him to have or to do something justly'. This, he says, is the meaning that hereafter he is going to treat as the word's 'proper or strict' meaning. Then he clarifies the reference of the phrase 'moral quality'. Such a quality can be 'perfect', in which case we call it a *facultas*, or 'imperfect', in which case we call it an *aptitudo*.[10] When Roman lawyers refer to one's *suum* (as in their defining principle of justice, *suum cuique tribuere*, which is synonymous with *jus suum cuique tribu*[*endi*]) they are referring, says Grotius, to this *facultas*. And '*facultas*' in turn has three principal meanings: (i) power (*potestas*), which may be power over oneself (called liberty: *libertas*) or power over others (e.g. *patria potestas*, the power of a father over his family); (ii) ownership (*dominium*) . . .; and (iii) credit, to which corresponds debt (*debitum*).[11] The last-mentioned meaning of *facultas* rather complicates the picture; the Roman law tradition had more of a hold on Grotius than on Suarez. But Grotius is still on the same side of the watershed as Suarez: *jus* is essentially something someone *has*, and above all (or at least paradigmatically) a *power* or *liberty*. If you like, it is Aquinas's primary meaning of '*jus*', but transformed by *relating it exclusively to the beneficiary* of the just relationship, above all to his doings and havings.

This shift of perspective could be so drastic as to carry the right-holder, and his right, altogether outside the juridical relationship which is fixed by law (moral or posited) and which

[8] *De Legibus*, I, ii, 5.
[9] Grotius, *De Jure Belli ac Pacis*, I, I, iii.
[10] Ibid. iv.
[11] Ibid. v.

establishes *jus* in Aquinas's sense: 'that which is just'. For within a few years Hobbes is writing:

> ... *jus*, and *lex*, *right* and *law* ... ought to be distinguished; because RIGHT, consisteth in liberty to do, or to forbear; whereas LAW, determineth and bindeth to one of them: so that law, and right, differ as much, as obligation, and liberty; which in one and the same matter are inconsistent.[12]

Pushed as far as Hobbes's purposes, this contrast between law and rights deprives the notion of rights of virtually all its normative significance. Hobbes wishes to say that a man has most rights when he is in the 'state of nature', i.e. a vacuum of law and obligation, since 'in such a condition, every man has a right to everything; even to one another's body'.[13] But we could just as well say that in such a condition of things, where nobody has any duty not to take anything he wants, *no one has any rights*. The fact that we could well say this shows that the ordinary modern idiom of 'rights' does not follow Hobbes all the way to his contrast between law and rights. Nor did Locke or Pufendorf; yet they did adopt his stipulation that 'a right' (*jus*) is paradigmatically a liberty.[14] Their successors are those who today defend the 'choice' theory of rights, which as we saw in the preceding section is one eligible way of accounting for most, but not all, of the modern grammar of rights. And even those who defend the 'benefit' theory of rights are far from using the idiom of Aquinas, since (in common with ordinary language-speakers and lawyers in all modern languages) they think of 'a right' as something beneficial which a person *has* (a 'moral [including legal] quality' in Grotius's terminology), rather than 'that which is just in a given situation', the ensemble of juridical relationships established, by rules, between two or more persons in relation to some subject-matter (act, thing, or state of affairs).

[12] *Leviathan* (1651), ch. xiv; in Raphael (ed.), *British Moralists*, vol. I, para. 56. Thus, for Hobbes as for Hohfeld, liberty is simply the negation of duty; and this 'liberty-right' is the only right Hobbes has in mind.

[13] Ibid., loc. cit., Raphael, para. 57.

[14] Locke, *Essays on the Law of Nature* (1663; ed. W. von Leyden, Oxford: 1954), p. 10 (f. 11): 'jus enim in eo positum est quod alicujus rei liberum habemus usum' (right is predicated on this, that we have the free use of a thing). Pufendorf, *Elementa Jurisprudentiae Universalis* (1660), I, def. xiii, para. 3; cf. def. viii, para. 1 and *De Jure Naturae et Gentium Libri Octo* (1672), I, c. 1, paras. 19–20.

There should be no question of wanting to put the clock back. The modern idiom of rights is more supple and, by being more specific in its standpoint or perspective, is *capable* of being used with more differentiation and precision than the pre-modern use of 'the right' (*jus*). But it is salutary to bear in mind that the modern emphasis on the powers of the right-holder, and the consequent systematic bifurcation between 'right' (including 'liberty') and 'duty', is something that sophisticated lawyers were able to do without for the whole life of classical Roman law. This is not the place to argue the translation of the Roman law texts. To establish how differently the term '*jus*' sounded in the ears of a Roman lawyer from the modern term 'a right', suffice it to cite one short passage from a students' manual of the second century AD, the *Institutes* of Gaius:

The *jura* of urban estates are such as the *jus* of raising a building higher and of obstructing the light of a neighbour's building, or of not raising [a building], lest the neighbour's light be obstructed ...[15]

Obviously, we cannot replace the word '*jus*' in this passage with the word 'right' (meaning *a* right), since it is nonsense (or, if a special meaning can be found, it is far from the meaning of this passage) to speak of a 'right *not* to raise one's building, lest the neighbour's light be obstructed'. In Roman legal thought, '*jus*' frequently signifies the assignment made as between parties of justice according to law; and one party's 'part' in such an assignment might be a burden, not a benefit— let alone a power or liberty of choice.

And in this, the vocabulary of Roman law resembles more than one pre-modern legal vocabulary. Anthropologists studying certain African tribal regimes of law have found that in the indigenous language the English terms 'a right' and 'duty' are usually covered by a single word, derived from the verbal form normally translated as 'ought'. This single word (e.g. *swanelo* in Barotse, *tshwanelo* in Tswana) is thus found to be best translated as 'due'; for 'due' looks both ways along a juridical relationship, both to what one is due to do, and to what is due to one. This is linked, in turn, with a 'nuance in tribal societies,

---

[15] *Inst.* II, 14 (as conventionally reconstructed; but the same use of '*jus*' to cover both '*altius tollendi*' and '*non altius tollendi*' is found in the *Digest*, viii, 2, 2, along with similar uses, e.g. '*stillicidium avertendi ... aut non avertendi*').

in that they stress duty and obligation, rather than the nuance of modern Western society, with a stress on right[s]'.[16]

Let me conclude this review of the shift of meaning in the term 'right' and its linguistic predecessors by repeating that there is no cause to take sides as between the older and the newer usages, as ways of expressing the implications of justice in a given context. Still less is it appropriate to argue that 'as a matter of juristic logic' duty is logically prior to right (or vice versa). But when we come to explain the requirements of justice, which we do by referring to the needs of the common good at its various levels, then we find that there is reason for treating the concept of duty, obligation, or requirement as having a more strategic explanatory role than the concept of rights. The concept of rights is not on that account of less importance or dignity: for the common good is precisely the good of the individuals whose *benefit*, from fulfilment of duty by others, is their *right* because *required* of those others in justice.

VIII.4 RIGHTS AND THE COMMON GOOD

The modern language of rights provides, as I said, a supple and potentially precise instrument for sorting out and expressing the demands of justice. It is often, however, though not inevitably or irremediably, a hindrance to clear thought when the question is: What *are* the demands of justice? The aspects of human well-being are many; the commitments, projects, and actions that are apt for realizing that well-being are innumerable even for an individual contemplating only his own life-plan; when we contemplate the complexities of collaboration, co-ordination, and mutual restraint involved in pursuit of the common good, we are faced with inescapable choices between rationally eligible but competing possible institutions, policies, programmes, laws, and decisions. The strength of rights-talk is that, carefully employed, it can express precisely the various aspects of a decision involving more than one person, indicating just what is and is not required of each person

---

[16] Max Gluckman, *The Ideas in Barotse Jurisprudence* (2nd ed., Manchester: 1972), p. xxv; also p. xlv n. 18, and p. 21; I. Schapera, 'Contract in Tswana Law' in Gluckman (ed.), *Ideas and Procedures in African Customary Law* (Oxford: 1969), pp. 319, 326; Gluckman, *The Judicial Process among the Barotse* (Manchester 1955), p. 166.

concerned, and just when and how one of those persons can affect those requirements. But the conclusory force of ascriptions of rights, which is the source of the suitability of rights-talk for expressing conclusions, is also the source of its potential for confusing the rational process of investigating and determining what justice requires in a given context.

The Universal Declaration of Human Rights, proclaimed by the General Assembly of the United Nations in December 1948, has been taken as a model, not only for the United Nations Covenants on Civil and Political Rights and on Economic, Social and Cultural Rights (1966) but also for the European Convention for the Protection of Human Rights and Fundamental Freedoms (1952), itself the model for the very many Bills of Rights entrenched in the Constitutions of countries becoming independent since 1957, especially within the (British) Commonwealth. Such thoroughly pondered documents deserve close attention from anyone wishing to think out problems of human life in community in terms of rights, human or natural, or legal.

Two features of all these documents are immediately noticeable. First: each document employs not one but two principal canonical forms: (A) 'Everyone has the right to ...' and (B) 'No one shall be ...'.[17] Now it is clear that the formal logic of rights-talk permits, by simple conversion of terms and appropriate negations, a transformation from one form to the other. Hence a single canonical form would have been possible. The decision to use two different formulae cannot be ascribed to logical ineptitude or mere love of stylistic variation. The rationale of the decision can be detected by attending to the second feature common to all these documents: namely, that the 'exercise of the rights and freedoms' proclaimed is said to be 'subject to limitation'. In some documents (e.g. the European

---

[17] Thus, in the Universal Declaration: Art. 3 'Everyone has the right to life, liberty and security of person'. Art. 4 'No one shall be held in slavery or servitude ...'. Art. 5 'No one shall be subjected to torture ...'. Art. 13(1) 'Everyone has the right to freedom of movement and residence within the borders of each state.' Art. 17(1) 'Everyone has the right to own property alone as well as in association with others'. (2) 'No one shall be arbitrarily deprived of his property'; etc., etc. Or again, in the European Convention: Art 5(1) 'Everyone has the right to liberty and security of person. No one shall be deprived of his liberty save in the following cases ... (a) ... (f) ...'.

Convention) these limitations are specified article by article, in conjunction with the specification of the respective rights. In others the limitation is pronounced only once, in generic terms. Thus Art. 29 of the Universal Declaration reads:

(1) Everyone has duties to the community in which alone the free and full development of his personality is possible.
(2) In the exercise of his rights and freedoms, everyone shall be subject only to such limitations as are determined by law solely for the purpose of securing due recognition and respect for the rights and freedoms of others and of meeting the just requirements of morality, public order and the general welfare in a democratic society.
(3) These rights and freedoms may in no case be exercised contrary to the purposes and principles of the United Nations.

The grounds of limitation specified in Art. 29(2) are referred to again and again in the particular limiting clauses in the European Convention and other documents. The point to notice is that the limitations, in Art. 29(2), are said to be on the exercise of the 'rights and freedoms' specified in the document. This suggests that the limitations might *not* be applicable to those Articles which do not purport to define a right but instead impose a negative requirement (which *could*, as we have observed, have been expressed as a right, but was not). This in turn suggests a differentiation in the guiding force of the various Articles, as criteria for just laws and decisions. The Articles expressed in form (B)—'No one shall be subjected to . . .' —are intended to be of conclusory force. But the Articles in form (A) have guiding force only as items in a process of rational decision-making which cannot reasonably be concluded simply by appealing to any one of these rights (notwithstanding that all are 'fundamental' and 'inalienable' and part of 'everyone's' *entitlement*[18]).

Some of the Articles cast in the peremptory (B) form do themselves contain internal qualifications: for example, Art. 9 'No one shall be subjected to *arbitrary* arrest . . .'. But some are quite unqualified: for example, Art. 5 'No one shall be subjected to torture . . .'. And none are subject (if this interpretation of the draftsmanship is correct) to the limitation on exercise of rights, stipulated in Art. 29. One's right not to be tortured (as we can

[18] See preamble and Art. 2 of the Universal Declaration.

indeed express it) is not a 'right' that one 'exercises' in the sense of Art. 29; acts of torture cannot therefore be justified by appeal to 'just requirements of public order'. The right not to be tortured, then, could be called an absolute right, to distinguish it from the rights that are 'inalienable' but subject 'in their exercise' to various limitations. Later in this chapter I consider whether it is reasonable to assert that some rights are absolute, i.e. whether this feature of the Universal Declaration can be justified (VIII.7).

For the moment, let us examine the specified grounds of limitation more closely. They are fourfold: (i) to secure due recognition for the rights and freedoms of others; (ii) to meet the just requirements of morality in a democratic society; (iii) to meet the just requirements of public order in a democratic society; (iv) to meet the just requirements of the general welfare in a democratic society.

The last-mentioned ground of limitation, (iv), attracts attention, not merely for its breadth and vagueness. Some theorists have treated rights as 'individuated political aims' which are not subordinate to conceptions of 'aggregate collective good'[19] or the 'general interest'[20] or 'general utility'.[21] Such an account of rights would give reason for concluding that the reference to 'general welfare' in Art. 29 of the Universal Declaration is inept. Now that conclusion is indeed correct, but not for the reason just suggested. In defining or explaining rights we must not make reference to concepts which are incoherent or senseless; and, as I explained in Chapter V.6, conceptions of 'aggregate collective good' are incoherent, save in limited technical contexts. The ongoing life of a human community is not a limited technical context, and the common good of such a community cannot be measured as an aggregate, as utilitarians suppose.

---

[19] R. M. Dworkin. *Taking Rights Seriously* (London: 1977), p. 91.

[20] Ibid., p. 269.

[21] Ibid., p. 191. But, Dworkin continues, 'I must not overstate the point. Someone who claims that citizens have a right against the Government need not go so far as to say that the State is *never* justified in overriding that right. He might say, for example, that although citizens have a right to free speech, the Government may override that right when necessary to protect the rights of others, or to prevent catastrophe, or even to obtain a clear and major public benefit (though if he acknowledged this last as a possible justification he would be treating the right in question as not among the most important or fundamental).'

The ineptitude of Art. 29's reference to 'the general welfare', as a distinct and separate ground for limiting rights, can be shown if we reflect on the first of the grounds proposed in that Article: to secure 'due recognition and respect for the rights and freedoms of others'. For amongst the rights proclaimed in the Universal Declaration are life, liberty, security of person (Art. 3), equality before the law (Art. 7), privacy (Art. 12), marriage and protection of family life (Art. 16), property (Art. 17), social security and the 'realization, through national effort and international co-operation ... of the economic, social and cultural rights indispensable for [everyone's] dignity and the free development of his personality' (Art. 22), participation in government (Art. 21), work, protection against unemployment, favourable remuneration of work (Art. 23), rest and leisure (Art. 24), 'a standard of living adequate for ... health and well-being ...' (Art. 25), education (Art. 26), enjoyment of the arts and a share in the benefits of scientific advancement (Art. 27), and 'a social and international order in which the rights and freedoms set forth in this Declaration can be fully realised' (Art. 28). When we survey this list we realize what the modern 'manifesto'[22] conception of human rights amounts to. It is simply a way of sketching the *outlines of the common good*, the various aspects of individual well-being in community. What the reference to rights contributes in this sketch is simply a pointed expression of what is implicit in the term '*common* good', namely that *each* and everyone's well-being, in each of its basic aspects, must be considered and favoured at *all* times by those responsible for co-ordinating the common life. Thus, when the human rights proclaimed in the Universal Declaration are spelt out, and amplified as in the subsequent United Nations Covenants,[23] there is no room left for an appeal, *against* the 'exercise' of these rights, to 'general welfare'. Either 'general welfare' is a reference to a utilitarian aggregation, in which case it is merely illusory, or else it is a dangling and confused

---

[22] See Joel Feinberg, *Social Philosophy* (Englewood Cliffs, New Jersey: 1973), p. 67.

[23] For example, the Covenant of Economic Social and Cultural Rights (1966): Art. 11 'the right of everyone to an adequate standard of living ... and to the continuous improvement of living conditions'; Art. 12 '... the right of everyone to the enjoyment of the highest attainable standard of physical and mental health ...', etc. etc.

reference to a general concept at the end of a list of (most of)[24] the particular components of that very concept.

What, then, are we to say about the other listed grounds of limitation: (ii) just requirements of morality in a democratic society and (iii) just requirements of public order in a democratic society? The argument of the preceding paragraph suggests that, given the breadth of the rights contemplated by the rest of the Universal Declaration, most of what these limitations import is already implicit in ground (i) in the list of grounds of limitation: viz. (i) due respect for the rights and freedoms of others. It must also be noted that neither 'morality' nor 'public order' is a term clear in its meaning (quite apart from any substantive controversies about the requirements of morality or public order). For in much modern usage, including legal usage, 'morality' signifies almost exclusively sexual morality and the requirements of decency, whereas, in philosophical usage, sexual morality (including decency) is merely one small portion of the requirements of practical reasonableness. This ambiguity affects the use of the term 'morality' even when it is conjoined with 'public' as in the frequent references of the European Convention and the later UN Conventions (1966) to 'public order or morals'. And as for 'public order', this phrase as used in the international documents suffers from the irremediable ambiguity that in common law systems it signifies absence of disorder (i.e. public peace, tranquillity, and safety), whereas the expressions *ordre public* and *orden público* used in the French and Spanish versions of those documents signify a civil law concept almost as wide as the concept of public policy in common law. For example, by using a version of the civil law concept of public order, the Second Vatican Council, in proclaiming the right to freedom of religious belief, profession, and practice, found that all the necessary limitations on this right could be expressed in terms of public order:

the protection of civil society, by civil authority, against abuses of this right must not be accomplished arbitrarily or with inequitable favour to any person or group, but must be according to juridical

---

[24] Perhaps the list needs to be eked out, at least in respect of some of the rights which it is to limit, by reference to 'public health' and 'national security', which are among the grounds of limitation specified in the later documents.

norms which are consistent with the objective moral order and which
are required for [i] the effective protection of the rights of all citizens
and of their peaceful coexistence, and [ii] a sufficient care for the
authentic public peace of an ordered common life in true justice, and
[iii] a proper upholding of public morality. All these factors constitute
the fundamental part of the common good, and come under the notion
of *public order*.[25]

In the face of these terminological problems, why not say that
the exercise of rights is to be limited only by respect for the
rights of others? The answer must be that although it would be
possible, given the logical reach of rights-talk, to express *any*
desired restriction on rights in terms of other rights, the
references to morality, public morality, public health, public
order, etc., in all the contemporary declarations of rights, are
neither conceptually redundant nor substantively unreasonable.

For, as we have seen, modern rights-talk is constructed
primarily on the implicit model of a relationship between two
individuals. So, in its primary signification (as distinct from its
inherent logical reach) modern rights-talk most fittingly concerns benefits or advantages to individuals (in the limiting cases,
to *all* individuals), 'not simply as members of a collectivity
enjoying a diffuse common benefit in which all participate in
indistinguishable and unassignable shares'.[26] But public morality and public order (even in the restricted, common law sense)
are both diffuse common benefits in which all participate in
indistinguishable and unassignable shares. Hence, there is
reason for referring to them specifically.

The fact is that human rights can only be securely enjoyed
in certain sorts of milieu—a context or framework of mutual
respect and trust and common understanding, an environment
which is physically healthy and in which the weak can go about
without fear of the whims of the strong. Consider, now, the
concept of public morality, in its oddly restricted, sexual sense.
Apart from such special arrangements as marriage, no one's
human rights include a right that other men or women should
not conduct themselves sexually in certain ways. But the great
majority of any community that is reproducing itself will spend

[25] Declaration *Dignitatis Humanae*, 7 Dec. 1965, para. 7.
[26] Cf. D. N. MacCormick, 'Rights in Legislation', in *Essays*, p. 205.

more than a quarter of their lives as children and then more than another quarter as parents bringing up children—in all, more than half their lifetimes. Now if it is the case that sexuality is a powerful force which only with some difficulty, and always precariously, can be integrated with other aspects of human personality and well-being—so that it enhances rather than destroys friendship and the care of children, for example—and if it is further the case that human sexual psychology has a bias towards regarding other persons as bodily objects of desire and potential sexual release and gratification, and as mere items in an erotically flavoured classification (e.g. 'women'), rather than as full persons with personal and individual sensitivities, restraints, and life-plans, then there is reason for fostering a milieu in which children can be brought up (and parents assisted rather than hindered in bringing them up) so that they are relatively free from inward subjection to an egoistic, impulsive, or depersonalized sexuality. Just what such a milieu concretely amounts to and requires for its maintenance is something that is matter for discussion and decision, elsewhere. But that this is an aspect of the common good, and fit matter for laws which limit the boundless exercise of certain rights, can hardly be doubted by anyone who attends to the facts of human psychology as they bear on the realization of basic human goods. And while all this could be, and sometimes has been, expressed in terms of human rights, there is no need to consider inept, still less redundant, the reference to public morality, preferred by contemporary legislators with impressive unanimity.

Similarly, public order, in its restricted, common law sense, concerns the maintenance, not so much of the psychological substratum for mutual respect, but of the physical environment and structure of expectations and reliances essential to the well-being of all members of a community, especially the weak. Inciting hatred amongst sections of the community is not merely an injury to the rights of those hated; it threatens everyone in the community with a future of violence and of other violations of right, and this threat is itself an injury to the common good and is reasonably referred to as a violation of public order. Rioting and bombing, and threats thereof, are not merely prejudicial to the rights of those killed or injured, but to everyone who has now to live in a community where such things happen.

The operation of a grossly noisy aeroplane can be said to violate the rights of those awakened and deafened by it, but the problem is quite reasonably described as one of public order or public nuisance and not pinned down to the rights of those who happen so far to have been affected. The same goes for the notion of public health, a component in the civil law conception of *ordre public*, and a partner of the common law conception of public order.

This long but by no means elaborate discussion can now be summarized. On the one hand, we should not say that human rights, or their exercise, are subject to the common good; for the maintenance of human rights is a fundamental component of the common good. On the other hand, we can appropriately say that most human rights are subject to or limited by each other and by other *aspects* of the common good, aspects which could probably be subsumed under a very broad conception of human rights but which are fittingly indicated (one could hardly say, *described*) by expressions such as 'public morality', 'public health', 'public order'.

VIII.5   THE SPECIFICATION OF RIGHTS

The foregoing section suggested general reasons for concluding that most assertions of right made in political discourse need to be subjected to a rational process of specification, assessment, and qualification, in a way that rather belies the peremptory or conclusory *sound* of '... have a right to ...'. This conclusion can be reinforced by attention to the logical structure of the assertions or claims made or recognized or conceded in Bills of Rights and in political discourse at large. To resume the vocabulary I employed in VIII.2, we can say that these claims assert two-term relations between a (class of) persons and a (class of) subject-matter (life, body, free speech, property or ownership of property ...). Before such assertions can reasonably be accorded a real conclusory force, they must be translated into specific three-term relations.

This translation involves specification of (*a*) the identity of the duty-holder(s) who must respect or give effect to A's right; (*b*) the content of the duty, in terms of specific act-descriptions, including the times and other circumstances and conditions for the applicability of the duty; (*c*) the identity or class-description of A, the correlative claim-right-holder(s) (in a Hohfeldian sense of 'claim-right'); (*d*) the conditions under which a claim-right-holder loses his claim-right, including the conditions (if any) under which he can waive the relevant duties; (*e*) the claim-rights, powers, and liberties of the claim-right-holder in the event of non-performance of duty; and, above all, (*f*) the liberties of the right-holder, including a specification of the limits of those liberties, i.e. a specification of his duties, especially of non-interference with the liberties of other holders of that right or of other recognized rights. Since (*f*) involves specifying the *duties* of right-holder A, it necessarily involves a specification of the claim-rights of B, and this specification in turn requires a complete specification of points (*a*) to (*f*) in respect, now, of B; which will require a similar specification in respect of B's duties of non-interference with C ...

Employing a useful contemporary jargon, we can say that people (or legal systems) who share substantially the same *concept* (e.g. of the human right to life, or to a fair trial) may none the less have different *conceptions* of that right, in that their specifications under (*a*) to (*f*) differ, partly because the circumstances they have in mind differ and partly because specification normally involves choices, by some authoritative process, from among alternatives that are more or less equally reasonable. As I said in relation to the lawyer's preference for two-term rights-talk (VIII.2), shifting and even competing specifications in terms of three-term rights can be intelligibly unified by their shared relationship to one topic, the two-term right (e.g. to life, or to a fair trial).

How is this process of specification and demarcation to be accomplished? How are conflicts of rights to be resolved? That is to say, how much interference with one person's enjoyment of his 'right', by other persons, in the exercise of the same right, and of other rights, is to be permitted? There is, I think, no alternative but to hold in one's mind's eye some pattern, or range of patterns, of human character, conduct, and interaction in community, and then to choose such specification of rights as tends to favour that pattern, or range of patterns. In other words, one needs some conception of human good, of individual flourishing in a form (or range of forms) of communal life that

/ fosters rather than hinders such flourishing. One attends not merely to character types desirable in the abstract or in isolation, but also to the quality of interaction among persons; and one should not seek to realize some patterned 'end-state' imagined in abstraction from the processes of individual initiative and interaction, processes which are integral to human good and which make the future, let alone its evaluation, incalculable (see VII.7).

So one will bear in mind, on the one hand, that art with all its (often competing) forms and canons really is better than trash, that culture really is better than ignorance, that reputation and privacy and property really are aspects of or important means to human well-being, that friendship and respect for human personality really are threatened by hatred, group bias, and anarchic sexuality, that children really do benefit from a formation that defines paths as well as illuminating horizons ... and, on the other hand, that servility, infantilism, and hypocrisy really are evils, that integrity and authenticity in self-constitution really is the indispensable centre to human well-being, that where 'paternalism' on the part of the political community is justified it is, like the educative function of parenthood itself, to be no more than a help and support to self-correction and self-direction, and that the resolution of all these problems of human rights is a process in which various reasonable solutions may be proposed and debated and should be settled by some decision-making procedure which is authoritative but which does not pretend to be infallible or to silence further rational discussion or to forbid the reconsideration of the decision. In short, just as the right of free speech certainly requires 'limitation', i.e. specification, in the interests both of free speech itself and of many other human goods, so too the procedure for settling the 'limits' of this and other human rights will certainly be enhanced in reasonableness by a wide freedom of cultural and political debate, in any society in which there is a sufficiently diffused respect for discussion and compromise as ways of being reasonable in community.

Human rights (not to mention the public order and morality which constitute a necessary framework for their enjoyment) can certainly be threatened by uses of rights-talk which, in bad faith or good, prematurely ascribe a conclusory or absolute status to this or that human right (e.g. property, contract, assembly, speech). However, if its logic and its place in practical reasonableness about human flourishing are kept in mind, the modern usage of claims of right as the principal counter in political discourse should be recognized (despite its dubious seventeenth-century origins and its abuse by fanatics, adventurers, and self-interested persons from the eighteenth century until today) as a valuable addition to the received vocabulary of practical reasonableness (i.e. to the tradition of 'natural law doctrine'). For first, the modern usage of rights-talk rightly emphasizes equality, the truth that every human being is a locus of human flourishing which is to be considered with favour in him as much as in anybody else. In other words, rights-talk keeps justice in the foreground of our considerations. Secondly, it tends to undercut the attractions of the 'calculations' of consequentialists (though, since many rights are not absolute, the real critique of such calculations must be made more directly: V.6). Thirdly, since rights must be and are referred to by name, modern rights-talk amplifies the undifferentiated reference to 'the common good' by providing a usefully detailed listing of the various aspects of human flourishing and fundamental components of the way of life in community that tends to favour such flourishing in all.

VIII.6 RIGHTS AND EQUALITY OF CONCERN AND RESPECT

It is sometimes argued that to prefer, and seek to embody in legislation, some conception or range of conceptions of human flourishing is unjust because it is necessarily to treat with unequal concern and respect those members of the community whose conceptions of human good fall outside the preferred range and whose activities are or may therefore be restricted by the legislation. As an argument warranting opposition to such legislation this argument cannot be justified; it is self-stultifying (cf. III.6). Those who put forward the argument prefer a conception of human good, according to which a person is entitled to equal concern and respect and a community is in bad shape in which that entitlement is denied; moreover, they act on this preference by seeking to repeal the restrictive legislation which those against whom they are arguing may have enacted. Do those who so argue and so act thereby necessarily treat with unequal concern and respect those whose preferences and legislation they oppose? If they do, then their own argument and action is itself equally unjustified, and provides no basis for political preferences or action. If they do not (and this must be the better view), then neither do those whom they oppose. Nor can the argument be rescued by proposing that it escapes self-stultification by operating at a different 'level of discourse': for example, by being an argument about entitlements rather than about good. For there is no difficulty in translating any 'paternalist' political preference into the language of entitlement, by postulating an entitlement of every member of a community to a milieu that will support rather than hinder his own pursuit of good and the well-being of his children, or an entitlement of each to be rescued from his own folly. Whether or not such entitlements can be made out, they certainly pertain to the same 'level of discourse'. Nor, finally, can the argument we are considering be saved by a stipulation that arguments and political programmes motivated, as it is, by concern for 'equal respect and concern for other people' must be regarded as showing equal concern and respect for everyone, even those people whose (paternalist) arguments and legislation they reject and override. For, on the one hand, such a stipulation is merely an *ad hoc* device for escaping self-stultification; if overriding someone's political preferences and compelling him to live in a society whose ways he detests were *ipso facto* to show unequal concern and respect for him in one context, so it would be in any other. And, on the other hand, there is no difficulty in supposing that a 'paternalist' political programme may be based on a conception of what is required for equal concern and respect for all; for paternalists may well consider that, for example, to leave a person to succumb to drug addiction on the plea that it is 'his business' is to deny him the active concern one would show for one's friend in like situation; or that to fail to forbid teachers to form sexual attachments with their pupils is to deny the children of negligent or 'wrong-headed' parents the protection that the paternalist legislator would wish for his own children, and is thus again a failure in 'equal concern and respect'. 'I wish someone had

stopped me from …': if this can rationally be said (as it can), ∧.
it follows necessarily that even the most extensive and excessive
programme of paternalism might be instituted without denial
of equal concern and respect to anybody.

The pursuit of any form of human community in which
human rights are protected by the imposition of duties will
necessarily involve both selection of some and rejection of other
conceptions of the common good, and considerable restrictions
on the activities of everyone (including the legislators themselves, in their private capacities as persons subject to egoism
and indifference to the real well-being of others). Some ways
of pursuing the common good through legislation do indeed
err by forgetting that personal authenticity, self-direction, and
privacy for contemplation or play or friendship are aspects and
important adjuncts of human well-being: VI.5, VII.3. Paternalist programmes guilty of this oversight should be criticized for
that—a failure in commutative justice—and not for the quite
different vice of discrimination, group bias, denial of equal concern and respect, a kind of refined selfishness, a failure in distributive justice. To judge another man mistaken, and to act on that
judgment, is not to be equated, in any field of human discourse
and judgment, with despising that man or preferring oneself.

The argument of this section has been dialectical. It has not
needed to consider whether the principle 'everyone is entitled
to equal concern and respect' is an adequately refined principle
of justice. I said earlier (VII.4) that everyone is equally entitled
to respectful consideration in the distribution of the common
stock and the incidents of common life, including legal protection and roles and burdens. But I also indicated that this does
not require 'equality of treatment' (i.e. identical treatment),
even in such distributions. And it would certainly be wrong
to suggest that any individual is bound or even permitted in
justice to show everyone equal *concern*; and the same is true of
those in authority in any particular community, with respect
to those within and those outside their community: VII.4, XI.2.

VIII.7   ABSOLUTE HUMAN RIGHTS

Are there then no limits to what may be done in pursuit of
protection of human rights or of other aspects of the common

good? Are there no fixed points in that pattern of life which
one must hold in one's mind's eye in resolving problems of
rights? Are there no 'absolute' rights, rights that are not to be
limited or overridden for the sake of any conception of the good
life in community, not even 'to prevent catastrophe'?[27]

The answer of utilitarians, of course, is clear: there are no
absolute human rights, for there are no ways of treating a
person of which it can be said, by a consistent utilitarian, 'Whatever the consequences, nobody must ever be treated in this
way'. What is more striking, perhaps, is the fact that, whatever
may be commonly professed in the modern world, no contemporary government or élite manifests in its practice any
belief in absolute human rights. For every government that has
the physical capacity to make its threats credible says this to
its potential enemies: 'If you attack us and threaten to defeat
us, we will kill all the hostages we hold; that is to say, we will
incinerate or dismember as many of your old men and women
and children, and poison as many of your mothers and their
unborn offspring, as it takes to persuade you to desist; we do
not regard as decisive the fact that they are themselves no threat
to us; nor do we propose to destroy them merely incidentally,
as an unsought-after side-effect of efforts to stop your armed
forces in their attack on us; no, we will destroy your non-
combatants precisely because you value them, and in order to
persuade you to desist.' Those who say this, and have been
preparing elaborately for years to act upon their threat (and
most of them acted upon it massively, between 1943 and 1945,
to say no more), cannot be said to accept that anyone has,
in virtue of his humanity, any absolute right. These people
subscribe to Bills of Rights which, like the Universal Declaration
and its successors, clearly treat the right not to be tortured as
(unlike most of the other 'inalienable' rights there proclaimed)
subject to no exceptions. But their military policy involves
courses of action which in all but name are torture on an
unprecedented scale, inflicted for the same motive as an old-
fashioned torturer seeking to change his victim's mind or the
minds of those next in line for the torture. Nor is this just a
matter of governments and soldiers; many of these governments
are freely elected, and their policy (as distinct from the dangers

[27] See Dworkin, quoted above, p. 213, n. 21.

of pursuing it) arouses scant controversy among their elec-
torates. And who does not notice the accomplished smoothness
with which the issue is avoided by many who write about rights?

In its classical representatives the tradition of theorizing
about natural law has never maintained that what I have called
the requirements of practical reasonableness, as distinct from
the basic human values or basic principles of practical reasonableness, are clearly recognized by all or even most people—on
the contrary.[28] So we too need not hesitate to say that, notwithstanding the substantial consensus to the contrary, there are
absolute human rights. For the seventh of the requirements of
practical reasonableness that I identified in V.7 is this: that
it is always unreasonable to choose directly against any basic
value, whether in oneself or in one's fellow human beings. And
the basic values are not mere abstractions; they are aspects of
the real well-being of flesh-and-blood individuals. Correlative
to the exceptionless duties entailed by this requirement are,
therefore, exceptionless or absolute human claim-rights—most
obviously, the right not to have one's life taken directly as a
means to any further end; but also the right not to be positively
lied to in any situation (e.g. teaching, preaching, research
publication, news broadcasting) in which factual communication (as distinct from fiction, jest, or poetry) is reasonably
expected; and the related right not to be condemned on
knowingly false charges; and the right not to be deprived, or
required to deprive oneself, of one's procreative capacity; and
the right to be taken into respectful consideration in any assessment of what the common good requires.

Because these are not two-term rights in need of translation
into three-term right–duty relationships, but are claim-rights
strictly correlative to duties entailed by the requirements of
practical reasonableness, the difficult task of giving precision
to the specification of these rights has usually been undertaken
in terms of a casuistry of duties. And because an unwavering
recognition of the literally immeasurable value of human
personality in each of its basic aspects (the solid core of the
notion of human dignity) requires us to discount the apparently
measurable evil of looming catastrophes which really do

[28] See e.g. Aquinas, *S.T.* I, q. 113, a. 1; I–II, q. 9, a. 5 ad 3; q. 14, a. 1 ad 3;
q. 94, a. 4c; q. 99, a. 2 ad 2. See also V.2, II.3, above.

threaten the common good and the enjoyment by others of *their* rights, that casuistry is more complex, difficult, and controvertible in its details than can be indicated in the foregoing summary list of absolute rights. That casuistry may be framed in terms of 'direct' choices or intentions, as against 'indirect' effects, and of 'means' as against 'incidents': V.7. But reasonable judgments in this casuistry are not made by applying a 'logic' of 'directness and indirectness' of 'means and ends' or 'intended and unintended', drawn from the use of those notions in other enquiries or contexts. Rather, such judgments are arrived at by a steady determination to respect human good in one's own existence and the equivalent humanity or human rights of others, when that human good and those human rights fall directly into one's care and disposal—rather than trade off that good and those rights against some vision of future 'net best consequences', consequences which overall, both logically and practically, one cannot know, cannot control or dispose of, and cannot evaluate.

NOTES

VIII. 2

Hohfeld's analysis of rights ... W. N. Hohfeld, *Fundamental Legal Conceptions* (New Haven: 1919). For common misunderstandings, see Finnis, 'Some Professorial Fallacies about Rights' (1972) 4 *Adel. L. R.* 377. For limitations of Hohfeld's analysis, see A. M. Honoré, 'Rights of Exclusion and Immunities against Divesting' (1959–60) 34 *Tulane Law Rev.* 453; Raz, *Legal System*, pp. 179–81. For problems in formalizing the schema, see P. Mullock, 'The Hohfeldian Jural Opposite' (1971)13 *Ratio* 158.

'Juridical acts' and 'natural acts' ... 'Juridical acts' are called by Hart 'acts-in-the-law' (*Concept of Law*, p. 96; 'Bentham on Legal Rights' in *Oxford Essays II*, p. 196), and the distinction is explained by him thus: '...[an] act may be called a natural act in the sense that it is not endowed by the law with a special legal significance or legal effect. On the other hand in the case of rights which are powers, such as the right to alienate property, the act ... is an act-in-the-law, just in the sense that it is specifically recognized by the law as having legal effects in varying the legal position of various parties': *Oxford Essays II*, p. 196. To prevent all commissions of crimes and torts being characterized as 'juridical acts' (and as exercises of Hohfeldian power!) I prefer the characterization in the text, though it is not perfect and may need to be supplemented or qualified by the notion that a juridical act is an act (usually involving one or more natural acts) which is *typically* done *in order to* affect legal relations, and which is regulated or defined by rules on the basis that it is *desirable* to enable officials or individuals to act effectively with that motivation: see Raz, *Practical Reason*, pp. 102–4; cf. p. 110. The problem of restricting the notion of power, so that we are not obliged to say that A has a power to make himself an offender by hitting X on the nose, has its parallel in the problem of restricting the notion of immunity lest we find ourselves having to

say that, by refusing to testify in court, A gains an immunity from being granted a reward of £10,000, or an immunity from being exempted from military service. It cannot be said that Hohfeldian analysis has mastered these problems. (It may be remarked, incidentally, that each of these problems of reconciling Hohfeldian definition with ordinary legal usage suggests that ordinary legal usage is rooted in the idea that a right is a *benefit*, not in the idea that it is a legally respected *choice*: see below.)

Is the bare Hohfeldian liberty legally or morally significant? . . . Hart argues, rightly ('Bentham on Legal Rights', in *Oxford Essays II*, 171 at pp. 179–82), that (i) it is analytically important to distinguish liberty (mere absence of duty) from claim-right, and (ii) it is important to see that a liberty unprotected by any claim-rights against interference cannot usefully be dignified with the name of a right. (This again suggests, though not to Hart, that common usage treats rights as distinctively *beneficial*, not merely as legally recognized *choice*.) The second of these two points is aimed at Hobbes's notion of a right, discussed in VIII.3, below: to like effect see G. Marshall, 'Rights, Options and Entitlements', ibid. 228 at p. 231.

Inadequacy of Hohfeldian analysis to account for lawyers' talk of 'two-term' rights . . . See D. N. MacCormick, 'Rights in Legislation' in *Essays*, 188 at pp. 200–2; A. M. Honoré, 'Rights of Exclusion and Immunities against Divesting' (1959–60) 34 *Tulane Law Rev.* 453; Raz, *Legal System*, at p. 180; and, less rigorously, L. L. Fuller, *Morality of Law*, pp. 134–7. What I am here calling 'two-term' rights are instances of legal 'institutions': MacCormick, 'Law as Institutional Fact' (1974) 90 *L.Q.R.* 102 at pp. 106, 110, rightly stresses the importance of *persistence through time* as the basic reason for lawyers' conceptions of 'things' or institutions, which are ways of conceptually ordering and controlling the ascription of Hohfeldian rights. J. L. Mackie pointed out to me the analogy with our common-sense account of the material world: the empirical consequences of a statement about material objects may be identical with those of some set of statements about phenomena, but are not exhaustively analysable into such a set; so too the practical legal consequences of any 'lawyers'-right' may be identical with those of some set of Hohfeldian rights, but are not exhaustively analysable into those.

Is the Hohfeldian claim-right holder the person with the remedy, or the beneficiary? . . . For the need to stipulate, and some problems about stipulating that he is the remedy-holder, see Finnis, 'Some Professorial Fallacies about Rights' (1972) 4 *Adel. L. R.* 377 at pp. 379–80). Hart's confidence, in all his defences of the 'choice' theory of rights (see the following note), that English lawyers would unhesitatingly express the clear rules of English law by saying that 'third parties have no rights under a contract', seems misplaced in view of the dicta of Lords Reid and Pearce (made without polemical or theoretical animus) cited in the text.

'Benefit or interest' versus 'choice or will' theories of rights . . . The most illuminating introduction to this very long-standing debate is (though I disagree with his preference for the 'choice' theory) Hart, 'Bentham on Legal Rights', loc. cit. *supra*. For criticism of Hart's preference see Marshall, 'Rights, Options and Entitlements', loc. cit. *supra*; MacCormick, 'Children's Rights: a Test-Case for Theories of Rights' (1976) 62 *Arch. R. S. P.* 305–16. Even for the strictly legal context, MacCormick provides good reasons for preferring some version of the 'benefit' explanation of rights: 'Rights in Legislation' in *Essays*, pp. 189–209. In his earliest defence of the 'choice' theory, Hart admitted that 'if there are legal rights which cannot be waived these would need special treatment': 'Definition and Theory in Jurisprudence' (1954)70 *L.Q.R.* at p. 49 n. 15. That 'special treatment' has not been forthcoming, and the existence of such rights does tell against the 'choice' theory.

VIII.3

The meaning of 'jus' *in Aquinas* ... For this extensively debated topic, see P. M. Van Overbeke, 'Droit et Morale: Essai de synthèse thomiste' (1958) 58 *Rev. Thom.* 285 at 304–11 and works there cited; to which add P.-D. Dognin, 'La justice particulière comporte-t-elle deux espèces?' (1965) 65 *Rev. Thom.* 399 at p. 412 n. On Aquinas's acquaintance with Roman legal terminology, see J.-M. Aubert, *Le Droit romain dans l'oeuvre de Saint Thomas* (Paris, 1955), pp. 87–139.

The meaning of 'jus' *in Roman law* ... For this difficult matter, see H. Maine, *Early Law and Custom* (1891), pp. 365, 390; W. W. Buckland, *A Text-Book of Roman Law* (3rd ed., P. Stein, Cambridge: 1966), p. 58; M. Villey, *Leçons d'histoire de la philosophie du droit* (Paris: 1957), chs. XI, XIV; Villey, *Seize essais de philosophie du droit* (Paris: 1969), pp. 149–55. Ibid., pp. 155–69 contains a detailed and valuable account of the debate about the meaning of *'jus'* between Pope John XXII (a canon lawyer and devotee of Aquinas) and William of Ockham, in the years between 1323 and *c.*1332. The novel definition of *jus* developed by Ockham can be seen from his definition of *jus utendi* (ibid., p. 166): 'A *jus utendi* is a lawful power of using an external object; a power which one ought not to be deprived of against one's will except for fault or other reasonable cause; a power such that, if one is deprived of it, one can institute legal proceedings against the person so depriving one' ('jus utendi est potestas licita, utendi re extrinseca, qua quis sine culpa sua et absque causa rationabili privari non debet invitus, et si privatus fuerit, privantem poterit in judicio convenire'). This can usefully be compared with modern 'choice' theories of right, and with Hart's notion of a right as a 'small-scale sovereignty'. Unfortunately, Villey's treatment of *jus* is marred by an exaggerated distinction between *jus* and *lex* (which are of course distinct notions but closely related), which leads him to misplaced distinctions between law and morality, and between justice and the principles of practical reasonableness: see Villey, 'Si la théorie générale du droit, pour Saint Thomas, est une théorie de la loi' (1972) 17 *Arch. Phil. Dr.* 427–31; for correctives, see ibid., pp. 424–5, and G. Kalinowski, 'Le fondement objectif du Droit d'après la "Somme théologique" de saint Thomas d'Aquin' (1973) 18 *Arch. Phil. Dr.* 59 at 64, 69–72; 'Sur l'emploi métonymique du terme "ius" par Thomas d'Aquin ...', ibid., pp. 333–6.

Hobbes on rights ... For the criticism advanced in the text, see also Marshall, 'Rights, Options and Entitlements' in *Oxford Essays II*, 228 at p. 231; Hart, 'Bentham on Legal Rights', ibid. 171 at pp. 179–82. Hobbes's claim that *jus* and *lex* were commonly confused is certainly not groundless, in relation to his contemporaries: see e.g. John Selden, *De Jure Naturali et Gentium juxta Disciplinam Ebraeorum* (1640), in his *Opera Omnia* (ed. D. Wilkins, 1726), vol. I: 'Jus peti nequit, unde auctoritas et imperium perspici nequit' (p. 133), or even more strikingly, 'Nulla obligatio juris inter pares' (p. 140). This is as far as possible from Aquinas's notion of *'jus'*, and simply equates *jus* with *lex* (a very voluntaristically conceived *lex*, too).

Locke on rights ... In *Two Treatises of Government* (1689), Locke uses the term 'a right' and its cognates in a loose and informal manner, but with an overwhelming predominance of the connotations of 'liberty' and 'power', rather than of 'claim-right' or of *'jus'* in its classical sense: see e.g. Second Treatise, paras. 87, 123, 128–9, 137, 190, 220; cf. paras. 7, 190.

VIII.4

Contemporary declarations and Bills of Rights ... See, e.g., Ian Brownlie, *Basic Documents on Human Rights* (Oxford: 1971).

'Public order' and 'l'ordre public' ... The marked difference in meaning of these terms was noted by the draftsmen of the Covenants of 1966: see UN General Ass. Records Annexes, Tenth Session (1955), Agenda item 28 (Part II), p. 48, quoted in Maurice Cranston, *What are Human Rights?* (London: 1973), p. 79. The common law conception is preserved in the interpretation of the Constitution of India, Art. 19(2); see Durga Das Basu, *Constitutional Law of India* (New Delhi: 1977), p. 45.

'Public morality' and 'morality' ... The international texts use both expressions and are sometimes grammatically ambiguous so that 'morality' may or may not be qualified by 'public'. The argument in the text concentrates on 'public morality' but there may be a case for allowing 'morality' as a ground of limitation in some contexts, e.g. in relation to incest and paedophilia generally, sado-masochistic practices, and suicide and complicity in suicide.

The rights of children and parents to a cerain sort of milieu ... Thus the Child and Youth Welfare Code (Presidential Decree No. 603 of 1974) (Philippines) provides, *inter alia*: Title I, Art. 3. 'All children shall be entitled to the rights herein set forth ... (3) Every child has the right to a well-rounded development of his personality ... (5) Every child has the right to be brought up in an atmosphere of morality and rectitude for the enrichment and strengthening of his character ... (9) Every child has the right to live in a community and a society that can offer him an environment free from pernicious influences and conducive to the promotion of his health and the cultivation of his desirable traits and attributes ...' Neither this nor the argument in the text exhausts the reasons for legislation concerned with sexual matters. Public decency is a related but distinguishable matter, concerned with the maintenance of (to be very summary) a certain 'distance' from other people's bodily features and sexuality, a distance that most people find essential to maintaining the integration of their own bodily nature and sexuality with their self-possession, friendship, etc.

VIII.5

Translating 'two-term' claims of human rights into 'three-term' relationships ... For the problem in relation to 'the right to life' and 'the right to one's own body', see Judith J. Thomson, 'A Defense of Abortion' (1971) 1 *Phil. Pub. Aff.* 47–66, and J. M. Finnis, 'The Rights and Wrongs of Abortion: a Reply to Judith Thomson' (1973) 2 *Phil. Pub. Aff.* 117–45 (both reprinted in, e.g., Dworkin (ed.), *Philosophy of Law* (Oxford: 1977)). For an outline of the complexities in relation to 'freedom of speech', see Finnis, 'Some Professorial Fallacies about Rights' (1972) 4 *Adel. L. R.* 376 at pp. 385–6. When thinking about freedom of speech, it is important to bear in mind the law about patents, copyright, contracts in restraint of trade and protection of trade secrets and intellectual property; misleading or dangerous advertisements, and consumer protection generally; libel, slander; treason; conspiracy to commit any and every crime; incitement to commit any and every serious crime; official secrets; etc., before thinking of the law about pornography.

'Paternalism' ... For the significance of the proportion of every human life spent in childhood, see Francis Schrag, 'The Child in the Moral Order' (1977) 52 *Philosophy* 167–77.

VIII.6

'Paternalism', 'liberalism', and equal respect and concern ... For the argument criticized in the text, see Dworkin, *Taking Rights Seriously*, pp. 272–7; I do not mention his distinction between 'external' and 'internal' preferences, since that is directed against utilitarianism, not against my position (which is roughly what he describes as an 'ideal argument of policy': p. 274). It is important to rebut Dworkin's interpretation of the requirements of equal concern and respect, since, properly understood, those requirements are a fundamental component of distributive justice: see VII.3, above.

Paternalism and violation of commutative justice ... To defend paternalism against the charge that it denies equal concern and respect is not to defend all forms of paternalism. Indeed, certain contemporary forms of paternalism seem particularly indifferent to (commutative) justice: especially (i) the new and radical paternalism that kills handicapped people (in the womb, in old age, or at other times) 'for their own good', 'because their life is, or will be, not worth living'; also, less strikingly, (ii) the paternalism that insists that the poor be given 'welfare benefits' only or mainly in kind, not in cash, treating the autonomy and self-direction of the recipients only as a cause of waste and folly, not as an intrinsic good.

VIII.7

'Absolute' rights ... Since 'inalienable' and 'inviolable' have been appropriated by manifesto writers and draftsmen of Bills of Rights for describing rights which are confessedly subject to exception-creating balancing and trade-offs with other rights or exercises of the same right, not to mention public order and morality, etc., it is necessary to use another term: here, 'absolute' or 'categorically exceptionless', after Feinberg, *Social Philosophy*, pp. 79, 86–8, 94–7.

The right not to be killed as a means to any end ... See G. G. Grisez, 'Toward a Consistent Natural Law Ethics of Killing' (1970) 15 *Am. J. Juris.* 64; G. E. M. Anscombe, 'War and Murder' in W. Stein (ed.), *Nuclear Weapons and Christian Conscience* (London: 1961), at pp. 46–51, also in R. Wasserstrom (ed.), *War and Morality* (Belmont, Calif.: 1972); Finnis, 'The Rights and Wrongs of Abortion...' (1973) 2 *Phil. Pub. Aff.* 117–45 (also in Dworkin (ed.), *Philosophy of Law*). The casuistry developed in relation to this absolute right can be extended, *mutatis mutandis*, to the other rights mentioned in the text.

IX
AUTHORITY

IX. 1 THE NEED FOR AUTHORITY

QUESTIONS about the need and justification for authority can arise in different ways. Someone reflecting on the fact of human freedom in moral choosing, or on the basic values of authenticity and freedom in practical reasonableness, may be moved to ask how any man can have authority to require one to choose what one would not otherwise have chosen. Orders and rules may weigh with me because of accompanying threats, or because of my uncritical conformism or my careerism. But can they have for me the authority of a fully critical conclusion of authentic practical reason? Someone else may raise a question about authority in reflecting more speculatively on human community. Is authority in a group required only because of the stupidity and incompetence of its members, their infirmity of purpose and want of devotion to the group, their selfishness and malice, their readiness to exploit and to 'free ride'? In a community free from these vices, would authority be needed, or justified?

It will be helpful to respond first to this last question. The human weaknesses recited in the question do indeed give good reason for having authority. But, more interestingly, it is also true that the greater the intelligence and skill of a group's members, and the greater their commitment and dedication to common purposes and common good (VI.8), the *more* authority and regulation may be required, to enable that group to achieve its common purpose, common good.

For, as I hinted in relation to the fifth requirement of practical reasonableness (V.5), the dedicated member of the group will always be looking out for new and better ways of attaining the common good, of co-ordinating the action of members, of playing his own role. And the intelligent member will find such new and better ways, and perhaps not just one but many possible and reasonable ways. Intelligence and dedication, skill and commitment thus multiply the problems of co-ordination, by giving the group more possible orientations, commitments, projects, 'priorities', and procedures to choose from. And until a particular choice is made, nothing will in fact be done. Moreover, in some forms of human community, that something be done is not just a matter of optional advantage, but is a matter of right, a requirement of justice. Somebody (e.g. parents) must decide how children are to be educated; in the political community, there must be decisions about the management and use of natural resources, about the use of force, about permitted forms or content of communication, and about the many other problems of reconciling aspects of justice with each other (VII.7), and of reconciling human rights with each other and with other 'conflicting' exercises of the same right and with public health, public order, and the like (VIII.4, 5). In the broad sense of 'co-ordination problem', these are all co-ordination problems which need a solution (VI.6). And for most though not all of these co-ordination problems there are, in each case, two or more available, reasonable, and appropriate solutions, none of which, however, would amount to a solution unless adopted to the exclusion of the other solutions available, reasonable, and appropriate for that problem.

There are, in the final analysis, only two ways of making a choice between alternative ways of co-ordinating action to the common purpose or common good of any group. There must be either unanimity, or authority. There are no other possibilities.

Exchange of promises (see XI.2) is not a third way; rather, it is a modality of the first way, unanimity. For there is no agreement without just that: some meeting of minds on what is to be done, or at least on what is the specific content of that promise. Even a unilateral promise is not binding unless accepted by the promisee. Moreover, the agreed co-ordination of action will occur only so long as the parties either retain their original unanimity, *or* acknowledge the authority of a rule requiring fulfilment of promises, *or* are held to their agreement by some authoritative person or body.

Now there is no need to labour the point that unanimity

about the desirable solution to a specific co-ordination problem cannot in practice be achieved in any community with a complex common good and an intelligent and interested membership. Unanimity is particularly far beyond the bounds of practical possibility in the political community. For here we have the most complex common good, which (subject to the principle of subsidiarity) excludes no aspect of individual well-being and is potentially affected by every aspect of every life-plan (VI.8). And the principle of subsidiarity (VI.5, VII.3) has wide implications here. For experience suggests that individuals and particular groups (this family, this firm, this university, this government department ...) should have a certain autonomy, a certain prior concern and responsibility for their own particular good, their own particular interests or speciality. Yet this concern of particular persons and groups for individual goods, for particular common goods and for particular aspects of the over-all common good, will enhance the over-all common good only if the resulting particular options are subject to some degree of co-ordination. And if the particular individuals and groups have as their *prior* concern (as they should) their respective particular interests, such over-all co-ordination can hardly be achieved save by some person or body of persons whose prior concern and responsibility is to care for the over-all common good. Again, the life of the political community is open-ended; its ends are never fully achieved and few of its co-ordination problems are solved once and for all. Finally, it must not be forgotten that unanimity is not a practical possibility in a community in which intelligence and dedication to the common good are mixed with selfishness and folly.

IX. 2 THE MEANINGS OF 'AUTHORITY'

A person treats something (e.g. an opinion, a pronouncement, a map, an order, a rule ...) as authoritative if and only if he treats it as giving him sufficient reason for believing or acting in accordance with it *notwithstanding* that he himself cannot otherwise see good reason for so believing or acting, or cannot evaluate the reasons he can see, or sees some countervailing reason(s), or would himself otherwise (i.e. in the absence of

RITTER LIBRARY
BALDWIN-WALLACE COLLEGE

what it is that he is treating as authoritative) have preferred not so to believe or act. In other words, a person treats something as authoritative when he treats it as, in Joseph Raz's useful terminology, an exclusionary reason, i.e. a reason for judging or acting in the absence of understood reasons, or for disregarding at least *some* reasons which are understood and relevant and would in the absence of the exclusionary reason have sufficed to justify proceeding in some other way.[1]

This is the focal meaning of authority, whether that authority be speculative (the authority of learning or genius) or practical (the authority of good taste, or practical experience, or office ...), and whether the authority be ascribed to a man, or to his characteristics, or to his opinions or pronouncements, or to some opinion or prescription which has authority for reasons other than that its author(s) had authority (e.g., as we shall see, custom or convention). I need say no more here about speculative authority, beyond observing in passing that a man's theoretical knowledge is often a good reason for treating him as having practical authority, but is not a necessary condition for so regarding him.

Before going further, it is as well to face up to some linguistic complications which, when not clearly understood, cause serious confusion between 'positivists' and 'natural law theorists' in jurisprudence. The foregoing two paragraphs have treated as focal or primary the meaning which the proposition 'X has authority' has when that proposition is asserted by a speaker (S_1) who treats X (or X's pronouncements, etc.) as authoritative not merely for others but also *for himself* (S_1), i.e. as giving anyone [relevant] including *him* (S_1) exclusionary reason for action in accordance with X (or X's pronouncement, etc.). But 'X has authority' may be said, truthfully, by someone (S_2) who does *not* regard X as have authority over or in relation to himself (S_2); for S_2 the truth of his proposition is established by showing that some people $(S_1$ and his fellows) in fact treat X as authoritative. In short, S_2 speaks as a historian, a sociologist or, in general, an observer. (He may, of course, be S_1 speaking as an observer.) Finally, 'X has authority' may be asserted by someone (S_3) *neither* in recognition of X's authority or authoritativeness in relation to himself (S_3),

[1] *Practical Reason*, pp. 35–48, 58–73.

nor by way of report about other people's attitudes to X, but rather by way of stating what is the case from the viewpoint of S_1 but without either endorsing or rejecting S_1's view. (S_3 may of course be S_1, speaking from a 'detached' or professional viewpoint.) Statements of this third type are very common in textbooks which explain the rules of a game, or of English or Russian or Roman law, and in professional opinions, advice, and arguments. In what follows I use the notation S_1, S_2, S_3 to refer to statements of the three types respectively, rather than, as above, to the speakers.

The difference between these three senses of 'X has authority' is found across the whole range of normative statements: for example, 'that is a binding promise', 'A has a legal duty to ϕ', and even (and above all) 'there is a rule the C must/may/has power to ϕ'. In all these cases one and the same grammatical form may be used to assert (S_1) what there is good reason to do, or what a sufficient reason is for doing ϕ, *or* it may assert (S_2) that a group considers that there is good reason to ϕ, *or* it may assert (S_3) what there is good reason to do from the viewpoint of a certain group or on the basis of certain rules or *if* certain rules give good reason for so acting (but without affirming or denying that that viewpoint is reasonable or correct or that those rules do provide good reason for acting). One and the same person may, even on one and the same occasion, make statements of all three types, switching his viewpoint without warning or grammatical indication. This is quite common in legal advocacy.

Joseph Raz has identified and explained these three types of statement. While stressing the importance of not trying to collapse S_3 into either S_1 or S_2, he clearly recognizes that S_1 and S_2 are 'basic' and 'primary'.[2] S_3, though widespread in discourse, is parasitic. And in discussing a closely related distinction between three 'properties or dimensions of norms' he says that 'beyond doubt the primary one' is the dimension or property of actually being a good reason (as distinct from being believed by some people to be a good reason, or being intended by some people to be taken as a good reason by

---

[2] *Practical Reason*, p. 172. For his account of the three types see pp. 171–7; see also his 'Promises and Obligations', in *Essays*, at p. 225.

others).[3] But to assert that something is or provides a good reason is to make an S_1 assertion. Thus, even for Raz's purposes, which lie within the 'formal part' of 'the philosophy of practical reason' (i.e. that part which is concerned with 'conceptual analysis', as distinct from the 'substantive or "evaluative" part'),[4] the primary and focal type of statement about authority and norms is the S_1 type. For our purposes in this book (which are sufficiently described by Raz's description of substantive practical philosophy),[5] this primacy of S_1 statements is even more evident. That is why the explanation of authority advanced in the first sentence of this section is an explanation of that form of recognition of authority which would be expressed by an S_1 statement.

But what is the importance of these technical distinctions between types of statement, or types of recognition of authority? It is this. As is already obvious from the opening section of this chapter, not to mention earlier chapters, my explanation of the need and justification for authority, and of its limits and its proper modes of operation, is going to be an explanation by reference to the common good (including justice and human rights); see, for example, the account of the authority of custom in the next section. Now to all such explanations, some 'positivists' in jurisprudence have made the following sort of objection:

'You claim to be explaining what it is for an authority, an authoritative custom, or a rule, to exist. But at best you succeed in explaining only what it is to believe that such an authority, custom or rule *ought* to exist. For on your explanation it would be *redundant* to say, e.g. "(P_1) an authoritative custom exists and (P_2) it is for the common good that it should

---

[3] *Practical Reason*, p. 84. 'Existential statements about norms are used for a variety of purposes, among which three are the most important. In saying that there is a norm one may state either that it is valid (that is, justified), or that it is practised, or that it has been prescribed by a certain person or body. These are the three dimensions of norms ...': p. 80.

[4] Ibid., p. 10. On 'conceptual analysis' see notes to I.4, above.

[5] Ibid., p. 10: 'Substantive practical philosophy includes all the arguments designed to show which values we should pursue, what reasons for action should guide our behaviour, which norms are binding, etc.' See also p. 11 on 'the most important branches of practical philosophy'.

exist." But it is odd and counter-intuitive to claim that P_2 is redundant when conjoined with P_1. Or again, on your explanation it would be *contradictory* to say "(P_1) an authoritative custom exists but (P_2) its existence is not for the common good". But it is odd and counter-intuitive to claim that P_1 contradicts P_2. We conclude that your method of explaining authority and rules is itself unsatisfactory, since it yields results which are counter-intuitive and inconsistent with ordinary language and common sense.'

To this 'positivist' objection the reply is now obvious. My programme of explanation does not commit me to condemning as either redundant or contradictory the conjunction of P_1 with P_2. Such a conjunction *does* entail redundancy or inconsistency if and only if P_1 is understood as an S_1 statement. But the positivist objection simply overlooks the fact that 'existential sentences about norms are used for a variety of purposes ...'.[6] The 'existential sentence' P_1 can perfectly well be understood as an S_2 or an S_3 statement, and someone who makes either of the conjunctive statements mentioned in the positivist's objection will of course intend the first half of his statement (i.e. P_1) in an S_2 or S_3 sense and the second half (i.e. P_2) in an S_1 sense. His meaning simply is: 'people treat this custom as justified, and indeed it is [or: is not]'; or perhaps, 'speaking from the lawyer's point of view, this is a legally authoritative custom; and, I may add, in my personal opinion it is [or: is not] for the common good that it be treated as such'; '"this is law; but it is too iniquitous to be applied or obeyed"'.[7] The fact that I systematically treat S_1 statements as primary, because the focus of my theoretical interest is in justificatory explanations, in no way requires me to regard any of those statements as objectionable (though the history of contemporary jurisprudence shows that they are open to misunderstanding): see II.2, XII.4. Hence this 'positivist' objection to my programme of explanation need not deflect us.

---

[6] Raz, ibid., p. 80.
[7] Hart, *Concept of Law*, p. 203, where the 'positivist' objection here under discussion is deployed in a compact form.

IX.3 FORMATION OF CONVENTIONS OR
CUSTOMARY RULES

In this section I show how an authoritative rule can emerge (i.e. begin to regulate a community) without being made by anyone with authority to make it, and even without the benefit of any authorized way of generating rules. The discussion will enable us to deepen our understanding of the relation between acknowledging the authority of a rule and following the principles of practical reasonableness. It will also enable us to understand more adequately both the distinctions and the connections between unanimity and authority in a community. For in studying the formation of custom we are studying the emergence of a substitute for unanimity under conditions which require a substantial degree of unanimity.

It will be convenient to conduct our discussion of the formation of custom by reference to the international community and the formation of customary rules of international law. For this is the context in which the problem of custom arouses most interest today, has been most debated, and found most difficult to explain satisfactorily. In what follows, I use the term 'custom' as shorthand for 'authoritative customary rule', and by 'authoritative' in this context I mean 'legally authoritative'. I use the term 'state' as a short form of reference to any entity acting in the sphere of international law as a subject or potential subject thereof.

There is a vast and confused literature on custom as a source of international law. It is generally agreed that custom involves some concurrence or convergence or regularity of practice amongst states. It is further agreed that such concurrence, convergence, or regularity is not enough to constitute custom. There must be a concurrence of deliberate practice, not induced by force or fraud or mistake. And, more positively, the practice must be accompanied by a certain attitude, belief, intention, or disposition: in the literature this is called the *opinio juris*. It is this last condition for the formation of custom that causes difficulty. For the classical accounts of the required content of the *opinio juris* are openly question-begging or paradoxical (but alternative accounts have not been forthcoming). As Oppenheim's treatise says: 'International jurists speak of a custom when a clear and continuous habit of doing certain actions has grown up under the aegis of the conviction that these actions are, according to international law, obligatory or right.'[8] But this is paradoxical, for it proposes that a customary norm can come into existence (i.e. become authoritative) only by virtue of the necessarily erroneous belief that it is already in existence (i.e. authoritative).

The method of analysis and explanation which I have been developing in this Part of this book (and which is only completed in the final chapters of this Part) enables us to offer an analysis of the formation of custom which makes intelligible something like the classic position of international jurists, a position which they themselves, however, have been unable to free from the paradox just mentioned. Technically speaking, the key to a solution of the problem lies in the distinction (expressed in the preceding section as that between S_1 and S_2 statements) between, on the one hand, practical judgments and, on the other hand, empirical judgments about the existence and extent of practices. As throughout this book, 'practical judgment' here refers to judgments made by any person, whether privately or in some official capacity, which explicitly or implicitly state that some action (including always omissions or forbearances) by some (potential) agent should (not) be done, or could (not) appropriately or justifiably be done (in any of the various senses of 'should', 'appropriately', or 'justifiably'): I.4.

At the root of the formation of custom, and in particular at the core of that factor in the formation of custom which is usually labelled the *opinio juris*, are two different but related practical judgments:

(*a*) in this domain of human affairs (e.g. passage of warships through coastal waters), it would be appropriate to have *some* determinate, common, and stable pattern of conduct and, correspondingly, an authoritative rule requiring that pattern of conduct; to have this is more desirable than leaving conduct in this domain to the discretion of individual states;

[8] Oppenheim, *International Law*, vol. I (8th ed., H. Lauterpacht, London: 1955), sec. 17. To like effect the International Court of Justice in the *North Sea Continental Shelf Cases*, *I.C.J. Rep.* 1969, p. 44.

(*b*) *this* particular pattern of conduct φ (e.g. innocent passage on the surface under flag to be permitted by coastal state)[9] is appropriate, or would be *if* generally adopted and acquiesced in, for adoption as an authoritative common rule of conduct.

These are both practical, not empirical, judgments, and they are not yet legal judgments. When the contents of a multilateral treaty, or the resolutions of an international body representative of states, are spoken of as sources or evidence of custom, what is really (or, at any rate, justifiably) being said is that the treaty or resolutions are evidence not of an opinion about what the law already is, but of *opinio juris* in the limited sense expressed in these two judgments. They are indeed judgments that might be made by anyone thinking about the relevant domain. They affirm that something is desirable (*a*) in general, (*b*) in particular. In a well-ordered international community, the frame of reference for assessing desirability would be primarily the common good of the whole community and its members (including considerations of justice and rights), and only secondarily the interests of the person or state making the judgments. Very commonly, of course, this ranking of the frames of reference is in fact reversed. This fact is an obstacle to the formation of custom, but only an obstacle, not insuperable.

The next step in the analysis is to observe that both the foregoing practical judgments are distinct from the empirical judgment that many (or few) states in fact subscribe to them. And this empirical judgment is, in turn, to be distinguished from two further empirical judgments: (i) that the practice of many (or few) states, in the relevant domain, is convergent in pattern and is of the pattern referred to in the second ((*b*)) of the aforementioned practical judgments; and (ii) that other states do (or do not) acquiesce in that pattern of conduct.

Empirical judgments of the three sorts just mentioned are prerequisites to the making of a new, practical judgment. This new practical judgment is a further aspect of the undifferentiated '*opinio juris*' of the classic treatises. (Indeed, it is the aspect

---

[9] Note that the relevant pattern of conduct φ may be procedural or 'framework' in nature: e.g. *negotiation of agreements*, as the appropriate and required method of settling disputed questions about (substantive) conduct in such-and-such a domain.

which, by its undue or even exclusive emphasis, renders the whole doctrine of those treatises paradoxical.) It affirms that the empirically widespread making of the two practical judgments ((a) and (b)), and the empirical concurrence of practice and generality (not necessarily universality) of acquiescence, together warrant the claim that a custom exists as an authoritative legal norm. Notice that the latter claim is a practical or S_1 statement; like S_2 statements it uses the indicative grammar of 'existence', but unlike S_2 statements it is not empirical. It expresses the view that the norm imposes *justified* requirements on all actors in the relevant domain. Even more obviously practical is the judgment that that claim is warranted in the circumstances. This judgment builds on the three empirical judgments mentioned above, but it relates the relevant empirical facts about state practice and opinion to some principle(s) about what is required for the common good of the international community. The action-guiding and requirement-imposing force of the legal norm which this judgment is affirming to be justified derives from some such meta-legal principle of practical reasonableness about the needs of international community. About this meta-legal principle I shall say more when I have completed and reviewed the analysis in outline.

The practical judgments identified in the preceding paragraph are to be distinguished from the empirical (S_2) judgment (often expressed in the same grammatical forms) that 'there is a legal norm requiring such-and-such', in the sense that states empirically do generally recognize such a norm, i.e. that the norm is more or less 'effective'. Those practical judgments are also to be distinguished, of course, from the (S_3) statements which neutral jurists make. Although juristic statements are, quite properly, the ones most frequently on lawyers' lips, I say no more about them here, since they are parasitic upon the attitudes of, and corresponding statements open to, those persons who consider that the relevant body of norms ought to be adhered to in practice, i.e. who actually use those norms to guide their own conduct: IX.2. Our problem about the formation of custom is to explain how a course of international practice can become a legal rule imposing requirements that *those* persons should and would recognize.

The distinctions made in the preceding four paragraphs can

now be summarized. For brevity and clarity we can use an *ad hoc* and elementary notation, merely as a shorthand: PJ signifies a practical (S_1) judgment, EJ an empirical (S_2) judgment, and JJ a juristic (S_3) judgment in the sense explained above:

PJ_0—(*a*) it is desirable that in this domain there be some determinate, common, and stable pattern of conduct and corresponding authoritative rule;

(*b*) this particular pattern of conduct, ϕ, is (or would be if generally adopted and acquiesced in) an appropriate pattern for adoption as an authoritative common rule.

EJ_1—there is widespread concurrence and acquiescence in this pattern of conduct, ϕ, by states.

EJ_2—the *opinio juris* (i.e. PJ_0) is widely subscribed to by states.

PJ_1—the widespread subscription to PJ_0, and the widespread concurrence or acquiescence in the pattern of conduct ϕ, are sufficient to warrant the judgment (PJ_2) that there is now an authoritative customary rule requiring (or permitting) ϕ ...

PJ_2—ϕ is required (or permitted), by virtue of an authoritative customary rule of international law.

EJ_3—states generally accept the rule that ϕ is to be done (or may be done) ...

JJ_1—according to international law, ϕ is required (or permitted) ...

What are the virtues of this analysis? Firstly, by differentiating between PJ_0 and PJ_1, it enables us to see that there need be no paradox or circularity in the classic notion that, it order to amount to an authoritative custom, a course of practice must be accompanied by a particular sort of attitude or *opinio*. Secondly, by differentiating between PJ_0 and PJ_2, it enables us to see that the legal judgment PJ_2, while in various ways dependent upon prior political or moral judgments PJ_0 (not necessarily made by the person now making the legal judgment), is quite distinct and 'positive' (*de lege lata*, not merely *ferenda*). Thirdly, by separating out EJ_1, EJ_2, and EJ_3 from the other judgments, the relation of authoritative rules to facts is clarified: an authoritative rule can be said to be a fact, but

it is more than the fact of concurrent practice, and more even
than the fact of concurrence of opinion; and it is a fact only
because it is treated as an exclusionary reason for action (i.e.
as more than a fact).

Fourthly, the analysis enables us to see clearly the real
problems involved in explaining (for practical reasonableness)
the formation of custom. The main problem emerges clearly
in PJ_1, the immediately proximate preliminary to the judgment
that a norm is in force and authoritative. For PJ_1, if it is not
to be a mere *non sequitur*, must have a suppressed practical
premiss; this premiss, I think, is the meta-legal or framework
principle PJ^m:

> PJ^m—the emergence and recognition of customary rules (by
> treating a certain degree of concurrence or acquies-
> cence in a practice and a corresponding *opinio juris* as
> sufficient to create such a norm and to entitle that
> norm to recognition even by states not party to the
> practice or the *opinio juris*) is a desirable or appropriate
> method of solving interaction or co-ordination prob-
> lems in the international community.

In turn, the clear identification of the meta-principle PJ^m
enables us to see that the formation of custom is possible only
because PJ^m enjoys wider favour among states than does the
PJ_0 relating to almost any particular problem of conduct. Just
as it is easier to get agreement that *some* rule would be desirable
($PJ_0(a)$) than to get agreement that *this* particular rule is
desirable ($PJ_0(b)$), so it is easier still to get agreement that the
international community needs methods of solving its interaction and co-ordination problems and that custom, *if* there
is sufficient acceptance that custom is an appropriate method,
is an appropriate method (since it often is the only practicable
method). And this way of expressing PJ^m shows that the desirability or appropriateness of accepting PJ^m is conditional upon
a sufficient number of other states also accepting PJ^m. This is
not a paradox or vicious circle!

Thus, although there are direct 'moral' arguments of justice
for recognizing customs as authoritative (e.g. arguments against
unfairly defeating reasonable expectations or squandering
resources and structures erected on the basis of the expecta-

tions), the general authoritativeness of custom depends upon the fact that custom-formation has been *adopted* in the international community as an appropriate method of rule-creation. For, given this fact, recognition of the authoritativeness of particular customs affords all states an opportunity of furthering the common good of the international community by solving interaction and co-ordination problems otherwise insoluble. And this opportunity is the root of all legal authority, whether it be the authority of rulers or (as here) of rules.

In short, the 'framework' practice of treating custom-formation as a source of authoritative norms is itself one instance of the pattern-of-conduct 'ϕ' in the analysis. In other words, the requirements, pre-conditions, and forms of custom-formation are themselves determined, in large part, by custom (i.e. by a framework custom whose source is similar in form to the customs for the formation of which it itself provides the framework). The authoritativeness of this framework custom derives not from some yet further custom, but from the opportunity of advancing the common good, the opportunity which is afforded by widespread (not necessarily universal) recognition of the framework custom, and of the particular substantive customs, as authoritative. But it is also very important to see that the authoritativeness of particular customs should not be explained by saying that their formation was 'authorized' by the framework custom. The framework custom does indeed regulate the making of PJ_1 judgments by states, and thus to some extent controls the emergence of customs, and determines the range of their authoritativeness (e.g. by determining what degree, if any, of prior protest exempts a state from adhering to the emergent custom). But it is artificial and unnecessary to say that the framework custom 'authorizes' states to make customs, or that it is 'the source' of the authority of particular customs. Both the framework custom and the particular customs which become authoritative within its framework derive their authoritativeness directly from the fact that, if treated as authoritative, they enable states to solve their co-ordination problems—a fact that has normative significance because the common good requires that those co-ordination problems be solved.

Finally, the analysis reveals the further problems that must be solved if custom-formation is to work at all well as an instrument of international order and community. For if it is to work, there must be a sufficient degree of agreement in answering these questions, amongst others:

(i) What actions of what persons in what contexts count as state practice?

(ii) What degree of practice counts as 'widespread' in a given domain, and for how long?

(iii) What expressions or silences, and whose, count as subscribing to the *opinio juris* ($PJ_0(a)$ and (b))?

(iv) To what extent can custom be localized geographically, granted that the interaction and co-ordination problems of the international community, in a given domain, are perhaps not peculiar to a particular geographical area (but perhaps have local variations)?

Answers to these and similar questions go to make up the content of the framework custom. Although they will reflect assessments of what is for the common good of the international community, they are none the less answers that have to be *adopted* by most members of the community if they are to *count as* answers. They therefore can change, i.e. be changed—not necessarily by the exercise of authority (custom is authoritative but not the result of anyone's exercise of international authority) but, authoritatively, by change in practice and opinion.

IX.4 THE AUTHORITY OF RULERS

The clumsiness of custom-formation as a method of generating authoritative solutions to co-ordination problems is obvious enough. Although the process does not require unanimity, it does require a substantial convergence of practices and of opinions, not merely on the desirability of *some* solution but on the desirability of a particular solution. And, as my analysis showed, there are numerous potential causes for doubt about whether an authoritative custom has emerged, whom it binds, and so on. The need for somebody, or some body, to settle co-ordination problems with greater speed and certainty is apparent in any community where people are energetic and inventive in pursuit of their own or of common goods, not to mention any community threatened with military, economic, or ecological disaster.

Authority (and thus the *responsibility* of governing) in a community is to be exercised by those who can in fact effectively settle co-ordination problems for that community. This principle is not the last word on the requirements of practical reasonableness in locating authority; but it is the first and most fundamental.

The *fact* that the say-so of a particular person or body or configuration of persons will in fact be, by and large, complied with and acted upon, has normative consequences for practical reasonableness; it affects the responsibilities of both ruler and ruled, by creating certain exclusionary reasons for action. These normative consequences derive from a normative principle— that authority is a good (because required for the realization of the common good)—when that principle is taken in conjunction with the fact that a particular person, body, or configuration of persons can, for a given community at a given time, do what authority is to do (i.e. secure and advance the common good).

Of course, this derivation of the relevant normative consequences is not indefeasible. That is to say, the conjunction of the principle with the opportunity is only presumptively sufficient to justify the claim to and recognition of authority. Someone who uses his empirical opportunity, or even his legally recognized authority, to promote schemes thoroughly opposed to practical reasonableness cannot then reasonably claim to have discharged his own responsibilities in reason, and may be unable to justify his claim to have created a good and sufficient exclusionary reason affecting the responsibilities of those whose compliance he is seeking or demanding. I take up the problem of unjust exercise of authority more fully in Chapter XII.

It is for political science to examine the empirical conditions under which particular persons, bodies, or configurations of persons can make stipulations for action, with empirical effectiveness. It will for example, be pointed out immediately that the state of affairs I am calling simply 'acquiescence', 'compliance', and 'effectiveness' is in reality more complex: while the mass of a population may passively obey, each 'for his own

part only' and out of fear of sanctions, there must also be a
class of more active, willing, 'consenting' supporters including
many if not most officials. But for present purposes it is quite
sufficient to say, in simple terms, that the motives or reasons
which people have for complying with and acting upon
stipulations presented to them as authoritative (and for being
willing to do so should occasion arise) vary widely—fear of force,
hope for (perhaps fraudulently suggested) profit, respect for age
or for wisdom or for numbers or for the fall of the lot, belief
in divine designation (charisma) or world-historic mission,
adherence to convention or custom (which in turn may desig-
nate blood-lineage, or lot, or age, or . . .) . . . Some of these
motives are more reasonable than others, either absolutely or
at least in given situations. Political science can say important
things about this relative reasonableness, and thus about the
legitimacy, for reasonable men, of various forms of constitution.
But, for an understanding of the authoritativeness of rulers, as
a concern of practical reasonableness, it is the sheer fact of
effectiveness that is presumptively (not indefeasibly) decisive.

In fact, political theorists pondering the location of authority
have frequently erred by carrying certain legal modes of
thought beyond the origins of law. The lawyer (reasonably,
as we shall see: X.3), when confronted by a claim to a certain
status, title, power, or right, inquires after the root of the alleged
title; he asks to be shown the conveyance or enactment or other
transaction which gave rise to the title, and in turn he will want
to be satisfied that those who made that conveyance or enactment had been given authority to do so by some further enactment or transaction which in turn . . . From this train of thought
arise the theories of governmental legitimacy and political
obligation which tacitly assume that the present authority of
particular rulers must rest on some prior authority (of custom;
or of the community over itself, granted away to the ruler by
transmission or alienation; or of the individual over himself,
granted away by promise or implied contract or 'consent').

The legalistic theories which seek to justify the authority of
rulers by reference to the prior authority of some presumably
self-authorizing transaction such as a 'contract of subjection'
or an act of 'consent', have often been reinforced by a train
of reasoning which employs the quite correct premiss that *all*

the members of a community are entitled in justice to a certain concern and respect. An argument along these lines became popular amongst scholastic writers in the sixteenth century. At the beginning of the seventeenth century, Cardinal Bellarmine formulated this argument with precision: Natural reasonableness requires that there be governmental authority; But natural reasonableness does not identify any particular man or class as the bearer of governmental authority; Therefore natural reasonableness requires that the bearer of governmental authority be the multitude, the whole community itself. (And the multitude, or community, then *transmits* its authority to representatives, be they kings, councils, or assemblies.) Bellarmine's 'syllogism' is helpfully clear; it reveals the fallacy in his theory, and in all such 'transmission' theories (which secular writers later developed, of course, into theories that governmental authority rests for its legitimacy on 'the consent of the governed'[10]). The argument's two premises are certainly correct; but the conclusion obviously does not follow from them.

Indeed, the conclusion is intrinsically implausible. For the need for authority is, precisely, to substitute for unanimity in determining the solution of practical co-ordination problems which involve or concern everyone in the community. To say 'the community has authority over itself' *either* amounts to saying that there is no authority in this community (so that co-ordination problems are solved by unanimity, or are dissolved by sheer force), *or* it amounts to saying something else, by way of a confusing legal fiction or ideological manner of speaking, about the location of authority in *some* communities; for example, that each member of such and such a community has an opportunity to participate in determining that location (though such acts of participation, while not devoid of significance, do not themselves amount to an exercise of authority, as every outvoted voter in a parliamentary election is well aware).

Consent, transmission, contract, custom—none of these is needed to constitute the state of affairs which (presumptively) justifies someone in claiming and others in acknowledging his authority to settle co-ordination problems for a whole community by creating authoritative rules or issuing authoritative

[10] American Declaration of Independence, 1776.

orders and determinations. Rather, the required state of facts is this: that in the circumstances the say-so of this person or body or configuration of persons probably will be, by and large, complied with and acted upon, to the exclusion of any rival say-so and notwithstanding any differing preferences of individuals about what should be stipulated and done in the relevant fields of co-ordination problems.

This emergence of authority without benefit of prior authorization requires, of course, the definite solution of a vast preliminary or framework co-ordination problem: *Whose* say-so, if anyone's, are we all to act upon in solving our co-ordination problems? Necessarily the solution will require virtual unanimity; *here* there will be no solution unless the preferences of the individual members of the community are brought into line. Such unanimity of practical judgment is, obviously, not easy to come by. Individual motivations for concurring in the relevant judgment will vary, and very commonly those who aspire to benefit from the judgment (i.e. who aspire to authority) will be busy ensuring that anyone who is failing to appreciate their claims to intrinsic fitness to rule will be supplied with some extrinsic motive to concur—fear or favour. The effort to bring everyone to at least an acquiescence in this judgment is usually very taxing and exhausting for all concerned, and makes clear to all what is indeed the case: that those general needs of the common good which justify authority, certainly also justify and urgently demand that questions about the location of authority be answered, wherever possible, by authority. I have been stressing that there are situations where this is not practically possible, and that the emergence of particular bearers of authority in such situations is, nevertheless, neither impossible nor unduly mysterious. Now it is time to recall that, very commonly, the first authoritative act of un-authorized bearers of authority is to lay down directions for ensuring that in future the location of authority (whether in themselves or in their successors) shall be determined, not by the hazards of those processes of arriving at unanimity from which they have just emerged as the beneficiaries,[11] but by authoritative rules.

[11] 'Beneficiaries': the *hereditas* can, however, be *damnosa*; in any event, authority is (in reason, as in modern British constitutional draftsmanship) responsibility.

Of course, some rulers are content to rule charismatically, and to leave their succession to the movements of a spirit which blows where it listeth (not perhaps without some huffing and puffing by those who would like it to breathe on them). But Weber was well justified in his tendency (contrary, perhaps, to some of his own methodological notions) to speak of the 'legal' type-form of rulership as the 'rational' type-form.[12] Once the problems of social order, and of authority as a rational response to such problems, have become the object of practically reasonable reflection in a community, 'constitutional' provision for the location of authority becomes a first priority. If the ruler does not make it his business to determine the location of authority for later times (not to mention for lower levels), thoughtful members of such societies will commonly make it their business to try, as best they can, to reach some understandings about it. The tendency of political thinkers to utter legalistic fictions about the original location of authority has its excuse, and perhaps its occasion (but not a justification), in the urgent need to legalize the devolution of undevolved authority.

It remains true that the sheer fact that virtually everyone *will* acquiesce in somebody's say-so is the presumptively necessary and defeasibly sufficient condition for the normative judgment that that person has (i.e. is justified in exercising) authority in that community. But to this perhaps scandalously stark principle there are two significant riders. First: practical reasonableness requires (because of the self-same desirability of authority for the common good) that, faced with a purported ruler's say-so, the members of the community normally should acquiesce *or withhold* their acquiescence, comply or *withhold* their compliance, precisely as he is, or is not, designated as the lawful bearer of authority by the constitutional rules authoritative for that time, place, field, and function—*if*, by virtue of custom or authoritative stipulation, *there are such rules*. The second rider

---

[12] *On Law*, pp. 336, xxxi: 'Indeed, the continued exercise of every domination (in our technical sense of the word) always has the strongest need of self-justification through appealing to the principles of its legitimation. Of such ultimate principles, there are only three ... (a) A domination can be legitimately valid because of its rational character: such *legal domination* rests upon the belief in the legality of a consciously created order and of the right to give commands vested in the person or persons designated by that order ...'

is this: while 'consent' as distinct from acquiescence is not needed to justify or legitimate the authority of rulers, the notion of consent may suggest a sound rule of thumb for deciding when someone should be obeyed even though general acquiescence is not likely, and for deciding when someone whose stipulation will be generally acquiesced in should nevertheless be treated as having no authority in practical reason. This rule of thumb is: a man's stipulations have authority when a practically reasonable subject, with the common good in view, would think he *ought* to consent to them.

The standing temptation of the lawyer, and of the political philosopher in a culture saturated with legal ideals and legalistic assumptions, is to treat these riders not as riders but as the fundamental principle—shutting his eyes to the fact which the lawyer and political philosopher, Sir John Fortescue, squarely faced during the turbulent emergence of nation-states in Europe: 'amongst *nearly all* peoples, realms have come into being by usurpation, just as the Romans usurped the government of the whole world'.[13] The fact that bad men happen to originate a government does not (Fortescue explained) affect the truth that governing power has its beginnings under, and by virtue of, the 'law of nature', and at all times was and remains regulated by that natural law. (Where Fortescue speaks of the law of nature, I have preferred to speak of the principles of practical reasonableness that call for co-operative life in the wide 'political' community, and for the authority that alone makes that life practicable.) In the very frequent case where bad men establish their rulership over a realm, there as else-where the law of nature itself (said Fortescue) operates to initiate the rulership, for the sake of human well-being: 'in one and the same act both the force of justice and the malice of wrongfulness effect the operation of the law of nature'—one can say that men establish governing power through the law of nature, but in the last analysis it is better to say (he concluded forcefully) that it is the law of nature that establishes that power through men, be they good or bad.[14] In these formulations,

---

[13] *De Laudibus Legum Angliae* (*c*.1470), c. 12: 'Sicet Romani orbis imperium usurparunt, qualiter fere in omnibus gentibus regna inchoata sunt'.

[14] Fortescue, *De Natura Legis Naturae* (*c*.1463) I, c. 18 (entitled 'Lex naturae statum regium in eius initio operata est, licet iniqui eundem statum primordiarunt').

his lawyers' jargon about powers being created by operation
of (natural) law does not obscure this English judge's moral
realism which refuses to trace the ultimate origin of authority
to any fiction of transmission, contract, or actual consent, or
to anything other than the principles of practical reasonableness
and the basic values of the common good, generating practical
conclusions ('I have the responsibility of ruling'; 'He has
authority . . .') from the sheer fact of ability to co-ordinate action
for the common good.[15]

IX.5   'BOUND BY THEIR OWN RULES'?

The foregoing section was not a defence of the rule of the few
over the many. For convenience, I referred often to 'the ruler'.
But nothing turned on the number of persons entitled, in a given
community, to participate in rulership. As the classics said, the
ruler may be one, or few, or many ('the multitude', 'the
masses'). There are social circumstances where the rule of one
will be best, and other circumstances where the rule of a very
narrow, or a very wide, class will be best. (The classical
'preference' for the rule of one—'mon-archy'—was not a
preference for life tenure of office, hereditary titles, or the
paraphernalia of royal courts, but expressed a concern for
effectiveness of co-ordination, for unity and consequently effectiveness in the pursuit of common good; and the preference was
carefully qualified by the proviso that the conditions must be
right—for where the conditions are wrong, the rule of one is
the absolutely worst form of rule: tyranny.) The discussion of
the best forms of rule under given conditions is for political
science. My concern is with the distinction, which all social
thought easily employs and recognizes and which legal thought
formalizes with convenient fictions, between acting in the
capacity of ruler and acting in the capacity of subject.
  Nothing in the notion of authority which I have been
expounding requires that authority rest in some permanently
or even quasi-permanently distinct governing personnel. The

---

[15] Thus there was sound philosophy behind the formula employed to claim jurisdiction for the Crown in British 'protectorates': 'Whereas by treaty, grant, usage,
sufferance and other lawful means, Her Majesty has power [sc. authority] and
jurisdiction in the said territories . . .' (emphasis added).

axiom that authority is required as a substitute for unanimity in no way entails that authority cannot vest in an assembly of all the sane adults of a community, or even in such an assembly determining issues only by unanimous vote. Provided that the determinations of such an assembly are treated by the members as authoritative after the determination, and after its members have returned to their own private affairs, we have co-ordination of action in the community by authority rather than by unanimity of judgment (for minds can change; assemblymen can come to regret their vote, and yet comply, and be bound to comply, with the determination). Of course, any requirement of unanimity amongst those who exercise authority tends to render authority inefficient as a substitute for unanimity amongst the members of the community: hence some form of majority rule will ordinarily meet with general acquiescence, at least 'in principle', i.e. as a method of generating authoritative determinations. But the axiomatic distinction remains conceptually clear: as Yves Simon said, imagining a small farming community practising direct, non-representative government by participatory democracy: 'Between [a] few hundred farmers scattered in their fields, busy with their own private affairs, and the same farmers gathered in an assembly in charge of the community's affairs, the qualitative difference is just as great as between the President of the United States and any of us United States citizens.'[16]

There is nothing mysterious about this distinction between the assemblymen in their 'collegiate capacity' (as John Austin aptly put it)[17] and each assemblyman in his individual capacity as subject to 'the assembly's' stipulations (i.e. the stipulations which have met the approval of that number of assemblymen— and according to that manner and form of expressing such approval—which wins general acquiescence, either merely *de facto* or, more usually, because of rules so providing). The distinction simply corresponds to two distinct though related human excellences which Aristotle summed up when he said that a citizen, in the focal sense of that word, is one who shares in rulership (whether in the deliberative assemblies or in the courts of law), and added that 'the good citizen must possess

---

[16] *Philosophy of Democratic Government* (Chicago: 1951), p. 151.
[17] Austin, *Province*, pp. 254, 259, 279, etc.

the knowledge and capacity requisite both for ruling and for being ruled, and the excellence of a citizen may be defined as consisting in a practical knowledge of the governance of free men from *both* points of view'.[18]

Just as it is obvious that each and every member of a governing assembly is bound by its authoritative stipulations, in so far as these stipulate what he is (not) to do, so it is obvious that a ruler who rules alone may stipulate what he is himself (not) to do, and is then bound by this stipulation. If we are to call these stipulations 'laws', and their obligation 'legal', so far as they touch and bind any mere subject, why should we not call them laws and their obligation legal so far as they touch a person who also rules? It will not do to object that a monarch may have the authority to relieve himself of his obligations by amendment or dispensation—for the question relates to his position, in reason's contemplation of law, *while* the law which embraces him is not thus amended or dispensed from. Nor is it helpful to declare that such a monarch's obligations must be merely 'political' or 'moral', not legal—for commonly they are obligations deriving not from this or that political 'factor', nor (directly) from any general moral rule, but directly and precisely from that very manner and form of acting which, in that society at that time, counts as authoritative laying-down-of-law.

The elementary distinction needed for present purposes—made clearly in medieval terminology and only gradually slipping out of English legal language during the two centuries dividing St. German, through Hale, from Blackstone—is that between the 'directive' and the 'coercive' force of authority. But when we speak of the coercive force of rules, we are beginning to speak of law (which, as we shall see, is not the same as saying that one cannot conceive of law without coercion).

NOTES

IX.1

It works to the common good that particular goods be properly defended by particular persons ... For insistence on this, and a vivid illustration, see Aquinas, *S.T.* I–II, q. 19, a. 10c; also Yves Simon, *The Philosophy of Democratic Government* (Chicago: 1951), pp. 41, 55–8,

[18] *Pol.* III, 2: 1277b14–16; also III, 7: 1284a1–3.

71. The first chapter of Simon's book also provides an excellent analysis of the reasons why, and differing ways in which, authority is natural to man, i.e. is required for his good but not (only) because of the deficiencies of individuals. Discount, however, his theory (taken from Maritain) of 'affective knowledge'.

Co-ordination problems ... The concept of co-ordination problem recently developed for analysis of games, strategies, and conventions is summarized by Edna Ullmann-Margalit, *The Emergence of Norms* (Oxford: 1977), p. 78. 'Co-ordination problems are interaction situations distinguished by their being situations of interdependent decision. That is, they are situations involving two or more persons, in which each has to choose one from among several alternative actions, and in which the outcome of any person's action depends upon the action chosen by each of the others ... The specific difference of co-ordination problems within this class is that in them the interests of the parties coincide.' Ullmann-Margalit rightly employs central case/focal meaning analysis here: 'When the coincidence of interests is perfect we speak of a *pure* co-ordination problem. In the non-pure co-ordination problems the convergence of the parties' interests is less than perfect, but still outweighs any possible clash of interests.' In my discussion, 'co-ordination problem' ranges from the pure to the very non-pure instances, approaching asymptotically the 'pure conflict case' where 'the parties' interests diverge completely and one person's gain is the other's loss' (loc. cit.). For a legislator or judge, considering the problems of social order generically, the pure conflict situation cannot be conceded to exist as between the members of a community: A and B may be in a pure conflict situation here and now; but A might have been in B's position, and vice versa; so, in advance or generically (i.e. for the purpose of selecting rules and conventions), people of A's and B's sorts have a convergent interest in containing, modulating, and conditioning the possible loss (and gain).

IX.2

'Exclusionary reasons' ... Joseph Raz has developed the concept in his *Practical Reason and Norms*. An exclusionary reason is a reason to exclude, or refrain from acting upon, a relevant reason for acting: see pp. 39, 42, 62; sometimes, as where someone is under orders, it is a reason for not acting on 'the merits of the case' at all—the order operates as a reason for not acting on an assessment of the pros and cons of the action ordered and alternative courses of action: see p. 42. As Raz rightly observes at p. 64: 'if authority is to be justified by the requirements of co-ordination [as he thinks it is: ibid.] we must regard authoritative utterances as exclusionary reasons. The proof is contained in the classical analysis of authority. Authority can secure co-ordination only if the individuals concerned defer to its judgment and do not act on the balance of reasons, but on the authority's instructions ...'. Raz, 'On Legitimate Authority', in R. Bronaugh (ed.), *Philosophical Law* (Westport: 1978), pp. 6–31, is a useful analysis of authority in terms of 'protected reasons', a protected reason being one that is both a reason to ϕ and an exclusionary reason for disregarding reasons against doing ϕ.

Distinction between S_1 and S_3 statements ... See also Raz, 'Kelsen's Theory of the Basic Norm' (1974) 19 *Am. J. Juris.* 94 at pp. 107–9. A similar point is made by, e.g., Winston Nesbitt, 'Categorical Imperatives' (1977) 86 *Phil. Rev.* 217 at p. 221: 'The judgment that from the point of view of etiquette one should do a certain thing is not "a 'should' statement based on rules of etiquette" ...; it is not a "should"-judgment at all, but a theoretical judgment about what etiquette requires, and is quite consistent with "But of course, it's nonsense that you should do any such thing". A "should" statement based on the rules of etiquette is not a judgment to the effect that one should from the point of view of etiquette do *A*, because the rules of etiquette require it ...'. See also Neil MacCormick, *Legal Reasoning and Legal Theory* (Oxford: 1978), p. 62.

IX.3

'Opinio juris' *as belief in obligatory character of the practice* ... Besides Oppenheim see
(amongst countless other sources) Judge Manley Hudson's Working Paper (dated
3 March 1950) on Art. 24 of the Statute of the International Law Commission: 'The
emergence of a principle or rule of customary international law would seem to require
presence of the following elements: (a) concordant practice by a number of States
with reference to a type of situation falling within the domain of international relations;
(b) continuation or repetition of the practice over a considerable period of time; (c)
conception that the practice is required by,' [surely too strong a requirement for the
opinio juris] 'or consistent with' [surely too weak a requirement] 'prevailing international
law; and (d) general acquiescence in the practice by other States': *International Law
Commission Yearbook 1950*, II, p. 26. Hudson's element (b) is rejected (so far as concerns
the modern world) by Tanaka J. (dissenting) in *Ethiopia* v. *South Africa*, *I.C.J. Rep.*
1966, at p. 291; already Suarez and the earlier jurists whom Suarez cites were clear
that custom can be established in a short period provided that knowledge of the custom
is quickly spread to all concerned (which is Tanaka J.'s point): *De Legibus*, VIII, xv,
8–9, reading *'princeps'* in the light of xiii, 1. Critical questions could also be raised
about the sense in which Hudson intended his element (d). The International Court
of Justice employed the classic doctrine of *opinio juris*, almost in Oppenheim's words,
in the *North Sea Continental Shelf Cases*, *I. C. J. Rep.* 1969, at p. 44. But in the *North
Sea Fisheries Case (Great Britain* v. *Iceland)*, *I. C. J. Rep.* 1974, at pp. 23, 26, can be
seen an understanding of custom-formation rather closer to that set out in our analysis.

'Appropriateness' of a practice as a solution to a co-ordination problem ... The text simplifies
matters here. A rational judgment of appropriateness, which is made both as a
component of the PJ_0 judgments and again (but now taking more facts into account)
as a component of PJ_1 judgments, will consider not only the intrinsic features (so to
speak) of the relevant co-ordination problem, but also the extent to which concurrent
practice in the relevant sphere has created structures (whether physical, economic/
financial, or of habit, 'goodwill', etc.) the dismantling of which would involve sheer
loss to many (for what gain? and to whom?). It will also consider whether (as is likely)
many have benefited from the regularity and concurrence of practice and the
consequent relative stability of expectations and predictions; and will ask whether it
would be reasonable for those who have so benefited (or who had the free opportunity
of so benefiting) to depart from the practice whenever they consider it burdensome
to them. These considerations tend in practice to reduce somewhat the difficulty
occasioned by the fact that, as D. K. Lewis stresses in his book *Convention: A Philosophical
Study* (Ithaca: 1969), p. 24, 'co-ordination problems' are typically 'situations of interdependent decision ... in which there are two or more proper co-ordination equilibria';
for his account of the relation between practice, opinion (expectations and preferences),
and convention, see ibid., p. 42. See also the analysis of 'conformative behaviour' in
David Shwayder, *The Stratification of Behaviour* (London: 1965), pp. 233–43, 247–80.

'Appropriateness' of custom as a method of settling both substantive and framework questions ...
This appropriateness does not derive from any abstract principle that what has always
been done ought to continue to be done; or from any principle that what a majority
of individuals or states want to be done (or to be authoritative) intrinsically ought
to be done (or to be regarded as authoritative). (Majority rule is often a highly
convenient, and therefore reasonable, principle of authority for a community to adopt—
but it is not, *pace* Locke, a 'natural law' principle; it must be *adopted*, by unanimity
or by authoritative, e.g. customary, rule: see Burke, *Appeal from the New to the Old Whigs*

(1791) in *Works* (1826), vol. VI, pp. 212–16, summarized in J. W. Gough, *The Social Contract* (Oxford, 2nd ed.: 1957), pp. 194–5; contrast Locke, *Second Treatise of Government* (1689), para. 96, and see the tangle of opinions recorded by Otto Gierke, *Natural Law and the Theory of Society, 1500–1800* (trans. E. Barker [1934], Cambridge: 1950), pp. 110, 120, 127, 247, 315, 321, 372, 387.) This judgment of appropriateness rests not only on the considerations mentioned in the text and the preceding note on appropriateness (which apply not in all but in many particular cases), but also on the consideration (parasitic, but reinforcing) that where this method of creating authoritative rules is accepted, those who take the benefits of the resulting system of practice, restraints, etc., will normally be acting unreasonably (partially, or unfairly) if in particular cases they claim to be free from the products of the method.

Failure to disentangle PJ_0 from PJ_2 judgments ... Hart's notion of the 'internal viewpoint' and the 'internal aspect of rules' has a close relationship to the notion of *opinio juris*; certain problems in understanding and applying Hart's notion arise from his conflation of elements which I have here tried to disentangle. See *Concept of Law*, pp. 86–8, 54–7, 99–100.

Defeasibility, or only presumptive sufficiency, of effectiveness as the basis of authority ... For this use of 'defeasible' and, especially, 'presumptive', see MacCormick, 'Law as Institutional Fact' (1974) 90 *L.Q.R.* 102 at pp. 123–7.

IX.4

Empirical conditions for effective rulership ... An early study is Aristotle, *Pol.* V: 1301a–1316b27. Hart, *Concept of Law*, pp. 111–14, 59–60, 197–8, 226, 86–8, 242, 247, regularly and sharply distinguishes between 'the ordinary citizen's obedience' and 'acceptance on the part of officials of constitutional rules' (though he fails to reserve the word 'acceptance' exclusively for the latter attitude of voluntary, critical acceptance of the rules as common public standards of conduct); likewise Raz, *Practical Reason*, pp. 124–6. Classical political science also regularly distinguished between the two classes of persons likely to be found in any society: those who need to be compelled to keep the peace, and those who freely make the law their own—as Aquinas says, *S.T.* I–II, q. 96, a. 5c, these are the two principal ways of being 'subject to law' (or 'subject to authority'). On the empirical concerns of political science as conceived by Aristotle, see Eric Voegelin, *Plato and Aristotle* (Baton Rouge: 1957), ch. 9, esp. p. 357.

Differing motives for compliance ... See Hart, *Concept of Law*, pp. 198, 226; *On Law*, p. 328.

Bellarmine's transmission theory ... His syllogism (in fact, of course, an enthymeme) actually runs: '[Political] power is of divine right, but divine right did not give it to any particular man; therefore it gave it to the multitude'; or again: 'apart from positive law, there is no greater reason why, out of many equals, one rather than another should dominate; therefore power belongs to the whole multitude': *Controversiarum de membris ecclesiae* (1588), III, c. 6, trans. Simon, *Philosophy of Democratic Government*, p. 166. For an earlier formulation, see Francisco de Vitoria, *De Potestate Civili* (1528), c. 7: 'Nam cum de iure naturali et divino sit aliqua potestas gubernandi rempublicam, et sublato communi iure positivo et humano, non sit maior ratio ut potestas illa sit in uno quam in altero, necesse est ut ipsa communitas sit sibi sufficiens et habeat potestatem gubernandi se.' For Cajetan's looser formulation in 1512, see Simon, op. cit., pp. 160–5. All these theorists took encouragement from some ambiguous and unsatisfactory remarks of Aquinas, especially *S.T.* I–II, q. 90, a. 30; Q. 97, a. 3 ad 3. For an elaborate discussion, which evasively recognizes that in the not infrequent case of a conquered people mere acquiescence suffices for 'transmission' of authority from the people to the new rulers, see Suarez, *De Legibus*, III, c. iv, para. 2; also paras. 3–5, 8; also c. ii, paras. 3, 4; c. iii, para. 6.

From transmission (or translation) theories to social contract theories ... See Otto Gierke, *Political Theories of the Middle Age* (trans. F. W. Maitland, Cambridge: 1900), notes 138–65, 305–8; for the distinction between the supposed contract of social union and the supposed contract of subjection to a ruler, see Gierke, *Natural Law and the Theory of Society, 1500–1800*, pp. 107–11 (sec. 16, para. iv). Generally, see Gough, *The Social Contract*, esp. ch. VI.

Usurpation and conquest as modes of acquiring authority ... The frequency with which authority (i.e., as always throughout this discussion, authority which ought to be respected by a reasonable citizen) is acquired by these methods is rightly stressed by David Hume, 'Of the Original Contract' [1748] (*Social Contract*, ed. E. Barker, Oxford: 1947, pp. 230–5). The US Dept. of the Army, *The Law of Land Warfare* (1956), para. 358, sums up the principle on which the International Regulations respecting the Laws and Customs of War on land, annexed to The Hague Convention IV (1907), implicitly proceed: '... military occupation ... does not transfer the sovereignty to the occupant, but simply the authority or power to exercise some of the *rights of sovereignty*. The exercise of these *rights results from the established power of the occupant and from the necessity of maintaining law and order, indispensable* both to the inhabitants and to the occupying force' (emphasis added). See also A. D. McNair, 'Municipal Effects of Belligerent Occupation' (1941) 57 *L.Q.R.* 33, stressing, at p. 36, that 'the morality or immorality of the occupation is irrelevant ...;' the occupying ruler acquires 'a right against inhabitants who remain that they should obey his lawful regulations for the administration of the territory ...' (p. 35). On the authority of usurpers, according to English law, see Honoré, 'Allegiance and the Usurper' [1967] *Camb. L. J.* 214; Finnis, 'Revolutions and Continuity of Law' in *Oxford Essays II*, 44 at pp. 46–7.

Fortescue on the origins of authority ... See also *De Laudibus Legum Anglie* (ed. S. B. Chrimes, Cambridge: 1942), cc. 12, 13, (and the analysis of c. 13 in Voegelin, *The New Science of Politics*, Chicago: 1952, pp. 41–5). The full title of Fortescue's treatise on natural law is significant: *De Natura Legis Naturae et de ejus Censura in Successione Regnorum Suprema* (i.e. ... and its judgment on the succession to supreme office in kingdoms). Despite the value of its teaching (aimed against a teaching of Cicero (*De Re Publica*, I, 25, 39) and Augustine (*De Civitate Dei*, XIX, 24) lying at the root of later social contract doctrine) that a people without authoritative rulership cannot be called a body, c. 13 of Fortescue's *De Laudibus* is not as wholly free from assumptions about transmission of authority as a reading of Voegelin's valuable analysis might suggest. By 1670, a similarly philosophically-inclined judge, Sir Matthew Hale C.J., is denying the frequency of conquest as an origin of authority and is looking assiduously for a 'consent of the governors and the governed': see his 'Reflections on Hobbes's Dialogue of the Common Law' in Holdsworth, *A History of English Law*, vol. V (London: 2nd ed., 1937), at p. 507.

IX.5

The ruler may be one, few or many (even 'all') ... Plato, *Statesman*, 291d–303d; Aristotle, *Pol.* III, 5: 1279a28; IV, 11: 1298a7–9; *Nic. Eth.* VIII, 10: 1160a32–35; 11: 1161a30; Aquinas, *De Regimine Principum*, c. 1, para. 11; Blackstone, I *Comm.*, p. 49.

Classical preference for monarchy ... The argument is simply from the need for efficiency (*not* to be contrasted here with justice) in co-ordination: Aquinas, *De Regimine Principum*, c. 2.; and the rule of one *bad* (self-interested) man ('tyrant') is the worst form of government, ibid., c. 3 (also Plato, *Statesman*, 302e–303b; Aristotle, *Nic. Eth.* VIII, 11: 1161a31–33). Plato particularly stresses that these questions about the form and number of the ruling authority are of little moment compared with questions of substance about what this authority *does*: loc. cit., and Voegelin, *Plato and Aristotle*, pp. 158–61.

Aristotle on citizenship as participation in government ... *Pol.* III, 1: 1275a22–24, a33, b17–22. (These pages of the *Politics* are the *locus classicus* on definition of terms in social science; and see I.3, above and XII.4, below.)

Single rulers may be bound by their own stipulations, just as members of governing assemblies are ... The argument in the text is that used by Vitoria, *De Potestate Civili*, 21.

Can laws made by a sovereign be binding upon him? ... This question is not of great practical moment in polities where governing powers are distributed amongst various persons and bodies, and the distribution is judicially supervised. Indeed, it has never been of great practical moment for lawyers, since sovereign monarchs of the sort supposed in the discussion will not lack powers of self-dispensation. But the question remains significant for uncovering basic assumptions and confusions about law and legal obligation—just as a critique of Austin's conception of law can most profitably begin by assessing the adequacy of his reason for asserting that a sovereign is legally illimitable; see *Province*, pp. 253–4. For the late scholastic ('voluntarist') view of obligation as a force whereby a *superior* by an act of will moves an *inferior* to the performance of a particular act, see Suarez, *De Legibus*, I, c. v, 24; c. IV, 7 (and see XI.8, below, and II.6, above). For the English legal doctrine that 'the King can do no wrong', see Blackstone, I *Comm.*, pp. 235–40, 243–4; esp. p. 237 'the King himself can do no wrong; since it would be a great weakness and absurdity in any system of positive law, to define any possible wrong, without any possible redress'; III *Comm.*, pp. 254–5; IV *Comm.*, p. 32.

The single ruler is under the 'directive' though not the 'coercive' obligation of the law ... The fundamental discussion is Aquinas, *S.T.* I–II, q. 96, a. 5 ('Is everybody subject to the law? Yes'), ad 3: 'A *princeps* is said to be "exempt from the law" in relation to the coercive power of law, for no-one is compelled, in the strict sense of the word, by himself (and the law only has its coercive force from the power of the *princeps*) ... But in relation to the directive authority of the law, the *princeps* is subject to the law made by his own will ... Before God's judgment, the *princeps* is not "exempt from law" in relation to its directive authority, and ought to fulfil the law freely, not under coercion (though he is above the law, in so far as he can change it if expedient, and grant dispensations from it adapted to place and season)'. The distinction is found in Bracton, *De Legibus Angliae* [*c.* 1250] I, 38 (and see Maitland, *The Constitutional History of England* [1888] (Cambridge: 1919), pp. 100–1; in Matthew Hale, *Pleas of the Crown* [*c.*1670] (1st ed. 1736) I, 44; Hale, 'Reflections on Hobbes's Dialogue of the Common Law' [*c.*1670], in Holdsworth, *A History of English Law*, vol. V, at pp. 507–8; and as a vestigial relic, in a discussion of 'the King can do no wrong', muddied with fiction and shifting rhetoric, in Blackstone, I *Comm.*, pp. 235, 237; and esp. IV *Comm.*, p. 33. For the undifferentiated proposition that the ruler should (save in extraordinary circumstances) be subject to the law, see already Plato, *Seventh Letter*, 337a, d; *Laws*, IV: 715b–d, 875d.

For an account of the *vis directiva*, the 'directive' force of law, see XI.4, below.

X
LAW

THE central case of law and legal system is the law and legal system of a complete community, purporting to have authority to provide comprehensive and supreme direction for human behaviour in that community, and to grant legal validity to all other normative arrangements affecting the members of that community (see VI.6). Such large claims, advanced by or on behalf of mere men, would have no plausibility unless those said to be subject to legal authority had reason to think that compliance with the law and with the directions of its officers would not leave them subject to the assaults and depredations of their enemies, inside or outside the community. The authority of the law depends, as we shall see at length, on its justice or at least its ability to secure justice. And in this world, as it is, justice may need to be secured by force; failure to attempt to resist by force the depredations of invaders, pirates, and recalcitrants will normally be a failure in justice. If 'effectiveness' is to be contrasted (as it need not be) with 'justice', the coercive force of law is not merely a matter of effectiveness.

Aristotle gave currency to a regrettable oversimplification of the relationship between law and coercion. He was aware that law typically has two modes of operation, directive and coercive. But he suggested that the need for coercion arises from the recalcitrance of the selfish, the brutish many whose unprincipled egocentricity can be moderated only by a direct threat to their self-interest. But the fact is that recalcitrance—refusal or failure to comply with authoritative stipulations for co-ordination of action for common good—can be rooted not only in obstinate self-centredness, or in careless indifference to common goods and to stipulations made for their sake, but also in high-minded, conscientious opposition to the demands of this or that (or perhaps each and every) stipulation. Practical reasonableness—

from the genuine authority of which conscience, in the modern
sense of that term, gets the prestige it deserves (V.9)—demands
that conscientious terrorism, for example, be suppressed with
as much conscientious vigour as other forms of criminality.

Not all lawful coercion is by way of sanction or punishment.
Even the most developed legal systems rightly allow a use of
force not only in resistance to forcible assaults but also for
expelling certain sorts of intruders. All allow the arrest of certain
suspected offenders or potential offenders, and of persons and
things (e.g. ships) likely otherwise to escape due processes of
adjudication. Judgments may be executed, and some other
classes of debts satisfied, by seizure, distraint, forced sale. But
the context of restrictions with which these measures of coercion
are surrounded in a mature legal system is best understood by
looking more closely at a threat and use of force employed for
a quite distinct purpose: punitive sanctions ('punishment').

The prohibitions of the criminal law have a simple justifying
objective: that certain forms of conduct including certain omissions shall occur less frequently than they otherwise would. But
the 'system' of criminal law is more than that set of prohibitions.
The 'goal' of the familiar modern systems of criminal law can
only be described as a certain form or quality of communal
life, in which the demands of the common good indeed are un-
ambiguously and insistently preferred to selfish indifference or
individualistic demands for licence but also are recognized as
including the good of individual autonomy, so that in this mode
of association no one is made to live his life for the benefit or
convenience of others, and each is enabled to conduct his own
life (to constitute himself over his span of time) with a clear
knowledge and foreknowledge of the appropriate common way
and of the cost of deviation from it. Thus the administration,
or working-out, of the criminal law's prohibitions is permeated
by rules and principles of procedural fairness ('due process of
law') and substantive fairness (desert, proportionality), which
very substantially modify the pursuit of the goal of eliminating
or diminishing the undesired forms of conduct: such principles
as *nulla poena sine lege* (and rather precise *leges*, at that), and
the principles which outlaw retroactive proscription of conduct
(at the known cost of letting some dubious characters slip
through the net), and restrain the process of investigation,

interrogation, and trial (even at the expense of that *terror* which a Lenin knows is necessary for attaining definite social goals).

One can rightly debate the details of these criminal law systems, and adjust them to changing circumstances. But, in their main features and intent, they are justified because the common good of the community is the good of all its members; it is an open-ended good, a participation in all the basic values, and its maintenance is not a simple objective like that of keeping a path free from weeds.

The legal sanction, then, is to be a human response to human needs, not modelled on a campaign of 'social defence' against a plague of locusts, or sparrows. There is the need of almost every member of society to be taught what the requirements of the law—the common path for pursuing the common good—actually are; and taught not by sermons, or pages of fine print, but by the public and (relatively!) vivid drama of the apprehension, trial, and punishment of those who depart from that stipulated common way. There is the need of the actually or potentially recalcitrant (which includes most members of society, in relation to at least some activity or other) to be given palpable incentive to abide by the law when appeals to the reasonableness of sustaining the common good fail to move. And there is the need to give the law-abiding the encouragement of knowing that they are not being abandoned to the mercies of criminals, that the lawless are not being left to the peaceful enjoyment of ill-gotten gains, and that to comply with the law is not to be a mere sucker: for without this support and assurance the indispensable co-operation of the law-abiding is not likely to be continued.

Quite distinct from the foregoing set of defining purposes or requirements, which derive from the 'psychology' of citizens, there is a further defining purpose or requirement, by reason of which legal sanctions constitute *punishment*, rather than merely the 'social hygiene' of quarantine stations, asylums for the insane, and preventive detention. Sanctions are punishment because they are required in reason to avoid injustice, to maintain a rational order of proportionate equality, or fairness, as between all members of the society. For when someone, who really could have chosen otherwise, manifests in action a preference (whether by intention, recklessness, or negligence) for his own interests, his own freedom of choice and action, as against the common interests and the legally defined common way-of-action, then in and by that very action he gains a certain sort of advantage over those who have restrained themselves, restricted their pursuit of their own interests, in order to abide by the law. For is not the exercise of freedom of choice in itself a great human good? If the free-willing criminal were to retain this advantage, the situation would be as unequal and unfair as it would be for him to retain the tangible profits of his crime (the loot, the misappropriated funds, the office of profit, the . . .). If those in authority allowed the retention of unfairly gained advantages they would not only lose the allegiance of the disadvantaged law-abiding but indeed forfeit their title, in reason, to that allegiance. For the authority of rulers derives from their opportunity to foster the common good, and a fair balance of benefits and burdens within a community is an important aspect of that common good.

Punishment, then, characteristically seeks to restore the distributively just balance of advantages between the criminal and the law-abiding, so that, over the span of time which extends from before the crime until after the punishment, no one should actually have been disadvantaged—in respect of *this* special but very real sort of advantage—by choosing to remain within the confines of the law. This restoration of the order of fairness is accomplished by depriving the criminal[1] of what he gained in his criminal act (in the presently relevant sense of 'gain'): viz. the exercise of self-will or free choice.

What is done cannot be undone. But punishment rectifies the disturbed pattern[2] of distribution of advantages and disadvantages throughout a community by depriving the convicted criminal of his freedom of choice, proportionately to the degree to which he had exercised his freedom, his personality, in the unlawful act. Such deprivation is very commonly by fine;

---

[1] Remember: not all who are defined as offenders by this or that legal system will actually be 'criminals' in the sense here relevant, that is, people who (a) really exercised their freedom in their unlawful act and (b) were not prior to that time themselves disadvantaged by a social order substantially unfair in some *relevant* respect.

[2] 'Pattern' here must be understood, not as a 'current time-slice' pattern (for that could never be 'rectified') but as the diachronic pattern whose justice is assessable only by examining how advantages and disadvantages are gained, incurred, and shifted over a stretch of time.

the removal of pecuniary means removes opportunities of choice. But deprivation of freedom may also be accomplished by actual imprisonment, or by the removal of civil liberties. There is no absolute 'natural' measure of due punishment: the 'law of talion' (life for life, eye for eye, etc.) misses the point, for it concentrates on the material content or consequences of criminal acts rather than on their formal wrongfulness (unfairness) which consists in a will to prefer unrestrained self-interest to common good, or at least in an unwillingness to make the effort to remain within the common way. But some unlawful acts are premeditated, some impulsive, some involve trivia while others are big choices, for high stakes, really pitting the individual's self-will against his fellows; accordingly, there emerges a rough and ready 'function' or, more crudely, 'scale' of *relatively* appropriate punitive responses.

Finally, sanctions are part of the enterprise of legally ordering society, an enterprise rationally required only by that complex good of individuals which we name the common good. The criminal is an individual whose good is as good as any man's, notwithstanding that he ought in fairness to be deprived of some opportunities of realizing that good. On the supposition (which I have been making, for simplicity, throughout this section) that the legal system and social order in question are substantially just, we are bound by our whole analysis of human good to say that one who defies or contemns the law harms not only others but also himself. He seized the advantage of self-preference, and perhaps of psychological satisfactions and/or of loot, but all at the price of diminishing his personality, his participation in human good; for such participation is only through the *reasonable* pursuit, realization, and enjoyment of basic goods. The punitive sanction ought therefore to be adapted so that, within the framework of its two sets of defining purposes already indicated, it may work to restore reasonable personality in the offender, reforming him for the sake not only of others but of himself: 'to lead a *good* and useful life'.[3]

[3] Rule 1, Prison Rules (England and Wales), S.I. 1964, No. 388.

X.2 UNJUST PUNISHMENT

The foregoing discussion of the role of coercion in the legal ordering of community is a fragmentary illustration of method in jurisprudence. The method is not squeamish about human evil. It is not restricted to the problems of an imaginary 'well-ordered' society. Nor does it suppose for a moment that those in authority are exempt from criminality and injustice. But someone pursuing this method will not participate in debates about whether 'we would call it punishment' if a judge knowingly sentenced an innocent man, using him as a scapegoat to avert civil commotion. The problem in jurisprudence is not to find or devise definitions which will extend to *all* circumstances in which, regardless of particular points of view, the word being defined could 'correctly' be employed. There is place in jurisprudence, of course, for stipulative definitions of words, in order to avert misunderstandings of discourse; and for lexical explorations, in order to assemble reminders of the complexity of human affairs, concerns, and reasonings. But the point of a jurisprudence such as is exemplified in this chapter is to explain certain human institutions by showing how they are responses to the requirements of practical reasonableness.

Authoritative institutions justified by the requirements of practical reasonableness may be, and quite commonly are, deflected to meet the requirements of individual or group bias. In other circumstances (e.g. the international community) these malign influences, or other practical obstacles, work to prevent the full development of such institutions. A sound jurisprudential method will recognize this, but will not water down its explanations of the links between human institutions and the values and requirements of practical reasonableness. So the explanation of punishment will refer to features which are absent from the punishment of scapegoats. This absence does not require us to amend the explanatory definition of punishment. Nor does that definition require us to forbid the use of the term 'punishment' in the scapegoat case. Still less does it require us to banish the study of abuse of authority to some other discipline. It simply requires us to recognize the unjust punishment of scapegoats for what it is: an abusive, corrupt use of a justified human institution or procedure, an abuse aptly referred to by a secondary or non-focal use of the term 'punishment', a term which in its focal use has a proper role in any satisfactory account of what is required for human well-being. The reasons for this role, and the corresponding features of the central case of the institution and the focal use of the term, have been set out in my account.

X.3   THE MAIN FEATURES OF LEGAL ORDER

Law needs to be coercive (primarily by way of punitive sanctions, secondarily by way of preventive interventions and restraints). But other main features of legal order will come into view if we pursue the question: Would there be need for legal authority and regulation in a world in which there was no recalcitrance and hence no need for sanctions?

Max Weber decided to define 'law' by reference to the problem of recalcitrance and the availability of authorized sanctions.[4] This was explicitly offered as a stipulative definition, and as such is unobjectionable. But it is significant that the complexity and richness of Weber's data, and of the Western language in which he had to discuss those data, overcame his definitional decision. For he felt obliged to distinguish, from among three 'pure types' of authoritative co-ordination (*Herrschaft*), one type that could best be described as *legal*. And the characteristics of this type, as Weber himself described them, had nothing in particular to do with coercion or with a staff of men authorized to impose sanctions. Indeed, he considered legal order to be most purely exemplified in the internal order of a modern bureaucracy, in whose workings coercion, even 'psychic' coercion, is characteristically replaced, in large measure, by a sense of duty motivated by a sense of the worth 'for its own sake' of compliance with the organization's internal rules. This departure from his own stipulated definition of law is evidence of Weber's sensitivity to data and language—for the many senses or facets of the term 'law' (and its equivalents

---

[4] 'An order will be called *law* if it is externally guaranteed by the probability that coercion (physical or psychological), to bring about conformity or avenge violation, will be applied by a *staff* of people holding themselves specially ready for that purpose': *On Law*, p. 5.

in German, etc.) simply reflect the many concerns, aspirations, and motivations of the societies which use that term for the purposes, and in the course, of the communal life and practices that in turn constitute Weber's sociological data (I.1).

For Weber, then, authoritative co-ordination is legal in character when it operates by way not of an attitude of obedience to persons but of a disposition to comply with 'the law', a legally established order of consistent, abstract rules (normally established intentionally) and principles to be applied to and followed in particular cases—so that those in authority are regarded as 'officials' whose office or authority is defined by these rules, and who are to be obeyed only while they act within their legal powers. Here we can leave Weber, observing that the features of law which he thus found, intelligibly clustered in a historically significant constant in many (not all!) phases of human social order, are features enabling us to distinguish law from politics, conventions, manners, etiquette, mores, games, and indeed from every other form or matrix of communal interaction—and to distinguish it with complete adequacy *even in the absence of any problem of recalcitrance* and hence of any need for coercion or sanctions.

The preceding paragraph's description of what is distinctive of legal authority and order does not in fact carry us much further than Aristotle's suggestive but teasing notion of 'the rule of law and not of men'.[5] Taking for granted the already-mentioned (VI.6) features of comprehensiveness, purported supremacy, and absorptive or ratificatory capacity (features which do not by themselves distinguish legal order from the charismatic personal governance of a sovereign administering 'palm-tree justice' by *ad hoc* decrees), we may now briefly list the main features which as a set (characteristically but not invariably found together) are distinctive of legal order. It will be evident from the list that the ways in which law shapes, supports, and furthers patterns of co-ordination would be desirable even in a society free from recalcitrance. Just as authority is not required exclusively by the malice or folly of man, so these features of legal order, though adaptable to handling problems of recalcitrance or negligence, are not neces-

[5] Cf. *Pol.* III, 10: 1286a9.

sitated exclusively, either individually or as a cluster, by the need to meet or remedy those human deficiencies.

Firstly, then, law brings definition, specificity, clarity, and thus predictability into human interactions, by way of a system of rules and institutions so interrelated that rules define, constitute, and regulate the institutions, while institutions create and administer the rules, and settle questions about their existence, scope, applicability, and operation. There is thus a characteristically legal 'circle', a sense in which the system (as the interrelated rules and institutions are significantly but loosely called) 'lifts itself by its own bootstraps'—a sense captured by the more scientific but still literally paradoxical axiom that 'the law regulates its own creation'. My analysis of custom-formation (IX.2) showed, of course, that the circle can be broken and the paradox avoided; but legal thought systematically avoids answering the question which I there answered: how an authoritiative rule can be generated without prior authorization.

The primary legal method of showing that a rule is valid is to show (i) that there was at some past time, t_1, an act (of a legislator, court, or other appropriate institution) which according to the rules in force at t_1 amounted to a valid and therefore operative act of rule-creation, and (ii) that since t_1 the rule thus created has not determined (ceased to be in force) by virtue either of its own terms or of any act of repeal valid according to the rules of repeal in force at times t_2, t_3 ... It is a working postulate of legal thought (so fundamental that it is scarcely ever identified and discussed) that whatever legal rule or institution (e.g. contract, settlement, corporation) has been once validly created remains valid, in force or in existence, in contemplation of law, until it determines according to its own terms or to some valid act or rule of repeal.

Thirdly, then, rules of law regulate not only the creation, administration, and adjudication of such rules, and the constitution, character, and termination of institutions, but also the conditions under which a private individual can modify the incidence or application of the rules (whether in relation to himself or to other individuals). That is to say, individuals may perform juridical acts which, if performed in accordance with rules in force at the time of the performance, count as making a contract or sale or purchase or conveyance or bequest, contracting a marriage, constituting a trust, incorporating a company, issuing a summons, entering judgment ... All the legal entities thus created have the quality of persistence through time.

Fourthly, we can say that legal thinking (i.e. the law) brings what precision and predictability it can into the order of human interactions by a special technique: the treating of (usually datable) past acts (whether of enactment, adjudication, or any of the multitude of exercises of public and private 'powers') as giving, *now*, sufficient and exclusionary reason for acting in a way *then* 'provided for'. In an important sense the 'existence' or 'validity' of a legal rule can be explained by saying that it simply is this relationship, this continuing relevance of the 'content' of that past juridical act as providing reason to decide and act in the present in the way then specified or provided for. The convenience of this attribution of authoritativeness to past acts is twofold. The past is beyond the reach of persons in the present; it thus provides (subject only to problems of evidence and interpretation) a stable point of reference unaffected by present and shifting interests and disputes. Again, the present will soon be the past; so the technique gives people a way of now determining the framework of their future.

Fifthly, this technique is reinforced by the working postulate ('no gaps') that every present practical question or coordination problem has, in every respect, been so 'provided for' by some such past juridical act or acts (if only, in some cases, by provisions stipulating precisely which person or institution is now to exercise a discretion to settle the question, or defining what precise procedure is now to be followed in tackling the question). There is no need to labour the point that this postulate is fictitious and, if taken literally, is descriptively misleading and would restrict unnecessarily the development of the law by non-legislative means. The postulate is significant simply as a reinforcement of the other four characteristics of law and legal thought already mentioned.

All this, then, stands as a sufficiently distinctive, self-contained, intelligible, and practically significant social arrangement which would have a completely adequate rationale in a world of saints. In the world as it is, these five constellated formal features of legal order are amplified and elaborated in order to meet the problems of fraud and abuse of power, and are supplemented by the law of wrongs and of offences, criminal procedure and punishment (X.1). So it is that legal order has two broad characteristics, two characteristic modes of operation, two poles about which jurisprudence and 'definitions of law' tend to cluster. They are exemplified by the contrast between Weber's formal definition of law and his extensive employment of the term 'legal'; and they can be summed up in the two slogans: 'law is a coercive order' and 'the law regulates its own creation'.

X.4 THE RULE OF LAW

The account just given of five formal features of law's regulation of its own creation and operation was more incomplete than the very brief account of punitive sanctions in section X.1. For it lacked any systematic account of the relation between these formal features and the requirements of justice and the common good. Such an account may best be developed through some consideration of the conditions under which we can reasonably say that the 'legal system' is working well.

The name commonly given to the state of affairs in which a legal system is legally in good shape is 'the Rule of Law' (capitalized simply to avoid confusion with a particular norm within a legal system). The Rule of Law, the specific virtue of legal systems, has been well analysed by recent writers; so my discussion can be brief. A legal system exemplifies the Rule of Law to the extent (it is a matter of degree in respect of each item of the list) that (i) its rules are prospective, not retroactive, and (ii) are not in any other way impossible to comply with; that (iii) its rules are promulgated, (iv) clear, and (v) coherent one with another; that (vi) its rules are sufficiently stable to allow people to be guided by their knowledge of the content of the rules; that (vii) the making of decrees and orders applicable to relatively limited situations is guided by rules that are promulgated, clear, stable, and relatively general; and that (viii) those people who have authority to make, administer, and apply the rules in an official capacity (a) are accountable for their compliance with rules applicable to their performance and (b) do actually administer the law consistently and in accordance with its tenor.

The eighth desideratum should remind us that what is loosely called 'the legal system' subsists in time, ordering the affairs of subsisting persons; it therefore cannot be understood as merely a set of 'rules' as meaning-contents. None of the eight desiderata is merely a characteristic of a meaning-content, or even of the verbal expression of a meaning-content; all involve qualities of institutions and processes. *Promulgation*, for example, is not fully achieved by printing ever so many legible official copies of enactments, decisions, forms, and precedents; it requires also the existence of a professional class of lawyers whose business it is to know their way around the books, and who are available without undue difficulty and expense to advise anybody who wants to know where he stands. Or again, *coherence* requires not merely an alert logic in statutory drafting, but also a judiciary authorized and willing to go beyond the formulae of intersecting or conflicting rules, to establish particular and if need be novel reconciliations, and to abide by those reconciliations when relevantly similar cases arise at different times before different tribunals. Or again, the *prospectivity* of the law can be secured only by a certain restraint in the judicial adoption of new interpretations of the law. At each point we see that the Rule of Law involves certain qualities of process which can be systematically secured only by the institution of judicial authority and its exercise by persons professionally equipped and motivated to act according to law. Obviously, much more could be said about this institutional aspect of the Rule of Law—of what historical experience has shown to be further desiderata, such as the independence of the judiciary, the openness of court proceedings, the power of the courts to review the proceedings and actions not only of other courts but of most other classes of official, and the accessibility of the courts to all, including the poor.

To complete this review of the content of the Rule of Law, before proceeding to inquire into its point, we need only observe that concern for the Rule of Law does not merely shape or modulate projects which a ruler already has in mind. It also works to suggest new subject-matters for authoritative regulation. Consider, for example, the extension of law into a field

such as consumer–supplier relations. Just as a rule authorizing
a tyrant to do what he wills *is* 'a rule of law' (in a thin,
rather uninteresting sense) but departs from the Rule of Law,
and *is* 'a constitution' (in a thin, uninteresting sense) but fails
to establish constitutional government, so likewise a rule such
as *caveat emptor* is 'a rule of law in respect of consumer–
supplier relations' but fails to extend legal order into that field.
The decision to extend legal order into the field, by way of
criminal law, contract and tort law, new institutions for inspec-
tion, complaint-investigation, arbitration, etc., is justified not
only by the desirability of minimizing tangible forms of harm
and economic loss but also by the value of securing, for its
own sake, a quality of clarity, certainty, predictability, trustworthiness, in the human interactions of buying and selling, etc.

And here we touch, at last, the reason why the Rule of Law
is a virtue of human interaction and community. It is the reason
that I touched upon in discussing the law of criminal procedure.
Individuals can only be *selves*—i.e. have the 'dignity' of being
'responsible agents'—if they are not made to live their lives for
the convenience of others but are allowed and assisted to create
a subsisting identity across a 'lifetime'. This is the primary
value of the predictability which the law seeks to establish
through the five formal features discussed above (X.3). But it
is also the primary value of that notion of *constitutional*
government (*Rechtsstaat*) which, often at the expense of some
certainty about the precise location of authority, seeks to
guarantee that rulers will not direct the exercise of their
authority towards private or partisan objectives. And the
motive of constitutional devices such as the so-called 'separation of powers' is characteristically expressed not merely by
reference to the unjust schemes of arbitrary, partisan, or
despotic rulers but also by appeal to the positive good of a
certain quality of association and interaction between ruler and
ruled: 'to the end it may be a government of laws and not of
men'.[6] Implicitly, a principal component of the idea of constitutional government (which itself is one aspect of the idea
of the Rule of Law) is the holding of the rulers to their side
of a relationship of reciprocity, in which the claims of authority

---

[6] Massachusetts Declaration of Rights [1779], Art. xxx (providing for the strict
separation of legislative, executive, and judicial powers).

are respected on condition that authority respects the claims of the common good (of which a fundamental component is respect for the equal right of all to respectful consideration: VII.3).

In short, the five formal features of law (X.3) are the more instantiated the more the eight desiderata listed above are fulfilled. The fundamental point of the desiderata is to secure to the subjects of authority the dignity of self-direction and freedom from certain forms of manipulation. The Rule of Law is thus among the requirements of justice or fairness.

X.5 LIMITS OF THE RULE OF LAW

Just as I followed my discussion of punishment (X.1) with a discussion of unjust punishment (X.2), so we should now briefly consider the abuse of the Rule of Law. Lon Fuller and his critics raised the question whether a tyranny devoted to pernicious objectives can pursue those ends through a fully lawful Rule of Law. The debate failed to clarify the relevant sense of 'can'. It is clear enough that 'logical' or 'conceptual' possibility is not, and should not be, the focus of discussion here. As we have to stress again and again in an age of conceptual dogmatism, concepts of law and society are legitimately many, and their employment is subordinated to matters of principle rooted in the basic principles and requirements of practical reasonableness (which themselves generate many concepts and can be expressed in many reasonable forms). Fuller himself seemed to rest with a very different but equally unsatisfying claim that as a matter of historical fact you will not find a tyranny that operated consistently through law. But Fuller's discussion had more underlying sense than his critics were willing to allow, who could see in it no more than either a 'logical' or a 'historical' claim.

The truly relevant claim, emerging in muted form in Fuller's references to 'reciprocity', is this. A tyranny devoted to pernicious ends has no self-sufficient *reason* to submit itself to the discipline of operating consistently through the demanding processes of law, granted that the rational point of such self-discipline is the very value of reciprocity, fairness, and respect for persons which the tyrant, *ex hypothesi*, holds in contempt.

The sort of regime we are considering tends to be (i) exploitative, in that the rulers are out simply for their own interests regardless of the interests of the rest of the community; or (ii) ideological, in that the rulers are pursuing a goal they consider good for their community, but pursuing it fanatically (cf. V.6, VII.7), overlooking other basic aspects of human good in community; or (iii) some admixture of exploitative and ideological, such as the Nazi regime. None of these types of tyranny can find in its objectives any rationale for adherence (other than tactical and superficial) to the disciplines of legality. For such regimes are in business for determinate results, not to help persons constitute them*selves* in community (cf. VI.5, VI.8, VII.3, VIII.5–6).

So it is a mistake to say, as some of Fuller's critics have said, that the Rule of Law (his set of eight desiderata) is simply an efficient instrument which, like a sharp knife, may be good and necessary for morally good purposes but is equally serviceable for evil. Adherence to the Rule of Law (especially the eighth requirement, of conformity by officials to pre-announced and stable general rules) is always liable to reduce the efficiency for evil of an evil government, since it systematically restricts the government's freedom of manœuvre. The idea of the Rule of Law is based on the notion that a certain quality of inter-action between ruler and ruled, involving reciprocity and pro-cedural fairness, is very valuable for its own sake; it is not merely a means to other social ends, and may not lightly be sacrificed for such other ends. It is not just a 'management technique' in a programme of 'social control' or 'social engineering'.

To this, however, we must add something not sufficiently emphasized in Fuller's account of the virtue of the Rule of Law, but not overlooked in Plato's. In any age in which the ideal of law, legality, and the Rule of Law enjoys an ideological popularity (i.e. a favour not rooted in a steadily reasonable grasp of practical principles), conspirators against the common good will regularly seek to gain and hold power through an adherence to constitutional and legal forms which is not the less 'scrupulous' for being tactically motivated, insincere, and temporary. Thus the Rule of Law does not guarantee every aspect of the common good, and sometimes it does not secure even the substance of the common good.

Sometimes, moreover, the values to be secured by the genuine Rule of Law and authentic constitutional government are best served by departing, temporarily but perhaps drastically, from the law and the constitution. Since such occasions call for that awesome responsibility and most measured practical reasonableness which we call statesmanship, one should say nothing that might appear to be a 'key' to identifying the occasion or a 'guide' to acting in it. Suffice it to make two observations, one practical, the other reflective. The practical corollary is the judicially recognized principle that a written constitution is not a suicide pact, and that its terms must be both restrained and amplified by the 'implicit' prohibitions and authorizations necessary to prevent its exploitation by those devoted to its overthrow. (I return to the question of 'implied' principles, their source, and their place in legal thought in XI.3 and XII.3, below.) The reflective observation one may add here is that at this point in our analysis we have visibly returned to the basic principle with which we began (IX.4): authority, of which legal rulership is one species, is the responsibility that accrues, as Fortescue said, 'by operation of the law of nature'—i.e. for the sake of the standing needs of the good of persons in community—from the sheer fact of power, of opportunity to affect, for good, the common life.

An exploration of the limits of the Rule of Law is an exploration not only of the judicial methodology developed to embody and buttress the Rule of Law, but also of the 'general theory of law' which, even when eschewing all concern with 'ideologies' and values, faithfully mirrors that methodology and thus, willy-nilly, the concern for values that informs the methodology. A judge unconscious of the limits of a methodology which suffices for normal times will respond inadequately to abnormal problems. In face of a revolution he will say, for example: 'A court which derives its existence and jurisdiction from a written constitution cannot give effect to anything which is not law when judged by that constitution.'[7] This proposition, like any unqualified statement of constitutionalism (whether

---

[7] *Madzimbamuto* v. *Lardner-Burke, N.O.* 1968 (2) S.A. 284 at 432 per Fieldsend, A.J.A. (High Court of Rhodesia, Appellate Div.). See my fuller discussion in [1968] *Annual Survey of Commonwealth Law* 108–12; and in 'Revolutions and Continuity of Law' in *Oxford Essays II*, 44 at pp. 54, 70.

judicial or jurisprudential), is self-defeating. For the proposition itself cannot be derived from, and applied in any particular instance simply by reference to, the constitution alone. Usually a constitution will be quite silent on this sort of question. (And why should the matter be affected fundamentally by the written or unwritten character of the constitution?) But even if a written constitution did contain a rule embodying the proposition, there would remain the question whether any given court derives its existence, jurisdiction, or authority from the written constitution alone, whatever that document may assert. Test the matter further. Suppose a constitution specifically provided that no rule or person should have any authority save by virtue of the constitution. There still would remain the question whether acceptance of one part of, or acceptance of authority under, a constitution requires one to accept the whole constitution, including the part which demands that the whole be accepted as exclusive. A constitution may stipulate, so to speak, 'All from me or nothing from me'. But it cannot thereby prevent anyone from raising the question whether he need accept *that* norm or stipulation. The very raising of the question shows that the answer cannot be determined by any positive rule (written or unwritten) of the 'system'—not even a rule stipulating that the question is illegitimate.

X.6 A DEFINITION OF LAW

Throughout this chapter, the term 'law' has been used with a focal meaning so as to refer primarily to rules made, in accordance with regulative legal rules, by a determinate and effective authority (itself identified and, standardly, constituted as an institution by legal rules) for a 'complete' community, and buttressed by sanctions in accordance with the rule-guided stipulations of adjudicative institutions, this ensemble of rules and institutions being directed to reasonably resolving any of the community's co-ordination problems (and to ratifying, tolerating, regulating, or overriding co-ordination solutions from any other institutions or sources of norms) for the common good of that community, according to a manner and form itself adapted to that common good by features of specificity, minimization of arbitrariness, and maintenance of a quality of reciprocity between the subjects of the law both amongst themselves and in their relations with the lawful authorities.

This multi-faceted conception of law has been reflectively constructed by tracing the implications of certain requirements of practical reason, given certain basic values and certain empirical features of persons and their communities. The intention has not been lexicographical; but the construction lies well within the boundaries of common use of 'law' and its equivalents in other languages. The intention has not been to describe existing social orders; but the construction corresponds closely to many existing social phenomena that typically are regarded as central cases of law, legal system, Rule of Law, etc. Above all, the meaning has been constructed as a *focal* meaning, not as an appropriation of the term 'law' in a univocal sense that would exclude from the reference of the term anything that failed to have all the characteristics (and to their full extent) of the central case. And, equally important, it has been fully recognized that each of the terms used to express the elements in the conception (e.g. 'making', 'determinate', 'effective', 'a community', 'sanctioned', 'rule-guided', 'reasonable', 'non-discriminatory', 'reciprocal', etc.) has itself a focal meaning and a primary reference, and therefore extends to analogous and secondary instances which lack something of the central instance. For example, custom is not *made* in the full sense of 'made'—for making is something that someone can set himself to do, but no one sets himself (themselves) to make a custom. Yet customs are 'made', in a sense that requirements of practical reason are not made but discovered. The way in which each of the other crucial terms is *more or less* instantiated is quite obvious. (If the term 'reasonable' arouses misgivings, see VI.1.) Law, in the focal sense of the term, is *fully* instantiated only when each of these component terms is fully instantiated.

If one wishes to stress the empirical/historical importance,[8] or the practical/rational desirability, of sanctions, one may say, dramatically, that an unsanctioned set of laws is 'not really law'. If one wishes to stress the empirical/historical importance, or the practical/rational desirability of determinate legislative

---

[8] Remember, incidentally, that empirical or historical *importance* can. in the last analysis, only be measured by reference to the values or principles of practical reason: I.1, I.4.

and/or adjudicative institutions, one may say, dramatically, that a community without such institutions 'lacks a real legal system' or 'cannot really be said to have "a legal system"'. If one wishes to stress the empirical/historical importance, or the practical/rational desirability, of rules authorizing or regulating private or public change in the rules or their incidence, one may say, dramatically, that a set of rules which includes no such rules 'is not a legal system'. All these things have often been said, and can reasonably be said provided that one is seeking to draw attention to a feature of the central case of law and not to banish the other non-central cases to some other discipline.

I have by now sufficiently stressed that one would be simply misunderstanding my conception of the nature and purpose of explanatory definitions of theoretical concepts if one supposed that my definition 'ruled out as non-laws'[9] laws which failed to meet, or meet fully, one or other of the elements of the definition. But I should add that it would also be a misunderstanding to condemn the definition because 'it fails to explain correctly our ordinary concept of law which does allow for the possibility of laws of [an] objectionable kind'.[10] For not only does my definition 'allow for the possibility'; it also is not advanced with the intention of 'explaining correctly our [sc. the ordinary man's] ordinary concept of law'. For the truth is that the 'ordinary concept of law' (granting, but not admitting, that there is *one* such concept) is quite unfocused. It is a concept which allows 'us' to understand lawyers when they talk about sophisticated legal systems, and anthropologists when they talk about elementary legal systems, and tyrants and bandits when they talk about the orders and the customs of their Syndicate, and theologians and moralists ... There is no point in trying to explain a common-sense concept which takes its meanings from its very varied contexts and is well understood by everyone in those contexts. My purpose has not been to explain an unfocused 'ordinary concept' but to develop a concept for use in a theoretical explanation of a set of human actions, dispositions, interrelationships, and conceptions which (i) hang together as a set by virtue of their adaptation to a

---

[9] See Raz, *Practical Reason*, p. 164.
[10] Ibid.

specifiable set of human needs considered in the light of empirical features of the human condition, and (ii) are accordingly found in very varying forms and with varying degrees of suitability for, and deliberate or unconscious divergence from, those needs as the fully reasonable person would assess them. To repeat: the intention has been not to explain a concept, but to develop a concept which would explain the various phenomena referred to (in an unfocused way) by 'ordinary' talk about law—and explain them by showing how they answer (fully or partially) to the standing requirements of practical reasonableness relevant to this broad area of human concern and interaction.

The lawyer is likely to become impatient when he hears that social arrangements can be *more or less* legal, that legal systems and the rule of law exist as a matter of degree ... and so on. For the lawyer systematically strives to use language in such a way that from its use he can read off a definite solution to definite problems—in the final analysis, judgment for one party rather than the other in a litigable dispute. If cars are to be taxed at such and such a rate, one must be able, as a lawyer, to say (i.e. to rule) of every object that it simply is or is not a car: qualifications, 'in this respect ... but in that respect', *secundum quid*s, and the like are permissible in argument (and a good lawyer is well aware how open-textured and analogous in structure most terms and concepts are); but just as they do not appear in statutory formulae, so they cannot appear in the final pronouncement of law. And the lawyer, for the same good practical reasons, intrinsic to the enterprise of legal order as I have described it in this chapter, extends his technical use of language to the terms 'law', 'rule', 'legal', 'legal system' themselves. To make his point propositionally he will say that a purported law or rule is either valid or invalid. There are no intermediate categories (though there are intermediate states of affairs, e.g. voidable laws, which now are valid, or are treated as valid, or are deemed to be valid, but are liable to be rendered or treated as or deemed invalid). Equipped with this concept of validity, the lawyer aspires to be able to say of every rule that, being valid, it is a legal rule, or, being invalid, is not. The validity of a rule is identified with membership of the legal system (conceived as a set of valid rules), which thus can be considered legally as the set of all valid rules, including those rules which authorized the valid rule-originating acts of enactment and/or adjudication which are (in this conception) the necessary and sufficient conditions for the validity of the valid rules.

There is no need to question here the sufficiency of this set of concepts and postulates for the practical purposes of the lawyer—though questions could certainly be raised about the role of principles (which have no determinate origin and cannot without awkwardness be called valid) in legal argumentation. Rather it must be stressed that the set is a technical device for use within the framework of legal process, and in legal thought directed to arriving at solutions within that process. The device cannot be assumed to be applicable to the quite different problems of describing and explaining the role of legal process within the ordering of human life in society, and the place of legal thought in practical reason's effort to understand and effect real human good. It is a philosophical mistake to declare, in discourse of the latter kinds, that a social order or set of concepts must either be law or not be law, be legal or not legal.

For our purposes, physical, chemical, biological, and psychological laws are only metaphorically laws. To say this is not to question the legitimacy of the discourse of natural scientists, for whose purposes, conversely, what we call 'law strictly speaking' is only metaphorically a set of laws. The similarity between our central case and the laws of arts and crafts and applied sciences is greater; in each case we are considering the regulation of a performance by a self-regulating performer whose own notion of what he is up to affects the course of his performance. But the differences still are systematic and significant; as I said before (VII.7, X.1), ordering a society for the greater participation of its members in human values is not very like following a recipe for producing a definite product or a route to a definite goal. 'Natural law'—the set of principles of practical reasonableness in ordering human life and human community—is only analogically law, in relation to my present focal use of the term: that is why the term has been avoided in this chapter on Law, save in relation to past thinkers who used the term. These past thinkers, however, could, without loss of meaning, have spoken instead of 'natural right', 'intrinsic morality',

'natural reason, or right reason, in action', etc. But no synonyms
are available for 'law' in our focal sense.

X.7 DERIVATION OF 'POSITIVE' FROM 'NATURAL' LAW

'In every law positive well made is somewhat of the law of
reason ...; and to discern ... the law of reason from the law
positive is very hard. And though it be hard, yet it is much
necessary in every moral doctrine, and in all laws made for
the commonwealth.'[11] These words of the sixteenth-century
English lawyer Christopher St. German express the fundamental concern of any sound 'natural law theory' of law: to
understand the relationship(s) between the particular laws of
particular societies and the permanently relevant principles
of practical reasonableness.

Consider the law of murder. From the layman's point of view
this can be regarded as a directive not to intentionally kill (or
attempt to kill) any human being, unless in self-defence ... The
legal rule, conceived from this viewpoint, corresponds rather
closely to the requirement of practical reason, which would be
such a requirement whether or not repeated or supported by
the law of the land: that one is not to deliberately kill the
innocent (in the relevant sense of 'innocent'). Now this requirement is derived from the basic principle that human life is a
good, in combination with the seventh of the nine basic
requirements of practical reason (V.7). Hence Aquinas says that
this sort of law is derived from natural law by a process
analogous to deduction of demonstrative conclusions from
general principles; and that such laws are not positive law only,
but also have part of their 'force' from the natural law (i.e.
from the basic principles of practical reasonableness).[12] Hooker
calls such laws 'mixedly human', arguing that their matter or
normative content is the same as reason necessarily requires,
and that they simply ratify the law of reason, adding to it only
the additional constraining or binding force of the threat of

---

[11] *Doctor and Student*, I, c. 4. As St. German remarks, ibid. 1, c. 5, English lawyers
are not used to reasoning in terms of what is and is not a matter of 'the law of nature';
instead they frame their reasoning 'in that behalf' in terms of what is and is not 'against
reason' (i.e. unreasonable).

[12] *S.T.* I–II, q. 95, a. 2c.

punishment.[13] Now Aquinas's general idea here is fundamentally correct, but vaguely stated and seriously underdeveloped;
and Hooker's clarifications and developments are not in the
most interesting direction.

True, some parts of a legal system commonly do, and certainly should, consist of rules and principles closely corresponding to requirements of practical reason which themselves are
conclusions directly from the combination of a particular basic
value (e.g. life) with one or more of those nine basic
'methodological' requirements of practical reasonableness. Discussion in courts and amongst lawyers and legislators will
commonly, and reasonably, follow much the same course as a
straightforward moral debate such as philosophers or theologians, knowing nothing of that time and place, might carry
on. Moreover, the threat of sanctions is indeed, as Hooker
remarks,[14] an 'expedient' supplementation for the legislator to
annex to the moral rule, with an eye to the recalcitrant and
wayward in his own society.

But the process of receiving even such straightforward moral
precepts into the legal system deserves closer attention. Notice,
for example, that legislative draftsmen do *not* ordinarily draft
laws in the form imagined by Aquinas: 'There is not to be
killing'[15]—nor even 'Do not kill', or 'Killing is forbidden', or
'A person shall not [may not] kill'. Rather they will say 'It
shall be [or: is] an offence to ...' or 'Any person who kills ...
shall be guilty of an offence'. Indeed, it is quite possible to draft
an entire legal system without using normative vocabulary at
all. Now why does the professional draftsman prefer this indicative propositional form? At the deepest level it is because he
has in his mind's eye the pattern of a future social order, or
of some aspect of such an order, and is attempting to reproduce
that order (on the assumption, which need not be stated or
indicated grammatically because it is contextually self-evident,
that the participants are to, shall, must, may, etc., act con-
formably to the pattern). More particularly, a lawyer sees the

---

[13] Richard Hooker, *Of the Laws of Ecclesiastical Polity* (1594), Book I, c. 10, sec. 10.
[14] Ibid.
[15] *S. T.* I–II, q. 95, a. 2c: 'Derivantur ergo quaedam [leges] a principiis communibus
legis naturae per modum conclusionum: sicut hoc quod est *"non esse occidendum"*, ut
conclusio quaedam derivari potest ab eo quod est "nulli esse faciendum malum" ...'.

desired future social order from a professionally structured view-point, as a stylized and manageable drama. In this drama, many characters, situations, and actions known to common sense, sociology, and ethics are missing, while many other characters, relationships, and transactions known only or originally only to the lawyer are introduced. In the legally constructed version of social order there are not merely the 'reasonable' and 'unreasonable' acts which dominate the stage in an individual's practical reasoning; rather, an unreasonable act, for example of killing, may be a crime (and one of several procedurally significant classes of offence), and/or a tort, and/or an act which effects automatic vacation or suspension of office or forfeiture of property, and/or an act which insurers and/or public officials may properly take into account in avoiding a contract or suspending a licence ... etc. So it is the business of the draftsman to specify, precisely, into which of these costumes and relationships an act of killing-under-such-and-such-circumstances fits. That is why '*No one may* kill ...' is legally so defective a formulation.

Nor is all this of relevance only to professional lawyers. The existence of the legal rendering of social order makes a new train of practical reasoning possible, and necessary, for the law-abiding private citizen (see also XI.4). For example, the professionally drafted legislative provision, 'It is an offence to kill', contextually implies a normative direction to citizens. For there is a legal norm, so intrinsic to any legal ordering of community that it need never be enacted: criminal offences are not to be committed. Behind this norm the citizen need not go. Knowing the law of murder (at least in outline), he need not consider the value of life or the requirement of practical reason that basic values be respected in every action. So Hooker is mistaken in suggesting that what the positive law on murder adds to the permanent rule of reason is merely the punitive sanction. As part of the law of the land concerning offences, it adds also, and more interestingly, (i) a precise elaboration of many other legal (and therefore social) consequences of the act and (ii) a distinct new motive for the law-abiding citizen, who acts on the principle of avoiding legal offences as such, to abstain from the stipulated class of action.

Thus, in a well-developed legal system, the integration of

even an uncontroversial requirement of practical reasonableness into the law will not be a simple matter. The terms of the requirement *qua* requirement (e.g., in the case we were considering, the term 'intentionally') will have to be specified in language coherent with the language of other parts of the law. And then the part which the relevant acts are to play in the legal drama will have to be scripted—their role as, or in relation to, torts, contracts, testamentary dispositions, inheritances, tenures, benefits, matrimonial offences, proofs, immunities, licences, entitlements and forfeitures, offices and disqualifications, etc., etc.

Now very many of these legal implications and definitions will carry the legislator or judge beyond the point where he could regard himself as simply *applying* the intrinsic rule of reason, or even as deducing conclusions from it. Hence the legal project of *applying* a permanent requirement of practical reason will itself carry the legislator into the second of the two categories of human or positive law discerned by Aquinas and Hooker.

For, in Aquinas's view, the law consists in part of rules which are 'derived from natural law like conclusions deduced from general principles', and for the rest of rules which are 'derived from natural laws like implementations [*determinationes*] of general directives'.[16] This notion of *determinatio* he explains on the analogy of architecture (or any other practical art), in which a general idea or 'form' (say, 'house', 'door', 'door-knob') has to be made determinate as this particular house, door, door-knob, with specifications which are certainly derived from and shaped by the general idea but which could have been more or less different in many (even in every!) particular dimension and aspect, and which therefore require of the artificer a multitude of choices. The (making of the) artefact is controlled but not fully determined by the basic idea (say, the client's order), and until it is fully determinate the artefact is non-existent or incomplete. To count as a door in a human habitation, an object must be more than half a metre high and need not be more than 2·5 metres, but no door will be built at all

---

[16] *S.T.* I–II, q. 95, a. 2c. There seems to be no happy English equivalent of '*determinatio*': perhaps Kelsen's 'concretization' would do; 'implementation' is more elegant.

if the artificer cannot *make up his mind* on a particular height. Stressing, as it were, the artificer's virtually complete freedom in reason to choose say 2·2 rather than 2·1 or 2·3 metres, Aquinas says that laws of this second sort have their force '*wholly* from human law', and Hooker names his second category '*merely* human laws'.[17]

These last formulae, so strongly emphasizing the legislator's rational freedom of choice in such cases, can be misleading unless one bears in mind that they enunciate only a subordinate theorem within a general theory. The general theory is that, in Aquinas's words, '*every* law laid down by men has the character of law just in so far as it is derived from the natural law',[18] or in St. German's words, already quoted, 'in *every* law positive well made is somewhat of the law of reason'. The compatibility between this theory and the subordinate theorem can be best understood by reference to one or two concrete examples.

A first example is hackneyed, but simple and clear. Consider the rule of the road. There is a sense in which (as the subordinate theorem implies) the rule of the road gets 'all its force' from the authoritative custom, enactment, or other determination which laid it down. For until the stipulation 'drive on the left, and at less than 70 miles per hour' was posited by one of these means, there was no legal rule of the road; moreover, there was no need for the legislator to have a reason for choosing 'left' rather than 'right' or '70' rather than '65'. But there is also a sense in which (as the general theory claims) the rule of the road gets 'all its normative force' ultimately from the permanent principles of practical reason (which require us to respect our own and others' physical safety) in combination with non-posited facts such as that traffic is dangerous and can be made safer by orderly traffic flows and limitation of speed, that braking distances and human reaction times are such-and-such, etc.

A second example is richer. If material goods are to be used efficiently for human well-being (cf. V.6), there must normally be a regime of private property: VII.3. This regime will be

---

[17] I–II, a. 95, a. 2c: 'ea quae sunt secundi modi, ex sola lege humana vigorem habent'; Hooker, loc. cit.

[18] I–II, q. 95, a. 2c: 'omnis lex humanitus posita intantum habet de ratione legis inquantum a lege naturae derivatur'.

constituted by rules assigning property rights in such goods, or many of them, to individuals or small groups. But precisely what rules should be laid down in order to constitute such a regime is not settled ('determined') by this general requirement of justice. Reasonable choice of such rules is to some extent guided by the circumstances of a particular society, and to some extent 'arbitrary'. The rules adopted will thus for the most part be *determinationes* of the general requirement—derived from it but not entailed by it even in conjunction with a description of those particular circumstances: VII.4, 5, 7.

Moreover, in the vast area where the legislator is constructing *determinationes* rather than applying or ratifying determinate principles or rules of reason, there are relatively few points at which his choice can reasonably be regarded as 'unfettered' or 'arbitrary' (in the sense that it reasonably can be when one confronts two or more feasible alternatives which are in *all* respects equally satisfactory, or equally unsatisfactory, or in-commensurably satisfactory/unsatisfactory). The basic legal norms of a law-abiding citizen are 'Do not commit offences', 'abstain from torts', 'perform contracts', 'pay debts', 'discharge liabilities', 'fulfil obligations', etc.; and, taking these norms for granted without stating them, the lawmaker defines offences (from murder to road-traffic offences), torts, the formation, incidents, and discharge of contracts, etc., etc. But this task of definition (and re-definition in the changing conditions of society) has its own principles, which are not the citizen's. The reasonable legislator's principles include the desiderata of the Rule of Law (X.4). But they also include a multitude of other substantive principles related, some very closely, others more remotely, some invariably and others contingently, to the basic principles and methodological requirements of practical reason.

What are these basic norms for the legislator? Normally they are not the subject of direct and systematic enquiry by lawyers. But it should be recalled that 'legislator' here, for convenience (and at the expense of some significant differentiations), includes any judiciary that, like the judge at common law, enjoys a creative role. Now the principles that should guide the judge in his interpretation and application of both statutory and common or customary law to particular issues are the subject of scientific discussion by lawyers. *These* principles are almost all 'second-order', in that they concern the interpretation and application of other rules or principles whose existence they presuppose. They therefore are not directly the concern of legislators who have authority not merely to interpret and supplement but also to change and abolish existing rules and to introduce novel rules. Nevertheless, the second-order principles are themselves mostly crystallizations or versions (adapted to their second-order role) of 'first-order' principles which ought to guide even a 'sovereign legislature' in its acts of enactment. Moreover, a legislator who ignores a relevant first-order principle in his legislation is likely to find that his enactments are controlled, in their application by citizens, courts, and officials, by that principle in its second-order form, so that in the upshot the law on the particular subject will tend to turn out to be a *determinatio* of that principle (amongst others).

Many of the second-order principles or maxims employed by lawyers express the desirability of stability and predictability in the relations between one person and another, and between persons and things. Such maxims[19] are obviously connected very closely not only with the formal features of law (X.3) and the desiderata of the Rule of Law (X.4), but also with the willingness of lawyers and indeed of men in society in every age to attribute authoritative force to usage, practice, custom (IX.3). And there is a corresponding first-order principle or set of principles to which any legislator ought to give considerable weight—that those human goods which are the fragile and cumulative achievements of past effort, investment, discipline, etc. are not to be treated lightly in the pursuit of future goods. More prosaically, the tangible expenses and waste of dislocative change are to be taken fully into account—the legislative choice between 'drive on the left' and 'drive on the right' is a matter of indifference in the abstract, but not in a society where by informal convention people already tend to drive on the left, and have adjusted their habits, their vehicle construction, road design, and street furniture accordingly.

[19] For example: 'qui prior est in tempore, potior est in jure, in aequali jure'; 'ex diuturnitate temporis omnia praesumuntur solenniter esse acta'; 'communis error facit jus' ('multitudo errantium tollit peccatum'; 'consensus tollit errores'); 'interest reipublicae res judicatas non rescindi'; 'ut res magis valeat quam pereat' ...

Starting with these second-order maxims favouring continuity in human affairs—i.e. favouring the good of diachronic order, as distinct from the good of a future end-state—we can trace a series of related second-order principles which include the principle of stability but more and more go beyond it to incorporate new principles or values. In each case these are available in first-order form to guide a legislator. Prose-form requires a linear exposition here which oversimplifies and disguises their interrelations: (i) compulsory acquisition of property rights to be compensated, in respect of *damnum emergens* (actual losses) if not of *lucrum cessans* (loss of expected profits), (ii) no liability for unintentional injury, without fault; (iii) no criminal liability without *mens rea*; (iv) estoppel (*nemo contra factum proprium venire potest*); (v) no judicial aid to one who pleads his own wrong (he who seeks equity must do equity); (vi) no aid to abuse of rights; (vii) fraud unravels everything; (viii) profits received without justification and at the expense of another must be restored; (ix) *pacta sunt servanda* (contracts are to be performed); (x) relative freedom to change existing patterns of legal relationships by agreement; (xi) in assessments of the legal effects of purported acts-in-the-law, the weak to be protected against their weaknesses; (xii) disputes not to be resolved without giving both sides an opportunity to be heard; (xiii) no one to be allowed to judge his own cause.

These 'general principles of law' are indeed principles. That is to say, they justify, rather than require, particular rules and determinations, and are qualified in their application to particular circumstances by other like principles. Moreover, any of them may on occasion be outweighed and overridden (which is not the same as violated, amended, or repealed) by other important components of the common good, other principles of justice. Nor is it to be forgotten that there are norms of justice that may never be overridden or outweighed, corresponding to the absolute rights of man (VIII.7). Still, the general principles of law which have been recited here do operate, over vast ranges of legislative *determinationes*, to modify the pursuit of particular social goods. And this modification need not be simply a matter of abstaining from certain courses of conduct: the principles which require compensation, or ascertainment of *mens rea*, or 'natural justice' . . . can be adequately met only by the positive creation of complex administrative and judicial structures.

In sum: the derivation of law from the basic principles of practical reasoning has indeed the two principal modes identified and named by Aquinas; but these are not two streams flowing in separate channels. The central principle of the law of murder, of theft, of marriage, of contract ... may be a straightforward application of universally valid requirements of reasonableness, but the effort to integrate these subject-matters into the Rule of Law will require of judge and legislator countless elaborations which in most instances partake of the second mode of derivation. This second mode, the sheer *determinatio* by more or less free authoritative choice, is itself not only linked with the basic principles by intelligible relationship to goals (such as traffic safety ...) which are directly related to basic human goods, but also is controlled by wide-ranging formal and other structuring principles (in both first- and second-order form) which themselves are derived from the basic principles by the first mode of derivation.[20]

In the preceding chapter (IX.1) I said that a principal source of the need for authority is the luxuriant variety of appropriate but competing choices of 'means' to 'end'. Now we can see how this range of choices is both increased *and* controlled by the complex of interacting 'principles of law'. True, the reasoning of those in authority frequently ends without identifying any uniquely reasonable decision; so the rulers must choose, and their choice (*determinatio*) determines what thereafter is uniquely just for those subject to their authority. But, having stressed that it is thus authority, not simply reasoning, that settles most practical questions in the life of a community, I now must stress the necessary rider. To be, itself, authoritative in the eyes of a reasonable man, a *determinatio* must be consistent with the basic requirements of practical reasonableness, though it need not necessarily or even usually be the *determinatio* he would himself have made had he had the opportunity; it need

[20] Hence the standing possibility of a jurisprudence which would disclose the 'jural postulates' of a particular legal system and trace their diverse relationships with universal rational requirements—the kind of jurisprudence adumbrated and practised by Sir William Jones, the first great English comparative lawyer, but eclipsed by the Benthamite misunderstanding of practical reason. See, e.g., Jones's *Essay on the Law of Bailments* (1781).

not even be one he would regard as 'sensible'. Our jurisprudence therefore needs to be completed by a closer analysis of this authoritativeness or 'binding force' of positive law (XI), and by some consideration of the significance of wrongful exercises of authority (XII).

It may, however, be helpful to conclude the present discussion by reverting to the textbook categories, '[positive] law', 'sources of law', 'morality'. The tradition of 'natural law' theorizing is not characterized by any particular answer to the questions: 'Is every "settled" legal rule and legal solution settled by appeal exclusively to "positive" sources such as statute, precedent, and custom? Or is the "correctness" of some judicial decisions determinable only by appeal to some "moral" ("extra-legal") norm? And are the boundaries between the settled and the unsettled law, or between the correct, the eligible, and the incorrect judicial decision determinable by reference only to positive sources or legal rules?' The tradition of natural law theorizing is not concerned to minimize the range and determinacy of positive law or the general sufficiency of positive sources as solvents of legal problems.

Rather, the concern of the tradition, as of this chapter, has been to show that the act of 'positing' law (whether judicially or legislatively or otherwise) is an act which can and should be guided by 'moral' principles and rules; that those moral norms are a matter of objective reasonableness, not of whim, convention, or mere 'decision'; and that those same moral norms justify (a) the very institution of positive law, (b) the main institutions, techniques, and modalities within that tradition (e.g. separation of powers), and (c) the main institutions regulated and sustained by law (e.g. government, contract, property, marriage, and criminal liability). What truly characterizes the tradition is that it is not content merely to observe the historical or sociological fact that 'morality' thus affects 'law', but instead seeks to determine what the requirements of practical reasonableness really are, so as to afford a rational basis for the activities of legislators, judges, and citizens.

NOTES

X.1

Aristotle on the dual operation of law and the need for coercion ... 'law [*nomos*] is a rule [*logos*], emanating from a certain practical reasonableness [*phronesis*] and intelligence [*nous*] and having compulsory force [*anagkastike dynamis*]': *Nic. Eth.* X, 9: 1180a21–22; for the whole discussion of the dual operation of law (i.e. in relation to the reasonable citizen and to the unreasonable), see 1179b30–1180b28. The medievals translated *anagkastike* in 1180a22 as *coactiva* (coercive) (cf. above, IX.5 and note).

'Conscientious objection' not a 'principle', or generally valid ground for exemption from law ... See note to V.9, above. A pungent brief discussion is Eric Voegelin, 'The Oxford Political Philosophers' (1953) 3 *Philosophical Q.* 97 at pp. 102–7. But when conscientious objection witnesses to basic values such as life or religion and is not radically incompatible with the genuine common good it may be tolerated notwithstanding the conscientious judgment of the rulers that the law objected to is really necessary. See e.g. Vatican Council II, *Gaudium et Spes* (1965), 79; *Dignitatis Humanae* (1965) 3, 7.

Punishment as the restoration of fairness ... See Finnis, 'The Restoration of Retribution' (1972) 32 *Analysis* 132; Paul C. Weiler, 'The Reform of Punishment', in Law Reform Commission of Canada, *Studies on Sentencing* (Ottawa: 1974); Herbert Morris, *On Guilt and Innocence* (Berkeley: 1976), pp. 32–6.

There is no 'natural' measure of due punishment ... This proposition is for Aquinas the classic illustration of his wider thesis that much just law is *not a conclusion* from principles of reason (natural law): see *S.T.* I–II, q. 95, a. 2c, following the hint given by Aristotle, *Nic. Eth.* V, 7: 1134b22–23 (quoted in note to X.7, below).

Compulsory measures of 'reformative treatment' ... Note that what is said in the text about reform applies to the 'free-willing' criminals who are the subject of the whole discussion of punishment in X.1. Many discussions, and measures, of reform are directed, in fact, towards offenders considered (sometimes *a priori*, sometimes not) to be immature, mentally ill, etc.—i.e. considered not to be 'criminals' in the sense I intend.

X.3

Weber on the 'legal' type of Herrschaft ... See Weber, *On Law* pp. 8–9, 336, xxxi–xxxii. On bureaucracy, the legal character of its internal order, and the bureaucrat's sense of duty, see ibid., pp. 1, 3; Weber, *The Theory of Social and Economic Organization* (ed. T. Parsons), pp. 328–36. For an excellent instance of Weber's working use of 'legal', 'rational', and 'bureaucratic', see *From Max Weber: Essays in Sociology* (ed. H. H. Gerth and C. W. Mills, London: 1948), pp. 298–9.

'Law regulates its own creation' ... For this most concentrated formulation of his jurisprudence, see Kelsen, *General Theory*, pp. 126, 132, 198, 354, 124.

What has been validly enacted (or transacted) remains valid until ... For the significance and source of this fundamental legal postulate, see Finnis, 'Revolutions and Continuity of Law' in *Oxford Essays II*, 44 at pp. 63–5, 76.

Law regulates the conditions under which individuals can modify the incidence or application of rules ... Here we touch on an interesting difference between contemporary analytical jurisprudence and its classical/medieval forerunners. In modern jurisprudence, e.g. Hart, *Concept of Law*, the law 'confers powers' upon citizens, e.g. to contract, to lease, to marry, etc., etc., and this is one of the fundamental 'functions' of the law. This manner of speaking, which is appropriate in a rigorously intra-systemic context, is quite novel. In Suarez (e.g. *De Legibus*, I, c. 17; III, c. 33, para. 1; V, cc. 19–34) or Hale (e.g. *On Hobbes' Dialogue of the Common Law* [*c*.1670], in Holdsworth, *History of English Law*, vol. V, pp. 507–8) there is certainly a recognition that the law 'does' more than merely command, forbid, permit, and punish (as the Roman lawyers (see *Digest* I, 3, 7 (Papinian)) and Aquinas (*S.T.* I–II, q. 92, a. 2) supposed); but the further 'effect' or 'force' of law is not 'power conferring' but rather 'laying down a definite form for contracts and similar acts-in-the-law, so that an act performed in other form may be treated as not valid' (*De Legibus*, III, 33, 1). In this perspective, a man can marry, buy, sell, promise, lend, etc., etc., without having any power to do so conferred on him by law, but the law may, for good reasons, *nullify* his acts (*lex irritans*). This perspective (in which the law has a moulding, *subsidiary* function) seems more appropriate to an analysis of the role of law within the wider context of human life and practical reason in society; it is revived in, e.g., Jonathan Cohen, 'Critical Notice of Hart's *The Concept of Law*' (1962) 71 *Mind* 395, and J. R. Lucas, 'The Phenomenon of Law' in *Essays* 85 at p. 91; see also A. M. Honoré, 'Real Laws', ibid. 99 at pp. 106–7.

The postulate of gaplessness of legal systems ... This is of course a lawyer's desideratum rather than a plain fact; as a description of the range and coverage of settled rules it is a fiction, but as a postulate of method it is central to legal thought. Formally it is secured by 'closing rules' such as 'whatever is not prohibited is permitted'; in legal process it is secured by the principle concerning *non liquet*, i.e. by the rule that a court cannot decline jurisdiction to settle a controversy on the ground that there is no law covering the matter in dispute. See generally J. Stone, *Legal System and Lawyers' Reasonings* (London: 1964), pp. 188–92.

X.4

The Rule of Law ... See Raz, 'The Rule of Law and its Virtue' (1977) 93 *L.Q.R.* 195; Fuller, *Morality of Law*, chs. II and VI; J. R. Lucas, *The Principles of Politics* (Oxford: 1966), secs. 24–31; Rawls, *Theory of Justice*, pp. 235–43; Alexander Solzhenitsyn, *The Gulag Archipelago*, Part VII (1976), ch. 3 ('The Law Today').

Desirability of reciprocity between ruler and ruled ... This principle is exploited but misconstrued by social contract theories. See e.g. Cicero, *De Legibus*, II, v, 11, reporting an argumentation, standard in his time, that the first lawgivers convinced their people that it was their intention to enact such rules as would make possible an honourable and happy life for them; so that 'those who formulated wicked and unjust commands, *thereby breaking their promises [polliciti] and agreements [professi]*, put into effect anything but "laws"'. Locke's use of the notion is very well known: *Second Treatise of Government*, e.g. sec. 134; see also Blackstone, I *Comm.*, 47–8. Less well known is Aquinas's cautious reference to the origins of the civil community in 'something like a kind of pact between king and people: *quasi quoddam pactum inter regem et populum*': see his *Commentary on the Epistle to the Romans*, 13, lect. 1 (para. 1041). See also the remarks of the sociologist Georg Simmel cited by Fuller, *Morality of Law*, pp. 217, 39.

X.5

Fuller and his critics on law and tyrannical wickedness ... See Fuller, *Morality of Law*, p. 154, appearing to assert that 'history does [not] in fact afford significant examples of regimes that have combined a faithful adherence to the internal morality of law [sc. the eight desiderata] with a brutal indifference to justice and human welfare.' Hart, in his review of Fuller's book, (1965) 78 *Harv. L. Rev.* 1281 at 1287–8, identifies and (rightly) attacks a special argument that the desideratum of clarity is incompatible with evil aims, but sees no further issue than 'the varying popularity and strength of governments'.

Rule of Law not a neutral tool of managerial direction ... See Fuller's useful clarifications in his 'A reply to critics', ch. 5 of the revised edition of *Morality of Law*, especially pp. 210, 214, and 216 n. The comparison of the Rule of Law with a sharp knife is to be found in Joseph Raz, 'The Rule of Law and its Virtue' (1977) 93 *L.Q.R.* 195 at 208; in other respects the article is a valuable study of the content and point of the Rule of Law.

'Social engineering' and 'social control' ... These misleading notions of the nature of law have been popularized by Roscoe Pound, e.g. *Social Control through Law* (New Haven: 1942). They are directly linked with that form of utilitarianism (associated with William James and Bertrand Russell: see note to V.7) which (in the spirit of John Rawls's 'thin theory of the good') maintains that every desire of every person is in itself equally worthy of being satisfied, so that, in Pound's words, op. cit., pp. 64–5, 'there is, as one might say, a great task of social engineering ... of making the goods of existence, the means of satisfying the demands and desires of men being together in a politically organised society, if they cannot satisfy all the claims that men make upon them, at least go round as far as possible'. Or again, '... we come to an idea of a maximum satisfaction of human wants or expectations. What we have to do in social control, and so in law, is to reconcile and adjust these desires or wants or expectations, so far as we can, so as to secure as much of the totality of them as we can': Pound, *Justice According to Law* (New Haven and London: 1951), p. 31; see also Pound, *Jurisprudence* (St. Paul, Minn.: 1959), vol. III, p. 334; and see J. Stone, *Human Law and Human Justice* (London: 1965), ch. 9. For a critique of this pure utilitarianism, see V.7, above.

Plato on abuse of legality ... See *Statesman*, 291a–303d; for accurate interpretation see Eric Voegelin, *Plato and Aristotle* (Baton Rouge: 1957), pp. 158–66.

Illegal acts for the sake of the values of legality ... For a partial formulation of this principle in the language of one polity see A. V. Dicey, *Introduction to the Study of the Law of the Constitution* (1908; 10th ed., London: 1959), p. 412: 'There are times of tumult or invasion when for the sake of legality itself the rules of law must be broken. The course which the government must then take is clear. The Ministry must break the law and trust for protection to an Act of Indemnity'. See also Blackstone's reference, I *Comm.* 250–1, to 'those *extraordinary* recourses to first principles, which are necessary when the contracts of society are in danger of dissolution, and the law proves too weak a defence against the violence of fraud and oppression ... [It is] impossible, in any practical system of laws, to point out beforehand those eccentrical remedies, which the sudden emergence of national distress may dictate, and which that alone can justify.' See also David and Brierley, *Major Legal Systems in the World Today* (London: 1968), p. 117: 'According to the court of Constitutional Justice of the German Federal Republic, one can imagine extreme circumstances in which the *idea* of law itself should prevail over positive constitutional law; the ... Court ... might then be led to appraise such "unconstitutionality".' See also Eric Voegelin, *Plato and Aristotle* (Baton Rouge: 1957), p. 161; *The New Science of Politics* (Chicago: 1952), p. 144.

'A constitution is not a suicide pact' ... 'No one could conceive that it is not within the power of Congress to prohibit acts intended to overthrow the Government by force

and violence': *Dennis* v. *United States* (1951) 341 U.S. 494 at 501 (and certainly neither the dissentient Justices nor later decisions suggest such a conception). In reaching, in the same year, a very different decision about the constitutionality of proscribing a revolutionary party, the High Court of Australia nevertheless affirmed the existence of an inherent self-protecting legislative power, arising 'on an essential and inescapable implication which must be involved in the legal constitution of any polity': *Australian Communist Party* v. *Commonwealth* (1951) 83 *C.L.R.* 1 at 260, also 187–8, 193.

X.6

The focal meaning of 'law' ... With the focal meaning of 'law' gradually constructed, and employed and identified, in this chapter, compare the 'definition of law' (*definitio legis*) offered by Aquinas, *S.T.* I–II, q. 90, a. 4c: 'quaedam ordinatio rationis ad bonum commune, ab eo qui curam communitatis habet, promulgata: a certain ordinance of reason, directed to the common good, promulgated by him who has the care of the community'.

Lawyers tend to regard legality in 'either–or', 'black-and-white' terms ... Fuller notices this, *Morality of Law*, p. 199, but fails to connect it with the very features of the legal enterprise which he himself underlines.

Laws of nature, studied by natural sciences, are for us only metaphorically laws ... See Suarez, *De Legibus*, I, c. i., para. 2 'non proprie sed per metaphoram'. Rules of art, he continues, are laws only *secundum quid* (para. 5). Finally, 'although iniquitous precepts or rules customarily go by the name of law ... none the less, speaking strictly and without qualification [*proprie et simpliciter loquendo*], only a rule which is a criterion of moral rectitude (in other words, a morally right and proper rule) can be called law ... For an unjust law is not a criterion of the rectitude of human conduct ... Therefore, it is not law, but partakes of the name of law by a kind of analogy [*per quandam analogiam*] in so far as it does prescribe a certain mode of action in relation to a given end' (para. 6). See XII.4, below.

Natural law is only analogically law, for our purposes ... For a stimulating argument (not in every respect beyond cavil) that in the Thomist analysis of law, natural law is law only by analogy of attribution (that is, by a loose form of analogy, not the strict analogy of proportionality) to the primary analogate which is human positive law, see Mortimer J. Adler, 'A Question about Law' in R. E. Brennan (ed.), *Essays in Thomism* (New York: 1942), pp. 207–36.

Law that is defective in rationality is law only in a watered-down sense ... This proposition is not offered as immediately applicable in a court of law (or other intra-systemic context); nor does it entail that a court or a citizen ought not to comply with such a law: see XII.3, and Aquinas, *S.T.* I–II, q. 96, a. 4c. The proposition is, however, offered as philosophically inevitable in any reflection upon law which seeks to answer questions about the place of law and legal system in man's effort to extend intelligence into action.

X.7

Positive law is derived from natural law in two ways ... Aquinas discovers this analysis in Aristotle, *Nic. Eth.* V, 7, 1134b18–24, Aristotle's principal discussion of *physikon dikaion* (natural right): see *in Eth.* Book V, lect. 12 (nn. 1016–23). In both Aristotle (loc. cit.) and 'Cicero' (*Rhetoric*, II, 14; 16; 19) Aquinas finds the important notion that (human, positive) law *includes* natural law (as well as many elements that are not of natural law, but are consistent with it and intelligibly, but *not* deductively, derived from it). Aristotle's distinction, in *Rhetoric*, I, 13: 1373b3–8, between particular law (written or unwritten) and universal natural law, is much less subtle and serviceable.

Legal systems can be promulgated without normative vocabulary ... For reflections on this, see A. M. Honoré, 'Real Laws' in *Essays*, 99 at pp. 117–18. Because the citizen/subject, the legislator, and the judge, all have different practical perspectives, there is no reason to take sides, or to adjudicate, in the debate about whether there is or is not a canonical form of legal rule, or a single method of individuating the units of meaning of which any 'legal system' is composed.

The legal drama ... For use of this figure, see Honoré, op. cit., p. 112; cf. Honoré, *Tribonian* (London: 1978), p. 36 ('the esoteric legal universe, neither natural nor supernatural'); also M. Villey, 'Le droit subjectif et les systèmes juridiques romains' [1946] *Rev. Historique de Droit* 201, 207, explaining the Roman lawyers' categorization of the objects of legal science as *personae, res,* and *actiones.*

'First-order' and 'second-order' principles ... For a lucid discussion of legal principles, employing this distinction, see Genaro R. Carrió, *Legal Principles and Legal Positivism* (Buenos Aires: 1971). Speaking historically, or sociologically, the principles discussed in the text exist mainly in the form of judicial customs; but very many of them are of such intrinsic or inevitable appropriateness for human life in society that judges do not need to demonstrate the existence of such a custom and can appeal, fully reasonably, to that appropriateness as the sufficient basis of their applicability in judicial reasoning.

The relation of determinationes *to natural law* ... See *S.T.* I–II, q. 95, a. 2c; q. 99, a. 3 ad 2; q. 100, a. 3 ad 2.

Do many laws relate to matters 'indifferent in themselves'? ... Aristotle launched the notion that *determinationes* relate to matters indifferent in themselves, in his set piece on natural right: *Nic. Eth.* V, 7: 1134b18–24: 'Political right is of two kinds, one natural, the other conventional [*nomikon*]. Natural right has the same validity everywhere, and does not depend on our accepting it or not. Conventional right is *that which in principle may be settled in one way or the other indifferently* [*diapherei*], though having once been settled it is not indifferent: e.g. that the ransom of a prisoner shall be a mina, that a sacrifice shall consist of a goat and not of two sheep ... [1135a1] Right based on convention and expediency is like standard measures—measures for corn and wine are not the same everywhere, but are larger in wholesale and smaller in retail markets ...' The notion of *adiaphora*, 'things naturally indifferent', became, via the Stoics, a scholastic commonplace; it was extensively used by Blackstone (see also Locke, *Two Tracts on Government* (*c.*1660/1; ed. P. Abrams, Cambridge: 1967). It is important to notice that the problem is much more complex than the simple Aristotelian and scholastic terminology suggests. For example, in Blackstone's *Commentaries* the category of 'things indifferent in themselves' shifts its meaning uneasily between (i) matters so 'indifferent' that legislation on them is unjustified (e.g. I, p. 126); (ii) matters so 'indifferent' that a legislator should be content with either performance or payment of penalty (e.g. I, p. 58) (for this 'purely penal law' theory, see XI.6, below); (iii) matters 'indifferent' in that, though of considerable moment in a given society, they are not of moment in all conceivable societies (e.g. I, p. 299); and (iv) matters 'indifferent' only in the sense that, though of great moment to social living, they would not be of great moment in the 'state of nature' which Blackstone (departing altogether, with Locke, from the Aristotelian and high scholastic tradition) postulates (e.g. I, p. 55). Moreover, Blackstone makes it clear that the matters in categories (iii) and (iv) include matters the regulation of which is of great moment, but which could be regulated in a variety of alternative but more or less equally reasonable ways (e.g. property to descend on intestacy to the eldest rather than the youngest son). (See further Finnis, 'Blackstone's Theoretical Intentions' (1967) 12 *Nat. L. F.* 163 at 172–4, 181.) Parallel distinctions can be found in Stoic writings: see Diogenes Laertius, *Lives of Eminent Philosophers* [*c.*225?], VII, 104–6 (Zeno).

'*Basic norms for the law-abiding citizen*' ... See A. M. Honoré, 'Real Laws', in *Essays*, at p. 118.

Creative role of judges ... To refer to this is not to dispute A. W. B. Simpson's pertinent observations, in 'The Common Law and Legal Theory,' *Oxford Essays II*, pp. 85, 86, that 'the production of [judicial] authority that this or that is the law is not the same as the identification of acts of legislation ... [Judges'] actions create precedents, but creating a precedent is not the same thing as laying down the law ... [T]o express an authoritative opinion is not the same thing as to legislate.'

'*General Principles of Law*' ... The thirteen principles listed in the text are evidenced in recent research: see the sources cited in R. P. Dhokalia, *The Codification of Public International Law* (Manchester: 1970), pp. 344–50. They are not themselves first principles of practical reason, and some of them contain elements contingent upon the existence of certain social institutions (e.g. courts). But they are so closely related to the first principles in combination with the basic methodological requirements of practical reasoning that they should be regarded as derivable *by reasoning* from natural law and thus, in a sense, a part of the natural law. At the same time, they are essentially principles for systems of positive law, and are in fact to be found in virtually all such systems. Hence they are the (or part of the) *jus gentium* in the sense explained (not without obscurity) by Aquinas, *S.T.* I–II, q. 95, a. 4c and ad 1; II–II, q. 57, a. 3; *in Eth.* V, lect. 12, no. 1019. The essence of Aquinas's concept of *jus gentium* is that the principles of *jus gentium* are part of the natural law by their mode of derivation (by deduction, not *determinatio*), and at the same time part of positive human law by their mode of promulgation. Aquinas's own examples of *deduced* principles of natural law (i.e. of *jus gentium*) may be found in *S.T.* I–II, q. 100, a. 1; a. 7 ad 1.

Analytical jurisprudence in Jones and Bentham ... Sir William Jones, *Essay on the Law of Bailments* (1781) has three parts, styled 'analytical', 'historical', and 'synthetical'. For Jones, to treat a set of rules *analytically* is to trace 'every part of it up to the first principles of natural reason' (p. 4); to treat it historically is to show the extent to which various legal systems conform to these first principles; and to treat it synthetically is to restate the law by way of (*a*) definitions, (*b*) rules, (*c*) propositions derived from the combination of (*b*) with (*a*), and (*d*) exceptions to the propositions (p. 127). The definitions are to derive principally from the experience and complexity of English law (i.e. of the legal system under particular study), while the rules 'may be considered as axioms flowing from natural reason, good morals and sound policy' (p. 119) as verified against the vast comparative learning of the 'historical' survey (pp. 11–116). With all this compare the programme announced five years earlier by Bentham in his *Fragment on Government* (1776), more or less closely followed thereafter by analytical jurisprudence: 'To the province of the *Expositor* it belongs to explain to us what, as he supposes, the Law *is*: to that of the *Censor*, to observe to us what he thinks it *ought to be*. The former, therefore, is principally occupied in stating, or in enquiring after *facts*: the latter, in discussing *reasons*. The *Expositor*, keeping within his sphere, has no concern with any other faculties of the mind than the *apprehension*, the *memory*, and the *judgment*: the latter, in virtue of those sentiments of pleasure or displeasure which he finds occasion to annex to the objects under his review, holds some intercourse with the affections' (Montague ed., Oxford: 1891, pp. 98–9; Bentham's italics). (Somewhat inconsistently, Bentham introduced, at pp. 117–22, the notion that an expositor could not properly, i.e. 'naturally', carry out his work of arrangement without first establishing a complete 'synopsis' or 'map' of the legal system, indeed for all legal systems, in terms of the tendency of actions to produce pain or pleasure. But this suggestion, not surprisingly, was not followed up extensively by Bentham —though cf. his *An Introduction to the Principles of Morals and Legislation* (1789; ed. J. Burns and H. L. A. Hart, London: 1970, pp. 5, 270–4)—and died with him.)

XI

OBLIGATION

XI.1 'OBLIGATION', 'OUGHT', AND RATIONAL NECESSITY

DISCUSSION of obligation is burdened by the cultural particularity of the word 'obligation'. Philosophers and moralists find the grammatical substantive form 'obligation' convenient for signifying a wide range of notions: that there are things, within our power either to do or not to do, which (whatever we desire) we *have* to do (but not because we are forced to), or *must* do, which it is our *duty to* do, which it is *wrong not to* do, or *shameful not to*, which one *morally* (or *legally*) *ought to* do, which (in Latin) *oportet facere* or (in French) *il faut faire*, one's *devoir* in French, *to deon* in the Greek of Aristotle and Euripides, *swanelo* among the Barotse of southern Africa (VIII.3). And the philosopher's decision to comprehend all these expressions or notions under 'obligation' does not seem unjustified: they all seem to relate to what can be experienced as a demand of conscience, a claim upon one's commitment, decision, action. Or again (since those experiences are characteristically related to the process of responsible rational assessment and practical judgment), all those expressions and notions may be related to some form or forms of rational necessity. The purpose of this chapter is to explore some of these forms of rational necessity, these (derivative) *requirements* of practical reasonableness.

On the other hand, the word 'obligation' etymologically relates particularly to the 'binding force' (*ligare*, to bind) of promissory or quasi-promissory commitments. And in several modern languages, as in English, obligations to other persons, deriving from particular roles, arrangements, or relationships, remain the central cases signified by the word. It thus becomes possible to say that there are things one ought to do which one has no obligation to do (since no one has a right to demand their performance). This serves as a warning that within the class of *rational necessity* we should expect to find significant sub-classes connected with a particular range of problems, those of justice and rights (other-directedness, owing, equality ... : VII.1). At the same time, we need not reserve the word 'obligation' exclusively to that particular range of problems. For the basic principles and requirements of practical reason-ableness which, as we have seen, underlie our response to those problems, are certainly wide enough to make good sense of the moralist's question: Has a man, irretrievably marooned alone on an island, an obligation not to drink (etc.) himself to death?

For the purposes of this book we need not tackle that particular moral question. Nor, incidentally, need we be con-cerned with the important moral distinctions between the obligatory and the meritorious or supererogatory, or between the excusable and the forbidden. At the same time we must set aside as spurious the categorizations of a textbook tradition which divides all moral thought between 'deontological ethics of obligation' and 'teleological ethics of happiness or value'. Finally, observe that I will not here deal with logical and grammatical refinements such as whether 'obligation' refers primarily to the act required or primarily to the relationship between the person-subject and the act required of him.

This said, it will be convenient to start the analysis by discussing that form of obligation with which the word has a particular affinity, and with which theorists of political (and therefore legal) obligation have often been peculiarly con-cerned: promissory obligation. To what extent, and why, do promises bind?

XI.2   PROMISSORY OBLIGATION

First, what is a promise or undertaking? Being a human practice, engaged in and maintained for diverse practical purposes, promising has its central cases (its focal meaning) and its secondary or borderline cases. Centrally, then, a promise is constituted if and only if (i) A communicates to B his intention to undertake, by that very act of communication (in conjunc-tion with B's acceptance of it), an obligation to perform a certain action (or to see to it that certain actions are performed), and (ii) B accepts this undertaking in the interests of himself, or of A or of some third party, C. In other words, the giving of a promise is the making of a sign,[1] a sign which signifies the creation of an obligation, and which is knowingly made with the intention of being taken as creative of such obligation. It is this that makes the giving of a promise distinct from the expression of an intention to perform an action—which is not to deny that there are circumstances in which the expression of an intention to perform an action, particularly when one is aware that one's addressee may rely on one, will create an obligation to perform it: only, *this* form of obligation is not strictly promissory (but rather, perhaps, an extended form of estoppel).

This definition of promising takes a stand on some issues controverted amongst philosophers (e.g. whether promises are complete and binding without acceptance, but can always be released from by their addressee). But it leaves aside many other controverted questions (e.g. as to the circumstances under which what would otherwise amount to a binding promise either fails to constitute a promise—say, because of fraud, mistake, or duress—or fails to bind—say, because it is to do an intrinsically wrongful deed). Moreover, it leaves aside borderline cases, upon which a mature law of contract must take a stand. Indeed, my definition is both wider and narrower than typically modern notions of legally binding contracts. For example, it includes no requirement of consideration, or of communication of acceptance by B to A. And on the other hand, a promise as defined above will not be constituted in circumstances where a legal contract is—for by getting on to a bus one concludes, whether or not one knows or intends it, a legally binding contract of carriage for reward and incurs in law the contractual obligation to pay; but one does not *promise* or *undertake* to pay. The informal human practice or institution of promising, not the law of contract, is my present concern.

The striking thing about promises is that their obligation is taken to be created by, or at any rate to arise upon, an intentional reference (express or implied) to that obligation. An expression signifying the undertaking of an obligation brings about (or at any rate tends to bring about) that obligation. But there

---

[1] In special circumstances, remaining silent can be significant and amount to a sign.

is no obligation-creating *magic* in uttering a sign signifying the creation of obligation. How, then, do promises bind?

A first level of explanation penetrates below the linguistic phenomena of signs and expressions of obligation, and points to the complex practice in which promissory undertakings are rooted. In this practice, expressions of obligation are not merely offered or given, they are accepted as such by other persons; subsequently and consequently, demands for corresponding performance are made, with express or tacit reference back to the prior giving of the promissory signs; criticism and reproach for non-performance, and threats and pressures, all likewise refer back to the undertaking given, as do self-criticism, apologies, demands for and offers of amends or compensation or restitution or recovery of losses and/or anticipated profits, etc. To give those linguistic signs that do amount to a promise (signs which may of course be very various in form and implicit in expression) is precisely to communicate a willingness to enter into and go along with that whole practice, i.e. by performing one's undertakings or at least by acknowledging the propriety of demands for performance, compensation, etc. It need not, incidentally, be assumed that there is only one 'promising' practice in any given community; there can indeed be many, containing the same basic elements in varying forms, some wider, some narrower, some more relaxed, others more stringent. Moreover, such practices can have a datable beginning. But it remains true, I think, that if someone utters a sign signifying the undertaking of an obligation, in a context in which no one is inclined to criticize him, etc., for non-performance, it seems odd to say that he *has* an obligation.[2]

Because it thus explains how some expressions purporting to signify the undertaking of an obligation do not bring into being any such obligation, while other, perhaps quite similar, expressions do (by virtue of their place in an interpersonal practice that involves more than merely linguistic signs), this first-level explanation has some explanatory power. An analysis which yields the conclusion that one is under a promissory obligation if and only if there is a social practice according to which one's expression of an undertaking is taken as justifying demands and

---

[2] Unilateral vows and oaths require a special analysis, not undertaken here.

pressure for performance, criticisms of non-performance, etc., is not a negligible analysis. But it fails to capture the significance or 'meaning' of promissory obligation, for it fails to give an account of the role of the notion of obligation in the practical reasonings both of the person under that obligation and of those other persons who take his being under an obligation as giving good (justifying) reason for their demands, pressure, criticisms, etc. This failure is readily brought to light by asking, for example: Granted that there is this social practice in which the linguistic or quasi-linguistic act of promising gives rise to such-and-such practical expectations, reactions, etc., why should I go along with the practice? Why not, at any stage along the way, *break the spell*?

In response to such questions, there emerges a second level of explanations, independent of but quite consistent with the first, and typically capable of giving reason for the attitudes, dispositions, reactions, etc. referred to in the first-level explanation. For example, Hume explains that 'the [promising-] conventions of men ... create a new motive ... After these signs are instituted, whoever uses them is immediately bound by his interest to execute his engagements, and must never expect to be trusted any more, if he refuse to perform what he promised'; in short, a man who uses the conventional form of words 'subjects himself to the penalty of never being trusted again in case of failure'.[3] Hume is here explaining the obligation of promises—in effect, the rational 'necessity' they create—and is doing so by implicit reference to the following sort of schema of practical reasoning: 'I have made what is conventionally regarded by my fellows as a promise. Given the expectations and attitudes that are part of that convention, I will never again be trusted by my fellows if I fail to perform as I promised and they expect. But it is in my own interests to be trusted (i.e. I want/need to be trusted). Therefore it is necessary for me to perform.' In short, continued trust in me being *impossible* without performance, performance is *necessary* if I am to get what I want (continued trust in me). And so, as Hume says,

---

[3] David Hume, *A Treatise of Human Nature* (1739), Book III, Part II, sec. V, 'Of the Obligation of Promises' (e.g. *British Moralists*, II, para. 541). I here ignore some peculiarities of Hume's treatment of obligation and motive: see II.5, above.

'interest is the *first* obligation to the performance of promises'.[4]

Just as, when we come to consider the obligation of laws, we will encounter again the first-level type of explanation, so we will then encounter again this second-level type of explanation. And it is not a negligible explanation. The schema of practical reasoning to which it appeals is quite genuine, applicable, and forceful. And who is there who does not reason thus, quite frequently? Still, as an explanation of obligation it leaves much to be desired. Someone sensitive to language will say that it is really an explanation, not of obligation, but of the 'prudential' *ought* (as in 'You ought to change your wet clothes'). Moreover, there are many circumstances in which failure to perform a promise, which everyone involved in the social practice would agree was a binding one, will in fact expose one to no more than a risk of 'never being trusted again'. And that risk may be quite remote, even negligible. Indeed, there are cases where (for lack of observers, or by skill in cover-up ...) there is no danger that the violation of obligation will even be known, let alone taken as an indication of general untrustworthiness. Yet, even in such cases, no one involved in the practice may doubt that there *is* an obligation; and there is no reason for the reflective analyst to adopt an explanation of obligation which would oblige him to say that when self-interested motives for performance are lacking, obligation, as a factor relevant to its subject's practical reasoning, is absent. And the same goes for all explanations of obligation in terms purely of self-interest, for example the argument (insinuated by Hume in tandem with that already discussed) that if I do not perform my obligations to others, others will not perform their obligations to me. For in all such cases it remains that my violation of obligation may go undiscovered or be disregarded, without thereby ceasing to be a violation of a subsisting obligation.

Still, the strategy of locating obligation as the conclusion of a train of practical reasoning, about what is *necessary* if one is to get what one wants, needs, or values, is a strategy that can

[4] Hume, loc. cit. (Raphael, para. 542). By 'interest' Hume means 'self-interest': see ibid., sec. II ('Of the Origin of Justice and Property') ad fin. (Raphael, para. 534). Hume goes on to refer sketchily to a 'new obligation' which arises 'afterwards', as an 'effect' of, *inter alia*, 'public interest': Raphael, para. 543; see also *Treatise*, Book III, Part III, sec. IX (ninth paragraph).

yield ampler and more powerful explanations. Though these better explanations could be called 'second-level', it will be convenient to call them 'third-level', in recognition of the extra explanatory dimension introduced by any reference to the common good. For these explanations will take for granted what we have previously laboured to explain: that every man has reason to value the common good—the well-being alike of himself and of his partners and potential partners in community, and the ensemble of conditions and ways of effecting that well-being—whether out of friendship as such, or out of an impartial recognition that human goods are as much realized by the participation in them of other persons as by his own (VI.4, VI.6, VII.2).

Now it is not difficult to establish that the practice or institution of promising-and-therefore-performing-or-accepting-the-justice-of-reproaches-etc. is greatly to the common good. The 'purchase' it gives one individual on another's action is a uniquely appropriate means of attaining both the (private) purposes of individuals and purposes conceived and executed as common enterprises for the advantage of the 'community' or the 'public' rather than of ascertained persons. For it provides an effective means of maintaining co-operation, once initiated, over the span of time necessary for the fulfilment of any human project (whether a straightforwardly attainable goal, such as building a bridge, or an essentially open-ended commitment such as undertaking to raise and educate a family and give mutual support in old age ...). Like the law, it enables past, present, and predictable future to be related in a stable though developing order; enables this order to be effected in complex interpersonal patterns; and brings all this within reach of individual initiative and arrangement, thus enhancing individual autonomy in the very process of increasing individuals' obligations. ('From status to contract ...' is a movement of, on the whole, increasing 'individual liberty'.) So if one is to be a person who favours and contributes to the common good, one *must* go along with the practice of promising. Similarly, and secondarily, if one is not to be a 'free-rider' who unfairly takes the benefits of beneficial social institutions but repudiates the burdens, then one *must* go along with the practice when one has promised, as much as when one has been promised.

And these necessities, unlike the necessity adverted to in the second-level explanation (in terms of the promisor's own reputation), are not affected by the fact that breach of the promise will go undetected either by the promisee or by others. For the practice of promising gains much of its value, as a contribution to the common good, precisely from the fact that the obligations it involves hold good even when breach seems likely to be undetectable. Someone who reneges on his promise simply because he judges that his non-performance will go undetected is therefore doing what he can to defeat the common good in this particular aspect.

To these necessities, derived from the needs of the common good at large, we must add a further necessity derived from the requirement of practical reasonableness (V.4) that one do as one would be done by (impartiality). One has no general responsibility to give the well-being of other people as much care and concern as one gives one's own; the good of others is as really good as one's own good, but is not one's primary responsibility, and to give one's own good priority is not, as such, to violate the requirement of impartiality. But one can incur responsibilities which give certain other people's claims upon one's care and concern a due measure of priority. Promising is one way of incurring such responsibilities. For the making of the promise creates a new criterion of impartiality, relative to the persons concerned and the subject-matter of the promise. The promise constitutes a special frame of reference, or vantage point, in relation to which the conduct of the parties can be assessed for its impartiality. That is to say: given the institution or practice of promising and its appropriateness for the common good as an instrument of co-operation, an impartial observer, with the common good and the interests of all concerned with the promise at heart, would use the promise as such a frame of reference. A promise thus gives each party (and normally, I think, a beneficiary who is not actually party in a strict sense: cf. VIII.2) a special *locus standi*, a right to claim performance. Performance is not merely an obligation in the general (philosophers' and moralists') sense (XI.1); it also is *owed* to the other party. Given the 'general justice' of the institution of promising, breach of promise is (presumptively) a commutative injustice (VII.5). Now all this is homogeneous with the third-level explanation in terms of the common good 'at large'. Indeed, it is a development of that explanation. For the good of an individual party to (or beneficiary of) the promise—the good which, by virtue of the promise, gains some priority of claim upon the care and concern of the promisor—is not something distinct from the common good. It is part of the common good. And that the good of ascertained individuals should be respected in the way required by these considerations is itself a further component of the common good—it is one of the conditions for the well-being of each and all in community.

Indeed, it is a truth of wide application that an individual acts most appropriately for the common good, not by trying to estimate the needs of the common good 'at large', but by performing his contractual undertakings, and fulfilling his other responsibilities, to ascertained individuals, i.e. to those who have particular rights correlative to his duties. Fulfilling one's particular obligations in justice, even within the restricted sphere of private contracts, family responsibilities, etc., is necessary if one is to respect and favour the common good, *not* because 'otherwise everyone suffers', or because non-fulfilment would diminish 'overall net good' in some impossible utilitarian computation, or even because it would 'set a bad example' and thus weaken a useful practice, but simply because the common good *is* the good of individuals, living together and depending upon one another in ways that favour the well-being of each.

All these *necessities*, derived from basic requirements of practical reasonableness, have a feedback into the obligation which is expressed, undertaken, argued about, etc., *within* the practice of promising. That is to say, the meaning of 'obligation' at the level of practice (i.e. in the uttering of promises, etc.) becomes charged with its meaning in the first, second, and third levels of explanation, whenever the people engaged in the practice are at all reflective. Then the expressions of and references to obligation which are integral to the practice will not have merely the force of moves in a game (though in Wittgenstein's sense of 'language-game' they *are* that) but will be regularly intended and taken as involving (and/or expressing the involvement of) the participants and their community, and relative to practical reasonableness itself.

Without presupposing that this third level of explanation of obligation is the deepest (cf. XIII.5), let me dwell for a moment on its strategy. It is an explanation parallel in form to the explanation offered (IX.3) for the authoritativeness of custom. For custom was explained as a complex practice involving (i) concurrent patterns of conduct, (ii) claims and opinions ('judgments') about (*a*) the appropriateness of uniformity of conduct in this particular field of action and (*b*) the appropriateness of *this* pattern of conduct, (iii) acceptance of the conjunction of the concurrence of conduct with the concurrence of claims and opinions as constituting an authoritative custom warranting compliance, claims, demands for compliance, reproaches for non-compliance, amends, etc. In this account, the authoritativeness of custom was explained (in third-level fashion, the first-level form of explanation being taken for granted) as deriving from (A) the need (for the common good) for some authoritative solution to co-ordination problems, taken with (B) a certain set of facts (about conduct, opinions, degrees of acceptance, etc.) which pragmatically afford an answer to that need (or afford an opportunity of answering to it).

So with promises. A certain set of facts affords an opportunity of answering to a standing need of the common good, the need for individuals to be able to make reliable arrangements with each other for the determinate and lasting but flexible solution of co-ordination problems and, more generally, for the realizing of the goods of individual self-constitution and of community. (Mutual trustworthiness is not merely a means to further distinct ends; it is in itself a valuable component of any common life.) The set of facts that affords this opportunity comprises (*a*) the framework fact that a practice (involving more than one party and extending over a span of time and applicable to many and various promises) exists or can readily be initiated (given the underlying facts about human foresight, memory, desire for security, ability to understand, co-operate, rely, etc.), whereby the intentional giving of certain signs will be linked by the participants with expectations of future performance, demands for that performance, etc., etc.; (*b*) the particular fact that a given individual has entered into the practice by voluntarily and intentionally giving the relevant signs; (*c*) the fact that if that individual, like others, goes along with the

practice by trying to perform as he promised to perform, even
when performance is at the expense of some ,inconvenience,
foreseen or even unforeseen, to himself, he will thereby not only
contribute to the well-being of the person for whose benefit his
promise was accepted (a contribution which might in the particular case be outweighed by the loss to his own well-being)
but will also be playing his part in a pattern of life without
which many of the benefits of community could not in fact be
realized.

Given these empirical facts and the aforementioned standing
need of the common good, that common good (including the
good of the promisee or other ascertained beneficiary) can be
realized with reasonable impartiality *only* if the individual per-
forms on his promise; and this necessity *is* the obligation of his
promise (both the general, moralists' obligation, and the obligation owed to the promisee or beneficiary). 'I *cannot* be one who
acts for the common good *unless* I go along with the practice
by performing on this promise.' Secondarily, 'I *cannot* be one
who is rationally impartial *unless* I take the burdens of the
practice as well as the benefits, and perform on this promise ...'.
The conclusion, in each case, is: '*Therefore*, I *must* perform ...'.
Both the authorities responsible for the common good at large,
and the promisee or other ascertained beneficiary, have the
right to demand that the promise be performed. Hence it is
appropriate that there be a judicially enforceable law of contract (and judicial doctrines of good faith, equity, etc.) and a
right of parties (and sometimes beneficiaries) to sue on the
promises covered by that law.

The reason for repeating and emphasizing this analysis of
obligation in terms of the necessity, given certain facts, of
determinate actions as means to valuable ends, is the pre-
valence, for many centuries, of an analysis of obligation, not
least of the obligation of promises, in terms of 'bonds' created
by 'acts of will': see XI.7. Suffice it to observe here that although
promissory obligations do not come into being without some
voluntary and intentional act such as might be said to manifest
an 'act of will' on the part of the promisor, the occurrence of
that act is only one of the several facts relevant to the emergence
of the necessity which we call obligation, and has no special
role in explaining the *obligation* of the performance promised.

The reason why *this* source of obligation, unlike some others, requires *inter alia* a voluntary act, and indeed a voluntary act intended to express willingness to create an obligation, is that the point of this institution, unlike others, is particularly to enable individuals to exercise a control over their own relationships in community. A practice or practical doctrine according to which obligation came into being whenever one made certain signs (whether voluntarily or not, and whether or not intending them to be signs with *that* significance), or whenever one expressed one's intentions of acting in the future, or whenever one expressed such intentions knowing that others might rely on one, would in each case be a practice or practical doctrine too restrictive of individual autonomy and self-direction, too cramping of human expressiveness and communication. So the willingness of the promisor to be bound (or to be taken as willing to be bound) is one of the necessary conditions of his being bound; but this fact itself has no peculiar explanatory power in an account of obligation.

XI. 3   VARIABLE AND INVARIANT OBLIGATORY FORCE

Though recent philosophers have often overlooked or minimized the fact, the obligation of promises is very variable, and is often quite weak. This is a fact about the practice as commonly understood and carried on. Without any expressed 'doctrine of frustration' or *clausula rebus sic stantibus*, people who make and receive promises commonly understand that a change in the circumstances of the parties, affecting the interests of one or both of them (especially but not necessarily if unforeseen at the time of the promise) may exempt from the obligation of performance and, quite often though not always, from the obligation of amends (and even of apology) for nonperformance. (If the promisee has been inconvenienced by this justified non-performance it will still be in order to express regret, as distinct from contrition.) A promise properly made is always an exclusionary reason, that is, always gives a reason for disregarding *some* reasons, which are genuine and relevant and which in the absence of the promise to do ϕ would have sufficed to justify not doing ϕ (see IX.2). But a promise is usually an exclusionary reason that can be defeated by some countervailing reasons, often by a wide range of readily available reasons (though never by *any and all* of the reasons that would, in the absence of the promise, have warranted not doing the thing promised). When it is intended by the parties that the promise shall afford a virtually indefeasible exclusionary reason, the promise will have to be expressed with solemnity and precision as being one that binds them 'for better for worse, for richer for poorer, in sickness and in health . . . till death . . .'[5] (and even such a form of words may be given a reduced obligation-creating significance by the practice in which it is rooted).

Of course, all this renders the practice of promising subject not only to obvious abuses and exploitation, but also to frequent bona fide differences of opinion about the strength of particular promissory obligations and even of promissory obligation in general. The practice is permeable by virtually all evaluative considerations, not only by those which in the third level of explanation give promises their obligatory force, but also by all other comparable considerations (whether incommensurable or not). That is to say, the feedback of considerations about individual and communal good is not only of considerations tending to show why it is necessary to perform promises in general and therefore this promise in particular, but is also of considerations tending to show that in this or that particular set of circumstances the general rule of obligatoriness can reasonably be considered inapplicable or supplanted. This feedback of various forms and requirements of practical reasonableness lends the extra-legal practice a flexibility without which it doubtless could not survive, but also an elusive variability or unreliability, of a sort that legal thought strives to exclude from legally regulated transactions.

This, then, is the first thing to observe about legal obligation. Whereas, at the level of language, common attitudes, and practice, the obligation of promises is understood by parties to promises as varying from one promise to another, the obligation of all laws and hence of all legally regulated transactions is understood by lawyers as being of the same legal force in every case. There are, legally speaking, no degress of legal obligation, just as there are (X.6) no degrees of legal validity.

[5] Book of Common Prayer (1662), Form of Solemnization of Matrimony.

The fact that, legally, all legal obligations are of the same strength can be obscured from casual view by the fact that many legal obligations are of variable content and incidence. The duty of drivers or manufacturers to take reasonable care, or of employers to fence machines adequately, is in each type of instance likely to involve conduct different at one time from another, at one place from another. But this sort of variability should be understood with precision. Consider, as a representative instance, the following provisions of the (English) Sale of Goods Act 1893, as amended by the Supply of Goods (Implied Terms) Act 1973:

s. 14(2). Where the seller sells goods in the course of a business, there is an implied condition that the goods supplied under the contract are of merchantable quality, except that there is no such condition—
(a) as regards defects specifically drawn to the buyer's attention before the contract is made; or
(b) if the buyer examines the goods before the contract is made, as regards defects which that examination ought to reveal.

s. 62(1A). Goods of any kind are of merchantable quality within the meaning of this Act if they are as fit for the purpose or purposes for which goods of that kind are commonly bought as it is reasonable to expect having regard to any description applied to them, the price (if relevant) and all the other relevant circumstances.

The seller's duty, then, is to supply goods 'as fit [for the usual purposes of purchasers of such goods] as it is reasonable to expect having regard to all relevant circumstances'. Such a duty is obviously variable in content, in two different ways: it will vary as the goods vary, and as other circumstances of the sale vary; and it will vary as the opinions of lawyers and judges vary concerning the relevance of particular types of 'circumstance'. But all these potential variations should not be allowed to obscure from our view the invariant elements which the law stipulates: if a seller is selling in the course of a business he has a duty to supply goods of a certain type of quality except as regards two defined types of defect; but if he is not selling in the course of a business then he simply does not have *any* duty of this type, though he has others; and if he does have this duty, the consequences of failure to conform to it, though not always the same, are well defined and, legally, inevitable.

There is simply no room for him to plead that, although he falls within the terms of s. 14(2) and his goods fail to meet the specifications of the provision, nevertheless his prima-facie duty was *outweighed* and *diminished* or *deferred* or in some other way *modified* by other considerations, however 'reasonable'. Of course, the law makes provision for exceptional circumstances in which the whole contract of sale is frustrated and the parties are relieved of their obligations (VII.4); but even here the legal method of analysing the situation produces the conclusion that what would otherwise have been the seller's duty is *not* his duty and has been *replaced* either by some *other* duty or by a legal liberty (*absence* of duty).

This invariability in the formal force of every legal obligation has as its methodological counterpart the legal postulate (shared by 'legalistic' moral thought) that there are no overlapping and conflicting legal duties; for any such overlap would oblige the lawyer to weigh one obligation against the other and to declare the weightier obligation to be the more binding. A lawyer will always seek to define (in terms of subject, subject-matter, act-description, time, and circumstance) the limits of each potentially applicable obligation so that the unique legal obligation in the situation under consideration can be identified, and all competing claims of obligation simply dismissed (for that situation). Hence the casuistical refinement of legal rules, their lists of conditions and exceptions, the unwearying legal effort for exhaustiveness and coherence of stipulation. The famous 'inflexibility' of the law goes far deeper than one would suppose if one merely called to mind, for example, well-known instances of criminal prohibitions so bluntly, naïvely, or widely drafted as to catch what all would agree is praiseworthy or at least acceptable conduct. Rather, the law's inflexibility is rooted in the invariance (in contemplation of law) of the action-guiding force of each and every obligation-imposing legal provision; and in mature legal systems this inflexibility should have as one principal consequence an exquisite refinement and narrowness of draftsmanship.

But my mention of the doctrine of 'frustration of contracts in exceptional circumstances' should remind us (if we had not already been reminded by the reference to 'reasonableness' at the heart of that refined commercial code, the amended Sale of Goods Act) that legal thought is not unaware of policies and principles which cannot be, or have not been, reduced to definite legal rules. That is to say, mature legal thought does not banish altogether those considerations, touching the common good, which in general are scarcely more closely definable than the basic values and principles discussed in earlier chapters of this book, but which in particular circumstances can lead reasonable men to agree on a course of action *not* provided for by the existing legal rules or the network of contractual or other obligatory arrangements subsisting under those rules. Nevertheless, unlike the informal social practice of promising, the legal system does not allow an unrestricted feedback of such 'value' or 'policy' considerations from the justificatory level of straightforward practical reasonableness back into the level of practice. Instead, the legal system systematically restricts such feedback by establishing institutions, such as courts, arbitrators, and legislatures, and then requiring that any shifting of the obligations imposed by existing rules and subsisting arrangements shall be authorized only by those institutions. Moreover, the institutions are themselves placed under legal rules (differing according to the nature and functions of the institutions) which make it obligatory that only in certain circumstances, and according to defined procedures and within certain limits, may they admit, accept, or act upon the 'extra-legal' policies, or upon the legally indeterminate (or not fully determinate, e.g. justificatory rather than strictly obligatory) principles. Thus the legal system buttresses and gives practical effect to a framework principle of legal thought, that legal obligation is of legally invariant force.

The black-and-white quality of legal obligation (like the all-or-nothing quality of legal validity)[6] is part of the data, which an explanation of law must take into account and explain (and not explain away). It is a feature of legal thought which obviously renders incomplete and unsatisfying any form of first-level explanation which is restricted to asserting that 'rules are conceived and spoken of as imposing obligations when the

---

[6] See X.6, above; also, e.g. Dworkin, *Taking Rights Seriously* (London: 1977), p. 79: 'The rule that unreasonable restraints of trade are invalid remains a rule if every restraint that is unreasonable is invalid, even if other reasons for enforcing it, not mitigating its unreasonableness, might be found.'

general demand for conformity is insistent and the social pressure brought to bear upon those who deviate or threaten to deviate is great'.[7] As I observed in relation to the analogous first-level explanation of statements of promissory obligation, such location of the 'logic of obligation' in a context of regularities of practice is not devoid of explanatory power. But over and above the general deficiency of first-level explanations—that they fail to uncover or explain the practical reasoning which by motivating and justifying the practice in the eyes of its participants gives the practice its specific unity and significance—there is a special deficiency in any explanation of a black-and-white, invariant obligation in terms only of 'social pressures' which must inevitably be very variable in their pressure and insistence.

The formal invariance of legal obligation equally renders inadequate all those forms of second-level explanation which account for the force and role of obligations and obligatory rules in practical reasoning by pointing to *human reactions to non-performance of the obligatory behaviour* (reactions which are standardly undesired by the person subject to the obligation, and which therefore give him a reason to perform-in-order-to-avoid-them). The most well-known forms of such explanation are, of course, the theories of legal obligation in terms exclusively of exposure to (the threat of, or liability to) sanctions. I stressed the importance of sanctions in any general account of law (X.1). But my remarks on Hume's theory of promissory obligation (XI.2) should make it clear why the threat of, or liability to, sanctions does not account for the nature and role of obligation in practical reasoning. This has, indeed, been elaborately shown by H. L. A. Hart;[8] his distinction between being obliged (under threat of unpleasant consequences) and being under an obligation in virtue of a mandatory rule was put forward not so much as an independent argument (which could be accused of verbalism) but rather as a summary reminder of features of the logic of obligation which give it a distinct place in the map of rational motivations of, or justificatory reasons for, action. But his own account of obligation (given in the last paragraph), when transposed from the first on to the second level of explana-

---

[7] Hart, *Concept of Law*, p. 84; also p. 214.
[8] *Concept of Law*, pp. 80–3.

tions (i.e. in his terminology, into an explanation from the 'internal point of view') suffers from analogous defects. The threat of adverse critical reactions to one's breaches of the law is variable in intensity and immediacy (as is one's own distaste for those reactions in differing contexts and circumstances).

In short, the 'directive' force of law is not to be reduced to, or explained by reference only to, the 'coercive' force of law (IX.5). In the next section I advance an explanation of that *vis directiva*.

XI.4   'LEGALLY OBLIGATORY': THE LEGAL SENSE AND THE MORAL SENSE

Obligation-imposing legal rules, as we saw earlier (X.7), are rarely drafted imperatively or even in terms of 'ought' or 'obligation'. Nevertheless, for analytical purposes they can be cast into the schematic form 'If p, q, r, then $XO\phi$'—where 'p, q, r' signify the circumstances under which the legal obligation arises, 'ϕ' stands for an act-description signifying the obligatory act (being or to-be) done by X, the relevant person-subject of the norm in those circumstances, and 'O' is a deontic modal operator signifying that ϕ is in those circumstances obligatory for X (rather than merely permitted or discretionary; and also rather than being actually the case or not the case or possible or necessary, as might be signified by some non-deontic operator).

Using this analysis, we can say that the problem discussed in the preceding section is the problem of explaining (i) how an obligation-imposing law provides a reason for action which would not exist independently of that law and is indeed provided by 'the law' or legal system itself, and (ii) why the obligation of such a law has, for legal thought, the black-and-white quality characteristic of legal obligations, i.e. how the modal operator 'O' has an all-or-nothing deontic force even when 'ϕ' stands for some vague or variably instantiated act-description such as 'supplying goods of reasonable quality'.[9]

---

[9] Notice that this section does not deal with those 'legal principles' which some writers (e.g. Dworkin, *Taking Rights Seriously*, London: 1977, ch. 2) consider to be legally binding although not legal *rules*. Such principles, while 'part of the law', do not legally require particular actions or decisions, although they (*a*) may *justify* particular decisions that particular actions are required, and (*b*) may be the subject of obligation-imposing rules *requiring* a judge to take them into account.

The answer to the problem consists in the correct identification of the law-abiding subject's practical reasoning, reasoning to which such a norm is directed and which such a norm is intended to direct in a distinctively 'obligatory' way.

The answer to the problem, then, consists in a third-level explanation similar in strategy to the explanations I offered in respect of custom (IX.3) and promissory obligation (XI.2). The relevant schema of practical reasoning runs something as follows (formulations could vary widely in detail):

Step *A*. For *all* co-ordination problems legally specified as appropriate for legal solution [including the problem of which such problems to specify and solve, and in what manner and form to specify and solve them] I must act in the legally specified way if I am to respect the common good.

Step *B*. Where a pattern-of-action has been legally specified as obligatory [i.e. where it has been legally stipulated that 'if p, q, r, then $XO\phi$'] the *only* way of satisfying the need postulated in step *A* is to act according to the pattern so specified [i.e. is to ϕ];

Step *C*. So, in the cases mentioned in step *B*, I must [ought to] act in the way specified as obligatory [i.e. where 'if p, q, r, then $XO\phi$' is a legal norm, and p, q, r, and I am X, then $O\phi$].

At first glance, this schema may appear empty and/or viciously circular. Step *A* will sound gratuitous or question-begging unless it is treated as a summary formulation of my earlier, rather elaborate contentions about the need for authority in community and for that authority to be treated as authoritative in practice, and about law as one form of authoritative solution to co-ordination problems (IX.1, X.1, X.3). But the appearance of vicious circularity in the schema derives particularly, perhaps, from the peculiar feature (mirrored in steps *B* and *C*) which legal obligation shares with promissory obligation, namely, that the obligation is standardly created by a sign which expressly or impliedly *signifies* that obligation. In steps *B* and *C* of the schema, the legal sign signifying a specific legal obligation is indicated by the formula '"if p, q, r, then $XO\phi$"'. (Recall that this is a schematic formula rarely adopted by drafts-

men, but well understood by lawyers as contextually signified
by a variety of legislative expressions and/or as derivable from
judicial precedent or practice, with or without the interpretative
assistance of accepted legal principles: see X.7.) When the
formula 'if p, q, r, $XO\phi$' appears in step C without enclosing
quotation marks, it refers not to the legal sign, the legal
stipulation of obligation, but to the rational necessity, given
steps A and B, of acting in the way characterized as ϕ.

The schema is not redundant. For if it were not possible to
find any means–end schema of practical reasoning generating
a conclusion such as C, then the legal signification or stipulation
'$XO\phi$' referred to in step B would be empty words (save as
a threat of sanctions). But since the schema is indeed available,
the notion of obligation which it generates is available for use
in the lawmaker's act of 'obligation'-stipulation, an act which
has its peculiar action-guiding relevance and force precisely
because it can play its role in a train of practical reasoning
whose conclusion it expressly anticipates. (Here again we are
observing the 'feedback' which we noticed in analysing the
practice of promising, and which is made possible by human
reflectiveness: XI.2.)

What then is the rational source and force of steps A and
B? Perhaps these steps can be more readily understood if I
translate the whole schema into the following simplified form:

A. We need, for the sake of the common good, to be law-
abiding;

B. But where ϕ is stipulated by law as obligatory, the *only* way
to be law-abiding is to do ϕ;

C. Therefore, we need [it is obligatory for us] to do ϕ where
ϕ has been legally stipulated to be obligatory.

It will be objected that the force of step A varies according
to circumstances; sometimes the common good may best be
preserved or realized by deviation from the law. That is true;
step A can take its place in the unrestricted flow of practical
reasoning and, since it is not itself one of the *basic* principles
or requirements of practical reasoning, will then vary in force
and applicability. Whence, then, the legally invariant force of
legal obligation? The answer is: from step B, taken together
with an interpretation of step A as an undiscussed postulate,

isolated by legal thought from the general flow of practical reasoning.

Step *B* proposes that if you are to have and retain the quality 'law-abiding citizen' you *must* perform each action which the law has stipulated to be 'obligatory', whenever and in all the respects in which such stipulations are applicable. This fundamental principle implicit in legal thought is not empty. It embodies the postulates that each obligation-stipulating law is a member of a system of laws which cannot be weighed or played off one against the other but which constitute a set coherently applicable to all situations and which exclude all unregulated or private picking and choosing amongst the members of the set. When you are confronted by an obligation-stipulating legal rule applicable to your circumstances there is no legally recognized rule or principle to which you can appeal to relieve you of your obligation. In this sense, at least, your allegiance to the whole system ('the law') is put on the line: either you obey the *particular* law, or you reveal yourself (to yourself, if not to others) as lacking or defective in allegiance to the *whole*, as well as to the particular.

In short, the law forbids any feedback (save through institutionalized channels and procedures) into step *B* from those general values and principles which can give step *A* a varying force; they can be systematically ignored by treating step *A* as a framework principle or postulate. Thus the law, as a system of practical reasoning offered to the man who wants (and sees the need) to be law-abiding, seeks to give an invariant force to the rational necessity expressed in step *C*, the law-abiding man's conclusion. That is why I have stressed that it is only 'in contemplation of law' that legal obligation is invariant in force. In fact, in strictly legal thought the basis and force of step *A* never becomes a topic of consideration (except perhaps in 'public emergencies' of the sort mentioned in X.5). That right or justice is to be done *according to law* is the judge's oath of office; it is a formulation of step *A* for intra-systemic legal purposes (rather than for private moral reasoning about the law) and so is not a subject-matter for judicial reasoning or pronouncement. But the formulae expressive of legal obligation have their specific intelligibility from the fact that they are self-consciously designed not only to fit into the recalcitrant citizen's sanction-dominated practical reasonings, but also and most characteristically to fit into and to give a special conclusory force to the practical reasonings of those who see and are generally willing to act upon the need (for the common good) for authority.

The law thus anticipates and seeks to capitalize upon, indeed to absorb and take over, the 'good citizen's' schema of practical reasoning, and to give it an unquestioned or dogmatic status. It tries to isolate what I have been calling 'legal thought' or 'purely legal thought' from the rest of practical reasoning. But the good citizen can always recover step A from its status, in legal thought, of undiscussed postulate or framework principle. By relocating step A in the whole flow of practical reasoning, one gives it as a premiss a moral force. Thus we can and should distinguish *on the one hand*, both (i*a*) the moral principle, embodied in this interpretation of step A, that laws provide directly applicable and authoritative guidance for the reasonable man and eliminate the need for him to weigh up (as the legislature had to weigh up) the pros and cons of many possible courses of actions, and (i*b*) the moral theorem, embodied in step C, that one of the forms of moral obligation is legal obligation, from *on the other hand* (ii) the legal principle (or theorem of strictly legal science) that legal obligation is invariant. The *equal* obligation in *law* of each obligation-imposing law is to be clearly distinguished from the moral obligation to obey *each* law.

For, like the obligation of promises, the moral obligation to obey *each* law is variable in force. It will vary according to the subject-matter of the law and the circumstances of a possible violation; for some subject-matters are in greater need of legal regulation than others, and some violations of law make a greater rent in the fabric of the law than others. On the one hand, the moral obligation to obey the law as such is usually, but in differing measures, reinforced by moral obligations that would exist in the same form (e.g. not to murder) or at least inchoately (e.g. to contribute towards the expenses of good government) even if the law did not re-enact them (as in murder) or concretize them (as in the law imposing income tax, estate tax, etc.): X.6. And on the other hand, the moral principles and theorems with which we have been dealing in this section (e.g. those in step *A* and step *C*) are all to be understood as giving *presumptive* and *defeasible* (IX.3) exclusionary reason for action. For simplicity I have omitted this qualification from the schema of practical reasoning, and from my elaboration of it. (The nature and effect of the defeating conditions will be examined in XII.2–3.)

Still, the reasons that justify the vast legal effort to render the law, unlike the informal social institution of promising, relatively impervious to discretionary assessments of competing values and conveniences are reasons that also justify us in asserting that the moral obligation to conform to legal obligations is relatively weighty. These reasons relate particularly to the extent, complexity, and depth of the social interdependences which the law, unlike promises between individuals, attempts to regulate. Such an ambitious attempt as the law's can only succeed in creating and maintaining order, and a fair order, inasmuch as individuals drastically restrict the occasions on which they trade off their legal obligations against their individual convenience or conceptions of social good. Moreover, just as promising creates a special frame of reference in which to assess impartiality, giving to the promisee (and to any ascertained beneficiary) a basis for claiming performance as a matter of right, so too the law creates a similar frame of reference and gives, at least to those directly responsible for superintending the common good, a right to demand compliance, not merely as something morally obligatory in the broad, moralists' sense, but as something morally owed 'to the community'. The law provides the citizen, like the judge, with strongly exclusionary moral reasons for acting or abstaining from actions.

Once it is understood that the schema of practical reasoning discussed in this section can be read both in the restricted, legal sense (in which its first premiss is a postulate detached from extra-legal practical reasoning) and in the unrestricted, moral sense, it should be clear that the schema satisfies the demands both of third-level strategies of explanation (which must display the location and role of the *explicandum* in unrestricted practical reasoning) and of specifically legal science, which reasonably insists both that legal obligation be understood as invariant and that legal obligation (whether or not it is *also* a form of moral obligation) be sharply distinguished from all those moral (or other) obligations which would subsist apart from or in the absence of the law.

This last-mentioned demand or insistence of legal thought is not of interest only to 'positivists'. A 'natural law' jurist can also make the demand, and can observe that it is satisfied by step *B* in the schema. This step expresses the fact that, wherever it reasonably can, legal thought looks to distinct sources for legal rules and obligations, viz. to the acts which lawyers treat as authoritative, i.e. as giving *now* (in the ambulatory present) good and conclusive (or at least determinate exclusionary) reason for acting *now* in the way *then* stipulated. This derivation of present sufficient reasons for action from past acts or facts, themselves identified by reference to other past acts or facts, themselves . . . etc., is thoroughly characteristic of legal thought: X.3. Those past acts or facts include the acts of deliberate or at least datable creation or amendment to which legal rules, *qua* legal, are always subject, in contrast to moral rules, which *qua* moral rules morally considered have no datable origins and cannot be amended. The dual role of the schema that I have been discussing goes to explain why legal rules, like promises, can generate moral obligations which (in a sense to be elaborated: XI.8) *are* subject to deliberate creation and amendment. It also, incidentally, helps to explain why it is often so difficult to tell whether a legal, especially an advocate's, utterance is intended to express the demands of unrestricted practical reasonableness in the situation, or is intended only from a professionally structured and systematically restricted 'purely legal' viewpoint—see the distinction between S_1 and S_3 statements, drawn in IX.2, above.

XI.5 CONTRACTUAL OBLIGATION IN LAW: PERFORMANCE OR COMPENSATION?

The foregoing section offered a schema of practical reasoning. When artificially isolated from the unrestricted flow of practical reason, the schema explains the specific action-guiding force of an obligation-imposing legal rule in contemplation of law; when integrated into the unrestricted flow of practical reasoning, it explains the specific moral force of such a rule. The remainder of this chapter seeks to consolidate the analysis of both these senses of 'legal obligation', i.e. the purely legal sense, and the moral sense. I do so, firstly, by considering two long-standing controversies in which lawyers have disputed with lawyers, and moralists with moralists, about these respective senses; and secondly, by using that discussion to clarify the precise role of the legislator's or, *mutatis mutandis*, promisor's 'will' in the creation and explanation of obligation.

The two controversies which we are to consider have very different origins and concerns, but raise overlapping and parallel questions. There is the controversy amongst lawyers about the legal obligation created by a contract: Is it to perform what was undertaken, or is it no more than an obligation to pay compensatory damages to the other party in the event of one's non-performance? And there is the controversy amongst moralists about the moral obligation to obey a legal-obligation-creating rule of law: Is it to do what that rule of law implicitly or explicitly directs the subject to do, or is it no more than an obligation to submit to the 'penalty' provided for by the law on certain conditions which concern the actions or omissions of the subject?

At the root of the lawyers' controversy is, it seems, the fact which we observed in the preceding section when discussing the appearance of circularity in the schema of practical reasoning which concludes: '*C*. Hence one must [is under an obligation to] ϕ when ϕ is stipulated by an obligation-imposing legal rule'. The schema requires one to identify those legal rules to which one *must* conform if one is to be a law-abiding citizen. Where there is a legislative text which employs distinctive terms, such as 'X shall ϕ, if p, q, r', the task of identifying the rules is relatively easy. But even in such cases, there will be problems about the range of circumstances in which the rule imposes the legal requirement to ϕ. Typically it will be for courts to interpret the rule and pronounce upon its scope. But the courts, typically, do not make such pronouncements for the purpose of enlightening the curious or conscientious; rather, they act only on the motion of a party who is seeking from the court some *remedy*, whether punitive or compensatory (e.g. damages) or compulsory (e.g. an order for specific performance). And they tend to use the availability of a remedy as an indication that a rule is of the obligation-imposing type. Thus it is easy to leap to the supposition that the boundaries of legal obligation are coterminous with the availability of remedies.

This supposition is even easier to arrive at in those areas of law in which the very content of the law is discoverable not from any legislative text using a clear terminology of obligation-stipulation but only (or primarily) from the pronouncements of judges in the act of granting or refusing enforceable remedies; here the availability of a remedy is often the principal, some-times the only, sign of the existence and extent of an obligation-imposing legal rule. And the supposition, finally, is reinforced by a practical lawyer's professional involvement with the concerns of those citizens who are only interested in the law to the extent that it may affect them adversely, and who care nothing for any train of practical reasoning which proceeds from concern for the common good or for the value of legal order as such.

From such roots emerges the view of an Oliver Wendell Holmes. Aspiring to 'wash with cynical acid' all idealistic fancies about the law, he argues that 'the test of legal principles' is 'the bad man's point of view'. 'What does the notion of legal duty mean to a bad man?' 'Mainly, and in the first place, a prophecy that if he does certain things he will be subjected to disagreeable consequences by way of imprisonment or com-pulsory payment of money.' So much for 'the widest concept which the law contains—the notion of legal duty'.[10] But, more specifically, 'the duty to keep a contract at common law means a prediction that you must pay damages if you do not keep it,—and nothing else'.[11] More precisely: 'the only universal consequence of a legally binding promise is, that the law makes the promisor pay damages if the promised event does not come to pass. In every case it leaves him free from interference until the time for fulfilment has gone by, and therefore free to break his contract if he chooses.'[12]

Discussions of this analysis of contractual obligation often focus on Holmes's references to prediction, and critiques of his

---

[10] The Path of the Law' (1897) 10 *Harv. L. Rev.* 457 at 461; also in Holmes, *Collected Legal Papers* (New York: 1920), p. 167.

[11] 10 *Harv. L. Rev.* at p. 462.

[12] Holmes, *The Common Law* (1881; ed. M. deW. Howe, Cambridge, Mass.: 1957), p. 236. For the link between the general strategy of analysing law from the 'bad man's' point of view and this analysis of contract, see ibid., p. 317.

argument often get little further than showing that it fails to reproduce or account for the 'internal point of view' of judges, who are interested not in predicting what they are about to do but in reasons they have for doing it. But, as the last passages quoted from Holmes make clear, his argument can readily be stated without any reference to prediction; for X to be under a contractual duty to ϕ means that X must *either* ϕ *or* pay damages—and this 'must' can (though it need not) be regarded as the conclusion of a genuine 'internal' schema of practical reasoning.

Reflection on Holmes's contention should begin with the recognition that a legal system certainly *could* interpret all its obligation-imposing rules in this disjunctive sense: *either* ϕ *or* undergo the stipulated 'penalties' (whichever you please). Or, more narrowly, it could construe all contracts in that sense. Still, the fact is that legal systems do not (though many do, of course, permit anyone to make such a disjunctive contract if he chooses to). It is a maxim of civil law systems that contracts are made to be performed, and common law systems have worked on the same principle. An executor or personal administrator, for example, is bound to carry out the contracts entered into by the deceased person whose estate he is administering, even when it would be more advantageous to the estate and its beneficiaries for him to refuse performance and pay damages for the breach. The reason judicially advanced for this rule is significant: 'the breaking of an enforceable contract is an unlawful act'.[13] And again: 'The administrator has ... a clear duty to perform. The moral duty is distinct. It is to perform the contract entered into by his intestate. The legal duty, in this instance, as ... it is in all cases where it is fully understood and examined, is identical with the moral duty.'[14] Similar reasons are advanced for other rules exemplifying the same general principle, for example, the rule that it is a civil wrong for C to incite A to break his (A's) contract with B, even when C is *not* inciting A to avoid paying damages for the suggested breach: in the view of the judges there is a

[13] *Ahmed Angullia* v. *Estate and Trust Agencies (1927) Ltd.* [1938] A.C. 628 at 635 (Privy Council).

[14] *Cooper* v. *Jarman* (1866) L.R.3 Eq.98 at 102, quoted and approved in *Ahmed Angullia's* case at p. 634 as 'both good law and good sense'.

'chasm' between cases where the act incited or induced was a breach of contract and cases where the act was the not entering into a contract, and there is this chasm precisely because the breach of contract is unlawful.[15] In short, allegiance to the legal system as a whole requires, according to the self-interpretation of these legal systems, that one perform what one undertook; offering or being willing to pay damages, or paying damages when assessed, do not suffice.

This virtually universal legal interpretation of contracts and contractual obligation has its significance, for us, as an indication that contracts are upheld by the law for the sake of the common good, which is positively enhanced (i) by the co-ordination of action, and solution of co-ordination problems, made possible by performance of contracts (in the ordinary, not the Holmesian, sense of 'performance'), and (ii) by the continued existence of a social practice which actively encourages such fully co-ordinated performance and discourages non-performance. If all contracts were interpreted and upheld in the Holmesian disjunctive sense, the common good of co-ordination might still, of course, be served to some extent. But it is served to a much greater extent if the law, as it does, (a) allows parties to enter into disjunctive contracts if they choose to, but (b) refuses to interpret other contracts disjunctively, and thus (c) allows the parties to a contract to know with precision what *unique* course of action is required of the other party by law, in all those cases (the great majority) in which it is to the advantage of each party *not* to give the other party a free option between more than one course of action (as Holmes's contract *does* give).

The ineptness of the Holmesian contract as an instrument for advancing the common good by collaborative works will be even more apparent when one observes that the duty to pay damages arises only, on his view, when a court has settled and ordered them, i.e. after the expense of social resources in litigation. And even then, what is this 'duty to pay'? Is it only a duty *either* to pay *or* to submit to the sheriff or bailiff when he comes to enforce payment by seizing one's goods? And is the 'duty to submit' only the duty to *either* submit *or* accept liability for assault and/or contempt of court? Without collaps-

[15] *Rookes* v. *Barnard* [1964] A.C. 1129 at pp. 1168, 1201.

ing the clear distinction between law and morals, it is possible to see and say that the law's ambitions are higher than this, and its distinctive schemata of thought quite different.

An important theoretical motivation for Holmes's construction, as appears from the immediate context of his formulation of it in *The Common Law*, was his desire (like Hume) to avoid and discredit any attempt to explain contractual obligation as the 'product' of an act (or acts or conjunction of acts) of will which could subsequently somehow 'bind' or 'subject' the (wills of the) parties. This motivation was entirely reasonable. But Holmes failed to see that contractual obligation, like legal obligation in general, can be explained as the necessity of a type of means uniquely appropriate for attaining a form of good (e.g. the standing availability of co-ordination of constructive action) otherwise attainable only imperfectly if at all. He failed to see, or at any rate to make sufficient allowance for the fact, that the social importance of law (as of the practice of promising) derives not only from its ability to mould the 'bad man's' practical reasoning, but also from its capacity to give all those citizens who are willing to advance the common good precise directions about what they *must* do *if* they are to follow the way authoritatively chosen as the common way to that good (it being taken for granted that having a defined and commonly adhered-to 'common way' is, presumptively, a peculiarly good way of advancing the common good).

XI.6   LEGAL OBLIGATION IN THE MORAL SENSE: PERFORMANCE OR SUBMISSION TO PENALTY?

It is now time to turn to the far more wide-ranging and long-standing controversy amongst moralists about the obligatory force of various common forms of legal stipulation. The controversy about 'purely penal' laws, which anticipates several of the debates of our contemporary analytical jurists, emerges in the later fifteenth century, and finds a classic expression in the work of Suarez at the beginning of the seventeenth century.

The term 'purely penal law' comes from an elementary analysis of the form of legal stipulations. Such stipulations may be in (or be analytically reduced to) one or other of three forms: (i) 'If p, q, r, then $XO\phi$'; this form was often, confusingly, labelled a *lex moralis*; (ii) 'If p, q, r, then $XO\phi$: the penalty for non-compliance is P'; this two-clause form was labelled *lex poenalis mixta*, since it combined a stipulation of action (or, of course, omission) with a stipulation of penalty; (iii) 'If p, q, r, and X does (not) do ϕ a penalty P is to be imposed on him'; this conditional directive to officials was labelled a *lex pure* [or *mere*] *poenalis*, since its formulation dealt only (*pure*, or *mere*) with the sanction.[16]

So elementary a piece of analysis could not be dignified with the name of 'theory'. The 'purely penal law theory' is the theory that asserts that some laws which might otherwise be interpreted as imposing a legal (and therefore, by the presumptive entailment we have been exploring, a moral) obligation on the subject to ϕ should rather be interpreted as imposing on him no more than the obligation to undergo the penalty P—or, in some versions of the theory, as imposing on him only the disjunctive obligation to *either* ϕ *or* undergo the penalty P. A law which should be so interpreted was a 'purely penal law'.

The reason for this description is as follows. The first systematic treatise devoted to the theory was Alphonsus de Castro's *De Potestate Legis Poenalis* (1550). In his version of the theory the decisive ground for interpreting a law as imposing only the obligation to undergo the penalty was simply the *form* of the law. If the legislative formulation was a conditional directive to impose a penalty (i.e. the *pure poenalis* form), then the law must[17] be interpreted as imposing on the subject no obligatory directive to do the act, ϕ, whose non-performance was the condition of the penalty. If, on the other hand, the legislator used the *poenalis mixta* form, incorporating an express direction to the subject to ϕ, then the law *must* be interpreted as imposing on the subject an obligation to ϕ. In short, for Castro the only class of enforceable laws that failed to impose on the citizen a straightforward obligation to ϕ was the class of laws

---

[16] The labels can be traced to Castro, *De Potestate Legis Poenalis* (1550); the distinctions are recognized by earlier authors: see Suarez, *De Legibus*, Book V, c. 4, para. 2.

[17] 'unless one can consult the lawgiver personally, and he tells you orally what he really meant': Castro. op. cit., Book I, c. 5.

pure poenalis in form.[18] (The modern reader will have observed that in Kelsen's 'pure theory of law' all laws are to be analytically rendered into the *pure poenalis* form, but are then to be interpreted as imposing on the citizen an obligation (purely legal, of course) to do the act whose non-performance is the condition for the application of the penalty.[19] The reader should reflect, not that Kelsen is wrong and Castro right, or vice versa, but that both the analytical reduction and the interpretative construction of a 'secondary norm' involve Kelsen in many more assumptions about the practical point and value of law than he is wont to admit.)

Castro's motive in linking obligation with verbal forms was to *limit* the effects of a notion of legal/moral obligation which, he said, he found widespread amongst laymen and ill-educated preachers and confessors—the notion that wherever a penalty is stipulated by the lawgiver there is no obligation on the subject to do (or refrain from) the act (or omission) to which the penalty is attached, and indeed no obligation to do anything other than to submit to the penalty if and when it is enforced. Castro's strategy was to restrict this wide exemption from positive obligation to the relatively narrow class of cases in which the lawgiver's formulae contained no directive to the subject at all.

This formalistic strategy is, of course, exposed to many objections. Above all, does not the lawgiver's use of the term 'penalty' (and/or of the machinery of criminal law enforcement) indicate an implicit directive to the subject to abstain from the penalized act or omission? Unless we admit the presence of this implicit directive, do we not extinguish the basic distinction between a *tax* (on conduct which the lawgiver regards as compatible with the common good) and a *penalty* (for conduct which he regards as inimical to the common good)?[20] In short,

[18] Such laws, according to Castro, impose only (*a*) an obligation on the judge to impose the penalty P, and/or (*b*) an obligation on the citizen to undergo P: ibid., c. 9. John Driedo, who anticipated Castro in his *De Libertate Christiana* (published posthumously in 1546), makes it clear that the latter obligation arises only 'when one has been caught': Book 2, c. 1.

[19] See Kelsen, *General Theory*, pp. 58–62.

[20] The point is made by two opponents of all 'purely penal law theories', Dominic de Soto, *De Iustitia et Iure* (1556), Book 1, q. 6, a. 5, and Louis Molina, *De Iustitia et Iure*, vol. III (1600), tr. 2, disp. 674. Cf. Hart's criticism of Kelsen and Holmes on similar lines, *Concept of Law*, pp. 38–9.

is it not 'verbal and childish'[21] to attend exclusively to the lawgiver's formulae in gauging his intention?

In reaction to Castro, there very soon emerged in a number of writers[22] a new version of 'purely penal law theory'. In this second version, the verbal form of a law was of little or no consequence; all laws imposing or concerning penalties were in substance directive or preceptive, incorporating a directive to citizens as well as to sanction-imposing officials, just as if they had been expressed in the *lex poenalis mixta* form. But 'directive' or 'preceptive' were given a special interpretation by these writers. The lawgiver, in their view, had two methods available to give action-guiding force to his directive: he could *either* attach to it the threat of a sanction P, to be imposed by his officials in the event of non-compliance with the directive, *or* attach to it a moral obligation (with the result that the non-complying subject would in the next life undergo the penalties imposed by God for sin). So if a lawgiver chose to stipulate a penalty P, he should be *presumed* to be withholding all moral obligation from his directive (express or implied) to ϕ. This presumption was founded on the lawyers' tag '*expressio unius est exclusio alterius*': 'And so the legislator who has power to oblige to both eternal [divine] and temporal [human] punishment, by invoking the latter seems to exclude the former'.[23] In a new sense, therefore, a law stipulating a penalty could be presumed to be 'purely penal', i.e. to impose no moral obligation on the subject.

It is hard to imagine a theory which detaches obligation more radically from all questions of the rational necessity of means uniquely appropriate to a common good. On this new version of the purely penal law theory, legal obligation (in both its

---

[21] Sylvester Prierias, *Summa Summarum de Casibus Conscientiae* (1515), s.v. 'inobedientia', para. 3, criticizing Castro's principal predecessors, Henry of Ghent (*c.* 1280) and the *Summa Angelica* (1486).

[22] Notably Martin de Azpilcueta, commonly called Navarrus (1557), and Gregory de Valencia (1592); but their views differ in various respects, and the synthesis in the text above is not to be attributed precisely to either.

[23] Navarrus, *Enchiridion sive Manuale Confessariorum* (1557), c. 23, n. 55. The presumption is not conclusive; contrary evidence as to the lawgiver's real intention is relevant if available.

purely legal sense and its moral sense)[24] amounts to nothing more than liability to sanctions human or divine; for this reason, if no other, it is (in both its senses) wholly at the disposition of the lawgiver to impose or withhold, in any degree, as he pleases.

Suarez, in his *De Legibus* (1612), objected to this second version of the theory on two closely related grounds: (*a*) because it eliminated from most enforceable laws all traces of a positive direction to the law-abiding citizen, and (*b*) because it assumed a reductionist account of obligation as equivalent to liability to penalty. But, while rejecting this radical elimination of differences commonly accepted and plainly relevant to practical reasonableness, Suarez (and his many followers) shared not only the new theorists' desire[25] that the consciences of citizens should not be burdened by too many and too onerous obligations, but also their belief that the intention of the lawgiver is decisive in determining the incidence of obligation. Thus there emerges in Suarez a third version of the purely penal law theory, skilfully combining elements of both the earlier versions, and foreshadowing Holmes in its principal analytical device.

In Suarez's account, a 'purely penal law' is one that, whatever its form, is to be interpreted as imposing on the subject (citizen) a disjunctive obligation: to *either* ϕ *or* submit to a 'penalty' P.[26] (It now seems desirable to enclose the word 'penalty' in inverted commas in stating the theory, since the theory's most obvious, though not most basic, difficulty is in explaining how P is a penalty at all; for the theory's essential contention is precisely that, in the case of a purely penal law, a citizen who fails to ϕ *has not violated the law at all* and *has not failed to comply with any directive* whether express or implied, obligatory or non-obligatory.) Suarez rejects the appeal to the tag *expressio unius est exclusio alterius*; not every law which stipulates or concerns a penalty is to be interpreted as 'purely

---

[24] This distinction between the senses of legal obligation is mine (XI.5), and is not explicit in the debates we are here analysing. I do not think the course of these debates would have been substantially affected if the participants had made the distinction.

[25] Expressed, e.g., by Blackstone in his discussion of 'purely penal law': I *Comm.* 58.

[26] *De Legibus*, Book I, c. 14, para. 7; Book III, c. 27, para. 3. Sometimes Suarez calls it a 'hypothetical precept', i.e. to submit to penalty if ϕ is not done: e.g. Book V, c. 4, para. 8. Not surprisingly, Suarez also recognizes 'purely penal' contracts, promises, or vows: Book III, c. 22, para. 6; Book V, c. 4, para. 8.

penal' in his view. Rather, the intention of the lawgiver to impose only the disjunctive obligation is to be declared explicitly, or else conveyed 'through tradition, custom or unwritten law'.[27] In the absence of any such customary principle of interpretation in a given community, Suarez suggests that Castro's criterion be used (i.e. that laws *pure poenalis* in *form* impose on the citizen no obligation to do or abstain from the acts referred to in the conditional clause). But Suarez avoids pure formalism by adding a proviso: the severity of the penalty or the intrinsic importance of the law's subject-matter[28] may indicate that the lawgiver (notwithstanding his form of stipulation) must have intended to impose a straightforward (not a merely disjunctive) obligation on the citizen.

What is the importance for us of these old theories? It is twofold. Firstly, they force us to refine our conception of the role of the lawgiver's will (his acts of choice or decision) in the imposition of legal and moral obligation. This point is developed in the following section. Secondly, they suggest a closer attention to the problems of conscience created by burdensome and insensitive laws, which are to be found today in legal systems that on the whole are just, as often as they were found by moral theologians in the legal systems of sixteenth- and seventeenth-century Europe. This point is developed in the next chapter.

XI.7 OBLIGATION AND LEGISLATIVE WILL

All versions of the purely penal law theory share the assumption that obligation is an effect of the lawmaker's will, is to be explained by reference to the moving force of his will, and can be imposed or withheld by him at his choice when he is indicating a rule or common pattern of action which he considers desirable for the common good. Some versions of the theory (e.g. Vazquez's[29]) propose that he can withhold all obligation from the pattern of action which he expressly or

[27] Ibid., Book V, c. 4, para. 8.

[28] i.e. the matters referred to in the conditional clause of the law: in my notation, ϕ. See ibid., Book V, c. 4, paras. 10, 12.

[29] *In Primam Secundae*, disp. 159, c. 2, 3. Vazquez's theory is a less formalistic version of Castro's, emphasizing legislative intention rather than legislative formulae.

impliedly is stipulating to the citizen. Others propose that he can regulate the degree of obligation. Others (e.g. Suarez's[30]) propose that, while obligation is essential if a stipulation is to count as a legal rule at all, this obligation may be directed by the lawgiver either (i) to the action, ϕ, which he desires or (ii) disjunctively to that action *or* the penalty (which amounts to saying that, on a certain condition, he can withhold all obligation from the stipulated pattern of action, ϕ).

A first difficulty, then, with all the purely penal law theories is that they almost inevitably trade in fictions. The fact is that very few lawmakers have any wish to distinguish between making conduct legally obligatory and subjecting it to a penalty, and even fewer have any will or intention about the moral implications of their enactments. Rarely do they go beyond the straightforward train of reasoning that common adherence to some single pattern of action ϕ is desirable for the common good, that ϕ should therefore be a legal requirement, and that a sanction P should be laid down (*a*) to indicate that it is henceforth a legal requirement, (*b*) to dissuade the recalcitrant from recalcitrance, and (*c*) with an eye to the range of pedagogical, retributive, and reformative considerations that I sketched in X.1, above. To look for a legislative intention to impose or withhold legal obligation in the moral sense, whether by looking to the drafting forms employed, or by searching behind them, is to look for something that typically is not there to be found. The upshot is a comedy of fictions: confronted by the stipulation of a 'disproportionately' severe penalty, some purely penal law theorists[31] presume that the severity indicates a legislative intention to impose a strict obligation to ϕ, while others[32] presume that it indicates the intention to impose no obligation to ϕ at all. Both presumptions are quite arbitrary, the latter (more popular) perhaps more so than the former.

A second difficulty goes a little deeper. All versions of the

---

[30] *De Legibus*, Book I, c. 14, para. 4; Book III, c. 20, para. 4.

[31] e.g. Castro, op. cit., Book I, c. 11; Suarez, op. cit., Book V, c. 4, para. 10.

[32] e.g. A. Lehmkuhl, *Theologia Moralis* (12th ed., Freiburg: 1914), vol. I, para. 312; J. Messner, *Social Ethics: Natural Law in the Modern World* (St. Louis: 1949), p. 211; for an early version of this line of thought, Alphonsus de Liguori, *Theologia Moralis* (1755), Book III, n. 616.

theory (and not just Castro's) muddy the distinction between tax and penalty. Now in various situations this distinction inevitably is hard to draw in practice: legislators imposing taxes can be uncertain whether they wish to discourage a certain form of conduct (e.g. smoking) or to raise revenue from it, or both. But it remains importantly desirable that law-abiding citizens should know where they stand in relation to any form of conduct they are considering: Is this (i) a form of conduct authoritatively declared to be incompatible with the authoritatively chosen common way (and *therefore* subjected to penalty) or is it (ii) a form of conduct which the legislator perhaps (*a*) approves but finds convenient as an occasion for raising revenue, or perhaps (*b*) disapproves of but is willing to concede to citizens (including the law-abiding) but only at a discouraging price? The distinction between (i) and (ii) is much more significant for the enterprise of ordering a community fairly through law than the distinction between (ii)(*a*) and (ii)(*b*). But 'purely penal law' theorists argue that the device of declaring an 'offence' and/or stipulating a 'penalty' is systematically ambivalent as between form (i) and form (ii)(*b*). In truth it is perhaps the legislator's most distinctive device for indicating form (i). Thus the 'purely penal law' theorists make legal regulation less finely tunable and so less apt as a way to the common good.

But the really basic difficulty lies in the very notion which gives the theory its perennial plausibility and .popularity. Obligation, it is argued, results from the lawmaker's decision to create an obligation-imposing rule. Can he not therefore decide to create a non-obligation-imposing rule, or a lesser-obligation-imposing rule, or a disjunctive-obligation-imposing ('either ϕ or P') rule? Does not power to do the greater include power to do the lesser? Only a rigorous analysis of the role of the legislator's will or decision in creating legal or legal/moral obligation will allow us to resist these rhetorical questions, as we should.

The necessary distinctions, though basic, are fine, as the failure of so many to see them shows. They can be made clear by reference to a legal analogy. (This analogy is intended to capture a single distinction, to rebut a single supposed entailment, not to be on all fours with law in general as it appears in the problematic of this section.) Consider a federal state,[33] in which the constitution requires lawyers to distinguish between 'federal' duties and 'provincial' duties, for example because 'federal' (i.e. central, as opposed to 'provincial') courts have exclusive jurisdiction in cases involving 'federal' rights and duties or obligations. A federal duty is one imposed by, under, or by virtue of federal law. Now suppose that a federal law stipulates that all persons who are certified to belong to class C shall have the duty to ϕ; and suppose further that under the constitution no provincial legislature could impose such a duty. This duty is imposed by federal law (and thus enforceable in federal courts). It remains a federal duty or obligation whether or not only federal officials have the power to certify that given persons belong to class C. Suppose that provincial officials are empowered by federal or provincial law to issue the relevant certificates: the duty of the certified persons to ϕ remains a federal duty. It will remain an exclusively federal duty even if the provincial officials are empowered to issue the certificates on criteria specified by provincial law, or by some foreign law, or in their own discretion. It will remain an exclusively federal duty whether the form of the provincially issued certificate is 'X is hereby certified to belong to class C', or 'X, being hereby certified to be a member of class C, shall ϕ', or 'X is hereby certified to be under an obligation to ϕ', or 'X is hereby required to ϕ'. None of these variations in verbal forms, or in width of delegation to non-federal officials, affects the *source* of the obligation, which is exclusively federal. The decisions of the non-federal officials to issue certificates are simply facts the occurrence of which attracts the federal obligation to a particular person—just as reaching the age of 18 is a fact which attracts federal obligations under federal laws relating to adults.

In short, although it is true that the decision (act of will) of a provincial official to bring it about that X is under an obligation to ϕ has the result that X is under that obligation, it is not true that therefore 'the source' of X's obligation is that

---

[33] The analogy could also be developed for a unitary state, in terms of a Minister, or local authority, or other functionary, empowered to classify persons for the purposes of an existing parliamentary enactment which imposes various obligations on various classes of persons.

official's act of will. Some official's act of will is indeed a necessary condition for X to incur this particular obligation; but that act of will has no more intrinsic importance (or explanatory significance in an explanation of X's obligation) than any other fact (e.g. turning 18) which is a necessary condition for X to incur that (or some other) obligation. And note that an official cannot decide to issue a certificate but to withhold the obligation that flows from that issue.

The foregoing analysis is not affected if we widen the range of choices open to the non-federal officials, e.g. to certify X as a member of class C, or class C_1, or class C_2, or class C_n, with the result that he would have the duty to ϕ, ... or ϕ_n, respectively. The only consequence of thus widening the range of options is that the officials' decisions can affect people in more various ways and are perhaps more difficult to make, and in these senses more 'weighty'; the decisions still are not 'the essential source' of the various obligations, any more than X's own decision would be 'the source' of his obligations under a federal law which imposed obligations on specified classes of persons but authorized and required people to *choose their own class* (whether periodically, or once for all).

By his decision to stipulate that ϕ is legally obligatory for X, a person with authority to make laws brings it about that (i) ϕ is legally obligatory and thus (presumptively) that (ii) ϕ is morally obligatory. But, as the foregoing analysis of the imagined federal legal situation should have helped to make clear, these consequences flow not from any 'force' of the law-giver's 'superior will', but from the interrelationship between (*a*) the fact that he has thus decided and (*b*) a 'higher' (or 'deeper') principle that makes that fact legally and/or morally significant.[34] In a strictly legal analysis, that further principle will consist in some law which imputes legal effect to specified types of legislative act (but which equally, though less commonly in the modern world, might impute normative effect to

---

[34] This explains how one should understand the *quia* ('because') in Aquinas's famous remark, still alive in English juristic parlance, that 'there are some things commanded because good, or prohibited because bad, but other things good because commanded, or bad because prohibited [*mala quia prohibita*]': *S.T.* II–II, q. 57, a. 2 ad 3; cf. I–II, q. 71, a. 6 ad 4.

events or facts which involve nobody's act of will or decision to impose such-and-such an obligation: see IX.3). And in the wider perspective of practical reasoning which includes but goes beyond the confines of legal reasoning, the relevant further principles will be the principles that the common good is to be advanced, that authoritative determination of co-ordination problems is for the common good, and that legal regulation is (presumptively) a good method of authoritative determination.

Hence, the question whether a lawgiver can withhold moral obligation from his stipulations, or modify the extent or degree of their moral force, is not to be settled by asking what moral obligations he can or does intend or 'will' to impose. Rather, that question is to be settled by asking what, in view of the common good, is the significance, for practical reasonableness, of certain facts—in this case, the fact that an authoritative lawgiver has decided and stipulated that ϕ is 'legally obligatory'. And the correct answer to that question is the one given in the preceding sections of this chapter, viz. that because of (a) the importance of law as a specific way of realizing a fundamental element of the common good, viz. a fair, predictable, positively collaborative, and flexibly stable order of human interrelationships, and (b) the fact that the law will not be effective for that purpose unless its subjects are generally willing to accept and act upon its stipulations (even when they would rather they had been otherwise), it follows (c) that where the authorized lawgiver stipulates that ϕ is obligatory, the effect, for the lawyer, is that ϕ is obligatory (there being no grades or degrees of legal obligation), and the effect for the conscientious citizen as such (whether or not he is also a lawyer) is that ϕ is (presumptively) morally obligatory. Thus the lawgiver's acts of will have their significance for the practical reason of other people only because they can take their place in a normative framework *which is not of the lawgiver's making*. That framework has no place for legislative 'intentions' (or 'acts of will') to withhold or modify moral obligations; for such intentions, if they had their intended effect, would seriously weaken the clarity and certainty and uniformity of application which are the very bases of law's utility as a specific way of realizing the common good. Therefore *these* intentions or acts of will are of no effect, i.e. are irrelevant to moral reasoning about one's obligations as a citizen.

To say this is not, of course, to deny that a legislator can expressly (or by a genuine implication) make a stipulation of which the correct legal analysis is that it is of the disjunctive sort identified by Suarez. But such legislative acts should be regarded by lawyers and citizens alike as muddled and abusive attempts to impose a tax on the doing of ϕ. They impose *no* form of obligation to do ϕ. So far as concerns the doing of ϕ, they are to be treated rather like a legislator's exhortations to do ϕ. Though such exhortations have some relevance to the citizen's own assessment of the requirements of the common good, they have *no* legal effect and hence do not create *any* degree of legal obligation in either the legal or the moral sense.

Nor, finally, does my basic argument against the 'purely penal law' theories in any way diminish the breadth and freedom of the legislator's authority to choose the obligatory pattern of action from amongst all the possible alternative patterns that might reasonably be made obligatory for the common good. Nor does it entail or suggest that the legislator is confined to crystallizing obligations that were somehow already 'there' (by virtue of 'natural law'): see X.6. If the analogy I developed with a certain federal legal situation seems to suggest such consequences, consider a further partial analogy. It sometimes happens that a central legislature, which has *exclusive* legislative jurisdiction over, say, the federal capital city, will provide for the criminal law for that city by simply enacting that the criminal law there shall be the criminal law of the surrounding province, whatever that law may be from time to time. In such a situation all the acts of choice about the *content* of the criminal law to be in force in the city are made by the provincial (i.e. non-federal) legislature—yet it remains true that that provincial legislature has *no* authority over the capital city, and no power to withhold, prevent, or modify the applicability of its laws to that city. The validity and obligatory force of the province's laws in that city are to be explained by reference essentially to the overriding federal law. So, too, in the analysis of law in general. The lawmaker's wide discretion to choose and mould the content of his subjects' obligations is not incompatible with the principles we have insisted upon, that the obligatory force of his acts of choice is not essentially[35] explicable by reference to those acts of choice as such, and is not his to impose, withhold, modify, or otherwise dispose of.

XI.8 'REASON' AND 'WILL' IN DECISION, LEGISLATION, AND COMPLIANCE WITH LAW

There the matter could be left. But a deeper understanding of the centuries-long debates among the moralists is available. *Why* did the purely penal law theorists (and indeed many others) attribute to acts of will a significance in the explanation of law that they do not truly have, and that seriously obscures the positively[36] explanatory role of the various relevant aspects of and appropriate means to the common good? In answering this it will be helpful to follow up the assumption or principle, shared by all parties to the debate, that the interplay of reasonableness and sheer decision in the politico-legal arena is illuminated by developing an analogy with an individual's own decision-making and action. We immediately notice that the most influential purely penal law theorist, Suarez, has developed an analysis of individual action (which he shares with Vazquez, another purely penal law theorist) in explicit opposition to the analysis offered by Aquinas, whose followers became the principal opponents of the purely penal law theory.

Like Aquinas, Suarez understands any free and deliberate human action in terms of a series (not necessarily chronologically extended) of interacting components. There is the intelligent grasp of an end, value, or objective: let this be attributed to one's 'reason', capacity to 'see the point' or understand the good of that end. But this will not result in action unless one is actively interested in, i.e. desirous of, that end, for oneself:

---

[35] But for the ambiguity of 'formal' in modern speech, it would be preferable to say 'formally': in short, our argument is aimed against the view, expressed by Locke in his sixth Essay on the Law of Nature, that 'the formal cause of obligation [is] the will of a superior' (von Leyden ed., Oxford: 1954, p. 185). Retaining the Aristotelian terminology used by Locke, our argument is that the will of a superior is one amongst several possible 'efficient', *not* formal, causes of obligation.

[36] Suarez of course allows the common good and justice a negative or limiting role in his account of law: a lawgiver's will does not have its moral effect if it is *unjust*: *De Legibus*, Book I, c. 9.

let this desire of the end be attributed to one's 'will', one's capacity to pursue objectives which one understands, or considers, to be valuable. Then there is the intelligent consideration of ways of achieving that end, and assessment of their respective efficacy, availability, advantages, and disadvantages: let this be attributed to one's 'reason'. But this consideration and assessment will not result in action unless one not only is attracted by the various respective advantages but also is willing to bring the potentially interminable process of comparing possibilities, advantages, and disadvantages to a close by choosing a specific means and *deciding* so to act: let this be attributed to one's 'will'. So far Aquinas and Suarez agree.[37]

But at this point in the analysis Suarez (like Vazquez) says: one's *decision* moves one to bestir oneself and carry out one's action. Decision being attributed by him, as by Aquinas, to 'will', we arrive at the same axiom as dominates Suarez's political and legal philosophy: it is will that moves man to action —in the political arena, the will of the superior; in the quasi-political arena of one's control over one's own faculties and limbs, one's own will. Aquinas, on the other hand, draws a distinction at this point. Between the decision, by which one settles, for oneself, what one is to do, and the physical or psychosomatic activity by which one actually executes one's own decision, Aquinas discerns by analysis a last component; he calls it *imperium* ('command', imperative). He attributes it to one's 'reason', and claims that what moves one to act is not, very strictly speaking, one's decision but this *imperium*, this 'direction to oneself'[38] Suarez protests: Aquinas's *imperium* is, he

---

[37] And Suarez would not dissent from Aquinas's view that 'reason' and 'will' are not to be personified or reified; it is only the person that acts; and, moreover, the alternating activations of the two capacities in question are psychologically entirely interdependent and only analytically distinguishable. 'Voluntas est in ratione' and 'est appetitus rationalis': *S.T.* I, q. 87, a. 4; I–II, q. 6 prol.; q. 8, a. 1; II–II, q. 58, a. 4c and ad 1.

[38] *S.T.* I–II, q. 17, a. 1: '. . . Hence, in conclusion, to order [or ordain: *imperare*] is an act of one's reason, presupposing an act of will in virtue of which one's reason moves [one], by way of the *imperium*, to the execution of the act.' Speaking more broadly, in the prologue to the same *Quaestio* 17, Aquinas refers to phases of action which are 'commanded by *the will*' (*imperatis a voluntate*). See also q. 90, a. 1 sed contra, and ad 3.

says, unnecessary and indeed impossible, 'certainly a fiction'.[39]

What, then, is the *imperium*, in Aquinas's analysis? It is an 'act of intelligence' by which one, so to speak, sets one's decided-upon course of action before oneself. Such an act of mind is necessary in order to guide, shape, direct the physical or psychosomatic activity which will carry one's intention into effect. So far, so good. But how can we say that this holding of the plan in one's mind's eye, however necessary it may be to the shaping of movement into 'an action', is what *moves* one to act? Certainly if, like Suarez both here and in the political context, we regard movement as the effect of a driving or pushing force,[40] we will be unable to accept Aquinas's claim about *imperium*. But Aquinas regards human movement not as the effect of a push (whether from within or from an external agent, for example a superior), but rather as a person's response to the attraction of (something considered to be) good. So for Aquinas, the final component in any deliberate action, viz. the actual bodily or other exertions, is an active response to (*a*) the good of the end and (*b*) the appropriateness of the means, both (*a*) and (*b*) being summarily held before one's attention by a representation (which could be expressed in propositions about what is-to-be or must be done) of the pattern of action which one has settled upon. This representation, the *imperium*, is to be attributed to one's reason rather than one's will, because it is representational (of a series of relationships between particular ends and particular means) and because it in turn enables intelligible (because intelligent) order to be brought into physical or psychosomatic exertions.

The *imperium* certainly presupposes 'exercises of will,' i.e. the desire of this particular end, the preference for these means, the sheer decision to bring deliberation to an end in choice.

---

[39] Suarez, *De Legibus* (1612), Book I, c. 5, para. 6; c. 4, para. 4. It is often overlooked that, in this, Suarez was preceded by the 'rationalist', Gabriel Vazquez, who argued elaborately that Aquinas's postulation of an *imperium* between one's decision and one's performance was 'unnecessary', 'inept', and 'futile': *in Primam Secundae*, disp. 49, c. 4 (on *S.T.* I–II, q. 17, a. 1). Indeed people were protesting along these lines within a few years of Aquinas's death.

[40] See, e.g., *De Legibus*, c. 5, para. 15: 'The first [of the characteristics of law that are to be found in the will not the reason] is that the law moves and applies [one] to action ...'; c. 4, para. 7: 'law does not merely enlighten, but also provides motive force and impels; and, in intelligent processes, the primary faculty for moving to action is the will'.

For without these exercises of will there would as yet be no plan of action and thus no fully determinate basis for exerting oneself in this way rather than that. But, granted those indispensable 'acts' of will (whose efficacy continues right through one's deliberation and one's action to its completion), it is the *imperium*, the fully determinate formulation to oneself of one's intention, that most directly moves one to act. For, being a representational 'act' of intelligence, there can (so to speak) shine through the *imperium* the attractiveness of the end or values at stake, and the adjudged appropriateness of the means selected; and it is *these* that account for one's carrying out this total action. Persons are moved by their perceptions and assessments of good, of value, of advantage; one's decisions mature into corresponding consummated actions not so much because, having being made, they somehow push one along 'of their own force', but rather because one can continue to express one's decision to oneself in a form that allows an understood relationship, between an end perceived as valuable and a means perceived as appropriate, to remain 'visible' to one, 'making sense' of one's exertions throughout their course.

There would be no point in taking sides in this debate about the 'faculties', were it not the case that Aquinas's analytical 'psychology' of the deliberate human act is simply one expression of his understanding of all such action by reference to the values which persons can seek and are seeking through action. At a decisive point in his explanation of obligation (itself the decisive aspect of law, for Suarez), Suarez allows the end and the means assessed as appropriate to it to drop out of view behind the sheer fact of decision.[41] To repeat: Aquinas regards the decision as a wholly necessary condition for any full human action; but he considers that the most precise reason for (and cause of) one's now acting is not that one has at some time (however proximate) decided so to act, but that one now sees the point of acting on one's decision: and this 'seeing the point' is accomplished by a rational representation-to-oneself-of-the-

---

[41] e.g. op. cit., Book I, c. 5, para. 21: 'if one has in mind the moving force in law, so that law is said to be the power in the ruler which moves and makes action obligatory, then in that sense, it is an act of will. If, on the other hand, we are referring to and considering that force in law which directs us towards what is good and necessary, then law pertains to the intellect'. Note the disjunction between the 'obligatory' and the 'good and necessary'.

selected-course-of-action, in a form homogeneous with and transparent for the intelligent grasp-of-value-and-assessment-of-means that has made one's decision a 'rational decision' rather than an 'impulse'. And as a Suarez denies this in his analytical psychology of individual action, so he correspondingly sees no need to explain obligation by setting in a framework of ends and means the ruler's decision that his subjects shall ϕ and shall be under an obligation to ϕ.[42]

In their politico-legal analysis, Suarez and Vazquez of course use a concept of *imperium*, command.[43] But there it is conceived by them primarily as an expression of the lawgiver's decision (to impose an obligation); the important thing for them is the act of will (decision) thus expressed and addressed to subjects. Again and again, Suarez makes the point that unless the lawgiver decides to make obligatory the pattern of action which he prefers, it will not be obligatory.[44] This proposition need not be denied. Suarez's mistake is to infer from it that what makes the conduct *actually* obligatory is, precisely and simply, the lawgiver's decision that it should be. The federal analogy should have put us on our guard against this inference. For Aquinas, on the other hand, the important thing about the lawgiver's *imperium* is not that it represents an act of decision, and indeed of decision to 'impose an obligation'; that fact is taken for granted. The important thing is that the expressed *imperium*, the promulgated 'intention of the legislator', represents to the subject an intelligible determinate pattern of action, which, having been chosen by the lawgiver to be obligatory, can actually *be* obligatory in the eyes of a reasonable subject because the ruler's *imperium* can (for the sake of the common good) be reasonably treated by the subject as if it were his own *imperium*.[45]

[42] By contrast, for Aquinas, obligation is simply a rational necessity of certain sorts of means to certain sorts of ends: *S.T.* I–II, q. 99, a. 1c; II–II, q. 58, a. 3 ad 2.

[43] See, e.g. *De Legibus*, Book I, c. 5, para. 13; Book II, c. 2, paras. 9, 14; c. 4, para. 1; c. 5, para. 13; c. 6, para. 6; etc.; *in Primam Secundae*, disp. 150, c. 3, no. 19; disp. 49, c. 2, no. 6. See notes to II.6, above.

[44] *De Legibus*, Book I, c. 4, paras 7, 8; c. 5, paras. 16, 19.

[45] See Aquinas, *S.T.* II–II, q. 50, a. 2c and ad 3; q. 47, a. 12c. Cf. Weber, *On Law*, p. 328: 'In our terminology domination shall be identical with authoritarian power of command. To be more specific, domination will mean the situation in which: The manifested will (command) of the ruler or rulers is meant to influence the conduct of one or more others (the ruled) and actually does influence it *in such a way that their conduct to a socially relevant degree occurs as if the ruled had made the content of the command the maxim of their conduct for its very own sake*' (emphasis added).

For, just as an individual's *imperium*, his formulated resolve to act, motivates his exertions by being transparent for the value of his objectives and the appropriateness of the chosen means to them, so in the eyes of the subject the ruler's *imperium* is compelling precisely by being transparent for the common good, for the needs of which the ruler's stipulation is treated by the subject (who recognizes the need for authoritative resolutions of social problems) as a relevant response.[46]

In short, in examining the purely penal law theories, with their attribution of all moving and obligatory force to the lawgiver's will, we are examining one limited aspect or offshoot of that vast movement of thought which has sought, with overwhelming historical success, to expel from the analysis of individual and political action all systematic attention to the intelligibility of the goods which are realizable in action.

XI.9   MORAL OBLIGATION AND GOD'S WILL

Those who founded legal obligation on the will of the ruler tried to be consistent in their understanding of obligation. They explained the obligation to act reasonably (i.e. morally) by appealing to a special exercise of the divine will, whereby God commands that good (the reasonable) be done and evil (the unreasonable) be avoided: II.8. For what could moral obligation consist in, if not in the movement of an inferior's will by a superior's?

Such an approach to the explanation of obligation is conceptually misdirected, because based on a reduction of the logic of practical reason to a kind of mechanics, in which one force moves or overrides another. Moreover, it invites the questions: Why should I obey God's will? How can obligation arise from what seems, after all, to be just one more *fact*? In the Suarezian tradition (which had antecedents, of course, and has followers to this day) such questions cannot be coherently answered. In

---

[46] This is why, at the very beginning of his treatise on law, Aquinas argues that 'law pertains to reason. For law is a rule and measure of action ... and the rule and measure of human acts is the reason, which is the basis [*principium*] of such acts. For ordering things to an end is the function of reason—and the end is the first *principium* of actions': *S.T.* I–II, q. 90, a. 1c. And, of course, the end or objective figures in one's practical reason(ing) under the description of 'good', 'valuable', etc.: q. 94, a. 2c; III.2, above.

II.5–6, above, I briefly traced the aftermath of the Suarezian impasse, down to its spectacular denouement in Hume's dismantling of the moral philosophy of several centuries. The grounding of ethical obligation in God's will becomes a prize specimen amongst conceptual fallacies collected for exhibition in elementary philosophy books.

Things are not, however, so simple: an unravelling of conflated issues is called for. Moreover, the topic should serve as a reminder that my explanation of obligation is as yet incomplete. For certainly it is possible to ask why the needs of the common good (taken as ultimate in this chapter) impose an obligation on you or me. It is possible to inquire, too, concerning the basic requirements of practical reasonableness which we discussed in Chapter V. Just what is meant by 'requirement'? And such questions are not merely conceptual or speculative. They arise, sometimes quite urgently, as part of or extensions to the effort to make practical sense of one's action and of one's life as a whole. There is room, therefore, for a deeper explanation, which I try to provide in Chapter XIII.

NOTES

XI.1

Obligation in Aristotle ... It is sometimes suggested that Aristotle has no concept of (what we would call moral) obligation at all. But for much evidence to the contrary, see *Gauthier–Jolif*, II, 2, pp. 568–75.

Obligation, 'ought', and supererogation ... See, e.g., Joel Feinberg, 'Supererogation and Rules' (1961) 71 *International J. Ethics* 276–88; Roderick M. Chisholm, 'Supererogation and Offence' (1963) 5 *Ratio* 1–14 (both in J. Thomson and G. Dworkin, eds., *Ethics*, New York: 1968).

Division of ethics into 'deontological' and 'teleological' ... Aristotle's certainly escapes this categorization: see J. M. Cooper, *Reason and Human Good in Aristotle* (Cambridge, Mass.: 1975), pp. 87–8. So does Aquinas's, and so does the ethics in this book.

XI.2

Promising and contract ... On the relationship between promises and the modern Anglo-American law of contracts (and its antecedents), see E. Allan Farnsworth, 'The Past of Promise: an Historical Introduction to Contract' (1969) 69 *Columbia L. Rev.* 576–607.

The focal meaning of 'promising' ... For much of the following analysis of promissory obligation, see G. E. M. Anscombe, 'On Promising and its Justice, and whether it needs be respected *in foro interno*' (1969) 3 *Crítica* 61–78. For a similar account, differing in details, see J. Raz, 'Promises and Obligations' in Hacker and Raz, *Essays*, pp. 210–27; in the same tradition, Grotius, *De Jure Belli ac Pacis* (1625), Book II, c. xi, paras. ii–iv.

Obligation based, via 'estoppel', on relied-upon expressions of intention to act ... See Neil MacCormick, 'Voluntary Obligation and Normative Powers' (1972) *Proc. Aris. Soc.*, Supp. vol. 46, pp. 59–78; *Australia* v. *France, I. C. J. Rep.* 1975, 253 at pp. 267–8, and the comment by Thomas M. Franck, (1975) 69 *Am. J. Int. L.* 612–20. Reliance rather than promise is increasingly the basis of American contract law, but this develops in tandem with a 'risk' theory of liability which bypasses, or at least radically reinterprets, the 'obligation' of contracts: see Roscoe Pound, *Introduction to the Philosophy of Law* (rev. ed., New Haven: 1954), pp. 159–68; for the origins of the risk theory, see Oliver Wendell Holmes, *The Common Law* (1881; ed. Mark deWolfe Howe, Cambridge, Mass.: 1967), p. 235; for criticism of Holmes's corresponding theory of obligation, see XI.5.

'First-level explanations' of promissory obligation ... See Raz, *Practical Reason*, pp. 52–3, 56–8, for exposition and criticism of the analogous 'practice theory of norms'.

'From status to contract' ... See Henry Sumner Maine, *Ancient Law*, 10th ed., 1884; ed. F. Pollock [1906], Boston: 1963), p. 165; on 'The Early History of Contract', see ibid., ch. ix; for the wider relevance of the main lines of Maine's analysis of contract, see Max Gluckman, *The Ideas in Barotse Jurisprudence* (Manchester: 2nd ed., 1972), ch. 6 and pp. xvi, xxiv. Both Maine and Gluckman show how the emergence of the modern concept of promissory contract is, in widely differing legal systems, (i) the struggle to detach the focal notion of an expressed and accepted intention to undertake an obligation from the notion that no obligation can arise without some transfer, or partial execution, or at least some formalities; and (ii) the struggle to admit that the obligations created by contract need not conform to any pre-existing type of proprietary or status obligation. It matters little whether or not this line of development is, as as a linear progression, universal: Leopold Pospisil, *Anthropology of Law* (New York: 1971), p. 150, gives some reason for thinking that it is not.

XI.3

Legal obligation is of invariant force ... Dworkin, *Taking Rights Seriously* (London: 1977), chs. 2 and 3, stresses that the obligation derived from legal *rules* is not a matter of weight. Although he also argues that there are legal *principles* which do create legal obligations of varying weight, he is primarily concerned to argue that such principles have legal weight precisely by virtue of their moral weight, and that 'legal theory' is a branch of moral or political theory or ideology. In this way, he minimizes the extent to which legal thought can and does insulate itself from the general flow of practical reasoning. The present chapter is not concerned to assert or deny that in 'sociological fact' all legal obligations are (treated as) of the same weight, or that in a moralist's 'theory of law' all legal obligations are of the same weight; its concern is to explain the practical reasons for a working postulate of legal thought, and the consequences of the postulate in legal reasoning.

No conflicts between duty-imposing rules ... Dworkin's view that 'such conflicts would be occasions of emergency, occasions requiring a decision that would alter the set of standards in some dramatic way', and his supporting reasons (op. cit., pp. 74–7), are to be preferred to Raz's view that 'conflicts' are commonplace ('Legal Principles and the Limits of Law' (1972) 81 *Yale L. J.* 823).

Explanation of obligation by reference to human reactions to non-performance ... The best attempt, supplementing Kelsen's with Hart's ideas, is Raz, *Legal System*, pp. 147–59. Other well-known sources are Hobbes, *De Cive* [1651], ch. XIV, paras. 1, 2; Austin, *Province*, pp. 14–15.

XI.4

Schematic representation of obligation-imposing rules ... For a fuller version on similar lines, see G. H. von Wright, *Norm and Action* (London: 1963), ch. V. In my notation ϕ corresponds to what is called 'a pattern of conduct' by Hart, 'a norm act' by Raz, 'an action-idea' by Alf Ross, 'a phrastic' by R. M. Hare, 'norm-contents' or more precisely 'generic acts' by von Wright ...

Moral obligation to obey the law ... M. B. E. Smith, 'Is there a prima facie Obligation to Obey the Law?' (1973) 82 *Yale L. J.* 950, argues that there is no obligation, even prima facie, to obey the law as such ('generically'); when confronted with a legal demand (e.g. to stop at a traffic light) one is morally entitled to start with a clean slate, i.e. to assess what is morally required in the situation apart from the fact that there is a rule of law demanding certain conduct in that situation. But in evaluating the fate of a society whose members showed this approach, i.e. who held that there was no prima-facie obligation to obey the law, Smith says (p. 960) 'we must assume that the members of that society accept other moral rules (e.g. "Do not harm others", "Keep promises", "Tell the truth") which will give them a moral incentive to obey the law in most circumstances'. He fails to see that all the arguments he brings against the generic obligation to obey the law could equally be brought against those other moral principles or norms—the general strategy of his argument being to postulate circumstances in which, if one started with a clean slate, one would conclude that there was no sufficient reason to do what a law stipulates, or, alternatively, that there was sufficient reason to do it even in the absence of that law. That general strategy would easily dispose of the obligations to keep promises, tell no lies, etc. Even on its own quasi-utilitarian terms, the strategy is unsound because it overlooks the drastic 'second-order' effects of everyone holding himself ready to start with a clean slate in each situation, i.e. ready to pick and choose amongst the options while prescinding from 'framework' considerations derived from past agreements and undertakings, general adherence to basic values, or authoritative stipulations in community. Some of these effects are well explored in D. H. Hodgson, *Consequences of Utilitarianism* (Oxford: 1967).

Exclusionary force of legal rules ... For very strong illustrations, consider two of Aquinas's teachings: (i) that a public official does not do wrong by carrying out a judicial sentence which he knows to be mistaken (not because the law applied was unjust, but because the defendant was innocent), since 'it is not for him to discuss the sentence of his lawful superior': *S. T.* II–II, q. 64, a. 6 ad 3; (ii) similarly, a judge must not defy the laws about evidence, proof, verdicts, etc., in order to bring about the acquittal of someone he *knows* (from legally inadmissible evidence) to be innocent. The most he can do is to subject the legally found 'facts' to stringent tests in an effort to find some error in the process of their determination: *S. T.* II–II, q. 64, a. 6 ad 3; q. 67, a. 2c. Note that Aquinas's older contemporary, Saint Bonaventure, disagreed with the rigorism of the second teaching.

XI.5

Obligation and penalty in contract ... Since the mid-seventeenth century, English law has treated 'penalties' (as distinct from genuine covenanted pre-estimates of damages) as irrecoverable: see A. W. B. Simpson, *A History of the Common Law of Contract* (Oxford: 1975), pp. 118–25. But the standard-form written contract of medieval Europe, the conditioned bond on which in English law the action of Debt would lie, might be regarded as a disjunctive contract, as Simpson seems to: ibid., p. 6. 'Performance of what may be called the underlying agreement is not imposed as a duty; instead performance is only relevant as providing a defence to an action of debt for the penalty': p. 112. But he also cites much evidence that the courts and jurists never lost sight of the underlying substantial agreement 'to which the obligee is primarily bound' (per Stanton J., in the Eyre of Kent, 1313–14, quoted ibid., p. 115). Indeed, rather inconsistently with his earlier remarks, Simpson concludes on p. 123 that 'the institution of the penal bond and the practice of the courts in upholding such bonds exemplified' 'the idea that the real function of contractual institutions is to make sure, as far as possible, that agreements are performed'—and here 'agreements' must refer to the 'underlying, substantial agreement' concealed 'beneath the legal form' (p. 112). So there is nothing Holmesian about the medieval technique, adapted to a time 'where men cannot trust each other, and the machinery of the law is weak' (p. 124).

Influence of the Summa Angelica *and other* Summae Confessariorum *on English Law* ... See Simpson, op. cit., pp. 337–405.

Holmes on contract ... See Mark deWolfe Howe, *Justice Oliver Wendell Holmes: The Proving Years 1870–1882* (Cambridge, Mass.: 1963), pp. 224, 233–40. Note the evidence (ibid., p. 234 n. 25) that Holmes did not himself accept that his analysis amounts to saying that the promisor undertakes a disjunctive obligation (to either perform or be liable in damages). The fact is that Holmes really wished to get rid of the concept of obligation ('duty') in this context: see ibid., pp. 236, 76–9.

XI.6

History of the 'purely penal law' theories ... A 'purely penal law theory' is first clearly formulated in Angelo de Clavasio's *Summa Angelica de Casibus Conscientialibus* (1486; at least 30 editions by 1520), a manual for confessors which influenced the development of English law (e.g. of contract) through the English law student's first and most long-lasting textbook, St. German's *Doctor and Student*. The theory was still producing confused textual echoes in the seventh and later editions of Blackstone's *Commentaries*. See I *Commentaries* (7th ed., 1775), 58 n., claiming misleadingly to follow Robert Sanderson's *De Obligatione Conscientiae* (1660). The best accessible discussion is William Daniel, *The Purely Penal Law Theory in the Spanish Theologians from Vitoria to Suarez* (Rome: 1968), which gives references and quotations from all the writers here cited. He effectively criticizes (p. 112) D. C. Bayne, *Conscience, Obligation and the Law* (Chicago: 1966), which is, however, of value. The history of the theory is, of course, considerably more complex than our brief account can suggest.

'Obligation' in the purely penal law theories ... Throughout the moralists' controversy about 'purely penal laws', 'obligation' signifies, primarily (since the disputants were moralists) the moral obligation to ϕ that presumptively is entailed by any legal obligation to ϕ, and secondarily the legal obligation itself as it might be recognized in a judge's reasoning or conclusions (to be sharply distinguished, of course, from 'legal obligation' in the restricted [Holmesian] sense of mere liability to penalty P in the event of failure to ϕ). Note, however, that even a moralist strongly opposed to the 'purely penal law' theories might surrender to the misleading simplification according to which one has a 'legal obligation' if and only if one is liable to P on failure to ϕ: see Dominic Soto, *De Justitia et Jure* (1556), Book X, q. 5, a. 7.

Motives of Castro's formalist strategy ... See Daniel, op. cit., pp. 46, 77–83, 164–70. Castro's principal follower in this respect was Gabriel Vazquez, *in Primam Secundae*, disp. 159, c. 2. To the objection that 'purely penal' stipulations do not deserve the name of law, Vazquez is inclined to reply that he agrees, or that they can be called laws because they impose an obligation on the judge to inflict a penalty: ibid., c. 3.

Navarrus, Gregory de Valencia, and the 'second purely penal law theory' ... See Daniel, op. cit., pp. 64–70, 82–8, 175–200, labelling the theory one of 'benign supposition' (sc. as to the legislator's intention (not) to bind). Suarez's objections to this version of the theory are discussed ibid. at pp. 188, 205: see Suarez, *De Legibus*, Book III c. 22, para. 10; Book V, c. 3, paras. 11–12. Daniel, op. cit., pp. 86–7, 91, rightly stresses the importance of the assumption of Navarrus and many others (encouraged by the unfortunate medieval legal, canonical, and theological idiom which distinguished between *obligatio ad culpam* and *obligatio ad poenam*) that (moral) *guilt*, like a human penalty, was a kind of sanction, which the legislator could either impose or withhold.

'Purely penal law theory' as a relief from burdensome laws ... See especially Daniel, op. cit., ch. 4, on the theological discussion of (i) the harsh Spanish laws, of the sixteenth century, forbidding the gathering of wood and (ii) sales tax (the *alcavala*, first imposed in Spain in 1341, and rising to 10 per cent or more in the sixteenth century).

Suarez and the 'third purely penal law theory' ... See Daniel, op. cit., pp. 88–92, 94–113, 158–62, 200–6. Suarez's theory has remained influential to the present day.

XI.7

Distinction between tax and penalty ... As Soto, Bartholomew Medina (1577), and others (see Daniel, op. cit., pp. 41–4) have been aware, the distinction, used also by the US Supreme Court (see e.g. *United States* v. *La Franca* (1930) 282 US 568 at 572), representing a tax as a compulsory contribution to the expenses of maintaining the common good, is too simple. There is a third category, of laws imposing a levy on conduct (e.g. the export of grain, the smoking of cigarettes) in order to discourage it (or: to allow it at a price: *lex concessoria*). Holmes boldly used the existence of borderline tax/penalty cases to buttress his denial of the distinction altogether (from the 'strictly legal' point of view, i.e. the 'bad man's' point of view, of course): 'The Path of the Law' (1897) 10 *Harv. L. Rev.* 457 at 461.

XI.8

Aquinas and Suarez on 'reason' and 'will' ... For Aquinas, see *S. T.* I–II, qq. 10–17. Useful syntheses are provided by S. Pinckaers in the Éditions du Cerf edition of the *Somme Théologique*, 1a–2ae, qq. 6–17 (2nd ed., Paris: 1962), pp. 408–49, and more briefly by Thomas Gilby in vol. 17 of the Blackfriars translation (1966), appendix I. Behind Aquinas in these matters lies Aristotle, *Nic. Eth.* esp. VI, 2:1139a17–b6 (notwithstanding Aquinas's misunderstandings of Aristotle on various points of detail: see *Gauthier–Jolif* on 1139b4–5 and III, 5: 1113a6–7). For Suarez, see *De Legibus*, Book I, cc. 5 and 6; Book II, c. 3, paras. 4–9, and the texts cited in T. E. Davitt, *The Nature of Law* (St. Louis: 1951), ch. VI; D. P. O'Connell, 'Rationalism and Voluntarism in the Fathers of International Law' (1964) 13 *Indian Yearbook Int. Aff.* Part II, pp. 3–32. The real differences between Aquinas and Suarez, stressed in the text, should not be taken to entail that Suarez was a pure voluntarist; rather, he inclines to the view (*De Legibus*, Book I, c. 5, paras. 20–2) that 'for law there are two requisites: impulse and direction, or (so to speak) goodness and truth, i.e. right judgement concerning the things to be done and an efficacious will impelling to the performance of those things; and so law may consist of both an act of the will and an act of the reason'. A good summary of similarities and differences is Walter Farrell, *The Natural Moral law according to St. Thomas and Suarez* (Ditchling: 1930).

Excursus on 'will' theories of obligation

Many accounts of obligation, both promissory and legal, have employed, more or less obscurely, the notion that it is created by the will—of the promisor, or of a superior whose will 'moves' the inferior's. Often this goes along with the notion that the subject's will is moved by the threat of sanction (or, sometimes, by prospect of reward): Bentham's *Of Laws in General* is a good example, and can be interpreted as both asserting and denying that sanction (or reward) is strictly essential to legal obligation in its formal essence (as distinct from its efficacy). (For similar ambiguity, or ambivalence, see Pufendorf, *De Jure Naturae et Gentium* (1672) I, c. vi, para. 9.) In *A Fragment of Government* (1776), ch. V, paras. vi, vii, Bentham had defined duty in terms of sanction: 'That is my *duty* to do, which I am liable to be punished, according to law, if I do not ... One may conceive three sorts of duties; *political, moral,* and *religious*; correspondent to the three sorts of *sanctions* by which they are enforced ... Political duty is created by punishment: or at least by the will of persons who have punishment in their hands ...' See also ibid., ch. I, para. xii, note, where duty is defined simply in terms of expressions of the will of a superior; likewise *Of Laws*, pp. 93, 294. See *Of Laws*, pp. 54, 134, 136 n., 248, 298, for passages emphasizing the importance of sanctions, in the absence of which 'obligation would be a cobweb' (p. 136 n.) [but would not be inconceivable?] and the law 'could not have any of the effect of what is really a law' (p. 248). On p. 298 Bentham wrestles directly with the question and concludes: 'an expression of will, and the expression of the motive relied on for the accomplishment of that will, may actually exist the one without the other ...' This is reflected in his formal definition of 'a law' in the opening sentence of his work (p. 1). In all, the evidence for a change of view after the *Fragment* is insubstantial, but the ambiguities are significant evidence of the strength of the will-theory of obligation.

At any rate, it is clear that in the vast jurisprudence of Francisco Suarez, for example, obligation as the motive force of superior will moving inferior will (and see II.6, above) is clearly and fairly firmly distinguished from liability to penalty or sanction (as one would expect of a theorist who still subscribes to the medieval distinction between the 'directive force' of law, and its 'coercive force'). On obligation as the motive force of superior will, see e.g. *De Legibus* (1612), Book II, c. vi, paras. 7, 10, 22 (where no reference to sanction is ever made). For the distinction between 'directive' and 'coercive' 'power' or 'binding force' of laws, see e.g. Book III, c. xxxii, paras. 5, 6 (which, however, confuses imposing an obligation with sucessfully inducing or 'obliging'), c. xxxiii, paras. 1, 8, 9; Book VII, c. xix, para. 3. Suarez's central proof of his version of the 'purely penal law theory' (see IX.6, above) is as follows: 'the lawmaker can make a law obliging in conscience and at the same time imposing a penalty on law-breakers, and he can also make a law obliging in conscience without attaching any penalty to violation; therefore he can also make a law which obliges only to [undergo] the due penalty ...': Book V, c. iv, para. 3. In short, the fact that one is liable to legally stipulated penalty in the event of failing to ϕ simply does not entail, in Suarez's view, that ϕ-ing is obligatory (whether legally or morally).

A special, but not historically insignificant variant of the will theory of promissory obligation was suggested by Hobbes in his *De Corpore Politico* (1650), Part I, c. 3 (Raphael, *British Moralists*, para. 102): 'There is a great similitude between what we call *injury* or *injustice* in the actions and conversations of men in the world, and that which is called absurd in the arguments and disputations of the Schools. For as he which is driven to contradict an assertion by him before maintained, is said to be reduced to an absurdity ... there is in every breach of covenant a contradiction properly so called. For he that covenanteth, willeth to do, or omit, in the time to come. And he that doth any action, willeth it in that present, which is part of the future time contained in the covenant. And therefore he that violateth a covenant, willeth the doing and the not doing of the same thing, which is a plain contradiction. And so injury is an absurdity of conversation [sc. actions and transactions], as absurdity is a kind of injustice in disputation.' The argument reappears in slightly different form at a critical juncture of the *Leviathan* (1651), c. 14 (*British Moralists*, paras. 59, 61), with particular reference to the duty, or state of being 'obliged', created by 'contracts' ('covenant' here being given a special meaning, more restricted than in the *De Corpore Politico*). In the *Leviathan* the argument from self-contradiction is simply juxtaposed with Hobbes's better-known view that 'the bonds, by which men are ... obliged ... have their strength, not from their nature, (for nothing is more easily broken than a man's word,) but from fear of some evil consequence upon the rupture'. The argument from self-contradiction has two obvious weaknesses. The first is its equivocation between willing to φ at a certain time and willing at a certain time to φ. The second is that where two propositions contradict each other, *either* may be false, and there is no *a priori* reason to prefer one to the other; but a promissory act of will must *a priori* be preferred to the violative act of will if the former is to be counted as obligation-imposing.

When Kant took up the argument from self-contradiction, he seems to have identified the first weakness (of equivocation) but not the second: see his *The Science of Right*, First Part, sec. 7: 'This right [to what has been promised] is not to be annulled by the fact that the promiser having said at one time, "This thing shall be yours", again at a subsequent time says, "My will now is that the thing shall not be yours." In such relations of rational right, the conditions hold just the same as if the promiser had without interval of time between them, made the two declarations of his will, "This shall be yours", and also "This shall not be yours"; which manifestly contradicts itself.' With this read secs. 10, 17, and 19 and Second Part, secs. 45, 46, and 47.

The whole strategy of explaining obligation in terms of acts of will inducing, blocking, or overriding each other fails because it has turned aside from the genuine 'logic of the will', which is the logic of practical reasoning, that is, of values and their realization, of the requirements of basic principles which *must* be satisfied if human goods (including the good of reasonableness) are to be as fully participated in as they can be. The rational necessity which we call obligation (in any of its forms) can be accounted for only by attending (as one in practice attends when 'willing' anything) to the goods at stake in compliance or non-compliance with a proposed or stipulated course of action.

In modern jurisprudence, the theory that attributes significance to 'acts of will' and their 'contents' is not advanced directly for the purpose of explaining obligation, but to explain the 'nature' or 'ontological status' of norms. See G. H. von Wright, *Norm and Action* (London: 1963) pp. 120–1, where von Wright announces his adherence to 'the *will-theory* of norms'. He asks (p. 148): 'Can commands or norms in general, ever contradict one another? I wish I could make my readers see the serious nature of this problem ... It is serious because, if no two norms can logically contradict one another, then there can be no logic of norms either ... So therefore, if norms are to have a logic, we must be able to point to something which is impossible in the realm of norms ...'. After further discussion he concludes (p. 151): 'The only possibility which I can see of showing that norms which are prescriptions can contradict one another [sc. so that their coexistence in a corpus of norms is logically impossible] is to relate the notion of a prescription to some idea about the unity and coherence of a will ... a *rational* or *coherent* or *consistent* will.' His 'will-theory' prevents him, however, explaining why inconsistency *is* irrational. Well known are Kelsen's struggles with the problem, which start and (after many attempts) end with the admission that in a pure will-theory of norms contradictory norms *can* coexist within the same system: see Kelsen, *General Theory*, pp. 401–6, 437; for the intermediate efforts, see *The Pure*

Theory of Law (Berkeley: 1967), pp. 72, 74, 205–8; for the final admission, (1963) XIII *Österreichische Zeitschrift für öffentliches Recht* 2 quoted in translation in Alf Ross, *Directives and Norms* (London: 1968), pp. 157–8.

XI.9

Moral obligation 'explained' by reference to God's will ... For example, see Suarez, *De Legibus* (1612), Book II, c. 6, paras. 5–24: e.g. 'the law of nature, as it is true divine law, may also superimpose its own moral obligation, derived from a precept, over and above what may be called the natural evil or virtue inherent in the subject-matter in regard to which such a precept is imposed' (para. 12); '... in view of the fact that no real [*propria*] prohibition or preceptive obligation is created solely by a judgment [i.e. as to the evil of a particular action], since such an effect cannot be conceived of apart from volition, it is consequently evident that there exists, in addition, the [divine] will to prohibit the act in question, for the reason that it is evil' (para. 13): '... and if no such prohibition existed, that action would not possess the consummate and perfect character (so to speak) of guilt ...' (para. 19); '... the mere dictate of intelligence apart from will ... cannot impose upon another being a particular obligation. For obligation is a certain moral impulse [*motio*] to action; and to impel [*movere*] another to act is a work of will' (para. 22). Since Suarez is under pressure from theological tradition to admit that an action can be identified as contrary to one's obligation, and that the doing of it can be described as guilty, *without reference to God's will*, his effort to be consistent with his own concept of obligation is only verbally successful; again and again in these paragraphs he is brought to the brink of saying that even without reference to any divine precept, acts (or their avoidance) can be obligatory (or guilty/sinful); this is betrayed in his repeated statement that the obligation imposed by the divine will underpinning natural law is 'some sort of *additional* obligation' (paras. 12, 13,) a 'special obligation' (paras. 11, 17, 22).

Antecedents of Suarez on the obligation-imposing force of God's will ... See Suarez, *De Legibus*, Book II, c. 6, para. 4, citing a number of fourteenth-century writers, most relevantly Ockham, *Super quatuor libros Sententiarum* (c. 1318), Book II, q. 19 ad 3 and 4, and Peter d'Ailly, *Quaestiones ... super libros Sententiarum* (1375), Book I, q. 14, a. 3. Between these and Aquinas, Suarez tries to hold a 'via media' (para. 5). Especially forthright for the view that obligation can derive only from the will of a superior is Suarez's great predecessor in the Spanish revival of scholasticism, Vitoria: see his *De eo ad quod tenetur homo cum primum venit ad usum rationis* (1535), Part II, para. 9, cited by Suarez, *De Legibus*, Book II, c. 6, para. 5; quoted in II.6, above.

XII

UNJUST LAWS

XII.1 A SUBORDINATE CONCERN OF NATURAL LAW THEORY

THE long haul through the preceding chapters will perhaps have convinced the reader that a theory of natural law need not have as its principal concern, either theoretical or pedagogical, the affirmation that 'unjust laws are not law'. Indeed, I know of no theory of natural law in which that affirmation, or anything like it, is more than a subordinate theorem. The principal concern of a theory of natural law is to explore the requirements of practical reasonableness in relation to the good of human beings who, because they live in community with one another, are confronted with problems of justice and rights, of authority, law, and obligation. And the principal jurisprudential concern of a theory of natural law is thus to identify the principles and limits of the Rule of Law (X.4), and to trace the ways in which sound laws, in all their positivity and mutability, are to be derived (not, usually, deduced: X.7) from unchanging principles—principles that have their force from their reasonableness, not from any originating acts or circumstances. Still, even the reader who has not been brought up to believe that 'natural law' can be summed up in the slogan '*lex injusta non est lex*' will wish a little more to be said about that slogan and about the effect of unjust exercises of authority upon our responsibilities as reasonable persons.

The ultimate basis of a ruler's authority is the fact that he has the opportunity, and thus the responsibility, of furthering the common good by stipulating solutions to a community's co-ordination problems: IX.4. Normally, though not necessarily, the immediate source of this opportunity and responsibility is the fact that he is designated by or under some authoritative rule as bearer of authority in respect of certain aspects of those problems: IX.4, X.3. In any event, authority is useless for the common good unless the stipulations of those in authority (or which emerge through the formation of authoritative customary rules) are treated as exclusionary reasons, i.e. as sufficient reason for acting notwithstanding that the subject would not himself have made the same stipulation and indeed considers the actual stipulation to be in some respect(s) unreasonable, not fully appropriate for the common good . . .: IX.1, IX.2. The principles set out in the preceding three sentences control our understanding both of the types of injustice in the making and administration of law, and of the consequences of such injustice.

XII.2 TYPES OF INJUSTICE IN LAW

First, since authority is derived solely from the needs of the common good, a ruler's use of authority is radically defective if he exploits his opportunities by making stipulations intended by him not for the common good but for his own or his friends' or party's or faction's advantage, or out of malice against some person or group. In making this judgment, we should not be deflected by the fact that most legal systems do not permit the exercise of 'constitutional' powers to be challenged on the ground that that exercise was improperly motivated. These restrictions on judicial review are justified, if at all, either by pragmatic considerations or by a principle of separation of powers. In either case, they have no application to the reasonable man assessing the claims of authority upon him. On the other hand, it is quite possible that an improperly motivated law may happen to be in its contents compatible with justice and even promote the common good.

Secondly, since the location of authority is normally determined by authoritative rules dividing up authority and jurisdiction amongst separate office-holders, an office-holder may wittingly or unwittingly exploit his opportunity to affect people's conduct, by making stipulations which stray beyond his authority. Except in 'emergency' situations (X.5) in which the law (even the constitution) should be bypassed and in which the source of authority reverts to its ultimate basis (IX.4), an *ultra vires* act is an abuse of power and an injustice to those treated as subject to it. (The injustice is 'distributive' inasmuch as the official improperly assumes to himself an excess of authority, and 'commutative' inasmuch as the official improperly seeks to subject others to his own decisions.) Lawyers sometimes are surprised to hear the *ultra vires* actions of an official categorized as abuse of power, since they are accustomed to thinking of such actions as 'void and of no effect' in law. But such surprise is misplaced; legal rules about void and voidable acts are 'deeming' rules, directing judges to treat actions, which are empirically more or less effective, *as if* they had not occurred (at least, as juridical acts), or *as if* from a certain date they had been overridden by an *intra vires* act of repeal or annulment. Quite reasonably, purported juridical acts of officials are commonly presumed to be lawful, and are treated as such by both fellow officials and laymen, unless and until judicially held otherwise. Hence, *ultra vires* official acts, even those which are not immune-for-procedural-or-pragmatic-reasons from successful challenge, will usually subject persons to effects which cannot afterwards be undone; and the bringing about of (the likelihood of) such effects is an abuse of power and an unjust imposition.

Thirdly, the exercise of authority in conformity with the Rule of Law normally is greatly to the common good (even when it restricts the efficient pursuit of other objectives); it is an important aspect of the commutative justice of treating people as entitled to the dignity of self-direction (X.4), and of the distributive justice of affording all an equal opportunity of understanding and complying with the law. Thus the exercise of legal authority otherwise than in accordance with due requirements of manner and form is an abuse and an injustice, unless those involved consent, or ought to consent, to an accelerated procedure in order to cut out 'red tape' which in the circumstances would prejudice substantial justice (cf. VII.7).

Fourthly, what is stipulated may suffer from none of these defects of intention, author, and form, and yet be substantively unjust. It may be distributively unjust, by appropriating some aspect of the common stock, or some benefit of common life or enterprise, to a class not reasonably entitled to it on any of the criteria of distributive justice, while denying it to other persons; or by imposing on some a burden from which others are, on no just criterion, exempt. It may be commutatively unjust, by denying to one, some, or everyone an absolute human right, or a human right the exercise of which is in the circumstances possible, consistent with the reasonable requirements of public order, public health, etc., and compatible with the due exercise both of other human rights and of the same human rights by other persons (VII.4–5, VIII.7).

XII.3 EFFECTS OF INJUSTICE ON OBLIGATION

How does injustice, of any of the foregoing sorts, affect the obligation to obey the law?

It is essential to specify the exact sense of this question. Any sound jurisprudence will recognize that someone uttering the question might conceivably mean by 'obligation to obey the law' either (i) empirical liability to be subjected to sanction in event of non-compliance; or (ii) legal obligation in the intra-systemic sense ('legal obligation in the legal sense') in which the practical premiss that conformity to law is socially necessary is a framework principle insulated from the rest of practical reasoning; or (iii) legal obligation in the moral sense (i.e. the moral obligation that presumptively is entailed by legal obligation in the intra-systemic or legal sense); or (iv) moral obligation deriving not from the legality of the stipulation-of-obligation but from some 'collateral' source (to be explained shortly). None of these interpretations is absurd, and a sound jurisprudence will show to what extent the answers to each will differ and to what extent they are interrelated.

An unsound jurisprudential method will seek to banish the question, in some of its senses, to 'another discipline',[1] or even declare those senses to be nonsense. Thus John Austin:

Now, to say that human laws which conflict with the divine law are not binding, that is to say, are not laws, *is to talk stark nonsense.* The most pernicious laws, and therefore those which are most opposed to the will of God, have been and are continually enforced as laws by judicial tribunals. Suppose an act innocuous, or positively beneficial, be prohibited by the sovereign under the penalty of death; if I commit this act, I shall be tried and condemned, and if I object

[1] Cf. Hart, *Concept of Law*, p. 205.

to the sentence, that it is contrary to the law of God, who has commanded that human lawgivers *shall not prohibit acts which have no evil consequences*, the Court of Justice will demonstrate the inconclusiveness of my reasoning by hanging me up, in pursuance of the law of which I have impugned the validity.[2]

I need not comment on the tone of this treatment of unjust law and conscientious objection. What concerns us is the methodological obtuseness of the words here italicized, the failure to allow that one and the same verbal formulation may bear differing though not necessarily unrelated meanings and express questions whose interrelations and differences can fruitfully be explored.

The first of the four conceivable senses of the question listed above is the least likely, in practice, to be intended by anyone raising the question. (Nevertheless, it is the only sense which Austin explicitly recognizes.) Someone who asks how injustice affects his obligation to conform to law is not likely to be asking for information on the practically important but theoretically banal point of fact, 'Am I or am I not likely to be hanged for non-compliance with this law?'

The second of the four listed senses of the question of obligation might seem, at first glance, to be empty. For what is the point of asking whether there is a legal obligation in the legal sense to conform to a stipulation which is in the legal sense obligatory? This objection is, however, too hasty. In my discussion of the formal features of legal order (X.3), of the Rule of Law (X.4), and of legal obligation (XI.4), I emphasized the way in which the enterprise of exercising authority through law proceeds by positing a system of rules which derive their authority not from the intrinsic appropriateness of their content but from the fact of stipulation in accordance with rules of stipulation. I emphasized the degree to which the resulting system is conceived of, in legal thought, as internally complete ('gapless') and coherent, and thus as sealed off (so to speak) from the unrestricted flow of practical reasoning about what is just and for the common good. I treated these 'model' features of legal system and legal thought not as mere items in some 'legal logic' (which as a matter of logic could certainly differ widely from that model!), but as practically reasonable

[2] *Province*, p. 185 (emphasis added).

responses to the need for security and predictability, a need which is indeed a matter of justice and human right. But all this should not disguise the extent to which legal thought in fact (and reasonably) does allow the system of rules to be permeated by principles of practical reasonableness which derive their authority from their appropriateness (in justice and for the common good) and not, or not merely, from their origin in some past act of stipulation or some settled usage. The legal system, even when conceived strictly as a set of normative meaning-contents (in abstraction from institutions, processes, personnel, and attitudes), is more open than the model suggests —open, that is to say, to the unrestricted flow of practical reasoning, in which a stipulation, valid according to the system's formal criteria of validity ('rules of recognition'), may be judged to be, or to have become, unjust and, therefore, after all, wholly or partially inapplicable.

In some legal systems this openness to unvarnished claims about the injustice of an existing or purported law is particularly evident, as in the United States of America. In others, as in English law, it is less obvious but still is familiar to lawyers, for example from the 'golden rule' that statutes are to be interpreted so as to avoid 'absurdity' or injustice, and from the debates, quite frequent in the highest courts, about the propriety of amending or abandoning even well-established rules or 'doctrines' of common law. Those who doubt or minimize the presence of open-ended principles of justice in professional legal thought will usually be found, on close examination, to be making a constitutional claim, viz. that the judiciary ought to leave change and development of law to the legislature. Conversely, those who stress the pervasiveness of such principles and minimize the coverage of practical problems by black-and-white rules will usually be found to be advancing the contradictory constitutional claim. In other words, what is presented[3] as a dispute about the 'legal system' *qua* set of normative meaning-contents is in substance, typically, a dispute about the 'legal system' *qua* constitutional order of institutions.

In short, even in well-developed legal orders served by a professional caste of lawyers, there are (and reasonably) quite a few opportunities of raising 'intra-systemically', for example

[3] As in Dworkin, *Taking Rights Seriously* (London: 1977), chs. 2–4.

before a court of law, the question whether what would otherwise be an indubitable legal obligation is in truth not (*legally*)
obligatory because it is unjust. On the other hand, since there
is little point in meditating about the legal-obligation-imposing
force of normative meaning-contents which are not treated as
having legal effect in the principal legal institutions of a
community (viz. the courts), it is idle to go on asking the
question in this sense (the second of the four listed) after the
highest court has ruled that in its judgment the disputed law
is not unjust or, if unjust, is none the less law, legally
obligatory, and judicially enforceable. It is not conducive to
clear thought, or to any good practical purpose, to smudge the
positivity of law by denying the legal obligatoriness *in the legal
or intra-systemic sense* of a rule recently affirmed as legally valid
and obligatory by the highest institution of the 'legal system'.
(Austin's concern to make this point, in the 'hanging me up'
passage, was quite reasonable. What was unreasonable was his
failure to acknowledge (*a*) the limited relevance of the point,
and (*b*) the existence of questions which may be expressed in
the same language but which are not determinately answerable
intra-systemically.)

The question in its *third* sense therefore arises in clear-cut
form when one is confident that the legal institutions of one's
community will not accept that the law in question is affected
by the injustice one discerns in it. The question can be stated
thus: Given that legal obligation presumptively entails a moral
obligation, and that the legal system is by and large just, does
a particular unjust law impose upon me any moral obligation
to conform to it?

Notoriously, many people (let us call them 'positivists') propose that this question should not be tackled in 'jurisprudence'
but should be left to 'another discipline', no doubt 'political
philosophy' or 'ethics'. Now it is not a purpose of this book
to conduct a polemic against anybody's conception of the limits
of jurisprudence. Suffice it to mention some disadvantages of
this proposal. Firstly, the proposed division is artificial to the
extent that the arguments and counter-arguments which it is
proposed to expel from jurisprudence are in fact (as we
observed in the preceding paragraphs) to be found on the lips
of lawyers in court and of judges giving judgment. Of course,

the arguments about justice and obligation that find favour in the courts of a given community at a given time may be arguments that would be rejected by a sound and critical ethics or political philosophy. But they are part of the same realm of discourse. One will not understand either the 'logic' or the 'sociology' of one's own or anyone else's legal system unless one is aware (not merely in the abstract but in detail) how both the arguments in the courts, and the formulation of norms by 'theoretical' jurists, are affected, indeed permeated, by the vocabulary, the syntax, and the principles of the 'ethics' and 'political philosophy' of that community, or of its élite or professional caste. In turn, one will not well understand the ethics or political philosophy of that community or caste unless one has reflected on the intrinsic problems of 'ethics' and 'political philosophy', i.e. on the basic aspects of human well-being and the methodological requirements of practical reasonableness. Finally, one will not well understand these *intrinsic* problems and principles unless one is aware of the extent to which the language in which one formulates them for oneself, and the concepts which one 'makes one's own', are themselves the symbols and concepts of a particular human civilization, a civilization which has worked itself out, as much as anywhere, in its lawcourts and law schools. This set of considerations affords the first reason why I would not myself accept the proposal to banish to some 'other discipline' the question of the moral obligation of an unjust law.

The second reason, not unconnected with the first, is to be found in the argument, developed in my first chapter and not to be repeated here, that a jurisprudence which aspires to be more than the lexicography of a particular culture cannot solve its theoretical problems of definition or concept-formation unless it draws upon at least some of the considerations of values and principles of practical reasonableness which are the subject-matter of 'ethics' (or 'political philosophy'). Since there can be no sharp distinction between the 'two disciplines' at that basic level, it is not clear why the distinction, if such there be, should be thought so very important at other levels.

The third reason is that (not surprisingly, in view of what I have just said) the programme of separating off from juris-prudence all questions or assumptions about the moral significance of law is not consistently carried through by those who propose it. Their works are replete with more or less undiscussed assumptions such as that the formal features of legal order contribute to the practical reasonableness of making, maintaining, and obeying law; that these formal features have some connection with the concept of justice and that, conversely, lawyers are justified in thinking of certain principles of justice as principles of *legality*;[4] and that the fact that a stipulation is *legally* valid gives some reason, albeit not conclusive, for treating it as *morally* obligatory or *morally* permissible to act in accordance with it.[5] But none of these assumptions can be shown to be warranted, or could even be discussed, without transgressing the proposed boundary between jurisprudence and moral or political philosophy—in the way that I have systematically 'transgressed' it in the preceding five chapters. Thus the state of the scholarly literature testifies, so to speak, to what a sound philosophy of practical reason establishes abstractly: the principles of practical reasonableness and their requirements form one unit of inquiry which can be subdivided into 'moral', 'political', and 'jurisprudential' only for a pedagogical or expository convenience which risks falsifying the understanding of all three.

What, then, are we to say in reply to the question whether an unjust law creates a moral obligation *in the way* that just law *of itself* does? The right response begins by recalling that the stipulations of those in authority have presumptive obligatory force (in the eyes of the reasonable person thinking unrestrictedly about what to do) only because of what is needed if the common good is to be secured and realized.

All my analyses of authority and obligation can be summed up in the following theorem: the ruler has, very strictly speaking, no right to be obeyed (XI.7); but he has the authority to give directions and make laws that are morally obligatory and that he has the responsibility of enforcing. He has this authority for the sake of the common good (the needs of which can also, however, make authoritative the opinions—as in custom—or stipulations of men who have no authority). Therefore, if he uses his authority to make stipulations against the common

---

[4] See Hart, *Concept of Law*, pp. 156–7, 202.
[5] See ibid., pp. 206–7.

good, or against any of the basic principles of practical reasonableness, those stipulations altogether lack the authority they would otherwise have *by virtue of being his*. More precisely, stipulations made for partisan advantage, or (without emergency justification) in excess of legally defined authority, or imposing inequitable burdens on their subjects, or directing the doing of things that should never be done, simply fail, of themselves, to create any moral obligation whatever.

This conclusion should be read with precision. Firstly, it should not be concluded that an enactment which itself is for the common good and compatible with justice is deprived of its moral authority by the fact that the act of enacting it was rendered unjust by the partisan motives of its author. Just as we should not be deflected from adjudging the act of enactment unjust by the fact that improper motivation is not, in a given system, ground for judicial review, so we should not use the availability of judicial review for that ground, in certain other systems of law, as a sufficient basis for concluding that a private citizen (to whom is not entrusted the duty of disciplining wayward officials or institutions) is entitled to treat the improper motives of the authors of a just law as exempting him from his moral duty of compliance. Secondly, it should not be concluded that the distributive injustice of a law exempts from its moral obligation those who are *not* unjustly burdened by it.

Understood with those precisions, my response to the question in its third sense corresponds to the classical position: viz. that for the purpose of assessing one's legal obligations in the moral sense, one is entitled to discount laws that are 'unjust' in any of the ways mentioned. Such laws lack the moral authority that in other cases comes simply from their origin, 'pedigree', or formal source. In this way, then, *lex injusta non est lex* and *virtutem obligandi non habet*,[6] whether or not it is 'legally valid' and 'legally obligatory' in the restricted sense that it (i) emanates from a legally authorized source, (ii) will in fact

---

[6] Aquinas, *S.T.* I–II, q. 96, a. 6c; he is referring back to the discussion in a. 4, which (having quoted Augustine's remark (see XII.4, below) about unjust laws not seeming to be law) concludes: 'So such [unjust] laws do not oblige in the forum of conscience (except perhaps where the giving of a corrupting example [*scandalum*] or the occasioning of civil disorder [*turbationem*] are to be avoided—for to avoid these, a man ought to yield his right)'. He adds that the last-mentioned 'exceptional' source or form of

be enforced by courts and/or other officials, and/or (iii) is commonly spoken of as a law like other laws.

But at the same time I must add that the last-mentioned facts, on which the lawyer *qua* lawyer (normally but, as I have noted, not exclusively) may reasonably concentrate, are not irrelevant to the moralist, the reasonable man with his unrestricted perspective.

At this point there emerges our question in the *fourth* of the senses I listed at the beginning of this section. It may be the case, for example, that if I am *seen* by fellow citizens to be disobeying or disregarding this 'law', the effectiveness of other laws, and/or the general respect of citizens for the authority of a generally desirable ruler or constitution, will probably be weakened, with probable bad consequences for the common good. Does not this collateral fact create a moral obligation? The obligation is to comply with the law, but it should not be treated as an instance of what I have called 'legal obligation in the moral sense'. For it is not based on the good of *being* law-abiding, but only on the desirability of not rendering ineffective the just parts of the legal system. Hence it will not require compliance with unjust laws according to their tenor or 'legislative intent', but only such degree of compliance as is necessary to avoid bringing 'the law' (as a whole) 'into contempt'. This degree of compliance will vary according to time, place, and circumstance; in some limiting cases (e.g. of judges or other officials administering the law) the morally required degree of compliance may amount to full or virtually full compliance, just *as if* the law in question had been a just enactment.

So, if an unjust stipulation is, in fact, homogeneous with other laws in its formal source, in its reception by courts and officials, and in its common acceptance, the good citizen may (not always) be morally required to conform to that stipulation to the extent necessary to avoid weakening 'the law', the legal

---

obligation to obey the law does not obtain where the injustice of the law is that it promotes something which ought never to be done (forbidden by divine law). Later he speaks similarly of unjust judgments of courts (for 'the sentence of the judge is like a particular law for a particular case': II–II, q. 67, a. 1c): e.g. II–II, q. 69, a. 4c, mentioning again *scandalum* and *turbatio*. See also II–II, q. 70, a. 1 ad 2 (the obligation *de jure naturali* to keep a secret may prevail over human law compelling testimony).

system (of rules, institutions, and dispositions) as a whole. The ruler still has the responsibility of repealing rather than enforcing his unjust law, and in this sense has no right that it should be conformed to. But the citizen, or official, may meanwhile have the diminished, collateral, and in an important sense extra-legal, obligation to obey it.

The foregoing paragraphs oversimplify the problems created for the conscience of reasonable citizens by unreasonableness in lawmaking. They pass over the problems of identifying inequity in distribution of burdens, or excessive or wrongly motivated exercise of authority. They pass over the dilemmas faced by conscientious officials charged with the administration of unjust laws. They pass over all questions about the point at which it may be for the common good to replace a persistently unjust lawmaker, by means that are prohibited by laws of a type normally justified both in their enactment and in their application. They pass over the question whether, notwithstanding the normal impropriety of bringing just laws into contempt, there may be circumstances in which it is justified to use one's public disobedience, whether to an unjust law itself or to a law itself quite just, as an instrument for effecting reform of unjust laws. And they pass over the question whether, in the aftermath of an unjust regime, the responsibility for declaring its unjust laws unjust and for annulling and undoing their legal and other effects should be undertaken by *courts* (on the basis that a court of justice-according-to-law ought not to be required to attribute legal effect to radically unjust laws), or by retrospective *legislation* (on the basis that the change from one legal regime to the other ought to be explicit).

Much can be said on such questions, but little that is not highly contingent upon social, political, and cultural variables. It is universally true that one has an absolute (liberty-)right not to perform acts which anyone has an absolute (claim-)right that one should not perform (VIII.7). But beyond this, one should not expect generally usable but precise guides for action in circumstances where the normally authoritative sources of precise guidance have partially broken down.

XII.4 'LEX INJUSTA NON EST LEX'

St. Augustine in his early dialogue on Free Will makes one of his characters say, rather breezily, 'a law that was unjust wouldn't seem to be law'.[7] Plato and Cicero had made the same point in less contorted a fashion,[8] and Aristotle often made similar remarks;[9] but the Augustinian formulation for long enjoyed more prominence. Aquinas quoted it, but at that point and elsewhere offered his own more measured renderings: unjust laws (by which he meant, as he carefully explained, laws defective in any of the ways mentioned in XII.2, above) are 'more outrages than laws',[10] 'not law but a corruption of law'.[11] More precisely, he says that such a law is 'not a law *simpliciter* [i.e. straightforwardly, or in the focal sense], but rather a sort of perversion of law'; but, as he immediately adds, it does have the character of law in one important respect: it is the command of a superior to his subordinates (and in this respect is calculated to render the members of the community 'good', through their compliance with it—not [of course] good *sim-*

---

[7] *De libero arbitrio*, I, v, 11: 'lex esse non videtur quae justa non fuerit'.

[8] Plato, *Laws*, IV: 715b: 'Societies [in which the winners of the competition for office reserve the conduct of public affairs wholly to themselves] are no constitutional states [*out einai politeias*], just as enactments, so far as they are not for the common interest of the whole community, are no true laws [*out orthous nomous*]; men who are for a party, we say, are factionaries, not citizens, and their so-called rights are empty words' (trans. A. E. Taylor); cf. also 712e–713a; *Statesman*, 293d–e; *Rep.* IV: 422e; Cicero, *De Legibus*, II, v, 11.

[9] E.g. *Pol.* III, 4: 1279a17–22; 5: 1280b7–9; IV, 4: 1292a31–34 ('... it would seem to be a reasonable criticism to say that such a rule-of-the-many is not a constitution at all; for where the laws do not govern there is no constitution ... an organization of this kind, in which all things are administered by [*ad hoc*] resolutions of the assembly is not even a democracy in the proper sense...').

[10] 'magis sunt violentiae quam leges': *S.T.* I–II, q. 96, a. 4c. Cf. q. 90, a. 1 ad 3: 'magis iniquitas quam lex'.

[11] 'non lex sed legis corruptio', *S.T.* I–II, q. 95, a. 2c. This is the phrase adopted by St. German, *Doctor and Student*, First Dialogue (Latin) (1523, 1528), c. 2 ('non sunt statuta sive consuetudines sed corruptele', rendered in the English version [1531] as 'no prescriptions statutes nor customs but things void and against justice'; the English of the Second Dialogue [1530], c. 15, is elliptical but happier: 'where the law of man is in itself directly against the law of reason or else the law of God and then properly it cannot be called a law but a corruption'.

pliciter, but good relative to that [tyrannical, unreasonable] regime).[12]

Thus Aquinas carefully avoids saying flatly that 'an unjust law is not a law: *lex injusta non est lex*'. But in the end it would have mattered little had he said just that.[13] For the statement either is pure nonsense, flatly self-contradictory, or else is a dramatization of the point more literally made by Aquinas when he says that an unjust law is not law in the focal sense of the term 'law' [i.e. *simpliciter*] notwithstanding that it is law in a secondary sense of that term [i.e. *secundum quid*].

Perhaps we can dwell on this a little. The central tradition of natural law theorizing in which the 'lex injusta ...' doctrine is embedded has not chosen to use the slogans attributed to it by modern critics, for example that '*what is utterly immoral* cannot be law',[14] or that '*certain rules* cannot be law because of their moral iniquity',[15] or that '*these evil things* are not law',[16] or that '*nothing iniquitous* can *anywhere* have the status of law',[17] or that '*morally iniquitous demands* ... [are] *in no sense* law',[18] or that '*there cannot be* an unjust law'.[19] On the contrary, the tradition, even in its most blunt formulations,[20] has affirmed that unjust LAWS are not law. Does not this formula itself

[12] 'lex tyrannica, cum non sit secundum rationem, non est simpliciter lex, sed magis est quaedam perversitas legis. Et tamen inquantum habet aliquid de ratione legis intendit ad hoc quod cives sint boni; non enim habet de ratione legis nisi secundum hoc quod est dictamen alicujus praesidentis in subditis: et ad hoc tendit ut subditi legis sint bene obedientes; quod est eos esse bonos, non simpliciter sed in ordine ad tale regimen': *S.T.* I–II, q. 92, a. 1 ad 4; see also the notes in this section, below.

[13] He does say that an unjust judgment of a court is not a judgment (*injustum judicium judicium mon est*): *S.T.* II–II, q. 70, a. 4 ad 2. But recall (p. 206) that in listing the meanings of *jus*, Aquinas had noted that even an unjust judgment can be called a *jus* (because it is the judge's *duty* to do justice): *S.T.* II–II, q. 57, a. 1 ad 1. What we see here (as so often in classical social philosophy) is not self-contradiction but a supple subordination of words to a shifting focus of interest.

[14] Hart, 'The Separation of Law and Morals' (1958) 71 *Harvard L. Rev.* 593, reprinted in Dworkin (ed.), *The Philosophy of Law* (Oxford: 1977), 17 at p. 33 (emphasis added).

[15] Ibid. (emphasis added).

[16] Ibid., p. 34 (emphasis added).

[17] Hart, *Concept of Law*, p. 206 (emphasis added).

[18] Ibid., p. 205 (emphasis added).

[19] Arthur C. Danto, 'Human Nature and Natural Law', in S. Hook (ed.), *Law and Philosophy* (New York: 1964), p. 187 (emphasis added), ascribing this 'dictum' to 'the Thomistic defenders of natural law'.

[20] E.g. Blackstone, I *Comm.* 41 (quoted in notes to II.2, above).

make clear, beyond reasonable question, that the tradition is not indulging in 'a refusal, made *once and for all*, to recognize evil laws as valid *for any purpose*'?[21] Far from 'denying legal validity to iniquitous rules',[22] the tradition explicitly (by speaking of 'unjust *laws*')[23] accords to iniquitous rules legal validity, whether on the ground and in the sense that these rules are accepted in the courts as guides to judicial decision, or on the ground and in the sense that, in the judgment of the speaker, they satisfy the criteria of validity laid down by constitutional or other legal rules, or on both these grounds and in both these senses. The tradition goes so far as to say that there may be an obligation to conform to some such unjust laws in order to uphold respect for the legal system as a whole (what I called a 'collateral obligation': XII.3).[24]

There is no need to repeat here the analysis of normative statements offered in section IX.2. It will be recalled that such statements may, in one and the same grammatical form, intend to assert (S_1) what is justified or required by practical reasonableness *simpliciter*, or (S_2) what is treated as justified or required in the belief or practice of some group, or (S_3) what is justified or required *if* certain principles or rules are justified (but without taking any position on the question whether those principles or rules *are* so justified). And it will be recalled how natural and frequent it is to shift from the expository (S_3) or sociological/historical (S_2) viewpoint to the fully critical (S_1) viewpoint within the space of a single sentence. *Lex injusta non est lex* is such a sentence: it implies (i) that some normative meaning-content has for some community the status (S_2/S_3) of law, (ii) that that law is unjust (a critical judgment of practical reasonableness, whether correct or incorrect), and (iii) that compliance with that law is (S_1) *not* justified or required by the derivative and defeasible principle of practical reasonableness that laws impose moral obligations.

Plato, Aristotle, Augustine, and Aquinas did not draw attention to the distinction between the intra-systemic expository

---

[21] Hart, *Concept of Law*, pp. 206–7 (emphasis added); and see p. 152, ascribing that view to 'the Thomist tradition'.

[22] Ibid., p. 207.

[23] And such references are not merely in the context of 'non est lex' formulations: see e.g. *S.T.* I–II, q. 94, a. 6 ad 3.

[24] *S.T.* I–II, q. 96, a. 4c and ad 3.

viewpoint, the historical/sociological viewpoint, and the viewpoint of unrestricted practical reasonableness. They took it for
granted, and shifted easily from one to another while treating
the last-mentioned viewpoint as their primary concern: 'we hold
that, in all such matters [pertaining to human passions and
actions], whatever appears to the mature man of practical
wisdom [the *spoudaios*] to be the case really is the case'.[25] They
did employ a technical device to signal their consciousness of
differing viewpoints, and of the consequently different intention. In modern times, the questions, as experienced, create a
between focal meaning ('X *simpliciter*', '*vere* X', 'X *proprie*', etc.)
and secondary meanings ('X *secundum quid*', 'X *secundum aliquem
modum*', 'X *secundum similitudinem*', 'X *cum aliqua adjectione*', etc.)
within one and the same discourse or theoretical discipline.[26]

Now this technical device is justified and indeed indispensable
in any philosophy of human affairs, given the variety of human
concerns and projects, reasonable and unreasonable (I.3). But
while it enables us to register the degrees to which the elements
of some complex concept are instantiated by various particular
states of affairs, all assessed from one viewpoint, the device does
not register, with all the explicitness that could be desired, the
difference between the meanings of propositions which results
from differences in *viewpoint* or theoretical or practical *purposes*.
The device does allow a use of terms which is the primary or
exclusive use from one viewpoint to be admitted as a secondary
use in discourse which is controlled by some other viewpoint.
But it fails (i) to make explicit what the difference of viewpoints
is, and (ii) to clarify the relationship of interdependence or
one-way dependence or, as the case may be, independence
between the different viewpoints and their respective usages.
Hence the need to supplement the traditional formulations (see
also X.2) in the way I have attempted in IX.2 and in the
present section.

[25] Aristotle, *Nic Eth.* X, 5: 1176a16–17; the first set of bracketed words is inserted by
Aquinas in his commentary *ad loc., in Eth.* X, lect. 8, para. 2062. See also *Nic. Eth.*
I, 8: 1099a11–15; III, 4: 1113a22–33; X, 6: 1176b26; and notes to V.1, above.
[26] The Latin phrases are all to be found in Aquinas's commentary on Aristotle's
discussion of 'citizen' and citizenship (*Pol.* III, 1: 1274b32–1275b34); Aquinas, *in Pol.*
III, i. See I.3–4, above.

NOTES

XII.2

Types of injustice of laws ... See Aquinas, *S.T.* I–II, q. 96, a. 4c; St. German, *Doctor and Student*, First Dial., c. 4; Suarez, *De Legibus*, Book I, c. 9, paras. 12–16.

XII.3

Consequences of injustice of laws ... See Suarez, *De Legibus*, Book I, c. 9, paras. 11–12, 20.

Unjust legislative motives may be disregarded if the enactment itself is reasonable ... See *De Legibus*, loc. cit.; *Doctor and Student*, I, c. 26.

Collateral moral obligation to obey the law ... See *S.T.* I–II, q. 96, a. 4. Such an obligation may arise from quite different sorts of reasons; e.g. from one's duty to one's family to avoid the punishment that would come from breaking the law.

Undoing the effects of unjust laws ... The celebrated debate between Hart and Fuller on this point comes down to a question of constitutional niceties, of purely symbolic implications, and of convenience in settling details: cf. (1958) 71 *Harv. L. Rev.* at pp. 618–20 (Hart) and 655 (Fuller); Fuller, *Morality of Law*, Appendix.

XII.4

'Lex injusta non est lex' ... A vigorous modern formulation is P. T. Geach, *The Virtues* (Cambridge: 1977), p. 128: 'University people argue mightily about whether laws that violate these principles are laws or (as Aquinas called them) mere violence. Of course it doesn't matter whether you *call* them laws or not: the question is what consequences follow. An unjust piece of legislation exists *de facto*, as an institution: but it is no debt of justice to observe it, though it may be imprudent to ignore it. And though a private person should not lightly judge a law to be unjust, its contrariety to the Law of Nature and the peace and justice of society may be so manifest that such a judgment is assured. A sufficient mass of unjust legislation may justify a man in deciding that the civil authority is a mere Syndicate. I think Old John Brown rightly so judged about the slave-owning U.S. commonwealths of his time. Rebellion, however, is another matter, because the evils it may bring about are so great: whether Old John Brown judged rightly about this is a matter we must leave between Old John Brown and his Maker ...'. Aquinas himself was something of a 'University person', and his account is (as I have tried to show) a little more nuanced than Geach's. But he would certainly have agreed that (except for some special purpose) 'it doesn't matter whether you *call* them laws or not: the question is what consequences follow'.

Aquinas on tyrannical laws and 'law' and 'good' simpliciter ... The passage from *S.T.* I–II, q. 92, a. 1 ad 4, translated in the text and reproduced in the footnotes, is Aquinas's reply to someone who objected (against his claim that the point of law is to make men good) that there are tyrannical laws, intended by their maker for his own benefit and not to make men good. Aquinas's reply significantly concedes that there are indeed such laws, and tries to show that, though not in the strictest sense 'laws', they share in the nature of law not only as being the directives of a ruler to his subjects *but also* as having (in a misdirected way) the same sort of social function. See also the body of the article which further illustrates Aquinas's resolute use of focal meaning: 'If the law-maker's intention bears on true good, namely the common good measured according to divine justice, the consequence will be for men through law [i.e. by complying with it] to become good *simpliciter*. If, however, the intention is not for good without qualification [*simpliciter*], but for what serves his own profit or pleasure, or against divine justice, then the law will make men good, not *simpliciter* but relatively [*secundum quid*], namely in relation to that regime. This sort of goodness can be found even in things intrinsically bad; as when we speak of a "good thief", meaning that he operates efficiently.'

Part Three

XIII

NATURE, REASON, GOD

XIII.1 FURTHER QUESTIONS ABOUT
THE POINT OF HUMAN EXISTENCE

WHAT further explanations are required? After all, the basic forms of human flourishing are obvious to anyone acquainted, whether through his own inclinations or vicariously through the character and works of others, with the range of human opportunities. And the general requirements of reasonableness (itself one of those basic forms of good) are, likewise, as obvious as the norms of rationality, principles of logic, and canons of explanation that are presupposed in *any* explanation, whether in our practical context or in natural science or analytical philosophy. (Which is not to say that the implications of those requirements, for anyone's commitments, projects or actions, are all obvious!) Certainly, an analytical exploration of possible and actual social structures, practical norms, individual virtues and vices, and the like, is both possible and not easily exhaustible. But would it not be a mistake to expect any deeper level of explanation of the practical reasonableness of community, authority, law, rights, justice, and obligation, once their explanation has been pursued from practice to self-interest, and thence to the common good which both friendship and rational impartiality require us to respect and favour?

The answer must be: No, we cannot reasonably rest here. There are further practical questions; and there also are further relevant theoretical questions about both the whole structure of norms and requirements of good that has been identified, and the whole structure of explanations already advanced.

The range of relevant further practical questions can be indicated as follows. The basic aspects of human well-being are really and unquestionably good; but after all, they are not abstract forms, they are analytically distinguishable aspects of the well-being, actual or possible, of you and me—of flesh-and-blood individuals. This is equally true of the common good; it is the well-being of you and me, considered as individuals with shared opportunities and vulnerabilities, and the concrete conditions under which that well-being of particular individuals may be favoured, advanced, and preserved. But of each and every individual person, and therefore of each and every community of individuals, it is true that his or her participation in the various forms of good is, even at best, extremely limited. Our health fails, our stock of knowledge fades from recall, our making and appreciation of play and art falters and finishes, our friendships are ended by distance, time, death; and death appears to end our opportunities for authenticity, integrity, practical reasonableness, if despair or decay have not already done so. We notice the succession of human persons (and of their communities), evidently separated beyond all contact with one another by time and distance; and the question arises whether my good (and the well-being of my communities) has any *further* point, i.e. whether it relates to any more comprehensive human participation in good.

That question is an extension of, or analogous to, some not yet adequately settled questions about friendship itself. An aspect of my well-being is the well-being of my friend; if he or she is ruined or destroyed, I am worse off. What then is to be said of (and done in) situations in which his or her well-being can be secured only by my ruin or destruction? 'What is the good of it?' This question does not question the good of my friend's good, either as his or hers or as an aspect of mine; but it asks whether *further* sense can be made of the whole situation, in which the limitation on one's participation in human good arises not from time and decay but from a kind of conflict of opportunities. Similarly, one who clearly sees his responsibilities to his family or his political community, and who does not doubt that they reasonably may require self-sacrifice of him, still may reasonably inquire whether there is any further *point*, to which both his reasonable self-sacrifice and the resultant well-being of his community (which itself will sooner or later come to an end) contribute. (By 'contribution' is not necessarily meant some cause of chronologically distinct effects; what is looked for might be some wider pattern in which the particular situation-and-response in question might 'take its place', corresponding to some less limited perspective in which it could be seen to 'make [more] sense'.)

Or again, each of us is an item not only in the succession of persons (and their communities) but also in a universe, indefinitely extended in space and time, of entities and states of affairs, many of which have intelligible patterns of flourishing and decay. Of each, and of the ensemble, it is possible to ask whether it too has a good, a point, a value—and, in any case, how that entity or state of affairs, or ensemble of entities and of states of affairs, relates to anybody's good, not to mention my good and my community's.

In the absence of any answers to such questions, the basic human values will seem, to any thoughtful person, to be weakened, in their attractiveness to reasonableness, by a certain relativity or subjectivity—not so much the 'subjectivity' of arbitrary opining, but rather the 'subjectivity' of the '*merely* relative to us' (where 'us' has an uncertain but restricted reference).

The urgency with which thoughtful persons press these questions is amply evidenced by the course of human speculation. In modern time, the questions, as experienced, create a ready market for interpretations of history which allow the questioner to believe that he and his community, race, class, or party are contributing to the attainment of some future plateau to which History will, with his assistance, progress. The assumption about the plateaux of progress, from which Humanity will not regress, can be seen in Mill as plainly as in Marx.[1] The assumption that the basic point of good actions, projects, and commitments consists in their realizing some future good condition of the (then-existing) human race, can be observed in many versions of utilitarianism. The defect (questions of fact and probability aside) in all such responses was noted, near the beginning of the period of their popularity, by Kant:

What remains disconcerting about all this is firstly, that the earlier generations seem to perform their laborious tasks only for the sake of the later ones, so as to prepare for them a further stage from which they can raise still higher the structure intended by nature; and

---

[1] J. S. Mill, *On Liberty* (1859), ch. 1.

secondly, that only the later generations will in fact have the good fortune to inhabit the building on which a whole series of their fore-fathers (admittedly, without any conscious intention) had worked without themselves being able to share in the happiness they were preparing.[2]

Still, Kant himself brushes the problem aside; he will not be deflected from his 'assumption' that 'nature does nothing un-necessarily' (not in the individual, who is mortal, but 'in the species, which is immortal'), not indeed 'by instinct or by the guidance of innate knowledge', but by the 'reason' which 'nature gives' man in order 'to reach its ends'.[3]

In these remarkable passages, Kant makes plain the usually half-expressed assumptions of much modern thought about the point of human life and human good. And, above all, he is resuming, but in relation to a supposed course of 'history', the most important themes touched upon two thousand years earlier in Stoic thought about *natura*. Since the Stoic speculations (and word-play) on *natura* are an immediate source of the rather unhappy term 'natural law', it is important for us to observe how those speculations are motivated by the same practical questions about the objectivity (as opposed to 'subjec-tivity' in the already indicated sense) of human goods.

If, for example, we attend to the word *natura* in its fifty-two appearances in paragraphs 16 to 48 of the first book of Cicero's *De Legibus*,[4] we can readily understand the Stoic opinion, reported by him in his *De Finibus*, III, 73: 'he who is to live

---

[2] 'Idea for a Universal History with a Cosmopolitan Purpose' [1784], trans. by H. B. Nisbet in Hans Reiss (ed.), *Kant's Political Writings* (Cambridge: 1970), p. 44.

[3] All the words, phrases, and ideas are to be found in the first four 'Propositions' in Kant's essay. The anxiety underlying the 'assumption' is revealed by the last sentence of the First Proposition: 'For if we abandon this basic principle, we are faced not by a law-governed nature, but with an aimless, random purpose, and the dismal reign of chance replaces the guiding principles of reason.' See also Kant's essay 'On the Common Saying: "This may be true in theory, but it does not apply in practice"', Part III, 'On the relationship of theory to practice in international right considered from a universally philanthropic, i.e. cosmopolitan point of view' [1792], ibid., pp. 87–91.

[4] Here Cicero is reporting Stoic opinions, explicitly bracketing out the Academic-sceptical opinions to which he himself adhered (with waverings towards Stoic ethics): see *De Legibus*, I, 39. The word-count includes *naturalis*, but excludes one use of *natura* to mean. neutrally, 'the concept of' (*natura iuris*: I, 17).

[as Stoic ethics commends]⁵ in accordance with nature [*convenienter naturae*] must reason on the basis of the whole world and its government. Nor can anyone judge truly of good and evil, save by knowledge of the whole plan of nature [*omni ratione naturae*] as well as of the life of the gods, and of whether the nature of man is or is not in harmony with universal nature [*utrum conveniat necne natura hominis cum universa*]'.⁶

Being scholastics, interested in establishing a technical vocabulary, the Stoics were aware that *natura* was a word with a variety of meanings and shifting references. So a characteristic elaboration of a Stoic ethics would refer (i) to the *prima naturae*,⁷ the primary inclinations, needs, or objects of natural impulse, which in human nature are to live (in health of mind and body) and to know;⁸ (ii) to the possibility of pursuing the *prima naturae* in a particular and appropriate manner, i.e. reasonably, i.e. by way of a plan harmonious with itself, with human *natura* and with universal *natura*;⁹ (iii) to the aspects of human and universal *natura* which reason (in natural philosophy: i.e. *physica*, the *explicatio naturae*)¹⁰ discovers by investigation and comparison, for example, the fact that familial affection, being conducive to procreation and education, is natural not only as instinctive but also as being consistent with the maintenance of particular human beings in being¹¹ or that there is a *cosmopolis*, a universal community of gods and men, into which each of us is born, and which it is therefore fitting (*conveniens naturae*) for each of us to prefer, as any whole takes precedence over its parts;¹² (iv) to the fact that virtue, i.e. living-according-to-reason, not only is guided by (*a*) the

---

⁵ See *De Finibus*, III, 26, 31, 34; *De Republica*, III, 33.

⁶ Likewise *De Finibus*, II, 34: for the Stoics the supreme good is harmony with nature (*consentire naturae*), which they interpret as meaning living virtuously, i.e. *honeste*, which they explain as living 'with an understanding of the natural course of events [*cum intelligentia rerum earum quae natura evenirent*], choosing those things that are in accordance with nature [*secundum naturam*] and rejecting contrary things'; similarly IV, 14.

⁷ Cicero, *De Finibus*, III, 21. Synonyms are *prima secundum naturam* (V, 18, 19, 45); *prima naturalia* (II, 34); *prima natura data* (II, 34); *initia naturae* (II, 38); *principia naturae* (III, 22, 23); *principia naturalia* (II, 35; III, 17); *res quae primae appetuntur* (III, 17); etc.

⁸ Ibid. III, 16–18.

⁹ Ibid. III, 23.

¹⁰ Ibid. III, 73; IV, 12.

¹¹ Ibid. III, 62.

¹² Ibid. III, 64.

principle that choice is to be in accordance with nature (*secundum naturam*)[13] and (*b*) the object of maintaining one's being *in statu naturae*,[14] but also is actually most characteristic of (natural to) men and gods, these being the only beings, in the whole of *natura*, whose proper *natura* it is to be reasonable;[15] and (v) to the final speculative inference that, by virtue of being reasonable, the human virtue of living-according-to-[human]-nature is also in accordance with the universal *ratio* (intelligence/intelligibility) which informs the whole of nature (the universe or cosmos), and which, being a governing or directive *ratio*, should be called the law of nature (*lex naturae*), establishing a universal rightness or justice (*jus naturale*).[16]

In such an elaboration, the phases of the argument are fairly distinct, or at any rate distinguishable; but it is virtually impossible to prevent the meaning or reference of *natura*, as used in one phase, from flooding into its use in the other phases. And it is the meaning of *natura* in phase (v) which is most pervasive, and which by implication and anticipation most helps forward the 'argument'. For the Stoic, human life has its meaning, choice its significance, practical reason its objectivity, just in so far as they fit into the vast divine plan (*logos*) of the cosmos, one aspect of which is the cosmopolis of gods and men in the harmony (*homologia*) of their respective communities.

Phases (i) and (ii) of the foregoing elaboration may have reminded the reader of my distinction between (i) the basic forms of human good, and (ii) the basic requirements of practical reasonableness. Indeed, there are obvious similarities. But the Stoic conception of ethics or natural law (in both its Hellenistic/Roman and its post-Renaissance formulations) differs in a fundamental respect from the conception advanced both in earlier chapters of this book and in the Platonic and Aristotelian teachings which the Stoics were recasting. In my explication of practical reasonableness, the fundamental term is 'good(s)'; in the Stoic explication, 'good' has virtually

---

[13] Ibid. III, 12.

[14] Ibid. III, 20.

[15] Cicero, *De Legibus*, I, 25.

[16] Cicero, *De Republica*, III, 18; *De Finibus*, III, 71; *De Legibus*, I, 18, 23; II, 10, 16; etc.

disappeared[17] (along with, correspondingly, the difference between practical reasoning and theoretical or speculative reasoning). Of course, the Stoics are more than willing to join in the great Hellenistic debate about the identity of the highest form of good (the *summum bonum* or *finis bonorum*). But their answer is: there is only one good for man, namely, virtue—living-according-to-reason/living-according-to-nature.[18] The Stoic will invent a whole series of neologisms to avoid calling the *prima naturae* 'good' or 'goods'. Boldly he will declare that, if you wish to compare one's choice of aim in life with a man aiming a spear at a target, then you must admit that the ultimate good, end, or aim that such a man has in view is *not* the target, *nor* the hitting of it, but the aiming straight![19] The concept of good (*notio boni*) is for the Stoic a concept which one only arrives at by a process of inference (*collatio rationis*) which takes off from a prior recognition of things as being in accordance with nature (*secundum naturam*).[20] Hence, he will not choose to formulate his basic practical questions in the way I formulated them at the beginning of this section.

But his teaching is a response to the same anxiety about the 'subjectivity' of human effort. To that anxiety he responds by pointing to the all-embracing order-of-things, intelligible because intelligently ordered; human intelligence has its objectivity and worth by understanding that order; human activity has its objectivity and worth by conforming to the order thus understood, by corresponding, in intention if not in effect, to the intentions of the superintending universal-intelligence. This imposing vision of order and reasonableness is taken as rendering superfluous all further questions, either about the point or good of the whole in itself, or about the point or good-for-man of conforming to it.

Certainly the Stoic thesis has more to commend it than Kant's. Kant postulates a future order-of-things by sheer extrapolation on the basis of nothing more than a hope (or anxiety) which even as hope is, on his own admission, 'disconcerting'. In the bad sense of the term, his thesis is a 'projection'; the

[17] The replacement was deliberate and occurred at the very beginning of the Stoic school: see Cicero, *De Legibus*, I, 55.

[18] Cicero, *De Finibus*, III, 36.

[19] *De Finibus*, III, 22; also V, 20.

[20] Ibid. III, 33.

identification and denunciation of such projections is perhaps
the principal *modus operandi* of the post-Kantian sceptic. But the
Stoic thesis, too, seems to be essentially an expression of piety
directed towards a world-order whose order might well be
regarded as not altogether admirable, and whose outcome
might equally be regarded as a matter of indifference to us.
And without the support of that piety, the Stoic cultivation of
virtue would be no more than the 'athleticism', the self-cul-
tivation whose vanity Augustine of Hippo remorselessly exposed. Indeed, the Augustinian critique of the athleticism of
virtue remains in many respects the most searching objection to
any theory of natural law (or of morality) that is restricted to
tracing the requirements of practical reasonableness and refuses
or fails to respond to the practical questions raised at the
beginning of this section.

XIII.2 ORDERS, DISORDERS, AND THE EXPLANATION OF EXISTENCE

Let me restate those practical questions in terms of that
'reasonableness' which is central both to the Stoic analysis
and to my own. To be reasonable (well-informed, intelligent,
consistent, free from arbitrariness . . .) is primarily understood as
obviously a good for me and for any person, a good as self-
evidently and underivatively good as life itself, as play, art,
friendship . . . But is the point of being reasonable simply to be
better-off, myself—to be flourishing in one more aspect (even
if that aspect be rather strategic or architectonic)?

The proper way to begin an answer to such searchingly
reflexive practical questions is to tackle the strictly theoretical
(non-practical) questions mentioned but not identified at the
beginning of the preceding section. The exploration of these
theoretical questions will occupy the next three sections; in
section XIII.5 the results of that exploration will be brought to
bear on the practical questions about the point of reasonableness, the reasonableness of self-sacrifice, the relevance of history
and the universe, and the most basic explanation of obligation.

Because the practical questions were, or could well be,
framed in terms of 'reasonableness', the theoretical questions
start with 'reason'. Reason, intelligence, the mind and its

powers, are to be understood not by trying to peer within
oneself but by reflecting upon the forms and cumulation of
explanations in any of the many fields in which it is possible
to advance from ignorance and confusion to some degree of
knowledge and clarity. It matters little which field is
selected for this reflection.

Consider, therefore, by way of example, the explanations
advanced in Chapter XI. In that chapter I was trying to
explain (i) certain judgments which (it was assumed) the
reader, like the writer, sometimes makes and (ii) secondarily,
certain terms and patterns of word-usage that actually obtain
in a number of cultures, including our own. The explanations,
first of promises and then of obligation(s) in general,
themselves fell into a recognizable and intelligible pattern:
analysis in terms of the practical context of word-usage could
be supplemented by analysis of rational necessities relative first
to self-interest and then to the common good. That is to say,
phenomena of existent practices, and the instruments and products of collaboration and interaction, all could be related
intelligibly to the principles which guide and shape reasonable
individual actions, projects, commitments, habits, and attitudes. The pragmatic state of affairs in human conduct and
culture and the order of practical reasonableness, while thus
related, remained nevertheless distinct; the pragmatic state of
affairs, as it actually exists, can be understood only if the effects
not only of human unreasonableness, inertia, ignorance, and
malice, but also of chance or coincidence are recognized
(cf. I.4).

Moreover, the explanatory reference to the common good was
itself a summary reference to an elaborate order of explanations in earlier chapters. There, too, I was concerned to
explain, first, the practical judgments which we find ourselves
making and, secondly, the cultural phenomena of language-
usage, customs, institutions, etc., concerning actual and possible
human activities. My explanations distinguished inclinations
from judgments of value; and distinguished good, considered as
a definite objective capable of complete attainment by definite
means, from value, considered as a form of good to which one
can be committed but which one can realize or attain only by
way of a participation which is never completed. Basic values

(treated in practical thinking as principles) were identified, and found to be, in their content, parallel with basic inclinations, drives, or urges. A multi-faceted notion of human flourishing was thus developed, such flourishing being understood as capable of realization in a multitude of particular ways, as well as in varying degrees of fullness. Friendship was identified as one aspect of this flourishing, and community as a 'means' indispensable to the realizing of most aspects of human well-being. Parallel with the urge to question, and to reject the unintelligible, were found to be the value of knowledge and understanding (including the understanding being accumulated in this series of explanations itself) and the value of establishing (partly by discovery and partly by commitment and *determinatio*) an intelligible order in one's own actions and one's own interaction with other intelligent beings.

The fact that human beings have a certain range of urges, drives, or inclinations; and the fact that these have a certain correspondence, parallelism, or 'fit' with the states of affairs that anyone intelligent would consider constitute human flourishing; and the fact that without reasonable direction the inclinations will bring about individual and communal ruin ('natural sanctions'); and the fact that certain psychological, biological, climatic, physical, mechanical, and other like principles, laws, states of affairs, or conditions affect the realization of human well-being in discoverable ways—all these are facts in an order, external to our own understanding, which our understanding can only discover. This order is often called the order of nature. But alongside this are (i) the order of human artefacts (including language, technologies, the formulations of laws, and the design and manifestations of institutions employed to exploit nature for real or supposed human good); (ii) the order of attitudes, habits ('second nature'), commitments, and principles of action, by which individuals shape their lives and interactions more or less intelligently; and (iii) the order of the operations of thought as such, the order of logic, of investigations, critiques, analyses, and explanations (including the reflexive explanation of this order itself, as well as of the others): VI.2.

The remarkable fact that there is an order of nature which, like the orders of human artefacts, actions, and thoughts, is amenable to human understanding calls for some explanation. Often it has been explained by attributing the order(s) to an ordering intelligence and will, creating or in some other way causing the whole world-order. Kant, for example, considered that, to have an orientation in the scientific investigation of nature, one must postulate 'that a supreme intelligence has ordered all things in accordance with the wisest ends'. 'Moreover,' he adds, 'the outcome of my attempts [in explanation of nature] so frequently confirms the usefulness of this postulate, while nothing decisive can be cited against it, that I am saying much too little if I proceed to declare that I hold it merely as an opinion.'[21] Hume, too, in his *Dialogues concerning Natural Religion* [1779], not merely concedes but forcefully stresses and strikingly illustrates the orderliness of the world, and seems to ascribe it to an 'internal, inherent principle of order'[22] which 'first arranged, and still maintains, order in this universe' and 'bears . . . some remote inconceivable analogy to the other operations of Nature and among the rest to the economy of human mind and thought'.[23]

But, as there is order, so there is lack of order in the world, in terms of all four orders: waste in physical nature, error in reasonings, breakdown in culture, unreasonableness in human attitudes and actions . . . 'The utmost . . . that the argument [from order] can prove', says Kant, 'is an *architect* of the world who is always very much hampered by the adaptability of the material in which he works, not *creator* of the world to whose idea everything is subject.'[24] 'Look round this universe', says Hume's protagonist: 'the whole presents nothing but the idea of a blind Nature, impregnated by a great vivifying principle, and pouring forth from her lap, without discernment or parental care, her maimed and abortive children!'[25] At any rate, he remarks in more measured terms, the proposition that the cause or causes of order in the universe probably bear some remote analogy to human intelligence, while

---

[21] Immanuel Kant, *Critique of Pure Reason* [1781, 1787], B854; see also B651. On the postulate as a 'regulative ideal' of reason, see B728.

[22] David Hume, *Dialogues concerning Natural Religion*, ed. Kemp Smith (2nd ed., London: 1947), Part VI, p. 174.

[23] Ibid., Part XII, p. 218.

[24] *Critique of Pure Reason*, B655.

[25] *Dialogues concerning Natural Religion*, Part XI, p. 211.

acceptable, is 'ambiguous, at least undefined' and 'not capable of extension, variation, or more particular explication' and 'affords no inference that affects human life, or [that] can be the source of any action or forbearance'.[26]

In short, *direct* speculative questions about the significance, implications, or source of the orderliness of things yield, *by themselves*, no clear or certain answers. But this is not the end of the matter. As well as the orderliness of the order(s) of things, there is their sheer existence—the fact that propositions picking out states of affairs are sometimes true.[27] Philosophical analysis has gradually refined our undifferentiated wonder (Why?) about the origin of things, by differentiating the fact that entities and states of affairs are *what* they are from the fact *that* they are. There thus remains an alternative route for investigation, starting with the sort of fact with which we start in the investigations by which we gain our knowledge of order, viz. the fact that this or that particular state of affairs exists (or existed, or will exist). If we are to understand a number of issues of importance in answering the practical questions raised at the beginning of this chapter, and in the history of theories of Natural Law, we must try to see what this alternative investigation yields (and has often been taken to yield).

Consider, for example, this state of affairs: Someone reading a sentence in this book tomorrow (the day after you, the present reader, read a sentence in it). Such a state of affairs may or not exist. If it does, its existence will be the factor, distinct from *what* the state of affairs is, that makes true a proposition picking out that state of affairs. (The proposition which may thus be made true can be variously stated, depending on the time of the statement: viz., as stated today,

---

[26] Ibid., Part XII, p. 227. See also Hume, *An Enquiry concerning Human Understanding* (1748), sec. XI.

[27] For a much ampler and more rigorous version of the argument in the rest of this section, see Germain Grisez, *Beyond the New Theism: A Philosophy of Religion* (Notre Dame and London: 1975), chs. 4 and 5. In order to avoid the ambiguities of the verb 'to be' and the noun 'existence', and the consequent well-known philosophical complications, Grisez uses the verb 'to obtain' to refer to the factor, distinct from *what* a state of affairs is, that makes true a proposition picking out that state of affairs. Since I am here only sketching the argument, I retain the less artificial word 'exists' (and its cognates), but giving it the sense just defined in the text (so that it corresponds to Grisez's use of 'obtains').

'Tomorrow someone will read a sentence in *Natural Law and Natural Rights*'; as stated at the time of that reading, 'Someone is reading a sentence in ...'; and as stated the day after tomorrow, 'Yesterday someone read a sentence in ...'.) Since the state of affairs which we are considering may or may not exist (or, retrospectively, might or might not have existed), it is reasonable to ask why it will exist if it exists (... is existing if it is existing; ... existed if it was an existing state of affairs). History, biography, sociology, natural sciences ... all proceed by raising such questions. What conditions or prerequisites will have (had) to be fulfilled for that state of affairs to exist?

Some of the prerequisites for this state of affairs are included in the state of affairs itself: for example, for someone to read the sentence, he has to be able to see the words on the page. But there are many other conditions, prerequisite to the existing of this state of affairs, which are not included in the state of affairs itself. There must be enough light to read by (but it might be sunlight or candlelight or electric light); there must be someone alive and conscious and able to understand English. There will be no one alive and conscious unless a very great many physical, physiological, and psychological processes are then going on (including many processes which one need not, however, understand or even be aware of in order to know that the state of affairs exists). There would be no one able to understand English if there were not a whole English-speaking culture. If we elaborate the state of affairs to include the fact that the sentence being read is being read with understanding, it is easy to see that in this instance the conditions that must be satisfied (i.e. the states of affairs that must exist) for the relevant state of affairs to exist include states of affairs in all four orders—the physical order, the cultural order, the order of meaning and thought, and the order of human choices, attitudes, and actions.

All these prerequisite states of affairs may or may not exist (might or might not have existed). And they in their turn exist only if further prerequisites not included in themselves are satisfied. That *all* these prerequisites and their own prerequites are so disposed (whether simultaneously or in temporal succession or both) as to provide what is required for the first-mentioned state of affairs to exist, is itself a state of affairs. This whole prerequisite state of affairs (which might or might not extend to include the whole universe)[28] can be said to cause the first-mentioned state of affairs.[29] But, just as we began by asking why the first-mentioned state of affairs will exist if it exists (is existing ...; did exist ...), so we can now ask why the whole causing state of affairs itself exists (or will exist ...; or did exist ...).

Must there be an answer to this question? The rationalists of the late seventeenth and the eighteenth centuries, against whom Kant and Hume were arguing on many fronts (and whose doctrines of natural law I have not reproduced or defended), considered that indeed there must. For is there not a 'principle of sufficient reason'? Leibniz had identified such a principle, and formulated it thus: 'No fact can be real or existent, no statement true, unless there be a sufficient reason why it is so and not otherwise, although these reasons usually cannot be known to us'.[30] But, in fact, this principle should not be conceded. No *reason* can be given or need be sought to explain why two identical individuals (e.g. two pins or two atoms) are distinct and different. No reason can or need be given for a choice that was really freely made as between eligible alternatives. And no reason can or need be given why it is *this* world-order *rather than some other* possible world-order that exists. (Leibniz held that *this* world-order exists because God chose it, but his principle of sufficient reason compelled Leibniz to offer a reason for *this* choice. The reason offered had to be that *this* is the best of all possible worlds.[31] But we must reject the very notion of a best possible world as 'merely incoherent, like the idea of a biggest natural number'.[32] For goodness, as I argued in V.7, has irreducibly distinct and

---

[28] For the sake of the argument, we should grant that this whole prerequisite state of affairs comprises an *infinite* number of states of affairs, notwithstanding that contemporary scientific cosmology tends to favour Einstein's view that the universe is not infinite. If an infinite series of states of affairs happens to exist, it is still reasonable to ask why.

[29] In saying this one stipulates a sense of 'cause', such that where state of affairs A includes conditions which are not included in state of affairs B, but which must be satisfied for B to exist, one calls A a cause of B. See Grisez, op. cit., pp. 54, 128; Richard Taylor, 'Causation' in *Encyclopedia of Philosophy* (ed. Paul Edwards, London and New York: 1967), vol. 2, p. 63.

[30] Leibniz, *Monadology* [1714], sec. 32.

[31] Ibid., secs. 53–5.

[32] P. T. Geach, *The Virtues* (Cambridge: 1977), p. 98.

incommensurable aspects.) So, in the absence of any universal, necessary principle such as that of 'sufficient reason', our question remains: Must we answer the question why the whole state of affairs causing the first-mentioned state of affairs to exist itself exists?

In Chapter III.4, I referred to some norms or principles of theoretical rationality, with which I compared the basic principles and requirements or norms of practical reasonableness discussed in Chapters III, IV, and V. These norms or principles of theoretical rationality underpin all our thinking, even in logic and mathematics: for although the basic forms of deductive inference, such as *modus ponens*,[33] cannot be theoretically 'justified', it would be quite unjustified, i.e. irrational, to refuse on that score to accept and use them—it is, in short, a principle of theoretical rationality that one ought to accept deductive arguments that seem valid, even though no justification of the inference is possible. As I said in Chapter III.4, there are many norms of theoretical rationality. Among them are certainly such norms or principles as: If a question of a certain form has been asked and answered, one can expect another question of the same general form to be answerable, and: If a theoretical question can be partially answered by positing a theoretical entity, and to do so allows the raising of further questions which, if answered, might well provide a more satisfying answer to the initial question, then one ought to posit such a theoretical entity—unless there are good reasons for not doing so.

Well, the substantive question on hand is of the same general form as questions that can be answered fairly satisfactorily: for it is simply the question 'Why does X exist?' (the question underlying much of the sciences), applied to the case where X is the whole set of states of affairs which initially explain why the particular state of affairs first under consideration itself exists. And it is possible (as we shall shortly see) to answer this further question about the whole causing state of affairs, by positing one or more states of affairs, of which we may have no experience, but the positing of which is fruitful of further questions, the answers to which can more adequately answer the substantive question on hand. This being so, it is rationally (not logically)

[33] If p then q; but p; therefore q.

necessary to entertain this answer, and to accept it unless there are reasons not to.

The explaining of the whole causing state of affairs is not the empty project of 'explaining a group' after all the group's members have been fully explained—of absurdly demanding to know, for example, why there is a set of five Eskimos standing at the street corner, *after* the presence of *each* of the five has been explained. Rather, it is a matter of explaining more fully the existing of one particular state of affairs. The existing of that (first-mentioned) state of affairs is partially explained by the already postulated causing state of affairs, but only on the assumption that that whole causing state of affairs exists; so the relation between 'member', 'group', and 'explanation' is quite different, here, from in the case of the Eskimos. And the only available explanation of the whole causing state of affairs is this: that there is some state of affairs causing that whole causing set of prerequisites or conditions of the first-mentioned state of affairs, but which is not itself included in that causing set of conditions precisely because, unlike all the members of that set, its existing does not require some prerequisite condition (not included in itself) to be satisfied. This newly postulated state of affairs can (and should, given the sense we are giving to 'cause') be called an uncaused causing.

In so far as it is causing, this uncaused causing might or might not be an existing state of affairs: otherwise it would not be the case, as it is, that the first-mentioned state of affairs (somebody reading a sentence in this book) might or might not be an existing state of affairs. In this respect— contingency—the uncaused causing state of affairs does not differ either from the first-mentioned state of affairs or from the whole causing state of affairs which can partially explain the existing of the first-mentioned state of affairs. Where the un-caused causing must differ, if it is to explain what needs to be explained, is in this: that to exist, it requires nothing not included in itself. (That is the fact about it that we signify by 'uncaused)'.

Since the uncaused causing might or might not be an existing state of affairs, its existing needs explanation. (In saying this, one appeals to the same principle of theoretical rationality as underpins scientific inquiry, and the whole of our present inquiry thus far.) The explanation of its existing can only be this: that the uncaused causing state of affairs includes, as a prerequisite to its existing, a state of affairs that exists because of *what* it is, i.e. because it is what it is. It will be convenient to label this last-mentioned state of affairs D. In the case of all states of affairs except D, we can describe the state of affairs, say *what* it is, without knowing *that* it is (i.e. without knowing whether it is an existing state of affairs). But, of D the argument requires us to say that *what* it is is all that it requires to exist. So, although the argument provides us with no further description of this state of affairs, of what it is, than that, still the argument does require us to say that we know *that* D exists. For what the whole argument shows, with rational (not logical) necessity, is that if *any* state of affairs, that might not exist, exists, then D *must* exist; without it, no state of affairs that might not exist could exist. But some state of affairs, that might not exist, does happen to exist (e.g. the reader reading this sentence). So D must (this is *not* logical necessity) exist.

To this line of argument, many objections have been raised. Since this is not a book on natural theology or the philosophy of God, I may be excused for doing no more than referring the reader to at least one place where the objections I am aware of are fairly and sufficiently dealt with.[34] The purpose of this section has been twofold. The first purpose has been to show how concern for the basic value of truth is essential if reasoning is to lead from questions about states of affairs which we experience to knowledge of the exisiting of a state of affairs which we do not as such experience. For principles of theoretical rationality, although they do not describe anything (as Leibniz's mistakenly unqualified principle of sufficient reason purported to), are objective, not conventional or relative to individual purposes or commitments. But one can choose to ignore or flout them; the cost is not self-contradiction but simply loss of knowledge of what one might come to know if one cared enough for the value of truth to adhere to principles which, as experience confirms, guide our reasoning towards

[34] Grisez, *Beyond the New Theism*, chs. 4–13. Chapters 6–13 alternately state and criticize empiricist, Kantian, Hegelian, and some contemporary relativist arguments and alternatives.

knowledge and away from ignorance.

The second purpose of the section has been to show that a truth-seeking reasoning can provide an explanation of the existing of things (including the orders of things, and the goods which we can make exist by our choices, actions, projects, and commitments, and the acts of understanding whereby we understand these orders and these goods), an explanation more securely based than the earlier-mentioned purported inference directly from order and good to transcendent intelligence and wisdom. The explanation that we have found warranted is, of course, incomplete. It affirms nothing about the explanatory state of affairs, D, other than that it has what it takes to make all other states of affairs exist. What more can be said about it?

XIII.3 DIVINE NATURE AND 'ETERNAL LAW':
SPECULATION AND REVELATION

Before answering the question what can be said about D, it may be as well to indicate why that question is worth tackling in this book, here. The reason is that arguments (which are rather common) about whether or not God is, or could be, the 'basis' or explanation of moral obligation, or of principles of practical reason, are quite futile in the absence of a clear grasp of (i) what reasons, if any, there are for speaking of anything that might be termed 'God' at all (I offered some reasons in the preceding section); (ii) what can be predicated of the entity termed 'God', in what sense any terms can be so predicated, and what reasons there are for so predicating them; and (iii) the precise questions in answer to which God or some aspect of God's causality is advanced by way of explanatory answer. Very commonly, none of these three sorts of clarification is made before argument is joined about whether, for example, God's 'will' is the basis of obligation, or could not possibly be such a basis ('For why *ought* we to obey God's will?'); or about whether God's 'goodness' is that basis, or could not possibly be ('How could one respect the author of the evils of this world?').

'God' is a term burdened with very varying associations. So the argument set out in the preceding section terminates in the affirmation of the existing, not of God (since I do not know what the reader understands by 'God'), but of D, of which all that has been affirmed is that it is a state of affairs which exists simply by being what it is, and which is required for the existing of any other state of affairs (including the state of affairs: D's causing all caused states of affairs).

And beyond this the argument will not, I think, take us. Still, it is philosophically possible to speculate that D's causing of all caused states of affairs, being an uncaused causing which determines between contingent possibilities, is in some respects analogous to the free choices of human persons. Of course, human choosing, unlike D's causing, requires many prerequisites; so the analogy must be imperfect. But the analogy may be justified in as much as human persons, by free acts of thinking, choosing, and using or making, bring into being entities (e.g. arguments, friendships, poems, and constitutions) that simply would not exist but for these not-wholly-determined human acts.

If there is any such analogy, then, D's uncaused causality can be described as an *act*, and can be thought of as presupposing something like our *knowledge* of the alternative possibilities available to be brought to realization by choice and creation. We only act freely when we know what the possibilities were, and when we know what we are doing. This knowledge is propositional: we can say what we are up to in doing what we are doing. The Augustinian and Thomistic speculation on Eternal Law is a development of the analogy in this respect: what we do is guided, shaped, directed by the formally (and often chronologically) prior plan we have in mind; if we are trying to get the members of a community themselves to act in the way we have it in mind for them to act, our plan of action can be presented as a law of their actions. So too the ensemble of caused states of affairs can be thought of as a quasi-community of entities or states of affairs which exist in intelligible orders in accordance with physical and other laws of nature (both 'classical' and statistical), with principles of logic and theoretical rationality, with requirements of practical reasonableness for human flourishing, and with the flexible norms of arts and technologies. Thus the theory of Eternal Law proposes that the laws, principles, requirements, and norms of the four orders be regarded as holding for their respective orders precisely because they express aspects, intelligible to us, of the creative intention which guides D's causing of the categorially variegated 'community' of all entities and all states of affairs in all orders.

The purport of the theory of Eternal Law can easily be misunderstood. *First*, it must not be treated as a theory which could guide investigation and verification of suggested norms in any of the four orders; rather it is a speculation about why those norms whose holding has been appropriately verified or established do hold. *Secondly*, the creative 'plan' of D which the theory hypothesizes (by a speculative inference not altogether unlike 'reading off' an artist's or architect's intention from his work) must not be imagined on some single model of 'law' or 'norm' drawn from any one of the four orders; rather, it must comprise elements as categorially diverse as the four orders which we directly understand. As it is a mistake to confuse the laws in human legal systems with laws of nature such as the classical and statistical laws of physics, so it is a mistake to suppose that the Eternal Law could be described on the model of any of the norms of any of the four orders. *Thirdly*, the sense of 'eternal' must not be misunderstood. To exist, D requires nothing other than to be what it is; thus D cannot be incomplete, cannot be changing in any sense of 'change' that we could apply to contingent entities or states of affairs in any of the four orders. But, for just the same reason, D cannot be 'static' or 'unchanging' in any sense applicable to such contingent entities or states of affairs. To say that D is eternal, and to call the act(s) and intention(s) of D eternal, is simply a way of indicating that D (and anything that can be predicated of D) neither develops nor declines, that D is outside the range of application of the concepts of change and changeless-ness, and hence of time. *Fourthly*, the speculation that the norms intelligible to us in any of the four orders are expressions or indications of D's creative plan in no way warrants the further speculation that D's creative plan is understood by us. All that we *know* about D is that D has what it takes to bring it about that every state of affairs which exists exists. But what states of affairs do in fact exist is not at all fully explained by the laws and norms of natural sciences, or of reasoning, or human arts, or of practical reasonableness and human flourishing. Much is coincidental, 'fortuitous'. Yet every state of affairs,

however 'fortuitous', requires D's creative causality if it is to
exist. So the speculation on the 'plan' of that causality, i.e. on
Eternal Law, suggests that much of that Law is quite unknown to us.[35]

The *fifth* and final point to be mentioned here is related to
the fourth. It concerns the relation between the supposed
creative plan or intention of D and the evils and disorders that,
as I have already stressed, are to be found in all four created
orders. A careful analysis of evils and disorders shows that
evil, strictly speaking, is a defect, a lack, the non-existing
of what ought (in terms of the norms of the relevant order) to
have existed but in fact does not exist. Evil is real, indeed,
but is not something that itself exists. Therefore it is not caused
by D. But D does cause all the states of affairs that involve evil;
in this sense D is responsible for evil. Does this entail that D's
creative causality is somehow defective? It does not; for we
could only judge D's causality to be evil or imperfect or
defective if we knew what the norms applicable to creative
causality are. But the creative causality of D is not a state of
affairs within any of the four orders whose norms we more or
less know. While we can speculate that the norms known to us
do reflect the plan 'underlying' creative causality, such an
assumption does not warrant an inference that that plan is
'captured' by the norms which we know (or could come to know
by any means imaginable to us). The norms in terms of which
we judge states of affairs to be evil, in any of the four
orders, are not applicable to D as creator. Thus we have no
ground to judge that D's creative causality is defective. In
short, if there is an Eternal Law, we do not know enough of it
to be able to judge D's creative performance defective
in terms of it.

---

[35] Thus Aquinas, *S.T.* I–II, q. 19, a. 10c; q. 91, a. 3 ad 1; q. 93, a. 2. The text
above, oversimplifies. Aquinas sometimes distinguishes between Eternal Law and
Providence: ibid. I, q. 22, a. 1; I–II, q. 93, a. 4, obj. 3; see also *Summa contra Gentes*,
III, cc. 97, 98, 113, 114: the distinction seems similar to that between the principles
of an art like seamanship and the incommunicable skill of the seaman in applying
them and adapting their application to unforeseen circumstances. The Eternal Law
(on Aquinas's conception of it) would be known by us imperfectly, not only because
its over-all point is unknown to us, but also because the boundaries between
External Law ('general') and Providence ('particular') are opaque to us (and, indeed,
Aquinas sometimes speaks of the Eternal Law as extending to all particular contingencies; *S.T.* I–II, q. 91, a. 3 ad 1; q. 93, a. 5 ad 3).

The foregoing discussion of the theological topic of Eternal Law has been in hypothetical form, since the speculation on creative causality, as analogous to an act of choice made in pursuance of a logically prior intention, is a speculation which (unlike the conclusion that D obtains and is an uncaused cause) cannot, I think, be rigorously established by philosophical argumentation. Verification of the speculation, and clarification of the meaning of the concepts employed in it, will depend upon some other mode of access to D. Inasmuch as the speculation suggests that D *acts* and *knows*, it suggests that D's existing is conceivable on the model of *personal life*. It therefore suggests that some sort of communication from or self-disclosure of D might occur. Whether this does occur is a question of fact, of experience and history.

It must never be overlooked that, for nearly two millennia, the theories of natural law have been expounded by men who, with few exceptions, believed that the uncaused cause has in fact revealed itself to be all that the foregoing analogue model of creative causality hypothesized, to be indeed supremely personal, and to be a lawgiver whose law for man should be obeyed out of gratitude, hope, fear, and/or love.[36] The supposed revelation of God has been conceived òf as more or less public and empirically accessible, i.e. as something more than an event in the intellectual or spiritual life of a meditating individual. But it also must not be overlooked that the originators of natural law theorizing, who did not suppose that God has revealed himself by any such act of informative communication, believed none the less that through philosophical meditation one can gain access to the transcendent source of being, goodness, and knowledge. Nor is this belief of Plato and Aristotle irrelevant to their development of a teaching about practical reasonableness, ethics, or natural right, in opposition to the sceptics, relativists, and positivists of their day. For at the foundation of such teachings is their faith in the power and objectivity of reason, intelligence, *nous*. And there is

---

[36] So the Ten Commandments of Israel are introduced by the words '"I am the Lord your God, who brought you out of the land of Egypt, out of the house of bondage ..."', Exodus 20: 2. And the second promulgation of the Commandments is ratified by the self-identification of '"The Lord, the Lord, a God merciful and gracious, slow to anger, and abounding in steadfast love and faithfulness ..."': Exodus 34:5; cf. also Deuteronomy 5:29; 5:33–6: 6.

much reason to believe that their confidence in human *nous* is itself founded upon their belief that the activity of human understanding, at its most intense, is a kind of sharing in the activity of the divine *nous*.[37]

Neither Plato's nor Aristotle's conception of the divine nature and causality is the same as the notion of D and D's causing expounded in this chapter (or as the Jewish and Christian notion of God and God's creation). But their conceptions certainly have a similarity to the speculative analogue model discussed in this section, and to the confirmation of that speculation by the public divine revelation(s) believed in by Jews and Christians; so much similarity, indeed, that Augustine of Hippo felt obliged to raise the hypothesis that Plato had had some access to the divinely inspired prophets of Israel.[38] In the end, Augustine rather preferred the vague suggestion that Plato's knowledge of the divine nature and causality had been revealed to Plato by God 'through His created works'.[39]

Neither of Augustine's hypotheses is too satisfactory. But the issue is not unimportant. For there has been pressure in some theological traditions to distinguish sharply between revelation and reason (or 'natural reason'), and to appropriate the term 'revelation' rather exclusively to the Judaeo-Christian orbit. Plato and Aristotle, on the other hand, do not trade on any such distinction. Certainly they think they have reasons, arguments, for judging that the ordered goods of this world (among them our own *nous*, power of understanding) are caused by something beyond this world.[40] These arguments are perhaps unsatisfactory to the extent that they proceed by too straight and narrow a path from the order of the world to an ordering intelligence.[41] But this need not concern us here, since they can in any case be treated as arguments towards the development of an analogue model for speculatively interpreting the possible or likely nature of the uncaused causing

---

[37] See Plato, *Rep.* VI, 508a–509b; VII, 514a–518e; Aristotle, *Meta.* XII, 7: 1072b13–25; *Nic. Eth.* X, 7: 1177b26–1178a1.

[38] *De Civitate Dei*, VIII, c. 11. The suggestion had been mooted by earlier Christian writers.

[39] Ibid., c. 12 (cf. c. 10), quoting Romans 1: 19–20.

[40] See Plato, *Rep.* VI, 509b.

[41] See e.g. Plato, *Laws*, X, 888d–889d; Aristotle, *Meta.* I, 984b7–24; and cf. XIII.2, above. Notice that they are well aware of evils and disorders; Plato indeed considers them more extensive than good and order: *Rep.* II, 379c.

which can be affirmed on the basis of a sound argument which these philosophers were moving towards but had not yet differentiated from the arguments in question. What does concern us here is that, besides their arguments, both Plato and Aristotle seem to claim a certain experiential access to the divine. In particular they both affirm, usually meditatively rather than argumentatively, that man can participate in the divine through the activity of his intelligence, firstly, inasmuch as one's wondering desire to know is the result of a divine attraction stirring one from one's incuriosity to a curiosity that can be satisfied by, and only by, a knowledge of the divine origin of things; and secondly, inasmuch as the act of understanding is itself a kind of sharing in the divine intelligence which by its practical exercise has made an intelligible world.

It is necessary to mention these matters because the distinctions later drawn by Christian theologians between natural law and divine law, and between natural reason and revelation, have given some encouragement to the supposition that 'natural law' or 'natural reason(ableness)' signify properties of a purely immanent world ('nature') or an intelligence which has no knowledge of, or concern for, the existence of any transcendent ('supernatural') uncaused cause. But this supposition is mere muddle and is not, and was not intended to be, entailed by the aforementioned distinctions. When, for example, Aristotle speaks of the 'right (or just) by nature' (*physei dikaion*),[42] or of what every person desires 'by nature' (*physei*), he is in no way contrasting 'by nature' with 'by divine appointment'. Indeed, he insists that when Anaxagoras first said 'that there is mind [*nous*] in nature [*physei*], as in animals, and that this is the cause of *all* order and arrangement, he seemed like a sane man in contrast with the haphazard statements of his predecessors'.[43] More pointedly, Aristotle opens his fundamental philosophical work with the affirmation that 'by nature [*physei*] all men desire to know'.[44] From there he proceeds not only to the affirmation (i) that the most desirable object of knowledge is 'the highest good in the whole of nature [*physei*]',[45] a good which he identifies

---

[42] *Nic. Eth.* V, 7: 1134b18–1135a5; cf. I, 3: 1094b11–16.

[43] *Meta.* I, 3: 984b15–17. And 'the first principle upon which depend the sensible universe and nature [*physis*]' is God (*ho theos*): XII, 7: 1072b14.

[44] *Meta.* I, 1: 980a22.

[45] Ibid. I, 2: 982b7–8.

as God,[46] but to the further affirmations (ii) that understanding [or thought] 'in the highest sense' is concerned with God;[47] (iii) that the supreme object of understanding or thought is God and that 'intelligence [or thought] [*nous*] understands [or thinks] itself through participation [*metalepsis*] in the object of under-standing [or thought]; for it becomes an object of understanding by being touched and understood, so that intelligence [*nous*] and the object of understanding are the same';[48] and (iv) that the best and most pleasant state, which is enjoyed only intermittently by us but always by God, is the contemplation (*theoria*) of that actuality which understanding has, as a divine (*theion*) possession, when it thus participates in its supreme object.[49] In these intense passages the subject of Aristotle's attention, *nous*, is intended by him to be taken as something in a sense shared between God and man, in that human understanding participates in the divine *nous* which is its source, its attracting mover, and its object, while the divine *nous* participates in the human *nous* which it moves, illuminates, and satisfies. And all this is Aristotle's unfolding of what, he says, everybody desires *by nature*.

Plato and Aristotle do not use the existence of God or the gods as an argument to justify their claim that there are objective norms of human flourishing and principles of human reasonableness. But their arguments in justifying that claim, and their reflection upon the nature, point, and source of those (and all such) arguments, lead them to affirm that there is a transcendent source of being (i.e. of entities and states of affairs, and of their existing) and in particular of our capacity and desire to understand being (or nature) and its many forms of good. Thus in realizing one's nature, in flourishing (*eudaimonia*), and (what is the same thing from another aspect) in recognizing the authoritativeness of practical reasonableness, its principles, and its requirements, one is responding to the

---

[46] Ibid. I, 2: 982b4–11, 983a6–10; XII, 7: 1072a26–b31.
[47] Ibid. XII, 7: 1072b19–20.
[48] 1072b20–23.
[49] 1072b23–27.

divine pull[50] and recognizing the mastery of God.[51] So when Plato speaks of God's law, his meaning is rather close to what a Christian theologian, such as Aquinas, means in speaking of natural law as the Eternal Law in so far as it is addressed to human practical reasonableness. Thus Plato:

God, as the old saying says, holds in his hand the beginning, end and middle of all that is, and straight he travels to the accomplishment of his purpose, as is (his) nature [*kata physin*]; and always by his side is Right [*dike*: justice] ready to punish those who disobey the divine law [*theiou nomou*]. Anyone who wants to flourish [*eudaimonesein*] follows closely in the train of Right, with humility ... What line of conduct, then, is dear [*phile*] to God and a following of him? ... Well, it is God who is for us the measure [*metron*] of all things; much more truly so than, as they [sophists, notably Protagoras] say, man. So to be loved by such a being, a man must strive as far as he can to become like that being; and, following out this principle, the person who is temperate-and-ordered is dear to God, being like him.[52]

Plato has no conception corresponding to Aquinas's differentiated[53] concept of divine law, i.e. the law which supplements the natural law and is promulgated by God for the regulation of the community or communities (Israel and then the universal Church) constituted through God's public self-revelation and offer of friendship. For Plato, while he would affirm that God can be apprehended by us in the act and experience of human understanding, has no conception of a revelation accessible to men without the effort of rational dialectic and contemplation—of the sort of empirical revelation, for instance, that would be 'folly to the Greeks' (but would be offered to them none the less).[54]

[50] Plato, *Laws*, I, 644d–645b; 803, 804b. See also *Rep.* VIII, 515c, e, on the dragging of the prisoner from the Cave, the pulling of him into the light of the Sun. For Aristotle, see *Eud. Eth.* VII, 14: 1248a16–28.

[51] *Laws*, IV, 713a, 716c; VII, 803c; VI, 762e; Aristotle, *Eud. Eth.* VIII, 3: 1249b6–21.

[52] *Laws*, IV, 715e–716d. See also *Rep.* VI, 600b.

[53] In the *Summa contra Gentes*, III, cc. 114–18, Aquinas also uses an undifferentiated concept of *lex divina*, embracing what in the *Summa Theologiae* (I–II, q. 91, aa. 1–5) he distinguishes as *lex aeterna*, *lex naturalis*, and *lex divina* (Old and New).

[54] As by Paul: 1 Corinthians 1: 22–4. Of course, on Aquinas's view, this revelation does not oppose reason; in going beyond what is accessible either to argument or to meditative rational experience, the revealed truths, he thinks, incorporate truths accessible to reason and answer questions raised, pressed, but found insoluble by reason. Correspondingly, the divine (i.e. revealed) law, for Aquinas, incorporates and repromulgates many elements of natural law: *S.T.* I–II, q. 100, aa. 1, 3; q. 99, a. 2.

In short, Plato and Aristotle consider that what I have called a speculative analogue model of D's nature and causality is in some measure verified in the experience of the true philosopher.[55] By this belief they are encouraged to treat reason as more than a skill, knack, or characteristic that men, unlike animals, happen to have; and to treat the nature or reality that both includes and is illuminated by man's understanding as more than a fortuitous agglomeration of entities and states of affairs devoid of any significance that could attract human admiration and allegiance. Practical reasonableness gains for them the significance of a partial imitation of God;[56] the basic values grasped by practical reason gain an objectivity;[57] and practical reason's methodological requirements of constancy and impartiality are reinforced by the worth of adopting the viewpoint of the God who 'contemplates all time and all existence'.[58]

Still, there is deep uncertainty in their knowledge of God's nature and relation to this world and its goods. This uncertainty could be illustrated in many ways. Suffice it here to take a representative instance. Aristotle quite often speaks of the friendship (*philia*) of God or the gods for men and of men for God or the gods;[59] but in his fundamental analysis of friendship he expresses his considered opinion: God is so remote from man that there can be no friendship between God and man.[60] Both the vacillation and the fundamental conclusion on this point entail a deep uncertainty about the content of human flourishing and the significance of human life. Very well known is Aristotle's uncertainty about the relation between contemplation of divine things and a practical life of all-round flourishing in the context of the *polis*. Not quite so well known is Aristotle's attempt to explain the reasonableness of self-

---

[55] Plato adds that *every* human being possesses the capacity of learning this truth: *Rep.* VII, 518; cf. VI, 505.

[56] See *Rep.* II, 383c; VI, 500; VII, 540a.

[57] See *Rep.* VI, 504b, 508b–e.

[58] *Rep.* VI, 486a.

[59] See *Nic. Eth.* X, 9: 1179a23–32; VII, 12: 1162a5; IX, 1: 1164b5; *Eud. Eth.* VII, 3: 1238b18; 10: 1242a32.

[60] *Nic. Eth.* VIII, 7: 1158b35, 1159a4.

sacrifice for one's friend;[61] the attempt seems laudable, inevitable, right; but the explanation offered is curiously inadequate. Every reader of Aristotle's *Ethics* becomes aware of
such uncertainties, though not all trace them to their roots.

This uncertainty of Plato and Aristotle corresponds to D's
objective inaccessibility to the argumentations and inferences of
rational inquiry. Without some revelation more revealing than
any that Plato or Aristotle may have experienced, it is
impossible to have sufficient assurance that the uncaused
cause of all the good things of this world (including our
ability to understand them) is itself a good that one could love,
personal in a way that one might imitate, a guide that one
should follow, or a guarantor of anyone's practical reasonableness.

XIII.4 NATURAL LAW AS 'PARTICIPATION OF ETERNAL LAW'

Most people who study jurisprudence or political philosophy
are invited at some stage to read Thomas Aquinas's 'treatise
on law' (Questions 90–7 of the First Part of the Second
Part of his *Summa Theologiae*). Here they read his definition of
natural law as *participatio legis aeternae in rationali creatura*:[62]
the participation of the Eternal Law in rational creatures. In
fact the treatment of natural law in that 'treatise on law' is
barely intelligible to one who has not read Aquinas's account of
the moral measure and significance of reasonableness;[63] or his
account of *prudentia*, practical reasonableness;[64] or any of his
discussions of particular moral questions, not to mention his
treatment of *beatitudo*, the happiness of human flourishing;[65] and
of *caritas*, friendship with God.[66] Still, what has been said
about the first two of these topics, in Chapters III–V of
this book, has sufficient similarities (as well as additions) to
Aquinas's line of thought to afford the present reader some
indispensable orientation and complementary material for

[61] Ibid. IX, 8: 1169a18–26.
[62] *S.T.* I–II, q. 91, a. 2c.
[63] I–II, qq. 18–21.
[64] I–II, q. 57, aa. 4–6; q. 65, a. 1; II–II, q. 47.
[65] I–II, qq. 1–5.
[66] I–II, qq. 62, 65; II–II, qq. 23–7.

understanding Aquinas's formal discussion of natural law. The present section, then, seeks to provide a summary elucidation of that famous phrase: *participatio legis aeternae in rationali creatura*.

The term *participatio* translates into Latin a number of Greek terms (especially *methexis*) which Plato used in a semi-technical manner, as well as the term *metalepsis* which, in the previous section, we observed Aristotle using, non-technically, to express the significance of the supreme activation of human intelligence as a kind of sharing in God's self-understanding. Aquinas is inclined to dissociate himself from Plato's semi-technical meanings as he understands them,[67] and is not here concerned with Aristotle's contemplative experience. Nor does he mean what I mean by 'participation' in a value, in earlier parts of this book (III.3). For Aquinas, the word *participatio* focally signifies two conjoined concepts, causality and similarity (or imitation). A quality that an entity or state of affairs has or includes is participated, in Aquinas's sense, if that quality is *caused by* a *similar* quality which some other entity or state of affairs has or includes in a more intrinsic or less dependent way.

Aquinas's notion of natural law as a participation of the Eternal Law is no more than a straightforward application of his general theory of the cause and operation of human understanding in any field of inquiry. His bases for inference are the power of human insight and the imperfection of human intelligence. The power of human understanding far exceeds (or rather is incommensurable with) what we would expect to be the intrinsic capacity of the brain-material, however complex, that is its substratum; understanding an equation, a series or an inference, or somebody else's intention and meaning, or that a proposition indeed answers a question or that a certain event really occurred, or that a certain scientific law really holds or that a pointer-reading verifies a scientific hypothesis about the universe—all this amounts to a unique capacity-in-action quite irreducible to any material conditions. On the other hand, it is not difficult to postulate an intelligence that would far exceed human intelligence; for our pursuit of understanding is laborious, developmental, and never nearly completed; we need images, figures, symbols, to help us

[67] See, e.g., *S.T.* I, q. 6, a. 4c.

understand even the most abstract terms and relations; and our learning and discovery are always harassed by oversight, muddle, and lapse of memory. Thus Aquinas follows Plato and Aristotle in postulating a 'separate intellect' which has the power of understanding without imperfection, and which causes in us our own power of insight, the activation of our own individual intelligences—somewhat as a source of light activates in us our power of sight.[68] He then relies explicitly on revelation ('the *documenta* of our faith')[69] to identify the supposed 'separate intellect' as God. In short (he concludes), 'it is from God that the human mind shares in [*participat*] intellectual light: as Psalm 4 verse 7 puts it "The light of thy countenance, O Lord, is signed upon us."'[70] The same scriptural quotation caps his account of natural law as a *participatio* of Eternal Law.[71]

So, for Aquinas, there is nothing extraordinary about man's grasp of the natural law; it is simply one application of man's ordinary power of understanding. None the less his account of this practical *participatio* of the Eternal Law draws attention to some related points worth recapitulating here.

Aquinas begins by drawing a sharp distinction (which runs through all his work)[72] between the intelligent nature of human beings, and the intelligible but not intelligent nature of animals, vegetables, and the rest of 'nature'. The latter participate in the Eternal Law 'somehow',[73] since that is the ultimate source of all their tendencies (*inclinationes*) (which have and follow intelligible patterns). Human beings, on the other hand, provide for themselves (and for others); so we can say that

---

[68] On this anaology, admitted by Aquinas to be inadequate, see his *Summa contra Gentes*, III, c. 53.

[69] *S.T.* I, q. 79, a. 4c.

[70] Ibid. He is quoting the Vulgate version of the Psalm, and considers the verse peculiarly relevant in relation to practical reasoning because it is preceded by the verse 'Many say: "Who showeth us good things?"': see *De Veritate*, q. 16, a. 3c.

[71] *S.T.* I–II, q. 91, a. 2c. In q. 93, a. 3 he remarks that *all* knowledge of truth is a kind of *irradiatio* and *participatio* of the Eternal Law. The quotation from Psalm 4: 6 recurs e.g. in q. 19, a. 4c, where Aquinas is arguing that reasonableness is the standard of moral judgment because our practical reason participates in the Eternal Law, the primary standard.

[72] See e.g. *S.T.* I–II, q. 1, a. 2c; q. 6, a. 1c; *De Potentia*, q. 1, a. 5c; *in Meta.* V, lect. 16, nn. 999–1000.

[73] 'Aliqualiter': *S.T.* I–II, q. 91, a. 2c; in ad 3 he remarks that their participation can be called (a following of) law only metaphorically (*per similitudinem*).

man is not only subject to God's providence, but is actually a participant (*particeps*) in it.[74] In brief, animals (and the rest of 'lower creation') are *not* subject to natural law. And their nature is not a basis for inference about the principles of human reasonableness.

Next, Aquinas specifies the basic manner in which the eternal reason is participated in us: through our 'natural inclination to the due [*debitum*] act and the due end'. This terse formulation needs expansion. It is elaborated a few pages later, when he explains that amongst our natural inclinations is the inclination to act *secundum rationem*, i.e. reasonably.[75] But the formula also looks right back to the beginning of Aquinas's discussion of human self-direction.[76] There his first exploration is of our inclination towards our last (or all-embracing)[77] end (*ultimus finis*), a completeness of flourishing (*beatitudo*) which will be found when our natural desire for understanding (i.e. for the satisfaction of our reason) is satisfied by that undying contemplation of God which, he says, can be anticipated only on the basis of revelation and can be attained only by a divine gift.[78] Finally, the formula in the discussion of natural law looks forward to his resumption of the Aristotelian meditation on the divine causality that underpins all our inclinations and capacities, including our desire to know and to be intelligent, reasonable, responsible, and our capacity to choose freely and responsibly.[79] All these themes Aquinas draws together in explaining this aspect of the participation of Eternal Law in us as natural law: 'every activity of reason and of will derives, in us, from that which is according to nature ... For all reasoning derives from principles [or sources: *principiis*] naturally[80] known; and all desire for things which are for an end derives from natural desire for an end beyond which

[74] See also I–II, q. 93, a. 5c; a. 6c.

[75] I–II, q. 94, a. 3c.

[76] See I–II, Prologue, and qq. 1–5.

[77] For the meaning of *ultimus* here as 'completely adequate, fully actuating, perfecting', see e.g. I–II, q. 3, a. 2.

[78] *Summa contra Gentes*, III, cc. 52–4; *S.T.* I–II, q. 5.

[79] *S.T.* I–II. q. 109, a. 2 ad 1; similarly I, q. 82, a. 4 ad 3; Aristotle, *Eud. Eth.* VII, 14: 1248a16–28.

[80] But not without experience; for the intelligence of each of us starts as a *tabula rasa*: *S.T.* I, q. 79, a. 2c. Like Aristotle (*Post. Anal.* B, c. 19: 99b14–100b17), Aquinas has no truck with 'innate ideas'.

is no further end [*ultimus finis*]; and so it must be that the first directing of our acts towards an end [or: the end] is through natural law'.[81]

Having thus stressed the inclinations which, prior to any rational control of ours, underlie all our effort, including our effort to make our efforts intelligent and reasonable, Aquinas turns to that aspect of our participation of God's practical reason which I mentioned earlier: our power of understanding. For, by this power, we grasp the basic forms of good (and thus the basic principles of natural law);[82] the data for this act of understanding include the desires and inclinations which we experience, but like all understanding, this act of understanding goes beyond the data as experienced, to concepts accessible or available not to experience but only to understanding. I have already indicated (briefly!) Aquinas's general account of the source of our power of illuminating the data of imagination and experience by the insights of common sense, natural science, philosophy, and practical reasonableness. So now he cites again the words of Psalm 4:7, and adds that 'the light of natural reason, whereby we discern what is good and what is bad (which is what natural law concerns), is simply the impress in us of the divine light'.[83]

This metaphorical language is not to be understood in a mystical way. There is a touch of mysticism (i.e. a suggestion of direct experience of God) in Aristotle's account of the participation of divine and human *nous* in contemplation. (To say this is not to comment on the validity of that account.) But Aquinas's account, though sometimes metaphorically expressed, works with no more than the ideas of causality and similarity. There is no suggestion that the mode of divine causality can be further explained, or that the causing or its source are experienced as such. The Thomist theory of participation is not a report of experience, but a theorem in the general explanation of all states of affairs by reference, ultimately, to creative uncaused causality. And so far as it concerns similarity, and also in its metaphorical colouring, the

[81] *S.T.* I–II, q. 91, a. 2 ad 2.

[82] I–II, q. 94, a. 2c; q. 10, a. 1c.

[83] I–II, q. 91, a. 2c. Some people are more receptive of this light than others, though every (sane and conscious) person grasps the general principles of practical reasonableness: q. 93, a. 2.

theorem is derived simply by taking the analogue model of divine intelligence, intentionality, life, personality, etc.; treating the model as verified; and then applying it in reverse to the explanation of the human inclinations, intelligence, deliberations and decisions, etc., on which the analogy was founded.

The account of the *source* of natural law thus focuses first on the experienced dynamisms of our nature, and then on the intelligible principles which outline the aspects of human flourishing, the basic values grasped by human understanding.[84] A few pages later Aquinas formulates one of the fundamental theoretical principles of his account of the *content* of natural law: 'all those things to which man has a natural inclination, one's reason naturally understands as good (and thus as "to be pursued") and their contraries as bad (and as "to be avoided")'.[85] It is certainly possible to raise the question: Whence this parallelism, this fit, this *convenientia*, of felt inclinations with valuable aspects of human well-being?[86] And it is easy to see what Aquinas's answer to this question would have been, had he bothered to raise it.

XIII.5 CONCLUDING REFLECTIONS ON THE POINT AND FORCE OF PRACTICAL REASONABLENESS

I have not presented natural law or the principles of practical reasonableness as expressions of God's will. And I have positively declined to explain obligation in terms of conformity to superior will. But what I have said in this chapter should show why appeals to God's will, and explanation of obligation by reference to it, cannot be refuted (as it often is supposed they can) by the apparently available question: 'But why should we obey God?' (cf. XI.9). For that question implicitly treats 'God' as referring simply to one more superior in an ascending series of superiors, of each of whom the question can reasonably

---

[84] In I–II, q. 93, a. 6c, at the end of his discussion of Eternal Law and immediately before his main discussion of natural law, Aquinas focuses on the two themes explicitly and together.

[85] I–II, q. 94, a. 2c.

[86] On the *convenientia* of *appetitus naturalis* with the nature of the being that has these 'appetites' or inclinations or tendencies (for this is, for Aquinas, a quite general metaphysical principle), see *S.T.* I, q. 78, a. 1 and 3; q. 80, a. 1c and ad 2; I–II, q. 26, a. 1c. This *convenientia* is not, for Aquinas, the decisive principle of ethical reasoning: cf. II.6, above.

be asked (so that it would seem arbitrary to treat the last member of the series as immune from the questioning). But the perspective of those who assert that God wills such-and-such, and that that will should be obeyed, is (or certainly can be) quite different.

To the extent that they follow something like the train of argument leading to the affirmation that D exists (XIII.2), those who speak of God intend to refer to an entity and state of affairs that by its existing explains the existing of all entities and states of affairs in all four orders of contingent being. Consequently, by 'D' or 'God' is meant (i) that which explains the very possibility of explanation, of there being answers to questions about any order of being, and in particular explains (a) the existing of any and every entity or state of affairs to be explained, and (b) the existing of all our powers of understanding and explaining, and (c) the order of entities or states of affairs (and the corresponding order of concepts) that afford or figure in the partial explanations available to us in every discipline or field of inquiry. By 'D' or 'God' is further meant (ii) that which explains the existence of the questioning subject; (iii) that which explains the existing of good states of affairs, and the opportunity of making them exist; (iv) that which explains our ability to recognize goods, to grasp values and their equivalent practical principles; and (v) that which explains our ability to respond to the attractiveness of those goods, to the rational appeal of the principles. How D (or God) thus is the explanation of all this is not known; what is considered to be known is simply that D (or God) is whatever is required to explain them. Already, therefore, it should be clear that to ask for an explanation of D (or God) is to miss the sense and reference of claims made about D (or God).

But those who claim to know what God wills in some human context, and that that will should be obeyed, are (as I have said) going beyond what can be affirmed about D on the basis of philosophical argumentation.[87] They are claiming (like Plato,

[87] Aquinas, who will not be suspected of minimizing the range of philosophical reasoning, says 'the will of God cannot be investigated by reasoning, except for those items that it is absolutely necessary for God to will. Now, as we have said before [q. 19, a. 3c], such items do not include what God wills in regard to creatures': *S.T.* I, q. 46, a. 2c.

but relying unlike him upon some definite revelation) that God positively favours both the basic goods and human adherence to the principles and requirements of practical reasonableness in the pursuit of those goods; that the evils and disorders of this world are not favoured so, but are merely tolerated by God for the sake of some positive good (what, and how attained, we do not know); and that friendship with God, some sharing in God's life and knowledge and love-of-goods, is available to those who positively favour what God positively favours. In the context of such beliefs—and it is only in such a context that claims about the authoritativeness of God's will for man are plausibly made—the question 'Why should God's will be obeyed?' has no bite.

After these preliminary remarks about a problem that is not mine (since I have asserted nothing about God's will), I can at last return to the practical problems raised at the beginning of this chapter: the possibility of a deeper explanation of obligation; the reasonableness of self-sacrifice in human friend-ship; the relevance of our limited place in human history and the universe; the point of living according to the principles and requirements of practical reasonableness. In view of all that has been said in this and earlier chapters, I can perhaps afford to be summary.

In the first place, what can be established, by argumentation from the existence and general features of this world, concerning the uncaused cause of the world, does not directly assist us in answering those practical questions.

In the second place, this limitation of 'natural reasoning' leaves somehow 'subjective' and 'questionable' the whole structure of basic principles and requirements of practical reasonableness and human flourishing discussed in Chapters III–XII. On the other hand, it does not unravel that structure or affect its internal order or weaken its claim to be more reasonable than any logically possible alternative structures.

In the third place, 'natural reasoning' can speculatively postulate that the uncaused cause exists in something like the mode of personal life, and that its causality has some analogy to the intelligent self-direction and intentionality of human creative decision. Such a model for thinking about the uncaused cause allows the further speculation that the uncaused cause might somehow disclose itself to human understanding, by an act of intelligible communication. This further speculation in turn permits the speculating thinker to hope that the uncaused cause might reveal itself to be lovable, and that the 'ideal observer' which practical reasonableness postulates as a test of arbitrariness might prove to have a real and substantial counterpart (cf. V.4).

In the fourth place, if these speculations and hopes were confirmed, a more basic account of obligation would become possible. For if the uncaused cause were revealed to favour the well-being of everyman, for no other reason than its (D's, God's) own goodness (in a sense of goodness going, now, beyond the perfection of being all that is required to make all states of affairs exist), the common good could be pursued by us for a new reason, viz. out of love or friendship for the personal being ('God') who not only makes possible whatever well-being of persons there can be and actually is, but also positively favours (though in ways often unintelligible to us) that common good. This would not entail that we no longer favoured the common good for its own sake, nor that we no longer loved our friends for their own sakes. Rather, it would mean that 'for their own sakes' would gain a further (and explanatory) dimension of meaning. For then other persons (and ourselves!) could be regarded not simply as persons whose good we happen to favour, rather inexplicably (in view of their inevitable imperfections), but as persons whose good is favoured also by one whose own goodness is unrestricted and whose love is in no way blind but rather is given knowing fully the true worth and all-explaining point of everything, of the existence of every person, and of the history of every community. And this would not only explain, in principle, how self-sacrifice in friendship can make sense; it also would account for our obligation to favour the common good.

For our earlier accounts of obligation terminated at the common good: those actions, projects, and commitments are obligatory which are necessary if the common good of persons in our communities is to be realized. This left an unanswered question: In what sense are we to take it to be *necessary* to favour that common good, which after all will end, sooner or later, in the death of all persons and the dissolution of all communities? That question could not be answered. For in friendship (VI.4) one values what one's friend values (save where he is mistaken in his valuation), for no other reason than that he values it. (No other reason is called for.) So if God could be recognized to be our friend (in, of course, an unusual sense of 'friend'), and to be one who favours the common good of human persons, we would have a new and pertinent reason for loving that common good, pertinent even though we could not see how that love would work out in the perspective of all times and all places. And, if we wanted to use the rather vague terms of contemporary philosophy textbooks, we could say that the considerations advanced in this paragraph show how 'God is the basis of obligation'.

In the fifth place, the foregoing speculations or anticipations, if verified, would enable a deeper understanding of the basic values with which our exploration of natural law began in Chapter IV. Here I propose to reconsider only three: practical reasonableness, religion, and play: cf. IV.2.

Plato has carried out such a reconsideration of those three basic human values, through the central philosophical myth in his last work, the *Laws* (*Nomoi*). The symbol in the myth is introduced in Book I immediately after a first theoretical account of a central meaning of *nomos*, law. Plato, through the Athenian stranger, has begun the parable by remarking that each human being is indeed one person, but has within him unwise and conflicting sources of direction, namely pain and pleasure, and their concomitants, aversion and audacity. But also there is *logismos*, reflective insight and reasonable judgment concerning the better and the worse among these basic movements in the psyche. And when this *logismos* is embodied in a public decree (*dogma*) of the *polis*, it is called *nomos*. To explain this, the Athenian stranger invites us to suppose that each of us is a puppet of the gods, created perhaps as a plaything (*paignion*), perhaps for some serious purpose—we do not know. What is certain is that all those basic movements within us are, so to say, the cords by which we puppets are worked, with opposite tensions pulling us in opposite directions; herein lies the division between virtue and vice. The myth is not to be understood mechanistically or as treating man as an automaton, for the account goes on to say that there is one

cord which works only with the support of man, and that each of
us ought to follow the pull of this cord against the pull of all
the others. For this is the golden and sacred cord of practical
reasonableness (*logismos*) or, 'to give it another name', the
common law (*koinos nomos*) of the *polis*. The pull of this cord is
soft and gentle. But the other cords are of iron and various
other materials. Against their hardness a man ought always to
co-operate with the pull of the *nomos*, lest the other pulls prevail
over him. One who understands all this understands self-
mastery and self-defeat; he has true understanding (*logos alethes*)
of the tensions in the soul; and he understands that the individual ought to live according to the golden cord of reason,
and that the *polis* ought to embody it in a law regulating both
the internal and the foreign relations of the *polis*.

Up to this point, Plato's discussion amounts to a compressed
anticipation, in deliberately undifferentiated language (playing
upon the various meanings and references of *nomos* and *logos*),
of the themes we have discussed in terms of natural law,
positive law, inclinations, practical reasonableness, and participation in the Eternal Law. This is one of the foundation texts
in the tradition of theorizing about natural law. But in Book VII
of the *Laws*, at the middle point of the whole work, Plato's Athenian returns to the symbol of the plaything (*paignion*) of God.

We should keep our seriousness for serious things [*spoudaion*], not
waste it on non-serious things. While God is by nature [*physei*] the
goal of all beneficent serious endeavours, man (as we have said before)
has been made as God's plaything, and this is, indeed, the finest thing
about man. All of us, men and women, ought to fall in with this
role, and spend our lives in playing this noblest of plays.

The usual view is that our serious work must be attended to for
the sake of our play. Thus people think that war is serious work which
ought to be well discharged in order to secure peace. In truth, however, in war we do not find, and we never will find, either real
play [*paidia*] or real formation [education: *paideia*]—which are the
things I count most serious for us human creatures. So it is in
peace that each of us should spend most of his life and spend it
best. This, then, is the right course: That we should pass our lives
in playing the games [or play] of sacrifice, song and dance, so that
we may gain the grace of the gods and be able to repel and defeat
our enemies when we have to fight ... [We are to bring up those
in our care so that they] will live out their lives as what they are by

nature [*physeos*], puppets for the most part, though having a little bit of reality, too.

Megillus: You give us a very poor opinion of the human race, Stranger.

Athenian: Do not be surprised, Megillus. Bear with me. The one who just spoke was looking and feeling towards God, when he was speaking.[88]

Perhaps the mood of Plato's symbolism is what the Christians would call pagan; man the plaything is not, perhaps, man the fellow player in the divine drama of history and eternity, who might be redeemed for friendship with God by God become man. But Christianity has not offered, nor has philosophy provided, any reason to doubt Plato's more fundamental point, that obligation, while real enough (and referred to again and again in the passages just cited), is not the framework or finally authoritative category of 'moral' thought. The requirements of practical reasonableness (which generate our obligations) have a 'point' beyond themselves. That point is the *game* of co-operating with God. Being *play*, this co-operation has no point beyond itself, unless we wish to say that God is such a further 'point'. By analogy with human friendship, we may be able to say that, but only in a special, restricted sense. For if we simply said that we act for the sake of God, we would suggest that God somehow needs us, needs creation, the success of creation, the achieving of the creative purpose. But D needs and lacks nothing. And has God been revealed as needing or lacking anything? So if we ask why God creates, no answer is available other than the one implicitly given by Plato: play—a free but patterned expression of life and activity, meaningful but with no further point.[89] Hence, even one who goes beyond Plato to accept that man is called to a friendship of devotion to God will grant that such friendship takes the form of sharing, in a limited way, in the divine play.

Practical reasonableness, therefore, need not be regarded as ultimately a form of self-perfection. That is not its final significance. Nor, on the other hand, are its requirements sheer

[88] *Laws*, 803b–c. In A. E. Taylor's translation the last words are finely rendered: 'Bear with me. I had God before my mind's eye, and felt myself to be what I have just said.'

[89] Cf. Proverbs 8: 30–1.

categorical imperatives; they gain practical force from the most basic explanation that can be provided for them—that they are what is needed to participate in the game of God.

Play, too, can now be more adequately understood. It is to be contrasted with business, with reponsibilities, with the serious things of life. But, in the last analysis, there is a play that is the *only* really serious matter. In such a 'final analysis', in which we seek an understanding going beyond our feelings, the 'serious things of life', even atrocious miseries, are really serious only to the extent that they contribute to or are caught up into a good play of the game of the God who creates and favours human good.

Finally, the assumptions about God necessary to justify the two preceding paragraphs would, if verified, entitle us to remove the question mark with which I originally introduced the basic human value of religion: see IV.2. In doing so, I spoke hesitantly, constrained by the anthropological and psychological evidence to postulate an inclination and a corresponding basic value which, however, I could describe only vaguely. The present chapter has illustrated some of the questions and concerns which exemplify, or provide the basis for, 'religious concern'; and my discussion suggests the conditions on which an adequate object of that wondering concern could be found. It only remains to avert a possible misunderstanding. The assumptions I am making or postulating in this section would entitle us to say that God is an unrestricted, 'absolute' value and that harmony with God ('religion') is a basic human value. They would not entitle us to say that religion is a more basic value than any of the other basic human values, so that 'for the sake of religion' one might rightly choose directly against any of those other values or ignore any of the other requirements of practical reasonableness: IV.4, V.5–6. There is nothing to justify treating God as an objective to be attained by the skilful disposition of concrete means. (The fanatic acts as if God were such an objective.) Due allowance made for the direct expression of religious concern (say, as Plato says, by 'sacrifice, song, and dance'), the human person's way of realizing the proposed friendship with God builds on all the requirements of practical reasonableness in the pursuit of, and respect for, all the basic forms of human good.

XIII.1

Stoic ethics based moral principles on theoretical knowledge of the universe ... Besides the cited texts from Cicero, see e.g. Diogenes Laertius, *Lives of Eminent Philosophers* [*c*.225?], VII, 87–9: 'Zeno [of Cyprus] in his work *On the Nature of Man* [early 3rd century BC] was the first [? Stoic] to declare that "life lived according to nature" [*homologoumenos te physei zen*] is the ultimate moral end ... Again, living virtuously is equivalent to living in accordance with experience of the actual course of nature, as Chrysippus states in the first book of his *Concerning Ends* [late 3rd century BC], because our individual natures are parts of the nature of the whole universe. And this is why the end [of man] may be defined as life in accordance with nature, i.e. in accordance with our human nature as well as with that of the universe—a life in which we refrain from every action forbidden by the law common to all things. But this law is nothing other than right reason, which pervades all things and is identical with God ... And this very thing constitutes the virtue of the truly happy man ... when all his actions promote the harmony of the spirit dwelling within individual man with the will of Him who orders the universe ... By the nature with which our life ought to be in accordance, Chrysippus understands both universal nature and more particularly the nature of man. Cleanthes, on the other hand, accepts the nature of the universe alone as the standard of all actions without referring to the nature of individual man.' The account I am giving of Stoicism is synthetic, ignoring important differences and developments within a school of thought that flourished for many hundreds of years and was strongly eclectic.

Hope and projection in Kant ... On the question 'What may we hope?', see Kant, *Critique of Pure Reason*, B833 ff. On the 'fictitious' character (from the viewpoint of pure reason) of the immortality we may hope for, ibid. A780/B808. For the origins of the idea that immortality, God, etc. are merely *projections* of human longings, relationships, etc., see L. Feuerbach, *The Essence of Christianity* (1841; trans. Marian Evans, 1854), *passim*; e.g. p. 226: 'The personality of God is nothing else than the projected personality of man'. On the idea of immortality, see e.g. p. 181: 'As God is nothing other than the nature of man purified from that which to the human individual appears ... a limitation ... so the future life is nothing else than the present life freed from that which appears a limitation or an evil'. For the exploitation of these ideas by Marx, see his 'Towards a Critique of Hegel's Philosophy of Right: Introduction' [1843/4].

Augustine's critique of the athleticism of virtue ... See his *De Civitate Dei*, Book XIX, cc. 5, 10, 25.

XIII.2

'Natural sanction' ... On the *poena naturae* ('self-avenging laws of conduct'), see Arnold Brecht, *Political Theory* (Princeton: 1959), pp. 431–3; cf. Plato, *Rep.* IX, 571a, 577c; Xenophon, *Memorabilia* IV, 4, 21–4.

The distinction between 'what' and 'that' ... The distinction is fairly clearly drawn by Aquinas in his early treatise *De Ente et Essentia* (*c*.1255) and is exploited in cc. 4 and

5 of that work, in an argument somewhat similar to Grisez's (which, however, works with 'obtaining' rather than 'existence'), to conclude to the existence of God.

'Sufficient reason' and 'the best of all possible worlds' ... Leibniz's 'great principle of sufficient reason' has three principal senses or applications: nothing happens without a cause; God cannot act without a motive; God must always act for the best (since there could be no reason to prefer the less good to the best). Four points may be noted here. (i) The Leibnizian argument for the existence of God starts with the principle in its first form, which Leibniz considers 'entitles' one to raise the question 'Why does something exist rather than nothing?': *Principles of Nature and of Grace* [1714], secs. 7–8. This is not the question with which my argument begins. (ii) One consequence of the principle for Leibniz is the 'identity of indiscernibles', the view that there never are two beings which are perfectly alike (i.e. lacking in any intrinsic difference): *Monadology*, sec. 9. (iii) In Leibniz's work the principle of sufficient reason is sometimes rendered as 'the principle of fitness [*convenance*]'. On the significance of fitness or *convenientia* in the natural law theorizing of the period, see II.6, above. (iv) Leibniz's successors, notably Christian Wolff, author of influential 'rationalist' treatises on natural law, debased the Leibnizian principle of sufficient reason and the Leibnizian theorem that this is the best of all possible worlds by taking 'best' to mean 'best for mankind': so the stars are to give us light. Leibniz's principle is unacceptable but Wolff's teleology is ridiculous, which helps to explain the thorough discredit into which theories of natural law soon fell.

Explaining states of affairs ... It is often supposed that an uncaused cause need not be postulated, because any causing state of affairs can be adequately explained by further causing states of affairs in a series which is either infinite or circular. But neither an infinite series of causes nor a circle of causes is capable of adequately explaining any state of affairs. See Grisez, *Beyond the New Theism*, pp. 59–67; Barry Miller, 'The Contingency Argument' (1970) 54 *The Monist* 368–71. Grisez suggests that the appeals to infinite or circular series, so obviously unsatisfactory as explanations, are usually merely the outposts of ('a symbolic way of suggesting') the central fortress of the sceptic, which is the claim (attended to in my text) that no explanation is required beyond the conditional explanations of science. The ways in which these scientific explanations demand to be completed by 'metaphysical' explanations, such as the one indicated in this section, are abundantly illustrated in Stanley L. Jaki, *The Road of Science and the Ways to God* (Chicago and Edinburgh: 1978).

Explaining the 'five Eskimos' ... The image is taken from a well-known objection by Paul Edwards, 'The Cosmological Argument' in Donald R. Burrill (ed.), *The Cosmological Arguments: A Spectrum of Opinion* (New York: 1967), pp. 114–22.

'D exists' ... Here the meta-predicable 'exists' is used in an unusual sense (as are all terms applied to D), unusual because in the case of D, *what* it is is all that it requires to exist, so that D's existing is only 'logically' distinct from what D is.

XIII.3

Eternal Law ... See Cicero, *De Legibus*, II, 9; Augustine, *Contra Faustum*, XXII, 27; *De Libero Arbitrio*, I, 6; Aquinas, *S.T.* I–II, q. 19, a. 4; q. 91, a. 1; q. 93, aa. 1–6; St. German, *Doctor and Student*, First Dial., c. 1; Richard Hooker, *Of the Laws of Ecclesiastical Polity* (1593), I, secs. ii–v.

Evil and creation ... For a careful and realistic treatment of obvious objections (e.g. 'pain is an evil and is not a mere lack'), see Grisez, *Beyond the New Theism*, ch. 19. As to pain, I may very briefly note that, while it is *felt* by us as an evil, it is *understood*, by anyone who reflects, as having a number of important functions, in particular as good for warning us of threats to our bodily constitution. Our understanding of it as, at least sometimes, a good does not diminish our horror of it; but, conversely, our dislike of it is not to be taken as a rational judgment on its character. This does not, of course, settle all objections based on pain; but it allows them to be tackled.

Aquinas on providence ... For a sophisticated explanatory account, see Bernard Lonergan, *Grace and Freedom: Operative Grace in the Thought of St. Thomas Aquinas* (New York: 1970), ch. 4.

Access to the God in contemplation: Plato and Aristotle ... For the view adopted in the text, and particularly for the analysis of *Metaphysics*, XII, 7, see *Gauthier–Jolif*, II, 2, pp. 848–60, esp. pp. 857–60; Eric Voegelin, *Order and History*: vol. 4, *The Ecumenic Age* (Baton Rouge: 1974), pp. 189–90, 228–38. On *Eud. Eth.* VIII, 3, see A. Kenny, *The Aristotelian Ethics* (Oxford: 1978), pp. 173–80.

XIII.4

Aquinas on 'participation' ... See *S.T.* I, q. 3, a. 8c; q. 8, a. 1c; q. 44, a. 1c and ad 1; q. 61, a. 1c; q. 75, a. 5 ad 1 and ad 4; q. 79, a. 4; q. 96, a. 1c.

Aristotle and Aquinas on God's moving the will ... For a discussion of this, and of the obvious problems concerning human freedom, see Lonergan, *Grace and Freedom*, ch. 5; Grisez, *Beyond the New Theism*, ch. 18. See also notes to V.2, above, on contingency, providence, and freedom.

XIII.5

Plato and the origins of theorizing about natural law ... See J. P. Maguire, 'Plato's Theory of Natural Law' (1947) 10 *Yale Classical Studies* 151–78.

God, man, and play ... For the history of the exegesis of *Laws*, VII, 803b–c and Proverbs 8: 30–1, see Hugo Rahner, *Man at Play* (London: 1964), esp. pp. 19–25.

INDEX

RITTER LIBRARY
BALDWIN-WALLACE COLLEGE

RITTER LIBRARY
BALDWIN-WALLACE COLLEGE